**To Jon Sutherland
You are the God of Thunder**

CONTENTS

INTRODUCTION

"I'VE BEEN THERE AND BACK, AND I KNOW HOW FAR IT IS."

—Ronnie Lane

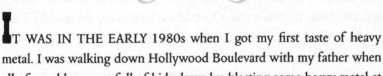

IT WAS IN THE EARLY 1980s when I got my first taste of heavy metal. I was walking down Hollywood Boulevard with my father when all of a sudden, a car full of kids drove by, blasting some heavy metal at nuclear volume. It seemed like everyone froze when they drove by. The music had everybody's attention, and it was very exciting. My father was less impressed. "They think they're cool if they play it loud," he told me.

By 1985, I was going to metal concerts on a regular basis. Every Sunday, I couldn't wait to get my hands on the *Los Angeles Times,* and tear through the Calendar section to see who was coming to town. Throughout the '80s, when a metal band was scheduled to play L.A., the promoters took out full-page ads in the paper announcing its upcoming arrival at such venues as the Forum, the Long Beach Arena, the L.A. Sports Arena. If it was a really big band, they could fill up the L.A. Coliseum, or Anaheim Stadium. If you were lucky enough to get tickets to a show, the wait for the actual concert always seemed like an eternity.

Once the night of a show rolled around, my parents would usually drop a friend and me in the parking lot, and pick us up after the show. They were usually pretty frightened by the sounds of shattering bottles, firecrackers, and vomiting.

I often felt like the kid in the movie *Almost Famous*, who is totally embarrassed when his mother drops him off at the Black Sabbath gig and reminds him, "Don't do drugs!" In fact, I was usually terrified my parents would come in the middle of a show and yank me out by my ear. Generally, they tolerated my teenage metal obsession, figuring it was a phase I'd soon grow out of. Usually the shows were over by 11, so they didn't have to wait too long for me. I was driving by the time Guns N' Roses had become successful, so thankfully my parents didn't have to wait until midnight before Axl Rose even *appeared* on stage.

On the night Mötley Crüe arrived to play at the Forum for the first time in 1985, my father came along with me. And he actually enjoyed himself. I was surprised when he told me how many encores the band would perform before they even hit the stage, and how the show was structured. How did he know this stuff? My father obviously saw what I couldn't see at the time: It was pure show biz.

My father wasn't put off by the profanity that Vince Neil spewed out during his stage raps. "He says all those dirty words on stage because that's what you kids like to hear," he told me. As we were leaving for the parking lot, my father asked me, "That singer guy, that's all he does? He doesn't play guitar or anything?" I told him, "No, Dad. He's just the singer. That's his job. You know, like Frank Sinatra?" My father shot me a dubious look. To even the most untrained ear, Vince Neil was no Frank Sinatra.

In the late Sixties in England, the genre of heavy metal would mutate from the blues, continue to grow and evolve, and eventually take on a life of its own. Artists as diverse as Black Sabbath, Led Zeppelin, and many others all had their roots deep in the blues, but from its influence they would invent an entirely new sound, taking the music to a new level of sonic overkill and density, often under the moniker of "heavy metal."

It's not completely certain who first used the term "heavy metal" as a description, but some critics have credited the Beat writer William Burroughs as the first one to use it long before the music actually came along. The legendary Lester Bangs was one of the first rock critics to describe bands such as Black Sabbath and Deep Purple as heavy metal in 1972.

The phrase also appeared in the 1968 Steppenwolf hit "Born to Be Wild" (songwriter Mars Bonfire claimed he heard the phrase "heavy metal thunder" in his high school chemistry class). However the term was derived, it became the perfect name for the sound it described. If you told people you were into heavy metal, they immediately knew what you were talking about.

Heavy metal and hard rock began developing at the same time rock and roll was becoming big business. Artists continued to break new ground while the record industry was turning into one of the biggest empires in the entertainment business. But even by the late 1960s, the music industry still wasn't entirely comfortable with the rock and roll revolution, and it certainly wasn't prepared for artists like Black Sabbath or Alice Cooper.

There were few ground rules in the music industry of the late '60s and early '70s. The people in charge of making the music, and those in charge of managing the artists, often flew by the seat of their pants. It would be a glorious time for the artists, shortly before the accountants and lawyers would take over the music business and make sales the only focus.

Although heavy metal's unique sound originated in the industrial cities of England, the decade of the 1980s saw a dramatic shift in where the new metal bands were coming from. The major record labels, with extensive operations in Los Angeles, began signing more bands from their own backyard.

In the '70s and '80s, being a rock star was the greatest job in the world. You could earn millions for playing your favorite music, sex was unlimited, sober was a relative term, and you could remain in a permanent state of adolescence. Mark Knopfler's words "Get your money for nothing and your chicks for free" were the M.O., pure and simple.

In the '80s, with the advent of MTV, bands like Twisted Sister and Mötley Crüe would become household names. Now metal bands had hit singles right alongside pop artists like Michael Jackson and Madonna at the top of the charts.

The critics, the music industry, and often the general public at large ridiculed heavy metal and bought into the stereotype that the bands were made up of musicians who couldn't play their instruments. Looking back, some of the best, most technically accomplished musicians in history came out of the heavy metal and hard rock genres. In today's music industry, artist development seems to be a thing of the past, and careers often last no longer than a single's chart run. Yet many of the bands in this book lasted for years, and in the case of artists like Ozzy Osbourne and Van Halen, for decades.

Out of all musical genres, metal has always received the least respect. Throughout the '70s and '80s, critics doled out praise sparingly. Even though the genre sold millions of albums, the suits who ran the music business didn't like it either.

Many bands that were clearly heavy metal shunned the term when describing their music, trying to distance themselves from it. Being a heavy metal band came to be seen as limiting, and many elements of the genre would eventually cross the line into self-parody.

No matter what ups and downs the music went through, there was always a strong core of metal fans to support it. As long as the bands stayed true to their roots and didn't treat their audience poorly, the fans would always be ready to buy their next record. Who cared what the critics and the suits thought? As long as there were pissed-off, adolescent, white males, there would always be a need for heavy metal. Or so the theory went. As invincible as the music seemed to be at the end of the 1980s, things came to a crashing halt in 1992 with the explosion of the Seattle music scene. The musicians who had driven heavy metal to the top of the charts were left terrified and bewildered. It wasn't just the musicians that were out of business. Many who worked with the bands—the managers, producers, road crews, hairdressers—had to face the fact that the party that raged in the heavy metal parking lot for decades was over.

Who was to blame, if anyone? It was easy to blame Seattle, but it clearly wasn't just one factor that brought the music crashing down. Many hard rock and metal bands had worn out their welcome by the '90s; the fact that the backlash against the music was so vehement proves it.

Perhaps the music mutated too far away from how it was originally conceived. Perhaps the fans finally decided they weren't going to put up with the arrogant behavior of the musicians. Finger-pointing and playing the blame game is common among heavy metal musicians, but there are no easy answers for why the music became so unpopular so quickly.

I grew up listening to heavy metal, and it was truly a surreal experience to write about how the music was created and the people who made it, from a perspective I could never have seen when I was a teenager.

When Seattle hit, many of the people who had been a part of the heavy metal landscape wanted to forget the music and everything else that went along with it. Indeed, there were many embarrassing moments that are difficult now to look back on. Nevertheless, heavy metal was an important part of rock history, and it should not be forgotten.

Behind-the-scenes accounts often fall into two traps. One is to see everything through rose-tinted lenses and overpraise the artists chronicled. The other is to reduce their lives to a tour of Babylon, with plenty of titillation and horror but little humanity or insight. To go either way entirely would be an inaccurate reflection. In writing this book, I wanted to address three key questions: What went right, what went wrong, and what the hell happened? There is a lot to learn from these musicians, good and bad. Those who made the music experienced plenty of highs and lows, and they have the scars to prove it.

Bang Your Head

 In the Beginning

Tony Iommi, guitarist for Black Sabbath, the band that started it all. "Let's face it," said former metal vocalist Ronnie James Dio. "Sabbath was the first heavy metal band, a band that stepped on buildings when they came to town." (John Harrell)

YOU CAN TELL WHAT BANDS HAVE STAYING POWER WHEN YOU GO INTO THE HEADSHOPS AND YOU SEE WHO'S PUTTING POSTERS OUT. IF YOU'VE GOT A BLACKLIGHT POSTER, YOU'VE BEEN IMMORTALIZED.

—Former Anthrax and White Lion drummer Greg D'Angelo

THE END OF THE 1960s was filled with equal amounts of promise and terror. The Woodstock festival, which began on August 15, 1969, in Bethel, New York, was the culmination of the peace-and-love generation; hundreds of thousands of hippies came out to celebrate. But by December 6, 1969, a similar festival at the Altamont Speedway in Northern California, headlined by the Rolling Stones, ended in violence and death when a Hell's Angels security guard killed a fan in the audience.

We would have a man on the moon before 1970, just as President Kennedy promised, but back on earth, the Manson slayings and the threat of Vietnam proved how inhumane the world could be. Musically, there was a new British Invasion brewing, but its message was a harsh reflection of a troubled world, not an escape from it.

The music that Black Sabbath and the other fledgling heavy metal bands were playing at this time was far removed from the feelings of hope and promise of the 1960s. The members of Black Sabbath may have looked like hippies with their long, wavy hair parted down the middle and their huge bell-bottoms swallowing up their feet, but there was nothing peaceful or flowery about their music.

In the '60s, the smell of incense filled the air, and everyone was singing about peace and love. And John "Ozzy" Osbourne wanted to puke. He thought to himself, What's all this flower shit? I got no shoes on my feet. Taking a trip to a magic land full of peace, love, and sunshine seemed as realistic to Osbourne as taking a trip to Mars. The world was taking a dark turn at the end of the '60s, and the music began to reflect that. "We got sick and tired of all the bullshit, love your brother

Led Zeppelin guitarist **Jimmy Page** playing a classic Les Paul guitar with a violin bow. When Page put his band together, he wanted a strong unit where everyone was a great musician. Led Zeppelin proved that great band line-ups are one in a million. (Neil Zlozower)

and flower power forever," said Osbourne. "We brought things down to reality." England became the giant petri dish where the germ of heavy metal music developed and grew.

Black Sabbath came out of Birmingham, England's second-largest city. The four original members, Osbourne, Tony Iommi, Terry "Geezer" Butler, and Bill Ward, grew up in working-class families within a mile of each other in the town of Aston. The entire area had been bombed heavily during World War II and was still struggling to rebuild and recover during the years that the members of the band were growing up.

Drummer Bill Ward had fond memories of his youth in Aston, recalling the steam trains coming into the city, the factories, the Victorian-style homes, and the 450-year-old local mansion Aston Hall. "There was a lot of pride coming from Aston," said Ward. "The people there were very resilient. Most people were just regular factory workers; they got by, and they made do. They would clean the front steps of their houses [and] make sure the brass was shining on the doors." It's not surprising heavy metal was born in a working-class environment. Heavy metal often carries the message of standing up for yourself, standing strong against impossible odds and overcoming them.

Growing up in Aston, there were only three options, according to Ward: Work in a factory, join a band, or go to jail. For Osbourne it was almost the last. He lived with his two brothers and three sisters in one room. His family barely got by. "It used to tear me apart to see my mother crying because she hadn't got enough fucking dough left to spend on bills and things." Eventually Osbourne turned to a life of crime. "I had to," he said. "It was down to basic survival." When he was caught burglarizing a clothing store and fined the equivalent of $60, Osbourne's father decided not to bail him out, figuring that spending a little time in jail would teach his son a lesson. He spent six weeks in jail, where he tattooed the letters O-Z-Z-Y on his own knuckles.

During his stay in jail, Osbourne was locked up in solitary for several days for fighting another inmate, leaving him with a lifelong fear of being alone. Mixed in with murderers and hardcore criminals, the only thing that kept Osbourne from being beaten or raped was his sense of humor. When he got out, he decided to try to make a living as a singer. Osbourne put up an ad at a shopping center where he used to cop dope, and guitarist Tony Iommi saw it. Iommi had once known an Ozzy, but he didn't think it could possibly be the same Ozzy he used to beat up in school. When Osbourne showed up at Iommi's door, it turned out it was.

Iommi had been playing the guitar since he was a teenager, first jamming with Sabbath drummer Bill Ward when both were fifteen. When he was eighteen, Iommi was working in a factory when he got an opportunity to tour Germany with a group of musicians. According to Iommi, he came home after working only half of his last day at the factory, but his mother forced him to go back and work a full day. The guy who normally operated the metal press at the factory had not shown up, so Iommi was asked to fill in until the end of his shift. Soon after he resumed work, his fingers were caught in the metal press machine. He yanked his hand out, leaving behind the ends of his right middle and ring fingers. Obviously, Iommi didn't go to Germany, and a doctor told him to find something else to do with his life besides music. Iommi wouldn't hear of it. He had an incredibly strong will and was determined to play again no matter what it took. Because of his injury, and being left-handed, he had to relearn the guitar from scratch without the tips of his fingers. Iommi made thimbles out of melted plastic to keep his fingers from being torn up by the guitar strings.

Unable to feel anything when he played, Iommi learned his way around the fretboard by ear, which could have strengthened his improvisational skills. The plastic tips, however, were clumsy and often slowed down his playing, making it harder to get around the fretboard quickly. He sometimes became so frustrated that he'd smash his guitar against the wall.

The manager at the factory brought over a Django Reinhardt album for Iommi to listen to. Reinhardt was a famous jazz guitarist whose left hand was paralyzed except for two fingers, and he inspired Iommi to keep playing. At first he played with only two fingers, which helped him develop a number of techniques he might not have discovered otherwise. Supposedly he was one of the first guitarists to play just the low strings of a major chord instead of all six strings, which produced the "power chord." "The guy had a lot of barriers to overcome just within himself," said Osbourne. "For a while he thought he would never play again, but he mastered it."

The four members of Black Sabbath first came together as a group in 1967, just as the blues-band scene in England was coming to an end. Most of the English hard rock and metal bands had strong roots in the blues, but each band gave it a unique interpretation that set it apart. On their debut albums, both Led Zeppelin and the Jeff Beck Group covered the Willie Dixon blues classic "You Shook Me," and the two versions sounded nothing alike.

Much of Sabbath's music grew out of jam sessions. When they got together to play, "nobody would know what was going to happen, which was incredible fun," says Ward. The songs on the first three Sabbath albums, *Black Sabbath, Paranoid,* and *Master of Reality,* were all born from their jam sessions. The band would plod along jamming, then a song would suddenly come together. There was a little arranging done afterward, but for the most part the way the song was written in the jam session was the way you heard it on the album.

Black Sabbath's sound was dark and morbid, more so than any other band at the time. They were one of the first bands to tune their guitars lower, often as much as three semitones, which gave their riffs more depth and texture and could make a single chord sound huge and oppressive. Many metal bands would later tune down their instruments, and the intense levels of volume and distortion at which Black Sabbath played is now standard for every hard rock and metal band. But what Black Sabbath was doing in the late 1960s was all new terrain. Never before had music sounded this dark, distorted, or loud. "I didn't hear Black Sabbath's music coming from anywhere else," says Richard Cole, Led Zeppelin's longtime tour manager, who grew up in the thick of the English music scene in the late '60s. "[They were] perhaps more original than Zeppelin in that sort of way. It almost came from nowhere." Ronnie James Dio, who sang with Black Sabbath from 1979 to 1982, said, "Let's face it, [Black Sabbath] was the first heavy metal band, a band that stepped on buildings when they came to town."

The band members' depressing upbringings in Birmingham couldn't help but seep into their music, and it's what helped create the sound of heavy metal. "It just seemed like the right thing to do, to go with those moods," says Ward. "Emotionally it was very satisfying for everybody, almost healing in a sense. Especially when you're real young and there's a lot of anger. Playing drums with Sabbath is the greatest transport one can have to deal with one's anger." It's doubtful a band like Black Sabbath could have come out of Beverly Hills.

In their early days, Black Sabbath had a tough time getting gigs, and they played wherever they could. They used to go to clubs where Jeff Beck was booked to perform because Beck was known for blowing off gigs, and if he didn't show up, Black Sabbath would be there ready to perform. A promoter in Birmingham named Jim Simpson started booking and eventually managing the band, but record labels wouldn't go to Birmingham to see a band; you had to be good enough to play in London. The Marquee Club in London was where countless bands got their start. (The Who, AC/DC, and Yes played there when they were getting started.) The club was a 350-capacity room that was usually packed and always sweltering. When Twisted Sister played there over a decade later, the room was so hot that guitarist Jay Jay French came offstage and wrote in his diary, "If this is hell, I'm becoming an atheist." Black Sabbath eventually got a gig at the Marquee in 1968, but legend has it the owner said they wouldn't be allowed to return unless they bathed first. "They were the dirtiest, grubbiest, most intimidating lot I'd ever seen," says Tom Allom, who engineered Sabbath's first album and went on to produce for Judas Priest. They may have looked like long-haired, dope-smoking hippies, but there was something foreboding about their presence. Only later, Allom adds, "I found out they were actually very nice!"

The members of Black Sabbath knew what they were doing was different, but they had no idea *how* different their music was from what was going on in England until they saw how much resistance they were meeting. Fourteen labels rejected the band before Jim Simpson finally managed to secure a deal. Vertigo was a subsidiary label set up by Phonogram and had originally passed on Black Sabbath, but needed them to help fill out a roster of priority artists like Rod Stewart, Manfred Mann, and Colosseum. The band went into the studio and recorded a demo under the name Earth on a four-track machine. The first song the band wrote together was "Black Sabbath," and soon the band would rename themselves Black Sabbath as well. The name was taken from a 1963 Italian horror film. Sabbath used to rehearse across the street from a movie theater where a horror film was playing. Osbourne thought: Isn't it strange that people pay money to get the shit scared out of them? Why don't we try and put that to music?

Black Sabbath's first album was recorded at Regent Sound in London.

It took only two days to record and another two days to mix. The entire album, including the cover photograph of a green witch in a psychedelic purple field, cost around £600 pounds, about $1,200. Allom, who engineered the album, recalls that it was very easy to record. "They were very proficient in the studio. Everything was first takes." Black Sabbath played at nuclear volume in the studio, and the producer, Rodger Bain, went crazy. "You can't turn it up that loud in the studio!" he screamed. "You won't be able to hear anything else; you won't be able to hear the drums!" He tried to get them to play at a lower volume, promising he'd turn up the mixes later, but the band wasn't interested. "We don't turn down, man, we turn up," they replied.

When Black Sabbath's self-titled debut album was released in February 1970, the label hyped the band as "Louder Than Zeppelin." Osbourne was just happy to be bringing home a record to his parents. The band members figured they would put out a couple of albums; then they'd head back to work in the factories. So everyone was quite surprised when the album went to No. 8 on the British charts. The song "Black Sabbath" was simple and startlingly effective. Osbourne perfectly described it as a song that has just three chords but "sounds like the gates of hell opening." It was also played in a swinging jazz beat, though it's played so slow you wouldn't know it. A number of British drummers, including Ward, played behind the beat—an influence taken from jazz—and that gave their music tremendous weight. Inside the sleeve of the first Black Sabbath album was a giant inverted cross, which the band members insist was the label's idea. Even though they wore steel crucifixes around their necks, they always wore them right side up. As the band was leaving for their first tour, Osbourne's father gave them the crucifixes to wear. "We were four guys who were traveling in a vehicle that was falling apart, going across the sea to Europe in freezing cold, snow, stormy seas," says Ward. "So the idea of having those crosses was [his] way of saying, 'Hey, God bless you, and try and be safe.'"

Black Sabbath had toured Europe extensively before the band was signed, and now they were coming to America for the first time. As with most bands in the early '70s, the scariest thing the musicians had to worry about was VD. One night Osbourne had to get so much penicillin shot into his rear end that he was hobbling and practically had to be helped to the stage. Sometimes on the road, Osbourne and Ward would get so drunk that the roadies would have to wheel them up to their rooms on luggage carts. Ward typically packed few clothes, but he made sure he packed "emergency booze" in case the drinks on the flight didn't come fast enough.

Because of their reputation, Black Sabbath attracted a lot of fans who practiced witchcraft. But the band was usually more worried about the Christian groups that protested their shows than the satanists who attended them. "I was always afraid that some of these people who said they had relationships with Jesus were going to pull the trigger," says Ward. "The witches would simply park their asses in the hotel corridors, light up candles, and just do their thing. But with the [Jesus freaks] I became more alert and watched out for that flash. You never know when there's a .45 coming out." Women were frightened of Black Sabbath as well, and the band didn't attract the best-looking groupies. "Honestly, other groups' *roadies* used to get better-looking groupies than we did," said Osbourne. "You'd turn over in bed looking for a glass of water, and there would be this *thing* lying there, looking like something Picasso painted on a bad day."

The band quickly followed up the success of their first album with *Paranoid,* which was recorded in July 1970 and released in September of the same year. The album was going to be called *War Pigs,* which was the title of a song about the insanity of the Vietnam War. Before they completed the album, the band realized they were one song short. When the band went out for a drink at the pub Iommi said he had an idea for a riff. They went back to the studio, and Iommi played the riff for the band. Within twenty-five minutes, they'd written the song "Paranoid," and it was added to the album at the last possible minute, right before the tracks were due to be completed. Geezer Butler wrote the lyrics to the song, as he did with most of Black Sabbath's songs. He liked the sound of the word "paranoid" but claims he had no idea what it meant. He was relieved when he found out the title fit the song's lyrics perfectly. "Paranoid" 's simple, classic riff would make it the band's trademark song.

Another track on the *Paranoid* album was "Hand of Doom," a song about heroin. The band drank, took psychedelics, and would eventually turn to cocaine, but heroin was a drug that scared them. At one of Black Sabbath's shows in America, after the lights came up and the crowd had dispersed, the band was horrified to see used needles all over the arena floor. They wanted the lyrics of the song to be hardcore and extreme, to show the horror of addiction.

Because of the dark nature of their music and lyrics, Black Sabbath became the rock and roll equivalent of a boogieman under the bed, a taboo to listen to, which of course is what helped make them so popular. Metallica vocalist James Hetfield liked the fact that when he told his friends his favorite band was Black Sabbath, they'd say, "Wow. My mom won't even let me own that album." As he put it, "Sabbath was forbidden, not the right thing to do."

The *Paranoid* album turned out to be Black Sabbath's biggest, selling more than four million copies in the States alone, and reaching No. 1 in England. When they returned to the States, they were now headliners. When they came to New York, they played the Fillmore East with Rod Stewart opening. Anxious to see Black Sabbath, the audience loudly booed Stewart in an effort to get him off the stage. That's when Black Sabbath knew they were really starting to get somewhere.

Black Sabbath released its third album, *Master of Reality*, in 1971. The band didn't have much material ready and wrote most of the songs, including their classics "Children of the Grave" and the weed-smoking ode "Sweet Leaf," in the studio. The album was written and recorded within three weeks. In addition to his punishing guitar work, Iommi also played flute on *Master of Reality*, adding haunting melodic passages to the song "Solitude." One night he and Butler smoked too much hash before going onstage, and Iommi tried to deliver a mournful melody with his flute, but since it wasn't up to his mouth, all the audience could hear was: "Psssfffttt! Psssfffft! Psssfffft!"

By this point, Black Sabbath had been playing and touring together for four years, and they were severely burned out. Small cracks in the band's surface began to grow larger. Before forming Black Sabbath, Iommi had played very briefly with Jethro Tull, where Ian Anderson was clearly in control of the band. When Iommi formed his band, he wanted to be the one in charge. Iommi and Butler had always had a close bond personally and musically. They didn't have to communicate in words; they were practically clairvoyant musically when they played together. But Osbourne and Iommi were never very close. Osbourne didn't play an instrument, and it was hard for him to get his musical ideas across to Iommi. Iommi didn't have the patience to listen, and Osbourne often felt Iommi was a bully. On later tours, Osbourne sang off to the side of the stage while Iommi stood in the center, making his dominance in the band clear.

By the *Black Sabbath Vol. 4* album, released in 1972, the band was partying hard and starting to lose its focus. Osbourne recalled that recording the *Vol. 4* album "was like one big Roman orgy. We'd be in the Jacuzzi all day doing coke, and every now and again, we'd get up and do a song." In the album's liner notes, the band thanked "the COKE-cola company." The album was originally going to be titled *Snowblind,* but Warner Bros., the group's American label, balked at the obvious drug reference.

Warner Bros. didn't think much of Black Sabbath's music to begin with. In fact, the first time any of the Warner executives came out to see the band live was in 1979, and then only because the label's baby act, Van Halen, was opening for them. Nor was Black Sabbath popular with the critics, and they endured years of bad reviews. In the '70s, Iommi said, "Nobody likes us except the public." But Black Sabbath's fans, like most metal fans, didn't let bad reviews influence their record-buying decisions. In fact, whatever the critics liked, metal fans usually avoided like the plague. "I don't give one fuck about a rock critic," said John Kalodner, the legendary A&R executive of Geffen Records and Sony Music.

"I was one, and I know they're full of shit. They mean nothing. The only thing that matters to me is the radio stations that play rock records and the kids who buy them." "Ultimately, it's the kids who make the decision," said Jon Bon Jovi. "Not the critics. Record-company guys are paid to tell you how great a record is; the critics are paid to tell you how bad it is. Both of them get their records for free. It's the kids who're gonna buy it and listen to it."

One of the few critics who understood Black Sabbath's music was Lester Bangs, now considered one of the greatest rock critics in history. In the '80s, metal magazines were overrun with sycophants and groupies who gave their favorite bands literary blow jobs because they craved the perks of access and were scared of being cut off if their reviews were too critical. Bangs turned down anyone in the music business who tried to woo him, and he was never afraid to call it as he saw it. If he liked a band, you knew he was sincere. While many critics dismissed heavy metal, comparing it to a group of grubby cavemen thumping their instruments, Bangs saw Black Sabbath's music as worthy of serious attention. "Despite the blitzkrieg nature of their sound, Black Sabbath are moralists," Bangs wrote in *Creem*. "Like Bob Dylan, like William Burroughs, like most artists trying to deal with a serious situation in an honest way. They are a band with a conscience who have looked around them and taken it upon themselves to reflect the chaos in ways they see as positive."

Black Sabbath would gain critical acclaim only after Kurt Cobain and many of the Seattle bands acknowledged their influence in the '90s. The band was clearly ahead of its time, and it took some time for the world to catch up. In the 1983 edition of *The Rolling Stone Record Guide,* each Black Sabbath album received a one-star review. In the revised 1992 edition, several of their albums received three stars.

But in the 1970s, Black Sabbath's day in the sun was still many years off. In 1974, Jim Simpson, who had managed the band early in their career, sued them for wrongful termination. After he filed suit, the band realized that their current managers had screwed them out of millions of dollars. The lawsuits went on for two years; the band spent a year off the road until their legal problems were straightened out. As Osbourne would later remark, "I liked the first four albums, but after *Sabbath Bloody Sabbath* [1973], we were just making albums to pay our lawyers."

With their *Sabbath Bloody Sabbath* and *Sabotage* albums, Black Sabbath's songs moved away from topical issues to reflect the brutal realities of the music business. "Killing Yourself to Live" was about the grind of life on the road. "The Writ" was a diatribe against their former manager; one line went, "You bought and sold me with your lying words." Even the title of the *Sabotage* album was a reference to the band's negative experiences in the music business. "You've got to be really careful of the business side of it, not to sign anything until you've had it read," said Iommi. "First thing to do, before you learn to play, is get a lawyer."

As Black Sabbath was coming together at the end of the 1960s, Led Zeppelin was rising from the ashes of the legendary British group the Yardbirds, which at various points had featured guitarists Jeff Beck, Eric Clapton, and Jimmy Page. When the Yardbirds fell apart while on tour in early 1968, Page was the band's guitarist. Already a legendary player, Page had made a good living as a studio musician for years. He played with the Rolling Stones, the Kinks, and the Who ("I Can't Explain"). He met future Zeppelin bassist John Paul Jones on the studio circuit. Jones was the ultimate pro, always dependable, and he had built up an impressive credit list backing up the Rolling Stones, Dusty Springfield, and Tom Jones, among others.

When the Yardbirds splintered, they were still under contract to do a Scandinavian tour, and Page wanted to put a band together called the New Yardbirds. It was the era of the "supergroup," and Cream, one of the first supergroups, had also just broken up. All three members of Cream, Eric Clapton, Jack Bruce, and Ginger Baker, were top musicians. Page wanted everyone in his band to be topnotch as well; there would be no "passengers" just along for the ride. Page asked Steve Marriott and

Steve Winwood to sing, but both declined. (Winwood later joined the short-lived supergroup Blind Faith with Clapton on guitar, which broke up six weeks after releasing its first album.) John Entwistle and Keith Moon toyed with the idea of leaving the Who to start their own band with Page, but Moon quipped that the whole enterprise would probably sink "like a lead balloon." His comment would eventually prompt Page to rechristen his new band Led Zeppelin.

Page next approached a pop singer named Terry Reid to be his vocalist but was turned down again. Page was growing weary that he would never find a singer. Reid recommended his friend Robert Plant, who was then singing in a band incomprehensibly named Hobbstweedle (it was the '60s, after all). Plant knew Page's rep as a studio musician, and he was nervous about meeting Page, but the minute they hooked up, they clicked. When Page heard him sing, he thought, Why isn't this guy a star yet? Plant recommended his old friend John Bonham to come in on drums (they had played together in a group called the Band of Joy). Bonham was a heavy hitter on the drums, a distinctive part of his sound. Bonham had worked in construction, and as Eddie Kramer, who engineered three Zeppelin albums, put it, "He had this bricklayer's ability to bang the drum immensely hard." For many heavy metal and hard rock drummers of this era, playing hard was often a matter of necessity. The P.A. systems at concerts were so terrible in those days, you had to play hard just to be heard.

John Bonham grew up in Birmingham, where he knew Bill Ward and Tony Iommi. Bonham was a big fan of Black Sabbath and was the best man at Iommi's wedding. As teenagers, Bonham and Ward's bands used to play at the same clubs. At one early gig, though, Bonham never even got to perform. His *soundcheck* was so loud they threw him out of the club. Before landing in Led Zeppelin, Bonham was fired from countless bands for playing too loud; he proudly listed the bands on his drum case. Bonham also played with his hands during drum solos. Sometimes he'd hit his drums so hard that they'd be covered in blood by the end of the show.

Bonham was backing up an American folksinger named Tim Rose, making forty pounds a week, when Page and Plant approached him. Bonham didn't want to give up his regular salary, but after much cajoling, he finally caved in and joined the band. For some time after, he was still nervous and would stay up nights wondering if he did the right thing walking away from forty pounds a week.

The four members of Led Zeppelin first got together to jam in a tiny room. The year was 1968. The first song they played was the jump blues classic "Train Kept a-Rollin'," and as Jones recalled, "The room just *exploded*. And we said, 'Right, we're on, this is it, this is gonna work!' "

Page was so excited about his new band that he booked studio time in October 1968, and Led Zeppelin recorded their first album on their own dime without the backing of a label. The first Led Zeppelin album was recorded in thirty hours and reputedly cost £1,750 to produce. The band tried to record the album as live as possible so they could recreate it live as well.

During the recording, Page began experimenting with microphone placement, a concept few guitarists even thought about back then. He would set up one mike right next to the amp speaker and another twenty feet away, explaining that "distance is depth." Page loved to tinker with different tones and sounds in the studio, and on later albums he would add layers and layers of overdubs like a tapestry. He strived to put his riffs together like an orchestral arrangement, which he called "the guitar army."

Led Zeppelin was managed by Peter Grant. Grant was a bear of a man whom no one with any common sense ever messed with. He was a former bouncer and professional wrestler who stood 6'5" and was grossly overweight. Grant grew up in the streets of England, where he learned how to hustle, be fast on his feet, and most important, make money. Grant started managing the Yardbirds when Page was a member. Page complained that the band was constantly being ripped off by promoters and losing money. But once the gigantic Grant began towering over promoters for the money, the Yardbirds collected.

In November 1968, Grant got Led Zeppelin a deal with Atlantic Records, and they signed for a then-astronomical $200,000 advance. It was a tremendous deal at the time mainly because it included a provision that gave the band complete control over their music.

Their second album, *Led Zeppelin II,* was written while the band was touring North America and England in 1969. Bits and pieces of the album were recorded all over L.A., London, Vancouver, and New York, whenever the band could find time to hit the studio. *Led Zeppelin II* was the band's first No. 1 album and the last No. 1 album of the 1960s. For their next album, *Led Zeppelin III* released in 1970, the band recorded an all-acoustic side that grew out of Plant and Page's love of Joni Mitchell, Crosby, Stills, Nash and Young, and other folk-rock artists. Although the songs were played on acoustic guitars, they were still heavy. *Led Zeppelin III* at first angered a lot of fans who felt they had made too radical a departure but today it is considered one of their finest records.

Despite the fact that Led Zeppelin's music was often complex and epic in nature, they usually worked quickly in the studio (Page claimed he did all the overdubs on the band's 1976 album *Presence* in a night). Page and Jones were trained studio musicians who knew how to nail a track quickly, and Jones and Bonham were an incredible team. "If you can't get it in a couple of takes with that rhythm section, you might as well give it up and go home," says Eddie Kramer.

They could have made spotless records if they wanted to, but Led Zeppelin often let their mistakes stay in. Some Led Zeppelin songs on close listening feature airplanes flying overhead, ringing telephones, and members of the band coughing in the background. "If it was an accident and it was good, it was taken as part of the record," says Kramer. "There were so many accidents and so many mistakes that were incorporated into the music that it became cool. We allowed the mistakes to happen and capitalized on them."

For their fourth album, the band decided not to put their name, or any other information, including the Atlantic logo and catalog number, on the album's cover. Instead of printing the band members' names on the sleeve, each member chose a symbol to represent himself, decades before Prince did. "We decided that on the fourth album, we would deliberately downplay the group name," said Page. "Names, titles, and things like that do not mean a thing. What matters is our music. We said we just wanted to rely purely on our music." Atlantic didn't want to give in to Led Zeppelin's demands. The band then threatened not to turn over the master tapes until they finally got their way. The album came out in November 1971, and most fans would dub it *Zeppelin IV*. The album featured the classic-to-be, "Stairway to Heaven," which, at the band's insistence, was never released as a single.

" 'Stairway' crystallized the essence of the band," Page told journalist Cameron Crowe, who toured with the band in the mid-1970s. "Every musician wants to do something of lasting quality, something which will hold up for a long time, and I guess we did it with 'Stairway.' . . . I don't know whether I have the ability to come up with more. I have to do a lot of hard work before I can get anywhere near those stages of consistent, total brilliance."

The fourth Led Zeppelin album would go on to sell more than 22 million copies, making it the fourth-biggest-selling album of all time. "Stairway to Heaven" would become one of the most played songs in music history. For many years, there was probably not an hour of the day it didn't play on the radio somewhere (one report claims "Stairway to Heaven" is the most requested song in the history of commercial radio).

In concert Led Zeppelin played up to three hours a night with no opening act. The band proved to be a powerful presence live, and Page and Plant were living, breathing rock and roll iconography onstage. As Cameron Crowe observed, Plant's shirt was "accidentally fallen open" as he sang; his wild blond mane and tight blue jeans were "accidentally perfect." A high-point of the show was when Jimmy Page played his guitar with a violin bow—a technique he had introduced in 1967 with the Yardbirds—on the song "Dazed and Confused," which would sometimes last up to half an hour live. Barring the use of lasers and dry ice in later tours, their stage sets were minimal. For many tours Bonham didn't even use a drum riser because he liked playing on the floor.

Led Zeppelin also had a very small road crew: thirteen people on staff for indoor gigs, twenty-seven for outdoor shows. When most British bands came to America in the 1960s, they would rent equipment and leave their own gear at home. Led Zeppelin was one of the first bands to bring their own gear with them, the idea being that the band would be as self-contained as possible.

Led Zeppelin's first tour to America in 1969 lasted six months and completely changed the nature of touring. Back then, bands usually came to a state and played not only the major cities but also practically every other city with a stage. When Led Zeppelin returned to America in 1970 for their second tour, the band and its management decided to play fewer dates in fewer cities with larger venues. In California the band played only L.A., San Francisco, and San Diego, ignoring the numerous cities in between. They'd consolidate their gigs into one place that they'd sell out and create a demand for tickets. Fans would have to travel hundreds of miles to see the band. This helped to build excitement and mystique around the band.

Led Zeppelin also set up base in big cities while touring America. They would stay in Chicago for two weeks, and from there they would fly to Indianapolis, play there and fly back, fly to St. Louis, play there and fly back. This was done to minimize the amount of time checking in and out of hotels, and to avoid the expense of constantly moving the band's road crew and entourage.

By 1973, Led Zeppelin was flying in a jet dubbed the Starship that was also used by the Rolling Stones and Alice Cooper. As many as ten limos would whisk the band and its entourage to and from gigs. Each band member had his own, manager Peter Grant had his own, and there were extras for photographers, record-company executives, and groupies.

For photographer Neal Preston, it was a dream come true to travel with his favorite band throughout the 1970s. Even though the Led Zeppelin camp trusted few outsiders, Preston witnessed a lot of the private mayhem surrounding the band and was able to photograph much of it, though many of his more explicit photos would never reach the public (some shots Preston didn't even print for over twenty years). "You just tucked those photographs away for a long time, never to see the light of day," he says. Another rock photographer, Neil Zlozower, was eighteen when he was hired by Atlantic Records to shoot a party with Led Zeppelin at the Continental Hyatt House, where the band always stayed when they were in Los Angeles. (The hotel would come to be known as the "Riot House.") Zlozower took some pictures of the band with a number of groupies they were close to at that party, including Jimmy's fourteen-year-old girlfriend, Lori Maddox. When *Circus* magazine sent Zlozower a photo request list soon after, he sent them the photographs he had taken at the Hyatt House. Candid, offstage photos of the band were not easy to come by back then. Zlozower soon found out why. Peter Grant blew a gasket when he found out what Zlozower had done. "You what?!?" he screamed. "You idiot! They're married! If their wives see those shots!" Zlozower got the photos back from *Circus,* and also had to give the negatives to Grant, which he regrets because those photos would now be worth a lot of money (then again, he would probably regret a thrashing from Grant more).

Rock photographers of this era were allowed to capture the fantasies that eventually hung on millions of teenage walls. The best rock photographers were self-taught, just like the best rock musicians. You didn't learn how to take a great live shot in school, just like you didn't go to school to learn how to lay down a hot guitar solo. It was all done by feel, and the fans knew what was authentic. Because they were fans themselves, Preston and Zlozower took shots the fans wanted to see. "The pictures that appealed to me were heroic pictures," says Preston. "Photos where the guitar players looked like gods."

In 1975, Neal Preston captured a classic shot of Jimmy Page chugging a bottle of Jack Daniels. Preston was sitting across the table from Page when he put the bottle of whiskey he was carrying around with him in his mouth, threw his head back, and took a huge swig. "The bottle stayed up in the air for what seemed like an eternity," Preston says. "Normally I would have shot a whole motor-drive sequence of photos, but I only took one frame. I guess that photo says a lot."

In the '60s and '70s, photographers had more freedom to shoot bands and create classic photos. Access to artists was almost total. When Zlozower started shooting bands, he could buy a concert ticket for six dollars, go all the way up to the front of the stage, and take as many pictures as he wanted. You didn't need special passes to bring in a camera, and there weren't squadrons of security goons in the arenas, only ushers. Eventually access to the artists would become much more restrictive. Photographers were permitted to shoot only the first three songs of a band's set. Some have said this rule started with Rod Stewart because after three songs he'd get so sweaty, his trademark rooster 'do would begin to wilt and he'd have to run backstage to blow-dry it up again. (Metallica prefers photographers to shoot the *last* three songs of its set, because those are the most intense.)

On the road, Neal Preston found that he got along best with Robert Plant and John Paul Jones. "Robert was basically a hippie," he says. "He was all about hippies, California, and Joni Mitchell." John Paul Jones usually took no part in the band's debauchery and didn't mind the fact that Plant and Page got most of the attention. "He was used to seeing pictures of the band where you couldn't really see him."

But Preston kept his distance from Page and Bonham. "People were scared of Jimmy," he says. "He was a volatile guy, he was mysterious, and he didn't trust a lot of people." It was rumored that Page dabbled in witchcraft and was well versed in the works of Aleister Crowley, a legendary necromancer whose writings on modern satanism were influential. (Page eventually bought and lived in Crowley's manor.) Page had also been an only child growing up and was used to spending a lot of time alone. "A lot of people can't be on their own," he said. "They get frightened. Isolation doesn't bother me at all. It gives me a sense of security."

Bonham, on the other hand, was a sweet guy when he was sober but an all-time terror when he was drunk, according to Preston. "He'd get on the Starship, he'd be sober in the morning, it was 'Hello,' 'How are you,' 'Good to see you.' Two hours into the flight, after drink, drink, drink, he'd remove your glasses off your face and stomp them into the ground." He was also jealous of the attention Plant and Page got, and wanted to be a star as well, like Ginger Baker was in Cream.

The insanity of Led Zeppelin's early tours would set a standard for wild behavior that bands tried to top for years. In 1969, they co-headlined a tour with Vanilla Fudge. Says Vanilla Fudge drummer Carmine Appice, "We had a great time. We were wrecking hotel rooms, abusing girls, probably all the same stuff Mike Tyson got arrested for."

In May, the two bands were staying at the Edgewater Inn in Seattle. The hotel was unique in that it rented fishing poles in the lobby and you could literally fish out of your hotel room window. It was here that the now-infamous "shark" incident took place. The story goes that a red-haired groupie was tied to a bed and with both bands watching, road manager Richard Cole took a freshly caught live red snapper, whipped her with it, and stuck its nose in her vagina. As Cole recalled in *Hammer of the Gods,* "I'm not saying the chick wasn't drunk; I'm not saying that any of us weren't drunk. But it was nothing malicious or harmful, no way! No one was *ever* hurt. She might have been *hit* by a shark a few times for disobeying orders, but she didn't get hurt." After the incident, Appice ran into Frank Zappa at an airport and told him the story. It soon became the lyrics to Zappa's song "The Mud Shark," and a legend was born.

The long drum and guitar solos that Led Zeppelin created on stage were a by-product of the 1960s, when bands like Cream would jam forever. They also came in handy when other band members wanted to get laid. In 1973, Led Zeppelin played several shows at New York's Madison Square Garden that were filmed and eventually released as *The Song Remains the Same.* "During the second Madison Square Garden show, Bonham was in the midst of his 'Moby Dick' solo, which gave the other band members twenty or more minutes of rest while he banged and battered the drums," recalled Richard Cole. "We had a teenage girl from Brooklyn in our dressing room, and as Bonzo took control of the crowd she was performing oral sex on the other band members." According to Cole, a security guard stood outside the dressing room door to make sure the camera crew couldn't film it.

While Led Zeppelin's offstage antics were becoming legendary, their musical contributions were largely dismissed by the press. Cameron Crowe called Led Zeppelin "the black sheep of English hard rock. Zeppelin would outdraw the Stones easily, but you'd never know it from the media coverage."

Led Zeppelin knew they were great musicians and were incredibly angry that critics panned them. Bonham was especially furious that he didn't get the recognition he deserved; he was particularly angry when Karen Carpenter placed higher than he did for "Best Drummer" in a 1975 *Playboy* music poll. "Zeppelin really had an us-vs.-the-world mentality," says Neal Preston. "Us vs. the critics, us vs. the hotels, us vs. everybody."

The band endured so much bad press that they eventually stopped granting interviews, with few exceptions. This would ultimately work in the band's favor, as Grant tried to build a mystique around the band. The less people knew about Led Zeppelin, the more mythical and larger-than-life the band became.

Led Zeppelin rarely did live television appearances, and Grant almost never allowed the band to be filmed or videotaped, with the exception of *The Song Remains the Same.* Grant didn't feel the video technology, as it was then, could capture their sound well. With tremendous foresight, especially considering how much MTV would later overexpose bands, Grant was able to preserve the band's mystery.

"If MTV had existed when Led Zeppelin was around, it might have burned out Led Zeppelin," said Rob Zombie. "But you only saw the band if you saw them live, which a lot of people never did, and they achieved legendary status. [Their career] just went on longer and longer."

When Led Zeppelin was gearing up for their 1972 tour, Grant told promoters the band would take 90 percent of all receipts. At the time, when a band played live, the money was split 50/50 between the band and the concert promoters. The promoters obviously weren't happy about it, but who was going to argue with Grant? Even if the promoters were only getting 10 percent, Led Zeppelin were such a strong live draw that the take was still guaranteed to be huge. To give you an idea how difficult it was for a band to achieve this, the Rolling Stones tried to get an 80/20 split for their 1969 tour but were able to get only 60/40 in their favor. Says Preston, "[Grant] had the, call it chutzpah, call it balls, call it whatever you want, of going to promoters and saying, 'You're lucky to be getting our band, so this is what you're gonna make if we sell out. It's not gonna be much, but you have our band.' " Grant wasn't just throwing his considerable weight around. Unlike many rock managers who took advantage of bands who didn't know any better, Grant protected Led Zeppelin zealously and made sure they got every penny due to them. His demands would end up setting a precedent. According to Carmine Appice, the music business changed "when Peter Grant changed the laws of promotions where the band made all the money."

Where Black Sabbath and Led Zeppelin's roots were deep in the blues, Deep Purple was the first metal band to combine the blues and classical melodies with the distortion and volume of hard rock. The band went through many personnel changes initially before arriving, in 1969, at a lineup that included Ritchie Blackmore on guitar, Jon Lord on keyboards, Ian Paice on drums, and two new members, singer Ian Gillan and bassist Roger Glover. Before joining Deep Purple, Gillan and Glover had played together in a band called Episode Six. Like Black Sabbath, the darkness at the end of the 1960s changed Episode Six's music as well. "We were a flower-power band," recalled Glover. "We wore beads and threw flowers out at the crowd. But by 1969, the music was getting tougher."

By 1971, Deep Purple was reputed to be the loudest band in the world. One reason for this was that the band had taken off so fast in America, moving up from clubs to arenas, and they had to buy more amps. When they hauled their giant P.A. system back home to England, they went back to playing smaller theaters yet kept the volume levels the same. At one show, reportedly, Deep Purple was so loud that several people were knocked unconscious when they walked past the P.A.

Ritchie Blackmore has also said he modified his Marshall amps to a 500-watt English rating (about 1,000 watts in American ratings), well beyond the normal capacity. But Blackmore grew tired of playing so loud and constantly having to fix blown amps. "I'd rather play a little amp anytime," he admitted. "I used to do the circuit with a little amp and played ten times better than I do now. I was fast and clean, but nobody took any notice except other musicians." Blackmore did get a lot of notice for his innovative playing, as well as his considerable ego. He held most rock guitarists in low regard, and once bragged he could "cut any guitarist alive."

Deep Purple's use of a keyboard player was one of the first in heavy metal. Despite the fact that Jon Lord's Hammond B-3 organ sounded heavier than most guitar players, keyboards were often disdained by metal bands. Some bands felt that synthesizers smoothed out their sound too much. In the 1980s, keyboards were associated with wimpy synthesizer bands like A Flock of Seagulls. Many later metal bands secretly used keyboards; they were usually just well hidden in the mix. Mötley Crüe used a lot of Hammond B-3 distorted organ hidden in the power chords of their *Shout at the Devil* album. According to Claude Schnell, who played keyboards in the band Dio, some bands had such disdain for keyboards that they even made their keyboard players ride in the crew bus away from the rest of the band.

Deep Purple peaked with their *Machine Head* album (a machine head is a tuning peg on a guitar) in 1972. For *Machine Head,* Deep Purple wanted to create a studio album in a live setting. The band wanted to capture the live energy that's so elusive to nail on record.

The album was engineered by Martin Birch (who later produced albums for Black Sabbath and Iron Maiden) and recorded in December 1971 in Montreux, Switzerland, at the abandoned Grand Hotel. The Rolling Stones mobile studio was parked outside the hotel. Inside the hotel, Deep Purple found the best place to capture their sound was the hotel hallway. The band had to brave a harsh snowstorm every time they wanted to go into the mobile studio and hear the playbacks.

The band also tried recording in the Pavilion, a theater near Lake Geneva, but the building began to crumble from the volume. Just as they were getting started, the Swiss police showed up and told them they had to find someplace else to play. The only thing the band was able to record there was the first four bars of a simple riff. It would eventually become the song "Smoke on the Water."

The lyrics for "Smoke on the Water" were based on a true event that happened to the band while they were in Switzerland. One night the members of Deep Purple went to see Frank Zappa and the Mothers of Invention perform at the Montreux Casino. The Casino was a huge building that housed restaurants, several nightclubs, and a convention center. During the concert, someone fired a flare gun. The flare hit the ceiling with a loud crack, then all hell broke loose. The electrical wiring lining the ceiling began to unravel and catch fire, setting off a domino effect of explosions. Within minutes, the entire building was in flames.

Singer Ian Gillan was having trouble walking that day because he was recovering from a bout of hepatitis, but he managed to flee to safety with his girlfriend. As the hall filled with smoke, making the exits difficult to locate, some fans panicked and threw themselves through plate glass windows trying to escape. Deep Purple's soundman in Montreux, Claude Nobs, knew the layout of the Casino and managed to rescue a number of people who were trapped in the passageways. The Casino blazed all night, the flames ultimately reaching 200 feet high. The smoke that spewed from the fire eventually descended over a tranquil lake nearby and lingered over the water for hours. By morning, the entire building had completely burned to the ground. The band watched the blaze from their hotel, and later that night, the title "Smoke on the Water" came to Roger Glover in his sleep.

Ian Gillan originally vetoed the title, figuring people would think the song was about smoking weed. The lyrics were written just like a conversation and explained exactly what had happened the night before: "We all came down to Montreux, on the Lake Geneva shoreline. . . ." The band never thought the song would be a hit, yet its signature riff has become a classic. It's one of the first riffs aspiring guitarists learn, almost criminal in its simplicity and instantly recognizable.

Deep Purple also became known for their long jams, and like Led Zeppelin, put them to similar use. One night when Blackmore went into a seventeen-minute guitar solo, Gillan sneaked a groupie underneath Jon Lord's Hammond organ and had sex with time to spare. "Thank God for the long solo," he said years after the event. To this day he doesn't know the girl's name, stating, "We weren't properly introduced."

While Black Sabbath, Led Zeppelin, and Deep Purple were creating a new style of music from the ground up, two American artists were about to drastically change the public's expectations for live bands, taking performances to a whole new level of theatrics. The days of touring with minimal lighting and no drum riser would soon come to an end, as the spectacle of the show for heavy metal acts would become as important, if not more so, than the music.

Born the son of a preacher man, **Alice Cooper** was more than just the original "shock rock" king. He was also a pioneer of rock and roll theatrics and paved the way for many artists to come, especially Kiss. (Neil Zlozower)

2

> "EVERYONE NEEDS A GIMMICK. LET'S SEE HOW FAR YOU GET WITHOUT ONE."
>
> —Alice Cooper

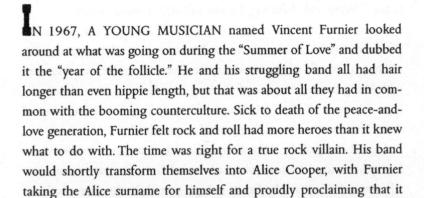

IN 1967, A YOUNG MUSICIAN named Vincent Furnier looked around at what was going on during the "Summer of Love" and dubbed it the "year of the follicle." He and his struggling band all had hair longer than even hippie length, but that was about all they had in common with the booming counterculture. Sick to death of the peace-and-love generation, Furnier felt rock and roll had more heroes than it knew what to do with. The time was right for a true rock villain. His band would shortly transform themselves into Alice Cooper, with Furnier taking the Alice surname for himself and proudly proclaiming that it was he who drove the final stake through the heart of the Woodstock generation. As far back as high school, Vincent realized if he couldn't fit in by being normal, he could stand out by being *abnormal.* He once said, "I fear mediocrity more than death."

The man who would eventually become rock and roll's prince of darkness was born in Detroit in 1948 with severe asthma. His family moved to Phoenix when he was three, hoping the dry, desert air would make it easier for him to breathe. Vincent's father worked as a used-car salesman but was often between jobs, making it tough for the family to make ends meet as they bounced around between Phoenix, Detroit, and Los Angeles. Compounding the family's problems was his father's heavy drinking. The elder Furnier eventually went on the wagon and become an ordained minister in 1961. He performed missionary work on the local Indian reservations, and sometimes the family would spend up to seven days a week in church.

When Vincent was thirteen, he came down with a severe case of typhoid. When the doctors told his parents he wasn't going to make it,

Vincent's father prayed for his son's survival, and eventually he pulled through after spending over a year in bed. His illness left him with a curvature of the spine and hunched shoulders. After a year in isolation, all Vincent wanted to do when he started high school was to fit in. Already an awkward teenager, self-conscious about his crooked teeth and "the cursed Furnier nose," he admitted, "I was not exactly a front-runner." Witty and charming, he was still able to make friends.

Furnier has carried a strong faith in God with him throughout his life, even after he became a rock star. Yet as a teenager, he stopped going to church because of the hypocrisy he found there. He was disgusted with being taunted because of his long hair. "I knew more about religion than most of them. I believed with more conviction than most of them. That I was even walking around was a miracle."

A great irony of the Alice Cooper band is that every member was a four-year varsity letterman who had met while on the track team. Usually the jocks beat up the freaks in high school. In this case, the jocks later became the freaks. In 1963, Vincent, Michael Bruce (guitar), Glen Buxton (guitar), Dennis Dunaway (bass), and Neal Smith (drums) formed their first band, called the Earwigs. The band worshipped the Beatles and played their first gig wearing "moptop" toupees, singing spoofs of the Fab Four's tunes with modified lyrics about the track team. They even hired girls to scream for them, just like Beatle fans.

When they practiced, the band would drive out to the desert with a case of beer, plug a power generator into the last telephone pole they came to on the road, and rehearse into the night. Their only audience was often a large group of stray cats whose countless tiny green eyes would stare back at them through the darkness. Sometimes, though, their loud, blaring music would wake up the migrant workers sleeping in the nearby orange groves, who would shout at them and call the police to shut them down. When the band recorded their first albums, their goal was to recreate the vibe of those late-night jams in the desert.

Going through several name changes during their early years, the

Earwigs became the Spiders and recorded what is now a highly collectable single called "Don't Blow Your Mind." They then became the Nazz, only to learn that Todd Rundgren already had a band by that name. So in the spring of 1968, they became Alice Cooper. Legend has it the band got their name when a Ouija board told Furnier that he was reincarnated from a seventeenth-century witch named Alice Cooper. The truth is actually much more mundane. The band liked it because it had a nice ring to it, like Baby Jane or Lizzie Borden, a combination of sweet and evil. Shortly after coming up with the name, they decided that Furnier would actually become the character of Cooper, a decision that several in the band would rue in years to come.

A fan of horror movies as a boy, Furnier always rooted for the villains—for Bela Lugosi's Dracula and Boris Karloff's Frankenstein, for the monsters like Godzilla and King Kong. Because of his struggles growing up, he equated being a villain with being an outsider, an underdog, just like heavy metal musicians and fans alike. With Cooper, Furnier now had a whole new persona he could step into at will. He could say and do outrageous things and blame them on Cooper, always being careful to refer to his alter ego in the third person. "Most people have a light side and a dark side," he would say. "My dark side gets to go onstage."

Like most parents of the time, Furnier's folks were shocked by the Beatles and the Rolling Stones. His goal was to come up with something that would *really* shock people and make those groups seem tame in comparison. It was guitarist Glen Buxton who first put dark circles under his eyes with cigarette ashes, and soon everyone in the band was wearing makeup, none more ghoulish than Cooper's thick, black, dripping eyeliner, which would become his trademark. His dirty mascara made him look like an evil harlequin whose eyes and mouth were bleeding (his early makeup also made his eyes look like they were crawling with worms). The band's stage clothes were also completely outrageous. One night they went onstage in plastic see-through pants; when they started to play, the pants fogged from sweat, obscuring their genitals from the audience. Their look was so outrageous for the time that many thought they were gay or, at the very least, transvestites.

By 1968, the band had moved to Los Angeles. They couldn't afford to live in Laurel Canyon, where a lot of rock stars like Joni Mitchell and Crosby, Stills, Nash and Young would eventually set up digs. Nor could they afford to live in Beverly Hills. Instead, they moved into a Topanga Canyon home that was literally sliding down the hill. The band played regularly at the Cheetah, a club located at the end of the Santa Monica Pier. They opened for the Doors when "Light My Fire" was on its way to becoming a hit single. Cooper and Jim Morrison became friendly and would often sit at the end of the pier, talking for hours. Already Cooper could see the burden of fame was affecting Morrison and couldn't remember a time when he wasn't drunk.

Alice Cooper wasn't welcomed to L.A. with open arms, however. People walked out on them in droves, and they quickly gained a rep as "the worst band in L.A." According to Cooper, they once cleared out a room of 6,000 people in three songs. Yelling "Fire" couldn't have emptied the room faster. It soon became trendy to say that you walked out on Alice Cooper. A few who couldn't stand to sit through even a couple of songs would buy tickets and simply not go to the gig. Then they would show off the ticket stub and brag that they had walked out on an Alice Cooper show.

At one show where the audience did its usual exodus, one of the few who stayed was an enterprising young man named Shep Gordon. Gordon had just come out to L.A. after graduating from the University of Buffalo in upstate New York and wanted to start managing bands. Michael Bruce's sister was an acquaintance of Gordon's and recommended he check out her brother's band. Gordon figured he would try to reverse what had just happened, with thousands of people rushing in to want to see the band instead of fleeing. The band was not an easy sell, to say the least. None of the local record labels was interested in signing them. The band had one meeting at Sound Records at which they were told they could have a deal, but only if they got rid of "that Vince guy."

During their time in L.A., Cooper had become friendly with the GTOs, "Girls Together Outrageously," a gang of groupies led by legendary "band-aid" Pamela Miller (who later became Pamela Des Barres). Miss Christine, a member of the GTOs, baby-sat Frank Zappa's daughter Moon Unit while Zappa was putting together his own label, Straight Records. Straight was an ironic name: Zappa was looking for "freak" bands to sign. He should have been careful what he wished for. Miss Christine introduced the Alice Cooper band to Zappa, who told them to come by his house the next day at seven o'clock. The band arrived at 7 A.M. the following morning and started jamming in Zappa's basement. He came down the stairs in his underwear, groggy and confused, with a mug of coffee in his hand. "I meant 7 at night!" he told them. Zappa, no stranger to weird music, found Alice Cooper's truly bizarre. He signed the band to Straight for $6,000. All our struggles are over, thought Cooper.

On September 13, 1969, Alice Cooper played the Toronto Rock 'n' Roll Revival festival. The Doors headlined the show, and it was the first time John Lennon performed solo without the Beatles. During the band's stage show, a trademark Cooper trick was to break open a pillow and fill the theater with feathers. While Cooper was thrashing his pillow about during the Toronto show, a chicken was thrown onstage. Cooper had never come across a live chicken in his life and figured if it had wings, it could fly. He threw it up in the air, expecting it to soar away to freedom. Instead, the bird fell straight into the audience, and a frenzy of hands began grabbing it. Before anyone could figure out what was happening, the chicken was torn to pieces. Its legs, wings, and head flew into the air, along with a healthy amount of blood. The next day, headlines across the world read that Alice Cooper had sacrificed a chicken and drunk its blood onstage.

With nothing left to lose, the band decided to move to Detroit, Cooper's original hometown. As hard as the band had tried, no one in Los Angeles had any idea what they were trying to do. But the minute they hit Detroit, Alice Cooper were immediately accepted and became kindred spirits with other revolutionary Motor City acts like the MC5 and Iggy Pop. "That was the original metal audience," said Cooper of the Detroit fans. They were middle-class, hard-working, hard-drinking kids. Aerosmith called the Detroit fans "the Blue Army" because when you looked out into the arena, you'd see waves of blue like a gigantic denim ocean. It's not surprising that Cooper became a star in a working-class environment: He always felt the band was an all-American phenomenon. "Our band is the epitome of everything that's American," he said. "We like girls with big tits, which is typically American. You can't find anybody in the band who'll eat gourmet food. Hamburgers, cheeseburgers, McDonald's, Jack in the Box—everything that's typically American for this period of time, we are. Beer, football, *everything.*"

There was, however, one more element that needed to be in place before Alice Cooper broke. They needed a hit record. The band had recorded two albums for Zappa's Straight label, *Pretties for You* and *Easy Action.* Both albums were musically abstract, and neither sold well. By 1970, Zappa sold his Straight label to Warner Bros. to offset its losses. For $50,000, Warner got James Taylor, Linda Ronstadt, and Alice Cooper. The record company wasn't exactly thrilled to get Alice Cooper, but Shep Gordon believed that if he could find the right producer for the band, they could fulfill the promise he had always seen in them.

Bob Ezrin was a native of Toronto. He began taking music lessons when he was five years old, studying classical piano, jazz piano, and composition. He first met Cooper while working as an assistant to Jack Richardson, producer for the Guess Who. Shep Gordon thought Richardson—who had his own production company, Nimbus Nine—would be the perfect producer for Alice Cooper. When Gordon brought in the first two Alice Cooper albums, everyone in the office was mortified. "Forget it," they screamed. "We're not doing this!"

But Shep Gordon would not take no for an answer. He got a partner, Leo Fenn, to keep pestering Richardson, who finally relented, saying, "If my assistant likes them, I'll talk to the band." Fenn got Ezrin's phone number and called him forty times a day. Ezrin hated *Easy Action* but finally agreed to go see the band at Max's Kansas City, a New York club.

When he arrived at the club, "I walked into an underworld filled with spandex, spider eyes, people who looked stranger than any group of people I've ever seen in my life," he recalls. The audience was all bone-thin with pasty white skin, black fingernails, long muttonchop sideburns, and tons of bracelets and rings.

Ezrin and Fenn sat down right in front. Cooper appeared onstage, his hair filthy and stringy, wearing mascara and high heels, and pounding a sledgehammer while singing a song called "Sun Arise." A policeman came in and threatened to break up the show, but Fenn stood up and screamed at him, "You have no right to stop this show! This show is not obscene! Stay off the stage!"

Alice Cooper's live performance completely assaulted Ezrin. After the band left the stage, he wondered aloud, "What the fuck was that?"

"I don't know, but I think I liked it," said Fenn.

"I think I loved it," said Ezrin.

Ezrin also knew that with a lot of work, the band could have hit singles. Never before had he seen an artist tap into so much adolescent pain and confusion and physically manifest it in songs and stage performance.

The next day, an ecstatic Ezrin called Nimbus Nine, saying the production company had to do the record. "You're fired," they replied. Now it was Ezrin who wouldn't take no for an answer. He flew back to Toronto, stormed into Jack Richardson's office, jumped on his boss's desk, and delivered his impassioned plea. Alice Cooper wasn't just about music, Ezrin said. It was a cultural movement with an audience that looked just like the band. They would be foolish not to jump on this.

Finally, the honchos at Nimbus Nine told Ezrin: If you like them so much, *you* do it. "That's how I became a record producer," he says. Like Mike Clink, producer for Guns N' Roses, Ezrin was the only one brave enough to work with Alice Cooper, and it would make both his and the band's career.

In the early stages of a band's development, having the right producer is crucial. The right producer for a hard rock or metal band often has to be like the band he works with: young, hungry, and maybe a little nuts. A good producer, like a good manager, is like an additional member of the band. He can become part of the trusted inner circle of a band and party with them until dawn. But he should also be disciplined and know when to crack the whip when the job has to be done. A band needs someone of a like mind who can bring out its best and be its reality check from making mistakes. Ezrin wouldn't just produce Alice Cooper's best work—he would play a strong hand in reinventing the band from the ground up.

Warner Bros. told Gordon and Ezrin that the label would not finance an Alice Cooper album unless it heard songs with commercial potential. Many had thought the band was Frank Zappa's in-house joke on the Straight label, so Alice Cooper was determined to prove itself musically. Ezrin and the band retreated to a barn in Pontiac, Michigan, for two months, rehearsing ten to twelve hours a day. There was a prison yard right next door to the property. Some days, they'd leave the barn door open so the prisoners hanging out in the yard could hear their music. If the prisoners in the yard liked the music and cheered for it, the band knew they were on to something.

Ezrin helped re-create the band from scratch, much like piecing together a Frankenstein monster. "We kept a lot of the madness—we just controlled it, aimed it," says Ezrin, who approached the process like Method acting. He once told Cooper, "Pretend you're desperate for a drink. Sing like a sponge."

At first, the band was apprehensive about the new musical direction in which they were headed. As Cooper recalled, "I argued with him every step of the way, even after I heard it on tape and knew it sounded good. I wasn't sure it was right for us. Then suddenly, 'Eighteen' happened, and it was a *sound*."

When the band performed "Eighteen," Ezrin thought Cooper was singing, "I'm edgy, and I don't know what I want." This is *great*, Ezrin thought. Let's put out a really edgy song. And it's even called "Edgy!" He eventually found out the song was actually called "Eighteen," and his instructions to the band to sound edgy fit perfectly.

In 1971, "Eighteen" was released as a single. Warner Bros. agreed that if the song did well, the band could record an album. It became an instant teen anthem, perfectly capturing the confusion of growing up, when you're legally an adult but mentally and emotionally still a child—something many rock stars, including Cooper, could relate to well into their twenties. But Gordon didn't leave things to chance. He reportedly paid people a dollar for every time they called a radio station requesting the song. The band even made hundreds of calls themselves, which "built up a phone bill a mile long," according to guitarist Michael Bruce. It all paid off when the song became a national hit, peaking at No. 21 on the charts. The band was loading up their equipment in Detroit when they first heard "Eighteen" on the radio. It was playing on an AM station. "That was the boner right there," said Cooper in his autobiography, *Me, Alice*. AM radio meant that *everybody* was listening.

With the success of "Eighteen," Alice Cooper were able to record their debut album for Warner Bros., *Love It to Death*, which included their hit single. They immediately began touring nonstop, and their fortunes reversed practically overnight. By the summer of 1971, the album and the tour had made so much money that the band was able to buy a forty-two-room mansion in Greenwich, Connecticut, recently vacated by actress Ann-Margret, where the band wrote music and lived together for the next several years.

" 'Eighteen' changed Alice Cooper from the group that destroyed chickens to the group that destroyed stadiums," proclaimed *The Village Voice*. " 'Eighteen' became our license to kill," added Cooper. "Probably the most dangerous thing anybody ever did in the business was give Alice Cooper a single." Yet even with the breakthrough of the *Love It to Death* album, Warner Bros. still wasn't fond of Alice Cooper and considered their success a fluke.

The theatrics that dominated Alice Cooper's live show had developed early on in the band's club days. "We started to incorporate theatrics into our show as a way of distracting the audience from the fact that we weren't very good musicians," said Michael Bruce. They also found it kept them from getting bored performing the same songs every night. Cooper especially was heavily influenced by Hollywood, not just its horror films but musicals like *West Side Story* as well. He felt there was a whole generation out there that wasn't even aware of Busby Berkeley, the famous musical director from the 1930s, and wanted to bring that style of old-time entertainment into a rock context. On the *Billion Dollar Babies* tour, he even had Kate Smith belting out "God Bless America" from the P.A. at the end of each show.

The addition of a giant boa constrictor would become an Alice Cooper trademark. The first snake, Kachina, was featured on the cover of the *Killer* album. Cooper liked the symbolism of the reptile. When he would bring the snake onstage, one person might see something deadly and dangerous, another something phallic and sexual. At first Cooper was terrified of snakes, but he became so comfortable with Kachina that he eventually posed nude with her lying in his lap for a photo that became a famous poster. The next snake after Kachina was named Angie Boa, after David Bowie's then-wife, Angie. One night when Angie had to be left at the Canadian border in quarantine, a substitute snake was brought in. Cooper tried rehearsing with it, but it kept opening its mouth uncomfortably wide whenever it got near his head. There was no snake that show.

Alice Cooper's live shows were well-rehearsed, and mishaps were rare, but one was particularly nasty. Cooper often brought out a sword as a prop, and one night, he accidentally rammed it through his leg. The audience went nuts, thinking it was part of the show. Like a pro, Cooper finished the gig. Back at the hotel, a doctor showed up to give him a tetanus shot. Even though he had just rammed a dirty, rusty sword through his leg, Cooper refused to get a shot—he was terrified of needles. Instead he grabbed a bottle of Jack Daniels and poured it over his wounds.

At first, the stage props were all "low-budget radical," as Ezrin put it. But as the band grew more successful, their stage show grew equally more complex. One of the band's early props was a huge, heavy, wooden electric chair with sheets of corrugated steel on the back. Cooper used to sit in it like a king when the band would rehearse. "He loved his electric chair," remembers Ezrin.

Cooper looked at their shows as a rock and roll morality play, and in the end, he had to be punished by being put to death. "Shakespeare would have been my biggest fan," he said. For the *Killer* tour, Cooper hung himself from a fake gallows built by the Warner Bros. prop department. On later tours he was decapitated in a guillotine built by magician James "The Amazing" Randi. Even though there was no way Cooper could have gotten hurt because of the fail-safes built into the apparatus, the band told the press that there was only one hinge preventing their frontman from losing his head. They wanted the audience to believe that the show they were watching could potentially be Cooper's last.

To choreograph the band's increasingly elaborate stage show, Cooper hired a Broadway producer who had previously worked with Liza Minnelli. The theatrics became such an important part of Alice Cooper that the band's lighting director got an equal cut of the tour dividends. According to some accounts, the band members were divided about the extreme theatrical direction they were moving in. When the band finally broke up in 1975, Cooper said it was because his bandmates didn't want to do his wild stage show anymore, but Michael Bruce said he didn't mind the extravagant theatrics as long as it didn't become "a dancing musical." Drummer Neal Smith countered, "The whole band was into theatrics 150 percent. We loved it. That's what made us different."

There was no question that Alice Cooper's theatrics would set a strong benchmark for countless bands to come. "I think we liberated a lot of acts that wanted to be theatrical but couldn't," said Cooper. "David Bowie used to come to our shows in England when he was a folk singer. Elton John was this nice piano player who came to our show at the Hollywood Bowl and sat in the front row. The next time I saw him he was in a Donald Duck outfit, wearing huge glasses and doing Dodger Stadium."

While Alice Cooper's stage show was becoming legendary, their music was catching on as well. With the *Killer* album, released in November of 1971, the band came close to cracking the Top Twenty, peaking at No. 21. But their real commercial breakthrough came the following year with *School's Out,* which zoomed to No. 2 on the album charts. With the song "School's Out," Cooper wanted to capture "the happiest, most exhilarating moment of the year . . . when the clock is one minute to three on the last day of school, and then it finally goes click." As with "Eighteen," it was another archetypal teenage anthem, and would become the band's first Top Ten single, peaking at No. 7 in the United States and No. 1 in England. The *School's Out* album featured a pair of women's panties stretched over the cover. When the band headlined the Hollywood Bowl, hundreds of panties rained down from the skies, dropped from helicopters.

On "School's Out," producer Ezrin employed a choir of children singing, "No more pencils, no more books . . ." "One of the best moments in rock history, I think, is when those kids come on that record," says Ezrin, who called a New York casting agency and had them send over "five stage-brat kids with their stage-brat parents. I had to explain to the parents why it was okay for this group of kids to sing with this group of completely twisted individuals. And the kids were scared to death, but I got them all to relax and by the end of it, the kids were all laughing and giggling. They loved Alice." A choir of children would become one of Ezrin's trademarks, and he would use it to great effect years later on Pink Floyd's "Another Brick in the Wall (Part Two)."

The following year, Alice Cooper settled in at their mansion in Connecticut to record their next album, *Billion Dollar Babies*. They finished it at Morgan Studios in England, where folk hippie singer Donovan was recording as well. Donovan walked down the hall to the Cooper session and put in a guest appearance on the *Babies* album, providing the echoing schizophrenic voice inside Alice's head on the title track, with the harmonies structured like the children's song "Row, Row, Row Your Boat." *Billion Dollar Babies* would prove to be their biggest seller to date, going to No. 1 in both the United States and United Kingdom.

By the time Alice Cooper set out on the *Billion Dollar Babies* tour, the band was sick of the road, having spent much of the past three years touring. With a No. 1 record, they hoped that by the end of the tour they would have made enough money to retire and get out. They scheduled sixty-four concerts in fifty-nine cities in ninety days—a grueling pace—and anticipated a gross of around $20 million.

Chicago Tribune journalist Bob Greene came along with them to write a book about the tour. What he saw was a band that was starting to fall apart right in front of him. Being the most notorious frontman in rock and roll had taken its toll on Cooper, and he drank heavily to deal with the pressure. "If Alice Cooper was destroying anyone, he was destroying me," Cooper recalled in his book. "It bothered me every time I was criticized. I made my own bed, and I was being paid handsomely to sleep in it. But even if you're grossing $20 million a year, it begins to drive you crazy when you get called a degenerate. I was tired of being the rebel. I was tired of being thrown out of church. I made my point, *all right*. Now what?"

When a fourteen-year-old Canadian boy was found dead in his room, having hung himself near a photo on his wall of Alice hanging from his stage gallows, the parents naturally blamed Cooper. It was one of the first incidents of heavy metal being blamed for teenage suicide, and Cooper and Ezrin were deeply troubled by the boy's death.

"I thought if we had anything to do with [the suicide], we needed to take a really close look at what we were doing," says Ezrin. "In fact, it changed my attitude toward what we were doing. Up until then, it was goofy and fun, but at that point, I started to take very seriously the responsibility of the rock star. We made sure from that point on that anything we did was really cartoony."

On the *Babies* tour, the band was now flying the Starship, the deluxe airplane that Led Zeppelin and the Rolling Stones used when they were on tour. The Starship's interior resembled a gaudy Las Vegas lounge. The plane had a giant couch, a study, a shower in the bathroom, and a large bedroom that was quite popular. In fact, it's probably the heavy metal and hard rock groups of the '70s that opened the first branch of the Mile High Club. The Starship also had one of the first VCRs and a videotape library before video technology was readily available. *Deep Throat* had recently come out and was a popular film on the Starship. The bands that used the plane had watched it so many times they had worn out two copies. Their first time on the Starship, the band put on *Deep Throat* before takeoff. As Greene wrote, "We sped down the runway and up into the air, just as Linda Lovelace was giving the first demonstration of her oral dexterity." Cooper preferred watching the Marx Brothers.

Tensions were high during the *Babies* tour, and Greene witnessed a lot of blowups among the band members. Bruce and Neal Smith constantly vented to Greene that they felt like a backup band and weren't getting the attention they felt they deserved. "I write No. 1 songs, and Alice ruins them," Bruce told Greene, complaining that the band was holding him back. "I wrote 'School's Out' and 'I'm Eighteen.' Then Alice takes them and puts his own weird lyrics in them, and they're not No. 1 songs anymore, they're just songs that fit the stage image we've built up."

Bruce had always resented Cooper and Ezrin making changes to his music, even though their changes took the band to a whole new level of success. Nor did Bruce get along with Shep Gordon, despite the fact that Gordon was also a big driving force in the band's success. "Shep doesn't care about the music," he said. "All Shep cares about is pushing

Alice, making Alice a bigger and bigger star on his own." Bruce wanted everyone in the band to be known equally, like the Beatles.

Yet in spite of the band's internal strife, Greene felt, "they did not hate Alice; they did not hate Shep. The band and the managers had been together for so many years that they were all virtually the only real friends they had. The years on the road, in their effort to achieve the heights, had made them absolutely dependent on each other for every kind of support."

Greene also felt that underneath all the ego battles and the complaining, the band was genuinely afraid of Alice leaving. "Now that they were on top, it seemed that the rest of the group was realizing for the first time that Alice really could, if he wanted, get along without them," Greene continued. "The same could not be said for the other four, who would be right back where they started without the Alice Cooper name."

Beside the emotional turmoil in the band, the tour also left them physically wrecked. The tour also wasn't the big financial windfall that everyone had hoped for either, grossing $4 million—huge by 1974 standards, but $3.5 million of it went toward touring expenses.

As anyone who's watched more than two episodes of VH-1's *Behind the Music* can tell you, the grind of being on the road has fractured many a band. Artists don't stay on the road anywhere near as long as metal and hard rock groups routinely did in the '70s and '80s, mainly because the process is too mentally and physically exhausting. Bands usually went from the stage to the hotel and back again, repeatedly, for years, and rarely had time to even see the world they were circling. It was all one big blur outside the window of the tour bus. Cooper used to say that whenever someone asked him where he lived, he'd point to the nearest Holiday Inn.

After the *Billion Dollar Babies* tour, the band decided to write a quick, no-frills record, do a small tour, and *then* take a much-needed break. The follow-up to *Babies, Muscle of Love,* was a big disappointment, both creatively and commercially. Ezrin didn't produce the album, supposedly because he was going through a divorce. As much as Bruce didn't get along with Ezrin and complained he streamlined their sound, he felt one reason the album didn't jell was because Ezrin wasn't behind the boards. The band also realized they had peaked with *Babies,* and it was a tough album to follow up.

Like most band breakups, Alice Cooper's was a train wreck that was a long time coming. Many heavy metal bands have a tragic figure, and in Alice Cooper, it was guitarist Glen Buxton. It was Buxton who taught Dennis Dunaway how to play the bass; he wrote the classic riff to "School's Out." Dunaway felt that it was Buxton's spirit that really drove the band, but he had been drinking heavily since he was fifteen and was up to a quart of whisky a day by his high school graduation. Years of alcohol abuse had wrecked his digestive system. He eventually had to be brought to the hospital for alcohol poisoning, and his pancreas had to be drained. Buxton looked far older than his twenty-six years, and by the *Billion Dollar Babies* tour he was seriously falling apart. He was no longer capable of playing, and two guitarists had to play behind a curtain for him. Buxton was also deteriorating mentally: During the *Muscle of Love* tour, he pulled a knife on their tour manager. As Buxton's behavior became more and more erratic, he became alienated from the rest of the band. Bruce felt that it was ultimately Buxton's downfall that gave Cooper the final incentive he needed to leave and pursue a solo career. Buxton died on October 19, 1997, from pneumonia.

Cooper's subsequent solo project, *Welcome to My Nightmare,* would be his rebirth. On the eve of the *Nightmare* tour, Cooper's four former bandmates signed legal agreements officially breaking up the original band. "Shep said we didn't have an employment contract so we couldn't force Alice back into the group," said Bruce. The band left the door open for Cooper to come back, but when the realization sunk in that he wasn't going to return, they all went their separate ways.

"Alice is a good guy, and I considered him my best friend," said Dennis Dunaway. "As far as not being on stage and not touring, that doesn't bother me as much as the fact that somebody who I thought was my best friend could just sort of eliminate me and eliminate everything that I had worked for creatively, overnight."

As Alice embarked on his new solo career, his former bandmates struggled to find a new identity. Bruce recorded a solo album that couldn't get an American deal. A year later, he formed Billion Dollar Babies with Smith and Dunaway. Their debut album went overbudget, ran late, and was completely ignored upon its release. They sank a lot of money into a tour that lasted only four dates. They built a huge stage like they'd used in the Alice Cooper glory days, but with the album flopping and the tour canceled, it ended up sitting in a warehouse. Bruce didn't realize what he had with Cooper until it was gone. "It was only then that I saw the writing on the wall," he said. "Okay, so maybe I had never really received the recognition I thought I deserved, but who was I without the band?"

Cooper himself was nervous about going out on his own, unsure if the fans would accept him as a solo artist. To alleviate his fears, he brought Ezrin back into the fold to produce the album, and Ezrin brought a hot new band in for him, including guitarists Steve Hunter and Dick Wagner, who had played with Lou Reed. In addition he spent close to half a million dollars to set up the subsequent tour. Cooper figured the *Nightmare* album would either be his greatest triumph or his most embarrassing failure. As luck would have it, *Nightmare* turned out to be a tremendous success. Despite some complaints that the chemistry of the original band was gone, *Nightmare* would become one of Cooper's quintessential albums, one of the first albums many of his fans bought or got into.

The song "The Black Widow" has a spoken-word introduction by Vincent Price, who leads Steven, a young boy who is the main character of the *Nightmare* album, through a spider museum. Price works himself into a frenzy, guiding the boy through all the different species of arachnids until he comes to the black widow, maniacally predicting how it will one day swarm the earth. The pitch to Price to appear on the record was simple: Ezrin called him and asked, "Mr. Price, how would you like to make your rock and roll debut?" He couldn't pass it up. The entire speech was written by Price and Ezrin over the phone and recorded in an hour from separate studios.

Right before the *Nightmare* album reaches its halfway point, the album softens with the ballad "Only Women Bleed." Many felt the song offered a grim view of being an abused woman. "Alice must have had some pretty good drugs back then, because he really put himself in a woman's position to write that song," said Lita Ford, who covered "Bleed." Ironically, Ike and Tina Turner also covered the song while they were married. Cooper claimed the lyrics were never really about domestic violence, but feminists latched onto the song. Gloria Steinem is rumored to have thanked Cooper by telegram for writing the song.

With Cooper's solo success, he discovered that he could exist and thrive outside the confines of a band. He would soon adopt a revolving-door policy, changing lineups between albums and tours. "When Alice decides to do a tour from one golf tournament to the other, he gets his band together, whoever it might be, and goes on tour as Alice Cooper," said former Guns N' Roses guitarist Slash. "So whoever is available and whoever is not is replaceable in Alice's mind." (Besides Cooper, Ozzy Osbourne, and Gene and Paul of Kiss would usually remain the focal points of their bands, while other musicians would come and go.)

Besides his triumph in going solo, it was also in the mid-1970s that Cooper's obsession with golf took hold. From the airplane, he'd look out the window and call to his road manager Joe Gannon, "Joe! There's a course down there! We gotta get in nine holes before the show tonight!" He even kept his clubs in the equipment truck. Cooper's love of golf continues to this day.

At this point in the '70s, Cooper also started becoming friendly with a number of old-time Hollywood stars such as George Burns and Groucho Marx. Marx, who often stayed up all night, would call Cooper whenever a Marx Brothers movie was coming on TV, invite him over, and tell him behind-the-scenes anecdotes while they watched the film together into the wee hours of the morning. Cooper loved old-time

Hollywood so much that he and Shep Gordon contributed to the campaign to save the famous Hollywood sign from decay. Cooper's donation helped preserve the second O in *Wood*, which he dedicated to Groucho's memory.

More and more, Cooper was stepping away from his stage persona in public, something Shep didn't want him to do at first. For years Gordon wouldn't let Cooper go on the *Tonight Show*, even though Cooper was dying to do the show, because it would have compromised his mystique. "Do you know how many people that's going to turn off?" asked Gordon. Michael Bruce said that when the band was at its peak with the *Babies* album Cooper felt trapped in his alter ego, locked into a role when the other guys in the band clearly weren't. Cooper got tired of being treated like the Antichrist by the unknowing public who didn't understand that the character was just part of his performance.

Little by little, Cooper began appearing out of character in public, playing golf with celebrities and eventually on television. In late 1976, *The Midnight Special* did a tribute to Alice Cooper. Instead of coming out in dripping black eyeliner with a dismembered baby doll in his hand, he appeared with no makeup at all, wearing shorts, a tanktop, and sneakers. His hair was its natural color, brown, instead of dyed jet black. Cooper looked like he just stepped off of a tennis court rather than out of a dungeon.

The fans were crushed; they really wanted to believe he was that monster on stage twenty-four hours a day. But keeping his onstage and offstage personas separate was something Cooper had always insisted on. He once said part of the reason he made that decision was from observing Keith Moon killing himself trying to be "Keith Moon" twenty-four hours a day. A lot of heavy metal and hard rock musicians have felt obligated to live up to the crazed rock-star stereotypes of groupies, drugs, wrecked hotel rooms—all the trappings that come with success in the music industry. The problem is that it gets harder and harder to top the last feat of outrageousness, and the stereotype becomes harder to escape. "I think [Cooper] drank more and more as there was increasing pressure on him to be more outrageous and upstage the last thing he did," said Bruce in his autobiography, *No More Mr. Nice Guy.*

It would take Ozzy Osbourne years to live down his "madman" persona, and much of his recent press has focused on his family life. Gene Simmons's onstage persona was such an extension of his personality that when Kiss took off their makeup in 1983 he felt lost without it.

Cooper was smart enough to realize that not separating who you are onstage with who you are offstage can be very dangerous. "If you're not careful, the whole world will push you into being that character," says Steve Hunter, who played guitar for Cooper from 1975 to 1979. "I knew when I got onstage with Alice and looked him in the eye, he was a different guy. I liked that."

Right as the Alice Cooper band was peaking, out of New York came a band called Kiss. Kiss was heavily influenced by Alice Cooper, so much so that in their early days they reportedly played as an Alice Cooper tribute band. What Michael Bruce saw in Kiss was a band that was more together than Alice Cooper had ever been. "They got four guys with makeup, four Alices," he said. "We couldn't even control the one Alice we had!"

Kiss was inspired by the success of Alice Cooper as well as that of the New York Dolls. Kiss wanted to be like the Dolls because of the quality and quantity of the women they attracted. The Dolls, headed by lead singer David Johansen and guitarist Johnny Thunders, were a short-lived but extremely influential band. Their provocative look—high heels, high hair, lipstick, and leather—was backed by a raw, sloppy, powerful sound. Along with being a major influence on the punk movement in New York, the Dolls also influenced a lot of late-1980s L.A. bands like Guns N' Roses.

The Dolls' self-titled album was produced by Todd Rundgren and recorded in a week, and it almost drove him to a nervous breakdown. Said Johansen, "In the end, Todd got so fed up with everyone saying,

'Turn me up,' that he just turned *everybody* up." Despite the Dolls' early promise, they fell apart in 1974, from alcohol and heroin abuse, just after releasing their aptly titled second album, *Too Much Too Soon*. The entire glam/glitter scene was laid to rest on October 11, 1974, at a concert called the *Hollywood Street Revival and Dance,* held at the Hollywood Palladium. The Dolls headlined the show, and a mock funeral was held for glitter and glam onstage.

With the Dolls self-destructing and Alice Cooper's original lineup falling apart, the four members of Kiss—Gene Simmons, Paul Stanley, Ace Frehley, and Peter Criss—saw an opening they could crash through like a semi. According to photographer Bob Gruen, "they figured there was no point in trying to be beautiful, because they couldn't compete with the Dolls, so they decided to be monsters."

Simmons was born Chaim Witz in Israel in 1949, and his father left the family when he was six. Like many children abandoned by a parent, Simmons learned to fend for himself at an early age and never let anyone stand in the way of what he wanted. If someone didn't live up to his standards, he'd move on without them without a second thought. "Anybody who held me back was gone in a second, and that includes women," he said. It was a pattern that would repeat itself throughout Simmons's life and career.

Simmons embraced his Israeli upbringing. "In Israel, religion takes a back seat to survival," he said. "There's a real difference between Israelis and American Jews. The latter strike me as being weak and spineless. Israelis, because they have no choice, come off much closer to Puerto Ricans and the Mafia than to anybody else. You have to have that backbone or you're dead, it's over. Being Jewish really gives you a sense of identity more than anything else. To be Jewish is to have a sense that your mind is your strongest feature. And therein lies real power." When Simmons was nine, he and his mother moved to New York, and his name was legally changed to Gene Klein.

Simmons met Paul Stanley through a mutual friend, Steve Coronel. Simmons was teaching grade school, but he clearly wasn't cut out for a life in the classroom. "I wanted to kill those little pricks," he once re-called. Stanley, born Paul Stanley Eisen, was from upstate New York and, like Simmons, was a middle-class kid. At their first meeting, Stanley was put off by Simmons's condescending arrogance. Eventually Coronel convinced them to play together, in spite of their initial dislike of each other, and they found that they clicked musically.

In 1970, Simmons and Stanley, along with Coronel, formed the band Wicked Lester. The next year, they were offered a deal with Epic Records, on the condition that they fire Coronel as their guitar player. Even though he had brought Simmons and Stanley together, Coronel was immediately dismissed. "There was no reason for the whole band to sink because of one guy," said Simmons, and this would be his M.O. throughout the history of Kiss.

Wicked Lester recorded an album, but it was never released. (Simmons and Stanley would buy back the rights from Epic when Kiss started getting popular, mainly to prevent pictures of them without makeup from being released.) Even with a major-label deal, Simmons and Stanley knew they were in the wrong band and were plotting to put something bigger together. While rehearsing with Wicked Lester, they were secretly auditioning other musicians. Scanning the want ads in *Rolling Stone* and other music magazines, they found an ad from a drummer named George Peter Criscuola who said he would do "anything to make it." At the same time, a guitarist named Paul Daniel Frehley advertised in *The Village Voice* that he had "flash and balls."

When Simmons and Stanley first talked to Frehley—who had a funny mustache and often wore a charcoal gray pinstripe suit, purple sneakers, and socks that didn't match—they hyped their new band, telling him they already had a record deal. The first song he played with the band was "Deuce," written by Simmons. Frehley loved it and immediately wanted to join the band, even after he found out there really was no record deal.

Everyone in the band decided to change their names at once. Gene Klein became Gene Simmons; Paul Stanley Eisen became Paul Stanley;

Peter Criscuola became Peter Criss; and since the name Paul was already taken, Frehley took the nickname Ace. They wanted to call the band a four-letter word, but since Fuck was out of the question, Kiss was the next best thing. Just as many thought Alice Cooper was a folksinger, Kiss's name was deceptive—at first, some thought they were a soft rock group, like Bread.

Simmons and Stanley were the main songwriters in Kiss. They had become close friends in spite of their early misgivings, though underneath their partnership there was still a rivalry. Simmons had a strong business mind and was supremely confident. He never tired of promoting himself or the band. Neither Simmons nor Stanley drank or used drugs. For Simmons especially, women and money would prove far more intoxicating than any controlled substance.

In many hard rock and heavy metal bands, there are class differences among members, and Kiss were a perfect example. Ace Frehley and Peter Criss came from a different world than Simmons and Stanley. Frehley and Criss had grown up on the streets, running around in gangs in the Bronx and Brooklyn. Where Simmons and Stanley were the businessmen of the group, Frehley and Criss were the band's true rockers. Criss was also volatile and dangerous. He would often fly into rages without a moment's notice and destroyed many a hotel room, often with his idol, Frank Sinatra, playing in the background. When Criss was in a good mood, he could be the life of the party, packing a huge entourage in his room. A split second later, he could become moody and distant, hibernating alone in his room for days. He loved guns too, which, considering his temper and unpredictability, was a bad idea. One Christmas, he shot up the tree in a rage. He once greeted Chris Lendt, Kiss's business manager, at the door with his gun clearly displayed in a holster. Criss told him he liked to wear it around the house to scare his wife. Lendt wasn't sure if he was kidding or not.

In their early days, Kiss lived and rehearsed in a giant loft on Manhattan's East 23rd Street, near Fifth Avenue, where they also showcased for record labels. Simmons and Stanley constantly practiced their stage moves during rehearsals, while Frehley would just lean against the wall while playing ripping leads. Simmons and Stanley kept going up to Frehley and nudging him with their guitars to get him to start moving along with them. The band first developed their makeup at a Long Island club called the Daisy, and their famous face designs evolved over time. At first, Frehley painted his face completely silver; Stanley painted his face all red. Simmons was supposedly the first to put makeup around his eyes, and the rest of the band soon followed with designs that reflected their inner personalities; soon they would lock down their trademark war paint.

On July 13, 1973, Kiss played a show at the Hotel Diplomat, a run-down, barely open building located in Times Square that was mostly frequented by hookers and junkies. In the audience was a television producer named Bill Aucoin who was looking to get into the music business. Stepping across gaping holes in the ballroom floor to meet the band after the show, Aucoin introduced himself and said, "Let's get together at my office and see whether there's something we can do."

Like Shep Gordon, Aucoin was a novice, and along with the band, would learn as he went along. Aucoin brought Kiss to mogul-to-be Neil Bogart. Bogart had a deal with Warner Bros. to distribute his acts. "Neil wanted to work with me and my associate at that point, Joyce Biawitz," says Aucoin. "She eventually became Joyce Bogart."

Neil Bogart loved over-the-top stage shows and personalities. Three of his biggest acts—Parliament, the Village People, and Kiss—would share that connective tissue even though none of them sounded remotely alike. Bogart himself was a larger-than-life character, a P. T. Barnum of rock and roll who knew how to hype and present everything in an outsized way. But according to Simmons, Bogart initially had cold feet about Kiss's makeup. As he recalled, when Bogart first came to see the band live, he told them, "I think this kind of garish stuff is over. Forget the makeup, and do it my way." But Simmons was adamant about keeping the makeup, telling Bogart, "We've got to do what we believe."

If the band couldn't wear the makeup, he told him, they'd walk. Bogart finally relented. "Okay, if you guys really believe in it, I believe in your belief."

As Aucoin recalls, everyone had second thoughts about the makeup at first, but it was Warner Bros., not Neil Bogart, who wanted the band to ditch it. "Warner Bros. never really liked Kiss," says Aucoin. "And they asked Neil to either get rid of this makeup band or certainly their makeup."

Kiss were rehearsing, getting ready to leave on their first tour, when Aucoin received a call from Bogart saying he was having a problem with Warner Bros., who had strong misgivings about the band wearing makeup. "Would you please ask them if they would consider taking it off?"

"Look, Neil, we've gone too far with this, and I really don't think the band's going to go along with it," said Aucoin. "I'll ask them as a courtesy to you, but I don't think it's going to happen." When he asked the band if they would consider taking off their makeup, they became worried. If they didn't, would they lose their record deal? "No, I don't think that's the case," Aucoin assured them. "We gotta stick to our guns. We can't be wishy-washy about it."

This did not sit well with Warner Bros. Soon a secret memo was distributed through the company that basically said the company liked Neil Bogart but was going to let Kiss slip through the cracks. They were certain Bogart would come up with another act that would be tremendously successful. The memo was leaked to Bogart, and he went crazy. He went to Mo Ostin and Joe Smith, then the co-presidents of Warner, and read them the riot act. "How could you do this to one of my first acts?" he screamed. "You're already working against me! This is not the kind of relationship I want to have!" Warner Bros. released Bogart from his contract, and he had to start over from scratch.

Bogart called his new label Casablanca Records. He had to mortgage his home to keep it afloat, and Bogart was forced to ask his friends and independent record distributors for loans. "That's how Casablanca kept going," says Aucoin. "Neil wouldn't give up. It's not like today, where if it doesn't work in a couple of weeks, next."

Bogart would not have been in this position if he had just let Kiss get dropped from Warner Bros. or if he had forced them drop the makeup, but he stuck with the band. "Neil didn't give in, and he fought," says Aucoin. "If he shook your hand and said we were gonna do it, you knew you were gonna do it."

The band knew from the beginning that the makeup was a big risk. "They could have been laughed right off the stage and were sometimes," says Fritz Postlethwaite, Kiss's tour manager from 1976 to 1979. "But they had the courage of their convictions to make it work."

Early on in Kiss's career, Aucoin told them if they were going to make a big deal of the fact that they wore makeup and not have it looked at with ridicule, it was important they not be seen without it. Everyone agreed, although, as Aucoin now says, "I don't think they realized at the time how much effort it was going to take to do that. At first when people tried to catch them without their makeup on, it was a lot of fun to hide." Sometimes magazines would get photos of the band without the makeup and have polls asking the fans if they wanted to see them. The fans usually voted no. When Kiss was at its peak, their fans loved the fact that they had no idea what the members really looked like.

"To tell you the truth, most magazines really didn't want to print pictures of us without makeup," Ace Frehley told *Guitar World* magazine. "They knew the band's mystique was selling a lot of magazines for them, and they didn't want to ruin that."

Kiss started wearing zinc oxide for the whiteface, then went to "clown white" by Stein's and Max Factor. For their lipstick and makeup, they'd use the cheapest they could find, with trashy names like *Broadway Red* (the song "Black Diamond," which is about hookers, was reputedly named after a cheap brand of makeup). At first the makeup took some getting used to. Criss would sweat profusely when he played the drums, and forgetting he was wearing greasepaint, would smush and smear the makeup when he wiped his face.

Kiss dyed their hair darker so there wouldn't be any highlights on-stage. No facial hair was allowed either, even in most of their post-makeup years, and they didn't have a blonde member until 1992. Later, other heavy metal bands started adopting height, hair, and look re-quirements when auditioning potential players. Often the wrong look could cost you a gig. Ozzy Osbourne wouldn't even consider hiring bassist Greg Chaisson because he showed up to the audition in sweat-pants and a baseball cap.

From the beginning, Kiss knew how to hype themselves. They made sure to play New York City only once a month even though they usu-ally needed the money. They wanted to give the impression that they were off playing somewhere else on tour. Their first big show was on December 31, 1973, with Iggy Pop and Blue Öyster Cult. The first Kiss tours were one-truck and one-tour-bus affairs, but the burn rate on money was still high. The joke in the Kiss camp was that they lost a lit-tle bit on each show but made up for it with volume.

The first time Fritz Postlethwaite ever saw Kiss play, "the opening chords were punctuated with bombs, and the pressure of the concus-sions was like standing in the dark and being hit in the chest with a medicine ball. It literally knocked the wind out of you." And in the small auditoriums and theaters they were playing in at the time, where the audience was much closer to the band, the effects were frightening. The pyrotechnician told Postlethwaite that his goal was to ensure there was not a dry seat in the first several rows.

Aucoin financed Kiss's first tour with his American Express card, which ran him $30,000 in debt. (Surprisingly, American Express never canceled his card.) It was a difficult tour to get through. For one show the band performed in a high school cafeteria with a bunch of lunch benches pushed together for a stage. Simmons was still practicing his fire tricks and was nervous when handling flash paper. Once he accidentally threw a burning piece of it into the audience, scorching off a fan's facial hair. Frehley would shoot bottle rockets off his guitar. One night a rocket flew in the direction of the road crew, and they had to scramble in all directions to get out of its path.

Kiss's self-titled debut album came out in 1974 with middling success. According to Aucoin, the album sold decently in the black community because it was thought the band was a black group done up in whiteface. Their second album that year, *Hotter Than Hell*, didn't fare much better commercially. Aucoin and the band went through many ups and downs before they made it, but Kiss wanted success more than anything, and all involved were willing to tough it out.

Kiss released six records over the next three years. Because albums that didn't sell could be returned to the label within six months, Casablanca wanted to make sure they always had fresh product in the stores. The label made sure the next Kiss album was already in stores before the last one started to come back.

Kiss's albums weren't selling well, but on the road it was a different story. The band was blowing away practically every band they opened for in concert. When they opened for Queen and Blue Öyster Cult in 1974, the promoter wouldn't let the band use the lighting rig because he feared their show would upstage the main acts. Kiss was forced to play with the house lights up. The audience kept chanting the band's name through most of Queen's set and continued well into Blue Öyster Cult's performance. Most bands they opened for wanted them kicked off their tours, but with Kiss on the bill, sold-out shows were guaranteed, which meant the headliners would get a percentage of the gate. Many of the headliners weren't doing well on tour and needed a strong opening act to save them, so they had to keep Kiss aboard whether they liked it or not.

Album sales improved slightly for Kiss with 1975's *Dressed to Kill*, which reached the Top Forty. The album had a bona fide hit with the anthem "Rock and Roll All Nite," which Simmons and Stanley wrote on tour in Eugene, Oregon. But it was still not enough. The band was at the make-or-break point in its career. With Casablanca Records teetering on the brink of financial ruin because of Bogart's manic overspending, the next album had to be a hit or it might mean the end of the band—and the label.

The decision to put out a live album at this point made little sense. None of the band's three studio albums had sold well enough to warrant a live album. Who was going to shell out for a double live LP when no one was buying the band's studio albums? At that time, live albums were also considered déclassé. "They were what the record company put out if you had nothing else, scraping the bottom of the barrel," said Deep Purple bassist Roger Glover.

But Kiss's concert tickets outsold their records by a substantial margin. If they were able to capture their live energy and excitement on vinyl, it was clear they had potential for a hit record. Kiss had built a hardcore following in Detroit, as had other artists like Alice Cooper and Aerosmith, and they decided to record their live album during several nights at Cobo Hall. (Kiss were so revered in Detroit that one local high school's marching band would play the band's songs during its football games.)

Kiss also put out a live album because they couldn't afford to record another studio album. Once the live recording was in the can, Bogart didn't have Kiss's advance money. Aucoin held up the master tapes until Bogart paid up, and Kiss's fourth album, *Alive*, was released in September 1975. The album was a huge success, breaking the Top Ten in November and saving Casablanca from bankruptcy. After several years of hard struggle, Aucoin got a huge check delivered to his office. When he saw it was for $2 million, he couldn't believe it. Aucoin had never seen so many zeros in his life; he counted them over and over. *Alive* became a blueprint for the gatefold-sleeve, double live albums that would flourish in the years to follow. Peter Frampton would release *Frampton Comes Alive!* in 1976. Like Kiss, his previous studio albums hadn't sold well, but *Frampton Comes Alive!* would sell more than 12 million copies and was No. 1 on the charts for ten weeks.

As for how live *Alive* really was, accounts are contradictory. "I do remember going back and redoing some of the vocal things, but I think by and large what you heard is what you got," said Gene Simmons. "It's anything but flawless," said Paul Stanley. "If we wanted a really flawless record, we would have doctored it up, but it's as close to live as it needs to be." But when asked about how live the album really was, producer Eddie Kramer said, "Only the drums were kept; everything else was replaced."

The not-so-well-kept secret about most live albums is they usually aren't live at all. There was a famous joke that the Who's *Live at Leeds* album was neither. Bands have always complained that they can't get their "live" sound in a studio album, yet most live albums are heavily patched up in the studio.

Without question, heavy metal and hard rock bands have always had to deliver in the live arena or there is no chance they will ever become successful. Building something out of nothing, like MTV could do with Milli Vanilli, was impossible then. Bands built their fan base on the appeal of their live shows. Even when albums weren't selling, bands could stay alive long enough for a commercial breakthrough if, like Kiss, they delivered onstage.

The money came, and went, fast. "As far as the live show was concerned, it was impossible to control the amounts spent," says Postlethwaite. "The best the business and accounting people could do was to simply document it." Limos and room service ran twenty-four hours a day. Ace Frehley always had at least $5,000 in his pockets and would sometimes spend thousands of dollars at toy stores, buying what he couldn't afford as a child.

The only thing that kept Kiss from drowning in red ink was the band's merchandising sales. During Kiss's biggest period, 1977 and 1978, they grossed $119 million, and according to Bill Aucoin, $52 million of it was made through merchandising. Gene Simmons once pulled aside Jefferson Starship singer Grace Slick and said, "Why don't you guys put out belt buckles and comic books? You could make $3 million a year just on the junk!"

Aucoin had each member's makeup design copyrighted so no one could reproduce them without permission. With their superhero personas, Kiss was the perfect band for merchandising overkill. The band was approached with countless offers and didn't turn many down. Eventually there would be Kiss radios, lunch boxes, makeup kits for kids, sleeping bags, dolls, and two comic books from Marvel. Much of the merchandise was geared toward younger fans. This would hurt Kiss later because they were sometimes perceived as a "kiddie band."

Kiss ultimately revolutionized merchandising in rock and roll. The concert tour shirts, which the kids bought in droves, would save countless bands when their stage shows became so unwieldy and expensive that the only way they could make a profit was through merchandising sales.

"The merchandising was the most profitable part of the tours," says Chris Lendt, the band's business manager for over ten years. "Concert tickets [then] were $5, $6, later $10—they didn't go up into the stratosphere like they do today. There were a lot of commissions that Kiss paid off the top to business managers, agents, then they split the money four ways after tour expenses were covered. So there wasn't a great deal left after those tours. If it wasn't for the merchandising, none of the Kiss tours would have been very profitable, if at all."

Aucoin controlled all the merchandising and licensing rights and had a separate company to make their deals. The merchandising profit was split 50/50 between him and the band at first; later, the four band members readjusted it to 60/40 in their favor.

Kiss was also one of the first bands to advertise its albums and concerts on TV and radio, do in-store appearances, and offer promotional materials with albums and through its fan club. "All this is taken for granted today," continues Lendt. "But in the '70s, what Kiss did with the record company, their management and the ad agencies was really quite revolutionary."

Others looked at the marketing of Kiss differently. "I think it was the mentality of let's make as much money as we can while we can," says photographer Neal Preston, who also worked with the band. But the attitude of "take the money and run" was not isolated to Kiss alone. As Cameron Crowe recalled about the music business in the '70s, "It all felt very fleeting. A lot of bands felt like we got to go out there and make as much money [as we can] now, because two years from now, nobody's gonna want to listen to this music, not knowing that this very music would be selling cars and presidential campaigns now."

Casablanca Records, now out from behind the financial eight ball, was thriving. By 1977, PolyGram had acquired half of the label. Not only would Casablanca have tremendous success with Kiss, the Village People, and Donna Summer, but that same year, RSO, also owned by Poly-Gram, would release the soundtrack to *Saturday Night Fever,* which topped the charts for six months and became the biggest-selling album in history at the time.

Outside the window of Bogart's office on the Sunset Strip was a giant billboard announcing that Kiss had sold out three nights at the Forum for their *Love Gun* tour. Having a billboard on Sunset Boulevard was a huge status symbol. Some artists had provisions put into their record contracts that upon the release of a new album, they had to have a billboard up on Sunset. At one point the billboards on Sunset featured so many bands that the movie studios had no room to advertise their upcoming films.

Even though the label featured mostly disco acts, Casablanca was as rock and roll a company as you could get. Walk into a record company today, and you won't hear any music playing, a telling detail about today's music business. At the Casablanca offices, they played their artists *loud.* "You walked into Casablanca, and the size of the speakers just assaulted your senses," recalled Jeff Wald, who managed Donna Summer. "And there was cocaine on people's desks and people getting loaded. By the time we got down to business, it was almost irrelevant." In the '70s, cocaine was so prevalent in the music business that some went to record labels to score.

Bogart was now wearing the L.A. uniform of prestige in the disco era: open silk shirts, gold chains, and a tall, frizzy head of hair that was popular among agents and show-biz execs. Brimming with success, Casablanca's parking lot was filled with Mercedes-Benzes.

There is some debate as to who was the real genius behind the success of Kiss. Certainly Simmons and Stanley deserve, and take, a lot of credit for being the driving forces behind the band. As far as Frehley was concerned, "When it came to orchestrating our career, setting up promotions, making sure we were in the right place at the right time, Bill and Neil Bogart were real geniuses. Paul and Gene are real smart guys—sometimes too smart for their own britches—and they wrote some tremendous songs, but I think it was really the management that was responsible for making the band happen."

"As far as what took place when I was around, the driving force behind Kiss was Kiss," counters Fritz Postlethwaite. "I truly believe the band came up with the concept and made it work." Postlethwaite concedes that Aucoin did a lot behind the scenes. "He was the fifth Beatle," he admits, and that Aucoin had strong opinions about the ideas Kiss came up with, always wanting to take the ones he liked even further.

One reason why Kiss was so successful was that Simmons was and is a workaholic. Says Bruce Kulick, who would become the band's lead guitarist in 1984, "That's Gene's oxygen. He doesn't like vacations; he hates Sundays." Simmons was so driven that Kulick once found himself working in the studio for three weeks straight without a day off. "Gene is pretty much a banker in disguise," said photographer Barry Levine, who shot Kiss throughout the 1970s. "If he wasn't playing bass, he'd be wearing a yarmulke and trading diamonds on 47th Street in Manhattan."

Besides money, one of Simmons's strongest driving forces has always been sex. Even though he's been with his girlfriend, 1982 Playmate of the Year Shannon Tweed, for eighteen years, and they have two children together, he disdains marriage and still brags about his ongoing sexual conquests.

On tour Simmons was especially insatiable, his conquests in the thousands. He admitted he wasn't picky. "I fuck everything that moves," he once said. "And if it doesn't move, we'll work something out." In a rare display of modesty, he admitted that if he weren't rich and famous, he wouldn't be getting so lucky. "That's really the biggest kick, that a guy who looks like me can get laid," said Simmons. "If there are uglier guys around, I don't know where they are." Barry Levine once walked into Simmons's hotel room and saw thirteen women lined up outside the bathroom, including a pregnant girl and twins, waiting to have sex with him inside. "It was almost like they had tickets and they were waiting for their number to be called, like at a deli."

Aucoin believes that Simmons has such an intense sex drive because he doesn't drink. Simmons chronicles his sexual exploits with a huge Polaroid collection, and, before video cameras were easily portable, he also made home videos with a huge camera that required two roadies to set up. With tremendous foresight, in light of the Tommy Lee and Pamela Anderson video debacle, Aucoin nipped Gene's videotaping in the bud, telling him he could get into a lot of trouble if the tapes of his sexcapades ever wound up in the wrong hands.

In spite of all this, women found Simmons very smooth and charming. Tweed first met Simmons at a Playboy Mansion party. He had just come off a movie in which he played a villain, naturally, and Tweed's first impression was: "He really looked like some slimy Arab with a harem somewhere. He had that sort of dark, brooding kind of come-hither look and I thought, 'Oh, great, this guy thinks he's really hot.' But we started talking, and the more we talked, the more I liked him."

Of the four members of Kiss, no one got more into his onstage persona than Simmons, who truly loved to play the monster. "To be fair, the most ridiculous Gene got was when he went into his character," remembers Postlethwaite. "He completely immersed himself like a Method actor or a person under hypnosis. Sometimes he used this excuse to cover bad behavior."

When he was under the spell of the demon, sometimes he'd mutter to Postlethwaite, "I want you to kill all living things everywhere for me." Often Simmons's demands were simply to test those working for him to see if they could deliver or not. He once commanded, "From now on, I want every dressing room and limousine to be at exactly 75 degrees when I step into it." On an airplane, he once told Postlethwaite to ask the pilot if he could quiet the engines because Kiss was on board. "Gene would demand a hamburger in the middle of the night, and he wouldn't care if you had to take a plane to get it," says Aucoin.

It was hard to tell whether Simmons really expected people to deliver the impossible or not, but they did have to consider his requests, because when things didn't go his way, his rage and cruelty knew no limits. One night, nothing during the show went right, and Simmons came over to his roadie on the side of the stage and spit on him between every song. By the end of the night, the roadie was in tears, covered in spit from head to toe.

Simmons thrived on control, and Criss, who loved to play practical jokes, devised a way to rattle Simmons's cage. Postlethwaite was also a drummer: He played drums for the band during soundchecks, and once when Peter was "ill" during a show, the band even considered putting him in Criss's makeup and costume to finish the set. They decided to call the show off early instead.

This time, Criss had the band's makeup man put Postlethwaite in Simmons's face makeup, an old costume of Simmons's and a black wig, without Simmons's knowledge. The band always ended their concerts at that time with the song "Black Diamond." At the end of the song, the drum riser would go up to the ceiling, and the band would turn to watch Criss for their cues. This time, though, Postlethwaite was up on the drum riser dressed as Simmons finishing "Black Diamond," hitting the cymbal crashes that were synched with the fireworks. Simmons turned to the drum riser and suddenly saw himself behind the drum set. He stopped playing in astonishment and began wandering around in a daze, almost walking off the edge of the stage before a roadie grabbed him.

After the show, Simmons and Bill Aucoin took off alone in a limo. Simmons was still in shock. "What's wrong?" asked Aucoin.

"I think I've lost my mind, Bill . . . I've snapped."

"What do you mean, you've snapped?"

"I looked back there, and I saw myself playing the drums," muttered Simmons. He was stunned, slumped in the back of the limo. "I think I've lost my mind."

Aucoin, who was in on the joke, couldn't contain himself anymore. "Oh no, that was Fritz!" he said.

Simmons went berserk. He never wanted to be anything less than the scary gargoyle he was on stage. To lose control in front of an audience was completely unacceptable, and he was angry at Postlethwaite for a long time after that. Soon a lot more control would slip out of his hands.

Kiss, pictured here in 1974, took a fast ride from New York bars to the top of the world, revolutionizing the music world with their over-the-top stage shows and rock merchandising along the way. From left to right: Peter Criss, Gene Simmons, Ace Frehley, and Paul Stanley. (Neil Zlozower)

On Fire

3

I FORGOT THE WORDS ALL OF A SUDDEN!

—Frank Sinatra on stage at the Sands

I FORGOT THE FUCKIN' WORDS!!!

—David Lee Roth on stage at the US Festival

HARD ROCK AND METAL dominated sports arenas throughout the 1970s. Going to a heavy metal show at any large arena or stadium was an experience unto itself. Outside the arena, thousands of young teenage males would sit in the back of their pickup trucks that were dented out of shape and encrusted in mud, their shirts off, showing off their torsos (devoid of muscle tone) no matter how cold the weather, blasting their favorite tunes.

Back then, a lot of parents gave their sons grief about growing their hair long, and this could be how the "mullet"—long hair in the back, short in the front and sides—developed as a compromise to having it long all over. If you were a young metalhead just starting to grow your hair out, you probably had a hair idol. Maybe you dreamed of the day you would have hair down to your waist like Ted Nugent or Steve Harris, the bassist in Iron Maiden. *Let's see . . . hair grows half an inch a month, six inches a year; by next year . . .*

Once inside the arena, saliva-drenched joints were passed around hand over fist. Any musician in the 1970s could have asked the audience for a puff between songs and been pelted with thousands of joints shooting out of the darkness like bullets. Hard rock and metal bands were moving up to the stadiums, playing big open-air festivals like California Jam or multiband bills at Anaheim Stadium, home of the Angels baseball team. The fans would line up a day in advance and sleep outside, rows of sleeping bags circling the stadium at least six bodies

With a virtuoso guitarist and the quintessential front man, **Van Halen** was one hard rock band that helped win the war against disco in the 1970s. From left to right: Alex Van Halen, Eddie Van Halen, Michael Anthony, and David Lee Roth. (Neil Zlozower)

deep. One fan recalled spending the night in line at Anaheim Stadium in the '70s, as another fan tiptoed through the sleeping bags, asking everyone to pour some of their booze into his thermos, which everyone was then allowed to drink from as he cried, "Exotic Elixir!"

The promoters were still getting only 10 percent, but with Led Zeppelin raking in so much money on tour, they were more than happy to take it. By 1975, Led Zeppelin were one of the world's top-grossing live bands. At the peak of Led Zeppelin's success, Peter Grant could be seen walking down the hotel hallway in his bathrobe at six in the afternoon, $100 bills falling out of one pocket, boulders of cocaine out of the other.

The year 1975 started out with a lot of promise as the band embarked on the *Physical Graffiti* tour, their first in two years. The double album, which included the epic masterpiece "Kashmir," was another No. 1 smash. Not only did Led Zeppelin headline three shows at the Forum with Linda Lovelace emceeing, but John Paul Jones and tour manager Richard Cole also got to spend time at Elvis Presley's mansion in Bel Air, where Presley gave them diamond watches and jewelry. The band had met the King the previous year when he was in town performing at the Forum (he used to tell his "Memphis Mafia," "I may not be Led Zeppelin, but I can still pack 'em in").

But things would soon take a turn for the worse. One night, Lynette "Squeaky" Fromme, a former member of the Manson Family, came to the "Riot House," where the band was staying, and demanded to see Jimmy Page. She was turned away, and a week later, she was arrested after attempting to assassinate Gerald Ford.

In July, Page and Plant went on vacation to Greece with their families. When Plant's wife Maureen lost control of the car she was driving, Robert and their two children were smashed into a tree, and she was badly injured. A farmer loaded everyone onto the back of his truck and drove them to a local hospital. Plant would later say that if he hadn't had the resources to fly his family out of the country for medical treatment, his wife would have died.

In 1977, Led Zeppelin was enjoying what would be its final U.S. tour, including six sold-out shows at the Forum. No one was needy for weed at these shows. As one fan in attendance recalled, the entire Forum had practically turned into one giant bong hit. On the last night of the Forum shows, Keith Moon came on stage and jammed on "Whole Lotta Love." These shows were the last time Led Zeppelin would ever play Los Angeles.

By then, the drug problems within the band were out of control. Page had fallen deeply into heroin addiction. The band traveled with a "tour physician," Dr. Larry, who had previously worked for the Rolling Stones. He carried a black bag that was reportedly full of Quaaludes and Valium. Whatever other drugs the band needed, he could provide as well (Led Zeppelin's code names for heroin and cocaine were "Henry" and "Charlie").

"Dr. Larry used to pull more chicks than anyone in the band," says Neal Preston. "One night while John Paul Jones played the introduction to 'No Quarter,' Jimmy comes over to me and says, 'Fucking Dr. Larry! He's got another one with him!' Dr. Larry was with three of the most beautiful girls you could ever imagine. It used to drive Jimmy nuts." Dr. Larry also had a barter system: He would trade girls for quaaludes.

The tour came to a violent end when the band played two shows at the Oakland Coliseum on July 23 and 24, 1977. The Friday before the shows, promoter Bill Graham received an urgent phone call from Led Zeppelin's road manager, Richard Cole. Even though they were making hundreds of thousands of dollars for the two shows, the band needed $25,000, and they needed it fast. Graham drove all around San Francisco to scrape up the money. He showed up at their hotel with the cash in a shopping bag, much of it in $1 and $10 bills. Graham was led to a guarded hotel room. When he walked in and saw a shady individual wearing a cowboy hat, he realized the money was for a drug deal. That weekend, Dr. Larry also tried to fill a large prescription for barbiturates. When the pharmacy refused, Led Zeppelin's goons started wrecking the place. As they were leaving, they dropped three $100 bills on the ground to take care of the damage.

Led Zeppelin's security entourage was a violent goon squad, and backstage at the Oakland shows, they beat a member of Graham's tour staff to a bloody pulp. Graham was so appalled that he swore he would never book Led Zeppelin again, which, considering his power, meant the band would never play the Bay Area again.

The night of Zeppelin's second show in Oakland, Plant's son Karac contracted a severe stomach virus. He died the next day. Plant took a great deal of time after the death of his son before even thinking about playing again. "I had a couple of bad knocks which, no matter what happens, will always have taken their toll on me," he said. "That kind of ramshackle 'I'll take on the world now' attitude was completely gone."

The mid-1970s would prove to be a more prosperous time for another British foursome. Brian May, Roger Taylor, Freddie Mercury, and John Deacon formed Queen in 1971 and after releasing three albums, *Queen I, Queen II,* and *Sheer Heart Attack,* had come a long way in developing their unique and eclectic sound and building a strong live following. But for guitarist May, choosing a career in music was a decision he agonized over. His family valued education highly, and May graduated from college with a physics degree before deciding music was his true calling. This so angered his father, who had given up his own dream of being a musician years earlier, that the two barely spoke for years. The other members of Queen would forgo their college educations to start the band with May. "We all had quite a bit to lose," he recalled. "It was certainly no fairy tale."

Like Eddie Van Halen and Jeff Beck, May built his own guitar, which he called the "Red Special." It took him eighteen months to complete with the help of his father. The neck of the guitar was made out of a piece of mahogany that a friend was going to throw out, and the body was built with oak from a fireplace mantle. It cost a grand total of $50, and May has played it throughout his career, using an English sixpence for a pick, the serrated edge making his playing sharp and meaty. Eric Clapton once said that May "can do things I could only dream of doing [on guitar]."

By 1975, Freddie Mercury was becoming legendary as Queen's flamboyant frontman. A born star, Mercury was at one with the stage from the beginning. "Freddie started out as a showman almost before he was a singer," said May. "I don't think any of us realized what potential he had for being a singer until he got into the studio."

The other members of Queen didn't know Freddie was gay until

1974. It was never an issue among the band or anyone who worked for them. "It was like saying, 'Oh, by the way, the sky is blue,' " says Neal Preston, who photographed Queen for years. "As far as me, Roger, and the guys on the crew, it meant more chicks for us!"

Even with three albums under their belt, when the band was preparing to record *A Night at the Opera,* they were broke and desperately in need of another hit. One day Mercury came into the studio with stacks of music paper, notes scribbled all over the pages. He had most of the song he wanted to record worked out when he presented it to the band, and he would sing new ideas to them to fill in the gaps: "Bum, bum, bum, bum, that's what happens here." It was like there was a giant symphony playing in his head as he explained, layer by layer, how to build what would eventually become "Bohemian Rhapsody." Originally, the operatic sections of the song were to be brief, but Freddie kept adding more and more layers. He'd come in each day with a new set of lyrics and announce, "I've added a few more Galileos here, dear."

"Bohemian Rhapsody" was a strong showcase for Freddie's vocal ability and musical inventiveness. There were reportedly more than 180 overdubs on the song, building layers of dense harmony. With the studio technology available in the 1970s, Queen had to bounce each successive take from one tape machine to another. Each time they would record a new voice over a previous dub, the tape would shed a little more oxide, becoming thinner and thinner. When they held the tape up to the light and saw it was almost transparent, they quickly made a copy to save the music.

When the song was finally completed, bassist John Deacon thought it was too long at six minutes-plus, but the other three members of Queen insisted the song remain uncut. Their decision not to compromise the integrity of the song would pay off in a big way. "Bohemian Rhapsody" became an instant sensation in England and remained at No. 1 on the charts for an astonishing nine weeks straight. The *Night at the Opera* album also reached No. 1 in the United Kingdom and No. 4 in America. With their inspired intuition and studio savvy, the band had finally broken through. Two years later, in 1977, they would practically invent the arena-rock anthem with "We Will Rock You." The song was designed for maximum audience participation, where everyone would stomp and clap along to its beat. Even today, whenever you stomp and clap that thunderous beat at a sporting event, Queen gets royalties.

After the mega-success of *Alive,* Kiss knew they had to come up with a hell of an encore to prove their success wasn't a fluke. In 1976, they enlisted Bob Ezrin, hot from working with Alice Cooper, to make *Destroyer.* Ezrin consciously set out to reinvent Kiss, something he would be called on to do again in the future. "That seems to be my role in their lives when they're at a crisis point, when they need something to push them forward or make some kind of change, to find a direction when they seem lost," he says. "Sometimes we were right, sometimes we were wrong. On *Destroyer,* we were extremely right."

Destroyer was an elaborate album, with plenty of bizarre experimentation. At first many fans didn't like it and blamed Ezrin for ruining the band (he co-wrote many of the songs and is responsible for the famous Spanish interlude in "Detroit Rock City"). Today many fans consider the album Kiss's best.

Kiss's manager, Bill Aucoin, always made sure that the band split everything four ways—money, decisions, music rights, etc.—and although Simmons and Stanley didn't like that arrangement, they had to abide by it for the time being. Ezrin recalls that it was "politically required" that Peter Criss have a song on the album, but the drummer simply was not a great writer. Finally, Criss brought in a semi-country ballad called "Beck," which he and pre-Kiss bandmate Stan Penridge had written years earlier, and which Ezrin rewrote and renamed "Beth." The rest of the band wasn't happy about recording a ballad. "It is Kiss, after all," says Ezrin, "and at that time, nobody was convinced that Kiss could get away with something of this nature."

The band wanted their first single on *Destroyer* to be a hard rock song, and they felt that "Detroit Rock City" was the obvious choice. "Beth" was chosen as the B-side of the single, and no one in the band thought that radio stations would play the track. But disc jockeys flipped the "Detroit Rock City" single over and started playing "Beth" like crazy, making the Criss-Penridge-Ezrin composition the biggest single of the band's career, peaking at No. 7 on the charts. Some people didn't even know it was Kiss on first listen.

Throughout 1976 and '77, Kiss was one of the biggest concert draws in the country. During the 1977 *Love Gun* tour, they headlined Madison Square Garden, which was a dream come true for the band and, in all likelihood, the highlight of their career. All of their parents came to one of the shows and pictures were taken backstage with the four band members wearing full makeup and costumes, towering over their folks. The pictures practically said, *Look, Ma, I made it.*

Many musicians who went on to form bands in the 1980s attended those Kiss shows, and headlining the Garden became their benchmark of success too, the ultimate peak of every musician's career. "If I never play another gig in my life, I'll know that Anthrax headlined the Garden, and I can die happy," said Anthrax guitarist Scott Ian. "We could have played the Christ Amphitheater in heaven, and it couldn't beat playing the Garden," says drummer Greg D'Angelo, who performed there with White Lion.

There's no better way for a new band to expand its audience than to open for a hot headliner, and many groups benefited greatly from opening for Kiss throughout the 1970s. Cheap Trick opened for Kiss right as they were hitting their stride with the *Live At Budokan* album and the "I Want You to Want Me" single. "They were an excellent 'little brother' act for Kiss," says former road manager Fritz Postlethwaite. "Cheap Trick were hard enough to be on a Kiss tour; they were loud and lewd enough to be respectable to a hard rock crowd, but pop enough to appeal to the younger fans." Cheap Trick has endured many ups and downs throughout their career; some joked that the band has spent more time coming back than they have on top.

Cheap Trick came out of Chicago and featured a bizarre combination of musicians. The lead singer and bassist, Robin Zander and Tom Petersson, were two good-looking rock and roll studs. The guitarist and drummer, Rick Nielsen and Bun E. Carlos, looked like nerds, making the band a pair of tens and a pair of twos. Zander's voice was pretty and eerie at the same time. He didn't look like the type of guy who had trouble getting laid, but when he sang, you could believe he truly lived the loneliness and heartbreak in Cheap Trick's lyrics.

Bob Seger opened a number of Kiss gigs in the mid-1970s as well and, surprisingly, went over very well with Kiss's fans. When Seger performed his life-on-the-road anthem "Turn the Page," it struck a chord with other musicians. The song captured the loneliness and hardship of touring. "We listened to 'Turn the Page' and knew that it was real and part of our lives," says Postlethwaite. "You can't help but identify with it."

Ted Nugent also opened for Kiss in the mid-1970s. Nugent was a pure rock and roller, strictly meat-and-potatoes. Ric Browde, who got his start as a producer working behind the scenes on several Nugent albums, says Ted made music for his Jeep. If it didn't sound good in the Jeep, the album couldn't come out.

Nugent is staunchly right-wing, "Rush Limbaugh with a guitar," according to Browde. An avid hunter, Nugent once nearly missed a scheduled performance at the Cal Jam Festival because he was on safari in Africa and was trapped in a storm that swept away many of his belongings. Even studio time had to be scheduled between hunting seasons.

With their ticket sales at an all-time high, Kiss put out another live album, *Alive II*, in 1977. The album was another double-record package: Three sides were live tracks, and one side contained new studio material.

Kiss often relied on studio musicians and outside songwriters, and Bob Kulick came in as an uncredited guest guitarist on *Alive II*'s studio tracks. Kulick had known the band for years and even auditioned for the lead guitarist slot the same day as Ace Frehley (Kulick's brother Bruce became Kiss's lead guitarist in 1984).

Kulick showed up to Electric Lady Studios in New York and found Frehley on the floor of the lounge, clearly unable to play. According to Kulick, Simmons and Stanley were happy to have a guitarist with a broader musical vocabulary than Frehley, but at the same time, if Kulick's playing got too radical, it would be obvious to the listener it wasn't Frehley. Kulick couldn't hear Simmons and Stanley's reactions in the control room, so after Kulick played a lead, the two would hold up a Kiss doll; if they nodded the doll's head, the solo was good. After Kulick laid down his solos, he came back to see Frehley. "How was I?" Frehley asked jokingly. "Best you ever played," Kulick assured him.

Throughout the mid-70s, if you twirled down the FM dial, you usually heard a lot of songs that would become today's "classic rock." Aerosmith were at the peak of their success in 1976. It was in February of that year that their song "Dream On" finally became their first Top Ten hit. "Dream On" first appeared on Aerosmith's debut album, released three years earlier. It was that song that kept them from being dropped from their label, CBS. At the beginning of the '70s, the major labels were still trying to figure out how to market hard rock and metal bands. CBS had built its foundation on artists such as Barbra Streisand and Paul Simon and the soundtrack to *My Fair Lady*. The label wasn't ready for a band like Aerosmith.

After Aerosmith's self-titled first album did lackluster business, label president Clive Davis declined to pick up the option for a second album. The band's management, Leber-Krebs, convinced the label to give Aerosmith an extension so the band could prove itself. "Dream On" was released as a single and eventually did well enough that the band was given the green light to record a second album, *Get Your Wings*.

Given time to grow, the band built a following by touring nonstop and, in 1975 and 1976, Aerosmith scored two hit albums back to back: *Toys in the Attic,* which featured "Walk This Way" and "Sweet Emotion," and *Rocks.* It was perhaps surprising that "Walk This Way" hit the Top Ten, considering that hidden deep in the rapid-fire lyrics was a song about masturbation, getting laid for the first time, and the fantasy of having two women at once.

Early in their career, Aerosmith often endured comparisons to the Rolling Stones, which superficially were somewhat easy to make. Lead singer Steven Tyler had a pair of Cinemascope lips, and lead guitarist Joe Perry had a similar presence to Keith Richards. And like Mick and Keith, Steven and Joe were prone to volcanic blowups. Lead singers and lead guitarists often butt heads and try to push the other out of the spotlight, and Tyler and Perry were no exception. Right after the band played its first gig in the fall of 1970, Perry and Tyler got into an argument, setting the tone for the rest of the band's career. "Joe, it's way too fuckin' loud!" Tyler screamed. "I can't hear myself sing right! You gotta turn down!"

Tyler and Perry made a perfect combination nonetheless. Tyler's singing and Perry's riffs were raunchy and reeked with feel. Tyler had attitude to burn, and as soon as they met, Perry knew he wanted to play with him. "Steven sure looked like a rock star, and he definitely acted like one, so we just assumed he already was one," he said. It was drummer Joey Kramer who came up with the name for the band when he was in high school. Just as millions of kids would do years later, he drew Aerosmith over and over again on his school textbooks.

Also in 1976, Blue Öyster Cult had a breakthrough single with "(Don't Fear) The Reaper," another surprise hit in that the lyrics dealt with death. The song peaked at No. 12 on the charts. Like Rush, Blue Öyster Cult was considered a "thinking man's metal band," or a metal band that intellectuals listened to and enjoyed (obviously, metal and hard rock still weren't taken seriously in many corners). Metal fans often didn't call their favorite bands by their full names (Zeppelin, Sabbath,

Crüe), and Blue Öyster Cult sounded better when referred to as B.O.C. But clearly the most pivotal new band of 1976 was Boston.

Boston was the brainchild of guitarist Tom Scholz, who graduated from MIT with a degree in mechanical engineering and worked for Polaroid as a product designer. In his spare time, he recorded songs in his basement, playing most of the instruments himself with help from vocalist Brad Delp and guitarist Barry Goudreau. When Scholz brought a tape of his music around to record companies, most couldn't believe it was just a demo. Tom Werman heard the tape when he worked A&R at Epic Records and remembered that it sounded so good that he thought he was on *Candid Camera* and someone was playing a joke on him. As good as the demo was, though, Boston was a tough sell at first. A number of other labels passed on the band. Epic, which eventually signed Boston, wanted a band that could tour. Eventually Scholz put a band together to audition for the label to prove his project was not just a technoid's mad basement folly.

Scholz admitted, "Boston existed on my basement tape recorder long before I could get five people together to take a picture for a band photo on the first album." One of their songs, "Rock and Roll Band," about building a fan base on the road, was "pure fantasy," according to Scholz, since Boston had never even played live, let alone toured. Eventually, Scholz hired Delp, Goudreau, bassist Fran Sheehan, and drummer Sib Hashian. Scholz was always considered the "genius" of the group, and most tiptoed around him, probably because they didn't feel they were on his intellectual level, while the rest of the guys in the band were considered "normal."

Boston's self-titled debut, released in 1976, went on to become the tenth-biggest-selling album of all time, with 16 million copies sold in America alone and over 50 million worldwide. The single "More Than a Feeling" was a huge radio hit, and the album reached No. 3 on the U.S. charts during a two-year stay there. The album was a landmark in terms of studio production. The guitar sound was incredibly ballsy yet impeccably clean, and there were endless layers of guitar and vocal harmonies. Scholz himself later developed the Rockman, a paperback-sized practice amp that enabled guitarists to reproduce Boston's sound. The Rockman became immensely popular with many bands. (Most of the guitars on Def Leppard's *Hysteria* were recorded through a Rockman.)

Boston followed up its debut two years later with *Don't Look Back.* Even though it hit No. 1 in September 1978, Scholz always felt the second album was rushed. He liked the first side of the album but felt the second wasn't up to snuff. Scholz argued that this was the reason *Don't Look Back* sold only half as many copies as the first album. He swore he'd never rush an album again, and he wasn't kidding. It would take eight years for another Boston album to come out. *Third Stage* was finally released in 1986, and with all the time Scholz had to perfect everything, it still sold only four million copies, the same as *Don't Look Back.* No matter how much time and money Scholz spent trying to make every little detail sound perfect on later albums, Boston never sounded better than they did on their debut album, which cost all of $28,000 to make.

The impact of the first Boston album was phenomenal. The 1992 edition of the *Rolling Stone Album Guide* claimed that "More Than a Feeling" ushered in "the long, cold winter of arena rock," its sound becoming "the cornerstone of Album Oriented Radio." By the '80s, a number of bands would have pop singles with heavy guitars, but according to Sony A&R executive John Kalodner, the Boston album in 1976 was the first time "where you could be really heavy and have pop singles." Kaldoner was inspired by this approach and signed Foreigner to Atlantic the same year, "and they took us further as being a [hard] rock band with singles."

Thin Lizzy would also enjoy a big single in 1976 with the song "The Boys Are Back in Town." Thin Lizzy was led by singer/bassist Phil Lynott. Lynott's mother, Philomena, grew up in Dublin, Ireland, but left for Birmingham, England, when she was seventeen. Wandering the streets of a city decimated during World War II, one night Philomena went to a dance at a local hostel where people trying to find their place after the war could meet and dance to big band music. She danced with a Brazilian named Cecil Parris. She and Cecil began dating, and Philomena lost her virginity to him, eventually becoming pregnant. Philomena gave birth to Phil on August 20, 1949. As she was recovering from her delivery, her racist landlords evicted her—they had found out her son was black.

The members of Thin Lizzy came together in late 1969 and would put out their first album in April 1971. Thin Lizzy went through a number of lineups, but the band always had great twin-guitar harmonies that included the likes of Scott Gorham, John Sykes, Brian Robertson, and Gary Moore, one of the most underrated guitarists in rock history. Many bands, including Iron Maiden and Judas Priest, copied Thin Lizzy's twin-guitar style—in which one guitarist is usually more controlled, the other wild and furious—but this part of their style had developed by accident. When Gorham was laying down a guitar track in the studio, the engineer put a long delay on one of his guitar lines. When the delay finally kicked in, it harmonized with what Gorham was playing. The band liked the sound so much that they began writing original harmonies immediately.

Thin Lizzy's riffs were sometimes based on traditional Irish melodies. A clever lyricist, Lynott took some of his words from Irish folklore as well. Lynott loved history, especially about Ireland, and wrote the song "Róisín Dubh (Black Rose)" as an homage to his homeland. He also wrote "Cowboy Song" about America's Wild West past. "The Boys Are Back in Town," the band's biggest American hit, was inspired by Lynott's adventures in New York City. The song was another surprise hit, but not because of the subject matter of the lyrics. In 1976 the band was recording their *Jailbreak* album. Their two previous albums had tanked, and they needed a hit single. One of their managers, Chris O'Donnell, picked "The Boys Are Back in Town," a song the band originally rejected, and suggested it for the album. Lynott and Gorham looked at each other and said, "Well, that's one guy that likes it!" so it wound up on the album. It became a Top Twenty hit and Thin Lizzy's best-known song. "Thank God our manager said he liked it," says Gorham.

When Thin Lizzy was starting out, Lynott never let the band stop playing until they had won over the crowd. Says Gorham, "Sometimes when you see things aren't going your way on stage, somebody will lean over and say, 'Hey man, we'll cut a couple of songs out and get the fuck out of here.' Phil wouldn't hear of that. To him, failure was not an option. He was the one who gave everyone a kick in the ass: 'We're gonna go up to the front of the stage, we're not gonna give up on these people, and we're gonna win this game.' I look back on it, and I really dig him for it." The band's motto was: "Leave the stage covered in blood, and watch the headliners slip all over it."

Many bands were scared to play in Ireland because of the ongoing violence there, especially after three members of a band called the Miami Showband were gunned down at a roadblock. But the war between the Catholics and the Protestants didn't stop Thin Lizzy from playing in Ireland or in England. "You came to a Thin Lizzy gig, and it was common ground," says Gorham. "It was: 'Leave your religion at the door.' " Thin Lizzy was the first Irish band to tour nationally in the '70s, opening the door for the Boomtown Rats and later U2. When Thin Lizzy toured America, they never were confronted with racism directly, but they did find that Phil's being black made it difficult for them to get on radio. Remembers Gorham, "They'd look at a picture of the band— here's a black guy playing with a bunch of white guys. How do we categorize this? Do we put this on soul stations because this guy is black? You think of that nowadays, and it's totally ridiculous.

"As far as flat-out racism, we never came across any of that," continues Gorham. "We were playing the Deep South, all over America—we never ran into any of that. The goal was always, 'Listen to the music.' The black issue never came up."

Other metal and hard rock bands with black musicians endured similar problems before and after Thin Lizzy. Sound Barrier was the first all-black metal band and also one of the first bands signed during the L.A. explosion in the 1980s. Journalist Jon Sutherland felt Sound Barrier was considered one of the most talented bands on the L.A. scene, but their record company, MCA, didn't know what to do with them. "They used to send out their singles with disco sleeves," says Sutherland. "They really screwed that band up." The label even had reservations about putting the band's picture on their album cover. "I've heard people say, 'They're pretty good for niggers' at Thin Lizzy and Sound Barrier shows, and it really pissed me off," says Sutherland.

In 1988, Living Colour, an all-black band best known for the hit single "Cult of Personality," toured with Anthrax in Europe. Said former Anthrax manager Jonny Z, "This [tour] is something we've wanted to do for a long time, but it just couldn't happen right now in the States. There is still a lot of racism among the American heavy metal music-biz ranks."

As it turns out, many minorities enjoyed metal and hard rock but felt they weren't invited to the party. "A lot of my black friends in high school were into Van Halen and the Scorpions," said Norwood Fisher from the band Fishbone. "But the way the industry was set up discouraged them from being a part of rock and roll, so they listened to it less and less."

Mike Kelley was a local fan who regularly came out to Los Angeles's Starwood Club. On a Monday night in 1976, he went to see a band called Straight Jacket play there. While Kelley was backstage, he heard a guitar player in the corner playing a song from a progressive group called Trapeze. This guy's playing one of my favorite songs, thought Kelley. He's gotta be cool. Kelley introduced himself and they started talking about music. The guitarist told him he was in a band called Van Halen.

"Oh sure, I know who Van Halen is."

"Yeah, we've been doin' the Top Forty thing. We're gonna be playing here two weeks from now doing our new gig, only originals."

Clearly nervous at the prospect of playing original material, the young guitarist, who introduced himself as Eddie, confided to Kelley, "I'm really scared. I've never done anything like this before." As Kelley got up to leave, Eddie said, "Be sure to come and see me."

As with many lead singer/guitarist combinations, Eddie Van Halen and David Lee Roth were from opposite worlds. Eddie and his brother Alex were born in Holland and moved to the United States when Eddie was eight. Their father, Jan Van Halen, played the clarinet but was unable to make a living as a musician and worked four jobs, including washing dishes, to put food on the table. When Eddie began playing guitar, his mother discouraged him because she didn't want him to struggle all his life like his father had.

One of the most important lessons Eddie learned from his father when he began playing is that feel is more important than the notes you play. Eddie had taken piano and violin lessons but said he never learned how to read music; he'd fool the teacher by watching his fingers and playing by ear. Most of the great rock guitarists played purely by ear and often couldn't explain what they were doing. "I can't play a scale," said Jimmy Page. "You think I'm kidding, but I'm not. I can't play a barre chord. It's unbelievable, isn't it?"

Eddie learned to play guitar by slowing down albums and practicing his favorite guitar solos note-for-note. His biggest influence was Cream-era Eric Clapton. Although his playing was stylistically similar to Jimi Hendrix's, Eddie insisted that his crazed whammy-bar abuse and end-of-the-world amp sound weren't influenced by Hendrix, although many didn't believe him. (The shadow of Hendrix has always been difficult for radical guitarists to step out of.) No matter who his influences were, you couldn't hear them in his playing. Eddie had something elusive that many rock guitarists couldn't achieve: a distinctive sound. He could play one note, and you immediately knew it was him.

David Lee Roth was born in Indiana and came from an affluent family. Growing up, Roth had a hard time forming attachments or making friends, and began developing his "Diamond Dave" persona early on. Even as a teenager, few people, if anyone, ever saw him outside of it. He was a rock star from the time he got up in the morning until he went to bed. Says a former employee, "Dave's ability to be normal may not have been anyone else's ability to be normal."

"The thing you gotta understand about David Lee Roth is there's two distinct different people," says photographer Neil Zlozower, who shot Van Halen in the '70s and '80s. "There's Dave, who's one of the nicest, most generous, coolest people you'd ever want to hang with, and there's David Lee Roth, who could be one of the biggest, most demanding pricks you'd ever want to deal with. I've dealt with him in both capacities."

Despite his fun-time alter ego, there has always been a strong undercurrent of anger and rage beneath the surface. As *Rolling Stone* once put it, underneath all the "forced zaniness" was "one bitter dude." One of Roth's most famous quotes (which Axl Rose later took to heart) was that he was "primarily motivated by fear and revenge. My songs, my interviews, the way I dress, every time we play, I'm dancing somebody in the dirt."

Roth hooked up with Eddie in 1973 when they were playing in different bands. Eddie and his brother Alex, who played drums, were in a band that went by a variety of names, including the Broken Combs and the Trojan Rubber Company. They were looking for a singer, and Eddie claims the reason they brought in Roth, who was with the Red Ball Jets at the time, was because he had his own P.A., and getting a singer with his own P.A. was cheaper than renting one. Michael Anthony came aboard as their bass player in 1974. Roth claimed it was his idea to call the new band Van Halen because it sounded like Santana. Alex joked that they came up with their name by voting, and Van Halen beat out Roth three to one.

In the beginning, the band rehearsed at the Roth family estate in Pasadena, California. The three-story house sat on a two-and-half-acre lot. It had nine bedrooms, a library, a study, fireplaces in five of the bedrooms, and a billiard room. There was also a vault where the previous owner kept artifacts from Europe. Like something out of an old Frankenstein movie, a bookcase would open to reveal the secret room behind.

Van Halen used the basement as their rehearsal space. The floor was covered with beer cans; the walls were padded with mattresses for soundproofing. Dave kept a big blackboard handy where he could write out the lyrics and sing off them like cue cards. Whenever Roth's father came downstairs, everyone had to scramble to hide their beer. One day Roth's father, an ophthalmologist, abruptly ended a rehearsal by coming downstairs and telling the band, "I have surgery at six o'clock in the morning."

Roth's father always wanted his son to have a backup plan; he told him that if the band didn't make it he had to go back to college. But Roth never seemed to have any doubt about his future. One day as he sat out by the pool, he listed to a friend all the rock stars who would be partying at the mansion once he was famous. "Rod Stewart's gonna be here, Mick Jagger . . ."

Years before Roth could send out the invitations, however, Van Halen had a hard time finding gigs. The band was too loud, for one thing. Eddie tried to quiet his amps by putting plastic covers over them, turning them against the wall, and padding them with Styrofoam. Throughout the '70s, when a band was just starting out, they had to know how to play Top Forty songs. Van Halen played songs from practically every band from Led Zeppelin to Aerosmith to Bad Company. They played disco covers such as KC and the Sunshine Band's "That's the Way 'I Like It',", and sang the horn parts, which is possibly how they developed their vocal harmonies. Dave was a big disco fan and tried to combine Eddie's end-of-the-world guitar playing with more danceable music.

But when Van Halen played covers, the way they played them was so distinctive that they sounded like original songs. "Back in the club days, it was always my fault we lost a gig, because for the life of me I could never make those Top Forty songs sound like the records did," said Eddie. "But it was a blessing in disguise, because I ended up only able to sound like me."

When the band couldn't get club gigs, Van Halen would play the Southern California backyard party circuit and advertise by cramming high school lockers with flyers. Wherever Van Halen played Hollywood, they brought with them a new influx of girls from Pasadena, which helped make them popular. They eventually moved all the way up to playing a 3,000-capacity theater without either a record deal or management.

For their stage shows, Van Halen stole lights from apartment complexes. They also made their own flash pots by putting gunpowder in coffee cans that were hooked up to car batteries. Sometimes they would malfunction, and in one quick *whoosh!*, someone would lose his eyebrows.

Van Halen was soon playing Gazzarri's as a cover band because it was a lot easier to get into than the other clubs on the Sunset Strip. Eddie and Alex were scared to move into bigger clubs like the Whisky or the Starwood. Gazzarri's was their comfort zone, but Roth kept pushing them to move forward. Like a director, he also pushed Eddie to develop a stronger stage presence. "You gotta move around more," he'd tell him. "Move your mouth with the notes." When the band played live, at the end of every song Roth wanted all the lights to shut off abruptly, leaving the stage pitch black. Every song had to end with a punch. "I really give Dave as much credit as I can give anybody in that band for breaking them," says Kevin Martin, whose band, A La Carte, played with Van Halen at the Starwood in the mid-1970s.

Throughout the band's tumultuous history, Eddie and Dave never really got along. They were as different as two people could be. Dave was often dictatorial and controlling; Eddie was insecure and passive-aggressive. Dave was flamboyant and loud; Eddie was painfully shy and quiet. Dave loved performing cover songs; Eddie always wanted Van Halen's albums to be completely original and was disappointed when their brutal cover of "You Really Got Me," instead of an original song, became their first single. "I'd rather bomb with my own shit than make it with someone else's," he once said.

Roth was always looking after the business end of the band. As he once said, "You have to watch where the money goes, and how it comes back." Eddie just wanted his music to be heard. He didn't have to worry about keeping a roof over his head because he still lived with his parents, and didn't move out until he hooked up with actress Valerie Bertinelli (they were married in 1981). If he was playing to 300,000 people or three, as long as he could keep making music, Eddie was happy.

Even though he got glowing press from guitar magazines, Eddie hated giving interviews. Like many rock guitarists who were shy and introverted, he'd rather let his music say what he felt. Roth was never at a loss for words. Like many frontmen, he had a semi-automatic mouth. His interviews were so entertaining that you could sell tickets to them. Roth's interviews seemed like they were part of the act. His schtick usually felt well-rehearsed, and once you asked Roth a question, many feet of tape would unravel before you could get to the next one. It was all sound and fury ultimately signifying nothing, but never did nothing sound so entertaining.

Eddie hated fame and being recognized, but Roth craved it, and he constantly needed an audience's approval. Eddie's greatest strength was that he was a phenomenal musician. Roth's greatest strength was that he made up for not being a great singer by being an incredible entertainer. Eddie took care of the music; Roth was in charge of the show, the clothes, and being the frontman. In a 1984 feature in *Rolling Stone,* the photo captions of Roth and Eddie summed them up perfectly: "The Rock Star" and "The Musician."

In the mid-1970s a friend convinced Steve Mercer to go to the Starwood for the first time, telling him, "Let me show you the real Hollywood." Mercer, like many teenagers, had to sneak out of his house to go to a show after his parents went to bed. He'd roll his parents' car down the street in neutral, starting it only when he was halfway down the block.

During the mid-'70s the clubs in L.A. had lost some of the popularity they had enjoyed in the '60s, when local bands like the Doors were first breaking onto the scene. At this time it was hard for a local band to get into the Whisky, which featured mostly touring acts, and Gazzarri's featured bands doing covers. For many young groups, the Starwood was the only game in town.

Located on Santa Monica Boulevard in West Hollywood, the Starwood was a club in which several bands could play at once. The rock bands played on the main stage, but there was also a disco room and numerous other rooms and corridors. Everyone filed in through the same entrance then split into their own factions.

The club's managers often compensated for booking unknown bands by giving them an unlimited guest list to invite hundreds of friends just to fill the club. Certain bands, like A La Carte, who played the Starwood frequently, drew a heavy-drinking crowd, so the club knew they'd make up for the small numbers with the increased bar business.

The Starwood later came to epitomize rock and roll of the 1970s and '80s, reeking of sex and decadence. "Even if we brought girlfriends, we had these wide-open spaces where we could lose them, find new ones, get phone numbers, and hump our brains out," says Brian O'Brien, drummer for A La Carte. "The whole thing about the Starwood was the sex and the drugs; the music was almost secondary. We were fucking without any regard to relationships, without any danger, nothing was going to stop us, we were invincible. We didn't need sleep; all we needed was to show up and have the time of our lives."

Bands used to go into the women's bathroom and create their own myths by writing on the bathroom walls. It never dawned on the women that the men themselves were the ones testifying how big their dicks supposedly were. On one wall at the Starwood, someone wrote: "David Lee Roth stuffs his pants with a handkerchief and half dollars."

The Starwood was also one of the easiest places to score quaaludes, which were all the rage throughout the 1970s. A local doctor supplied the Starwood regulars, and his offices became known as "Camp Quaalude." Every Saturday morning, the line in front of his office would stretch for blocks. The cops would drive by and think the kids were lining up for concert tickets. One night the club was raided, and a box of more than 4,000 'ludes was discovered. On the side of the box was written: "For distribution at the box office." (Slash claims he sold the best quaaludes at the Starwood, adding, "I think the statute of limitations has run out by now.")

Fans from all over Southern California started to gravitate to the Starwood as it became ground zero for L.A.'s burgeoning rock scene. Celebrities started coming as well. In one corner you'd see Erik Estrada; in another you might catch a glimpse of Gene Simmons. One night when Simmons and Paul Stanley came to the club, the lighting man shined the spotlight in the VIP balcony and announced that Kiss was in the building. It was hard for them to wave at their fans and cover their faces at the same time. "Back then, the Starwood was the only place the public could see Kiss without their makeup, except nobody knew what they looked like," says Brian O'Brien. "You'd see Gene Simmons pointed out to you every once in a while. 'Oh, he's not that bad-looking; I heard they were really ugly.' "

The Starwood was also a popular hangout for children of celebrities. One night, Zsa Zsa Gabor came to the Starwood dressed in mink and pearls, and furiously dragged her drunken daughter home. John Belushi was a fixture on the L.A. club scene and would enter the Starwood surrounded by a huge entourage, like a boxer walking into the ring. He always wanted to be a rock star and was a strong supporter of the local music scene. One night, Belushi jammed for hours at a private party with Aerosmith, imitating Joe Cocker as he sang. He later complained to Aerosmith that he wanted to do an Aerosmith skit on *Saturday Night Live* but that producer Lorne Michaels wouldn't let him unless he dressed up like a bee.

One night in May 1976, Gene Simmons came out to the Starwood to check out guitarist George Lynch's early band, the Boyz, with an eye to potentially nurturing and signing them. Simmons loved the show and told Lynch he was interested in getting them a record deal. He then excused himself to watch the next band, which was Van Halen. Once he saw them, he forgot about getting the Boyz a record deal.

Simmons took Van Halen to Bill Aucoin to get them a management deal, and according to Roth, Aucoin told them, "Great band, but you gotta get rid of the singer." Aucoin says he flew the band out to New York, and they didn't perform well because they were nervous. He now feels if he saw them in familiar surroundings—the Starwood or the Whisky—he would have signed them.

Surprisingly, many Starwood regulars agreed with Aucoin's assessment of Van Halen's singer. Says Mike Kelley, "Van Halen started getting really popular at the Starwood. More and more people would come to see them, but the consensus among every musician and anybody who was hip was the same: 'Good band, incredible guitar player—will never, ever get a deal with this lead singer. Impossible; it will never happen.'"

In the Starwood days, Roth's stage presence wasn't yet as cool as it would later become. He wasn't confident with his stage raps and told corny old jokes, borrowing heavily from singer Jim Dandy Mangrum of Southern rock band Black Oak Arkansas. "At the time, Black Oak Arkansas was dead, gone, over with, and not too recently in the grave," continues Kelley. "And all of a sudden, this band comes out with a singer who looked, sang, talked, and acted just like Jim Dandy. It was very out of place."

"He aped a lot of Jim Dandy's moves," adds Brian O'Brien. "He kind of had this beer gut with the open shirt, sort of a Robert Plant deal but with a little more gut and the real long hair." Before they had a record deal, the band's future producer, Ted Templeman, even tried to convince Van Halen to replace Roth—with none other than Sammy Hagar. The other members of Van Halen refused. Sure, Roth was a pain in the ass to deal with, but he was their singer, and from the beginning, Eddie decided Van Halen would be a *band.* Eddie even made sure the royalties were split four ways even though he wrote all the music.

In spite of anyone's initial misgivings about Roth as a singer, Van Halen was a tough band to beat on the club scene, and everyone knew it. "Van Halen was so cocky," says A La Carte guitarist Kevin Martin. "Hardly anyone was really friends with them. You were either in their inner circle or you weren't. In retrospect, I guess they deserved to have a 'tude. They knew how hot they were."

A La Carte and Van Halen were especially fierce rivals for the Starwood crown. A La Carte once had the misfortune of being on the same bill as Van Halen, and as Brian O'Brien recalls, "They took a piece of our ass, and it was brutal." Roth, in turn, referred to A La Carte derisively as "A La Fart."

A band by the name of Wolfgang (which later became Autograph) was another fan favorite at the Starwood. "They smoked all of us, really," says Quiet Riot lead singer Kevin DuBrow. "They got a better response than us and Van Halen, and nobody paid any attention to them at all." Stormer was another local legend on the club scene. Their guitarist, Jimmy Bates, was an amazing player, but he was fat and bald and sexually unappealing. "Van Halen had the tunes, and they had a sex god with David Lee Roth," says former Great White drummer Gary Holland. "Overall, they were the better package."

Marshall Berle, nephew of Milton, was handling the reopening of the Whisky in 1976 when he got a call from Kim Fowley telling him to check out a new local band named Van Halen. Fowley, on the L.A. scene since the 1960s, was the self-proclaimed Svengali who put together the groundbreaking all-female group the Runaways (a master of hype and hustle, Fowley once hired a limo to drive The Runaways two blocks to a record signing). Berle got David Lee Roth's number, called him, and asked if the band wanted to play the Whisky. Roth was ecstatic and invited Berle to the Pasadena Civic Auditorium, where the band was playing. The place was so packed that Berle couldn't get in.

Van Halen had recorded a thirty-song demo, produced by Gene Simmons. Like Boston's first demo, it was so good that it could have come out as an album on its own. But the band had no idea how to shop their demo or get it into the right hands, so it sat around collecting dust until Berle heard it and was impressed enough to begin working his connections for the band. Berle had previously run the music department at the William Morris Agency, where he represented a band called Harper's Bizarre, who had had a Top Twenty hit with "The 59th Street Bridge Song (Feelin' Groovy)" in 1967. The band was led by singer Ted Templeman, and Berle had remained friendly with him over the years. Templeman was now a hot producer who had built his rep with Van Morrison, Montrose, and the Doobie Brothers. Berle was also friendly with Mo Ostin because Reprise Records, which Ostin ran at the time, had its offices at William Morris when Berle worked there.

Berle set up a show at the Starwood a year after Simmons first saw them at the club in May 1977, and invited Templeman and Ostin to see Van Halen. All he told the band was that some important people were coming to see them, so play good. The gig was on a rainy Monday night, and the club was mostly empty save for Berle, Ostin, and Templeman. Despite the fact that the club was deserted, "they came out and just kicked fucking ass, man," recalls Berle. The show was over, and Templeman and Ostin asked, "Can we go back and talk to them?" Right then and there, they offered the band a deal. "Within a week, we were signed up," said Eddie Van Halen. "It was right out of the movies."

When Van Halen signed with Warner Bros., a lot of local hard rock bands hoped they would get signed too. But Van Halen proved to be an anomaly in the age of disco. "I thought after Van Halen's success, the doors would open wide for everybody," says George Lynch, who went on to play in Dokken. "It might have closed some opportunities offered to us, because Van Halen had done so well. People thought, 'Well, that already happened—what's next?' They thought another style of music would come along."

"When Van Halen got a deal, a lot of people were jealous," says W.A.S.P. guitarist Chris Holmes, who grew up in Pasadena and knew Eddie from high school. "I said fuckin' cool, man, at least *somebody* got out of here." Says A La Carte's Kevin Martin, "I remember how jealous I was. But having said that, everybody knew it was going to happen."

The first Van Halen album took less than a month and just $50,000 to record. Templeman went for raw energy in the studio. "I believe the concept was to make as much of a live album as possible," says Berle. "I know that's what Ted was striving for and what the band wanted." The band kept overdubs to a minimum, and almost every song ended abruptly without a fadeout, just like the band performed them live.

One of Templeman's greatest strengths as a producer was allowing bands to be themselves and not branding his personal stamp on their music. None of the bands he worked with, from the Doobie Brothers to Van Morrison to Van Halen, sounded anything alike. "I think that's the mark of a good producer," he said. "You recognize the artist, you don't hear the producer." Templeman didn't have to give Van Halen much advice anyway. He mostly helped them structure their songs. Obviously, Eddie didn't need help laying down a solo. You just stepped back and made sure the tape was rolling.

Eddie became known for a two-handed technique dubbed "finger-tapping," in which his right hand tapped out extra notes on the fretboard. This created licks impossible to play with just your left hand. Eddie didn't invent the technique but, without question, revolutionized it. In the club days, he would go out of his way to protect it from being stolen by turning his back to the audience so they couldn't see what his hands were doing.

At Templeman's suggestion, Eddie's live guitar solo, featuring his fingertapping techniques, wound up on the album. The track was called "Eruption," and as many music journalists have put it, it changed guitar playing in a minute and forty-two seconds. No less than Frank Zappa even thanked Eddie for reinventing the instrument. To learn "Eruption" note for note was a big deal, and countless guitarists wore down their turntable needles trying. So many guitarists adopted two-handed tapping after Van Halen that it became as common a technique as bending a string.

Many great guitarists are often identified by their favorite instruments, such as Jimmy Page and Slash with their Gibson Les Pauls. Eddie wanted his own distinctive instrument as well. He built his favorite guitar, a red and white Stratocaster, out of spare parts that cost about $150. He reputedly finished his guitars with spray-paint. He would experiment on an Ibanez Destroyer, and whenever he played the guitar live it seemed to grow bigger in size every gig because of each successive paint layer.

The day before Van Halen embarked on their first tour as an opening act, the band had lunch with several Warner Bros. executives. Roth drove his old, beat-up clunker of a car to the meeting. He was so confident the band would make it that he left it in the parking lot and never came back for it. "There was never any doubt as to where this was all going," says Berle. "We were just trying to keep up with it."

On their first tour, Van Halen opened for Journey. The tour started in Milwaukee. On the first night, as Berle settled into his hotel room several floors below the band, he was gazing out the window when he saw a TV set falling to its death, landing on the concrete below with a loud crash. The band later thanked the Madison, Wisconsin, Sheraton Inn on the *Women and Children First* album because they completely wrecked the hotel's seventh floor. They blasted each other in the hallways with fire extinguishers, flooding the carpets with water. The water seeped down into the hotel rooms below, causing irate guests to check out. Van Halen was eventually banned from the entire Holiday Inn chain and had to check into hotels under pseudonyms (David Lee Roth liked to check in under the name "Hugh Jazz.").

In a larger live arena, the gawky early performances of the Starwood era were long gone. Now Roth had the audience in the palm of his hand and owned the stage. Van Halen were masters of faking spontaneity. With his band Talas, Billy Sheehan opened forty shows for Van Halen in 1980. The first night he saw Van Halen perform, he thought they were the greatest band in the world. Several shows into the tour, he began to notice it was the exact same show. But even though he knew that Roth was going to tell the exact same joke in the exact same spot, it was still hilarious every night. "It dawned on me what the brilliance of that was," says Sheehan. "It's done in every other arena of show business, but in rock it wasn't done that much. When Dave brought it in there, it was a whole new ball game."

Soon Van Halen would add the infamous brown-M&Ms clause in their tour rider. The clause stated that they had to have a bowl of M&Ms backstage with all the brown ones removed. They eventually made *Esquire*'s dubious-achievements list for trashing their dressing room one night when the brown ones weren't removed. But Roth explained that the reason the clause was in the contract was to make sure the promoters were paying attention to the band's requirements. If the brown M&Ms weren't removed, chances were the stage wasn't set up right either.

When Van Halen made it, Eddie bought several rare Les Paul guitars with his first royalty check. He and Alex also retired their father from working. Jan Van Halen would burst into tears of happiness when he saw his sons play. He had never made it as a musician and, like a lot of parents, lived vicariously through his children.

Meanwhile, Roth was discovering that money was not making him any happier. Mark Danziesen, a drummer who went on to play with the

Riverdogs and Little Caesar, met Roth right as Van Halen was taking off. Danziesen was just a local musician playing around town and asked Roth what it would take for his band to get a record deal. Roth told him, "Well, you know, I got a record deal because I wanted to get away from my troubles and get them behind me, get some money. . . . Man, that's when your troubles *start*. So don't get a record deal. Believe me, you don't want a record deal. I'm in more hell now [than before]."

Roth was also not amused by the countless singers who ripped him off throughout the '80s. "Don't blame me for the errors of my bastard sons," he said, referring to the Bret Michaels and Vince Neils who followed in his wake. "Sometimes I'm flattered, usually not."

Likewise, even after Van Halen became successful, Eddie wasn't happy that other guitar players stole his licks. "It's kind of like incest," he said. "We're bound to have a couple of retarded kids after a while." As Slash put it, "It really bummed me out when everyone ripped off Eddie's whole trip. Now I think *he* doesn't know exactly what he's doing!"

Eddie complained that a lot of guitarists hated him because of his talent and once said, "The more people that hate you, the better you are. I mean, no other guitarist is gonna hate another guitarist if you're no good. You're no threat." Just as when Jimi Hendrix became successful, many guitarists were scared Eddie would put them out of business. "I was pertrified when I heard Eddie Van Halen," says former Kiss guitarist Bruce Kulick. "I never heard anything so intense but with that Eric Clapton tone. It freaked me out."

A lot of kids just learning to play in the '70s and early '80s had a hard time accepting the fact they would never be as good as Eddie Van Halen. "God, he was so disgustingly brilliant," said Pat Smear of Nirvana and the Foo Fighters. "He ruined my fucking life when he came out. I thought, 'I suck, I should stop playing.' I thought that this was it. I'm through; I'm completely worthless; I've been wiped out. I surrender!" A lot of players like Pat kept on playing anyway, and their bands would eventually take over the musical landscape.

By April 1980, Eddie Van Halen was on the cover of *Guitar Player* magazine, a true honor for any guitarist. Eddie was asked where he saw himself thirty years in the future. "I don't know what's gonna happen in the future," he replied. "Maybe somebody else in the band will get egoed out and quit or something. But I'd love Van Halen to be forever."

"IS EVERYBODY CRAZY YET?!?!" After his exit from Black Sabbath, **Ozzy Osbourne** not only established a successful solo career for himself, he became a heavy metal icon as well. (Neil Zlozower)

4

"RANDY (RHOADS) WAS AT ABOUT **80** PERCENT OF WHERE HE WAS GONNA GET TO AT THE TIME OF HIS DEATH. THAT'S THE TRAGEDY — HE NEVER PEAKED. AT LEAST HENDRIX HAD TIME TO DEVELOP BEFORE HE PASSED AWAY."

—Max Norman, producer of *Blizzard of Ozz* and *Diary of a Madman*, on the late Ozzy Osbourne guitarist Randy Rhoads

AS THE 1970S WERE DRAWING to a close, the decade proved to be a true Renaissance for rock music. There were countless bands that played what was considered heavy metal and hard rock, and almost none of them sounded alike. Originality and sincerity were crucial for a band to maintain a following. "There was more heart, more feeling that went into the music," Saint Vitus guitarist Dave Chandler said about the '70s. "It was hard to find two bands that sounded the same."

The groupies, drugs, wealth, and spoiled-brat behavior that many rock stars in the 1970s had adopted were already becoming clichés. In the summer of 1978, Joe Walsh of the Eagles had a Top Twenty single as a solo artist, "Life's Been Good," that hilariously described the rock star life. "I live in hotels, tear out the walls/I have accountants pay for it all."

Walsh never thought the song would become a hit—he didn't think it was as funny as everyone else did. "It might have been a little too close to the truth," he said. "But I really did tell the truth, and it was a hit because at the time it was important that somebody did." Many rock stars were apparently too close to the lifestyle Walsh described to see how accurate the song really was.

Aerosmith, one of the biggest bands of the mid-'70s, began to embody all the worst rock and roll stereotypes of the decade. The endless touring schedules bands endured throughout the '70s was also a big reason Aerosmith burned out. The nonstop pace of album-tour-album-

A local legend in his native southern California, **Randy Rhoads** went on to national prominence for his revolutionary guitar playing in Ozzy's solo band. His life was tragically cut short by a plane crash in 1982. (Neil Zlozower)

tour made it difficult for Steven Tyler to compose lyrics. "You get on the road, and you're just cut away from reality," said guitarist Brad Whitford. "You can only write so much about the road, and Steven is a storyteller, really." Tyler was so used to living in hotels that when he was between tours and wanted breakfast, he'd roll out of bed, pick up the phone, and dial O, forgetting that his home didn't have room service.

Aerosmith began to crumble from drug abuse. Their live performances at the end of the 1970s were usually terrible. The band was too stoned most nights to play well and wouldn't hit their stride as a live band until they got sober a decade later. As Tyler recalled, "We started to see how screwed up we could get before we walked onstage, just to see if we could get away with it," and often they couldn't. "It got to the point where as long as we did 'Back in the Saddle,' 'Toys in the Attic,' 'Sweet Emotion,' 'Walk this Way,' [and] 'Dream On,' it didn't matter if we sucked," said Perry.

By 1977's *Draw the Line* album, the band was completely unfocused.

Producer Jack Douglas thought the album title was appropriate: "the coke lines, heroin lines, drawing symbolic lines, and crossing them—no matter what." The record came in six months late. The band booked huge blocks of studio time, even kicking out Bruce Springsteen so they could record, and never showed up.

In 1978, it was clear Aerosmith wouldn't stay together much longer. That year the band appeared in the film *Sgt. Peppers Lonely Hearts Club Band,* a disastrous musical that featured thirty Beatles songs performed by an all-star cast. The Beatles declined to star in the film, so the Bee Gees, along with Peter Frampton, were given the job. Aerosmith played "the Future Villain Band," and they performed "Come Together" on a gigantic pile of money that represented the corporate greed of the record business. In the movie, disco represented the forces of good, and the hard rockers were the bad guys (Alice Cooper also played one of the villains).

A month after Aerosmith released their *Night in the Ruts* album in November 1979, Perry departed to try out a solo career. No one could have predicted that less than ten years down the road, not only would the band have an unprecedented comeback, but they would be sober as well.

The music business was transformed in 1978 by the success of one album. With the hit film *Saturday Night Fever* and its smash soundtrack, the disco movement came out of the underground and would become a nationwide phenomenon. The film opened in December 1977 and was an immediate sensation. With the relentless promotion of PolyGram, two Bee Gees songs from the soundtrack, "How Deep Is Your Love" and "Stayin' Alive," both hit No. 1 on the charts before *Fever* opened in theaters.

The *Saturday Night Fever* soundtrack was the *Star Wars* of the record business. All a record label needed was one huge hit like it to cover its losses for the entire year. With the subsequent breakthrough of the *Grease* soundtrack, as well as Casablanca's continued success with Donna Summer, the Village People, and Kiss, PolyGram sales topped $1.2 billion at the end of 1978, the first time a record company had scored over a billion in annual revenues. Both PolyGram and Casablanca figured that the hits would keep coming at this level, forever.

In the 1970s, labels often overshipped records, and stores would take them because there was no limit on how many unsold albums they could return later. By 1979, disco was heading downhill, albums were being returned to the labels in droves, and a record-industry crash followed. Casablanca's shipping practices started the derisive joke about an album being such a disaster that it shipped gold, (500,000 copies) then got shipped back platinum (1,000,000 copies). Bill Aucoin liked to say the joke actually started with the Kiss solo albums.

By 1978, the members of Kiss were severely burned out and needed time away from one another. It was decided that each member of the band would record a solo album, and all four would be released on the same day. Neil Bogart was against the idea until he realized four albums would equal four times the money. Distributors ordered a million units of the solo albums, 250,000 copies per member.

There was no question that Ace Frehley's album was the best of the four. "Each band member had an ego, and they needed to express it," says Eddie Kramer, who produced Frehley's album. "Ace aced everybody else's because, a) we had a hit single, b) it was the best produced, c) we had the best material and the best playing. We blew all the other records away, and I think the rest of the band was quite jealous frankly." Frehley's album was also the only one of the four that had a Top Forty hit, "New York Groove."

The Kiss solo albums sold roughly 600–700,000 copies per member, which would have been a tremendous success if the albums hadn't been overshipped. One former PolyGram executive said in Fredric Dannen's *Hit Men*, "[Bogart] pressed so many that we were getting killed on the returns. We were already way behind in September, yet Neil persuaded everyone that Christmas would take care of it. So he pressed another quarter million and lost even more!"

After the solo albums, the band's next studio release was 1979's *Dynasty*. The album got off to a promising start. Kiss actually released a disco song called "I Was Made for Lovin' You," written with future Bon Jovi and Ricky Martin songwriter Desmond Child. It was Child's first big hit as a songwriter for hire, and it almost broke the Top Ten. The *Dynasty* album peaked at No. 9 on June 23, 1979.

With their album starting off well and their previous 1977–78 tour a huge success, the *Dynasty* tour was planned as Kiss's biggest extravaganza yet. The stage show was so huge that the band needed a day off between shows in different cities just to transport everything and erect it. The tour had eleven trucks, and it could take up to six hours just to get the band in and out of a gig. But Kiss had peaked with their previous tour; their popularity was starting to cool off. The band expected to perform multiple nights in the major cities like New York and Chicago, but ticket sales were slow, and additional nights were canceled. Some of the shows on the *Dynasty* tour sold out, but most didn't. Some nights the band sold only half to three-quarters the house capacity. Kiss was now saddled with a very expensive show they couldn't make their money back on. The way the tour was budgeted, they could make money only if they were playing multiple dates and selling them out, which wasn't happening.

One casualty in the Kiss camp would be the departure of Peter Criss, who left the band just before they recorded their 1980 release, *Unmasked*. Criss was pictured on the cover of the album, but the drums were played by session drummer Anton Fig, who now plays in David Letterman's band. Sales for *Unmasked* were lukewarm, and the album never cracked the Top Thirty. Kiss didn't tour America for *Unmasked* except for a sole date at the Palladium in New York, a small theater. The show sold out, but Kiss didn't want to add a second show, because they were afraid they wouldn't sell enough tickets. It was at the Palladium show that they unveiled Criss's replacement, Paul Charles Caravello, who soon changed his name to Eric Carr. After a disastrous attempt to turn him into "the Hawk," complete with a feathery chicken suit, Carr's alter ego became "the Fox." Carr was the band's drummer for the next ten years.

Big changes were going on at Kiss's label as well. In February 1980, PolyGram bought out the other 50 percent of Casablanca and pushed Neil Bogart out (Bogart sold his stock in the company for $15 million). With record and ticket sales declining in the States, Kiss headed to Australia, where they did a number of sold-out stadium shows. The tour was backed by media mogul Rupert Murdoch, and all the newspapers he owned covered it. When the band landed at the airport, the runway was closed down and no other planes were allowed to land. Nine limos, a 727 jet, and a helicopter were on call for the tour. "There was very little the band didn't have at their disposal," says Aucoin. "This was the first time that they effectively took over a country!"

After the success of Pink Floyd's *The Wall,* in 1979, many bands wanted to make an epic album. Kiss was ready to make their great concept record with *The Elder.* This was the stab at artistic legitimacy they'd always wanted. "We actually did [*The Elder*] for the critics," admitted Simmons. "You should never go for respect, because on the day that critics and your mom like the same music that you do, it's over."

Bob Ezrin produced the album, and he and Simmons wrote a script together for it, like Ezrin had done with *The Wall.* *The Elder* told a Tolkien-esque sword-and-sorcery story of a young warrior fighting against evil. *The Elder* was designed as one of the first multimedia concepts. There would be an *Elder* movie and the songs on the album were to be the soundtrack (the album's full title was [*Music From*] *The Elder*).

Everyone who was involved in the album now agrees that it was a major mistake. Frehley wanted nothing to do with it and refused to come to the studio where the band was recording. Ezrin feels, in retrospect, that Frehley was "dead right" in not wanting to be involved in the album. "It had nothing whatsoever to do with Kiss and we should have figured that out," says Ezrin who cowrote six of the album's eleven tracks. What little Frehley played on *The Elder,* a handful of guitar solos, he recorded in his home studio, which the band dubbed "Ace's Bomb Shelter," in this case a fitting name for where he was hiding out.

Ezrin could usually convince Kiss when he thought they were making a mistake, but he was grappling with a drug problem at the time of *The Elder* and wasn't much help. Another problem with the album, among many, was Simmons and Stanley's rivalry—they were competing with each other instead of trying to work together.

In the original Kiss lineup, Frehley and Criss were close friends, and when the original four were together, manager Bill Aucoin insisted everything was an equal vote among them. With Criss out of the band, Simmons and Stanley had more leverage. According to Frehley, Eric Carr didn't vote because he was a "hired gun" who could have been easily replaced if he made waves. It was now easy for Frehley to be outvoted by Simmons and Stanley on decisions the entire band used to make. When Frehley finally heard the finished product, he became so angry that he smashed his cassette copy against the wall. He even pleaded with the band to shelve the album, but was outvoted.

The Elder was released in 1981. To call it a complete and utter disaster is putting it mildly. Plans for a massive *Elder* tour never got off the drawing board, and an *Elder* movie was never made. With Kiss's popularity fading rapidly in the States, *The Elder* was the worst possible album they could have made.

Frehley claims he went over the deep end with booze and drugs after the failure of *The Elder,* and left the band in 1982. He totaled his DeLorean the same year while driving drunk 100 miles per hour against traffic on the Bronx River Parkway. Six months later, he was busted for driving drunk again and lost his license for several years.

Years after the fallout cleared from *The Elder,* Ezrin gave it another listen when Simmons sent him a copy on CD. Halfway through the album, he turned to his wife and said, "You know something? I should have been killed before being allowed to finish this. This is one of the worst crimes that's ever been perpetrated on music!"

Kiss would follow up *The Elder* with one of their strongest albums, *Creatures of the Night* in 1982, but it came almost too late to revive their careers. At first, the *Creatures* album sold poorly, but it has gone on to become one of the band's all-time classics. Following the *Creatures* tour, Kiss took a radical step and went without makeup for their next album, *Lick It Up*, released in 1983. Reports vary as to whether it was the band's decision to take off the makeup or whether they were pressured by the label, but regardless, it was a move that the band had to make to revitalize itself. Vinnie Vincent, who filled the guitar slot in Kiss from 1982 to 1984, said, "No matter how many records Kiss would have done, I think if the makeup was still on they'd be fighting an element that they were old hat, yesterday's news."

AC/DC's success with the *Back in Black* album made them a hard rock anomaly at the dawn of the 1980s. When they wrote "It's a Long Way to the Top (If You Wanna Rock and Roll)" early in their careers, little did they know how well it would describe their journey to success.

Angus and Malcolm Young formed AC/DC in 1973. The guitar-playing brothers were born in Scotland; their family immigrated to Australia in 1963. Singer Bon Scott, who would join the band in 1974, was also born in Scotland but had also moved with his family to Australia when he was six.

Playing up his tough-guy exterior, Scott often wore vests two sizes too small to make his muscles look bigger. In reality, he was usually a friendly and down-to-earth character. "Bon didn't have a mean bone in his body," said one of his early friends. "He never looked for trouble, but if it happened, he wouldn't walk away."

Beginning in their club days, Angus wore the same outfit every gig, his Catholic schoolboy uniform, and he was effectively the band's mascot. Angus is also one of the shortest musicians in rock, and apparently could still fit into a schoolboy uniform well into his adulthood.

AC/DC would become the living embodiment of the old cliché: If it ain't broke, don't fix it. Musically, they never strayed from their formula of simple, powerful blues-based rock. Angus has played the same model guitar his entire career, a Gibson SG, which fit his tiny frame perfectly. He went through several SGs a year because they would become drowned in his sweat and short out.

Like many of the best hard rock and metal bands, AC/DC also had an incredibly solid rhythm section, with Cliff Williams and Phil Rudd on bass and drums, respectively. Rudd played behind the beat, which gave the music more weight and tension. "It's as if the music's hanging on by its fingernails," says Tony Platt, who engineered the albums *Highway to Hell* and *Back in Black*. "It almost feels like it's going to fall to pieces at any moment, and that adds to the excitement." Williams was a simple bass player, but he always had the right notes at the right time. "[Williams] plays very little but holds the band together like Krazy Glue," said fellow bassist Billy Sheehan, a huge AC/DC fan who went on to play with David Lee Roth's solo band.

In the studio, AC/DC kept their recordings as natural as possible. Beau Hill produced a number of bands in the '80s, including Ratt and Winger. Before he'd start an album, nine times out of ten, the bands he worked with would mention AC/DC's *Back in Black* as a prime example of a record that they would love to emulate. Many '80s bands tried to make their albums sound big by drowning them in reverb; Hill often used AC/DC as a perfect example of a band that could sound huge without effects or studio trickery.

"The truth is, AC/DC has no reverb, no effects, no slap, no echo," says Hill. "From a technical point of view, making records without that stuff is so much easier. The reverb times, the delay times—to get them to all act in harmony with one another is hard. Making a dry, in-your-face rock and roll record like AC/DC is a lot easier."

Says Tony Platt, "The main thing with AC/DC was to try and get a sound that was like a very heavy acoustic sound so you could hear the strings, you could hear the chords, but at the same time, it nearly takes your head off. The best way to describe it is a nice, clean, dirty sound." With AC/DC, the goal was to record an album that sounded great cranked up to oblivion and also had the same punch at a lower volume as well.

Eddie Kramer was first on board to produce the band's 1979 album *Highway to Hell*. The band didn't click with Kramer, though, and told their label, Atlantic, that they wanted to work with Robert John "Mutt" Lange. Lange was a native of South Africa and had previously produced the Boomtown Rats and Graham Parker. Atlantic was against the band working with Lange because he had never produced a hard rock band before, but the band wanted to work with someone who could bring something different to the process. As Malcolm Young put it, "We learned a lot. You really need an outsider, because we can all go too far and disappear up our own anuses."

Most of AC/DC's previous albums were recorded in three weeks each. The band spent three months working on *Highway to Hell*, toiling for fifteen hours a day. Lange was famous for being meticulous in the studio, something a band like AC/DC wasn't used to. Says Platt, "If Mutt and I ever had any clashes, it was over the fact that he was looking for the perfect take, and sometimes I'd say to him, 'But Mutt, that feels great!' With AC/DC, they are very instinctive, organic musicians. They knew which take was the one."

Bringing Lange on board was the best move the band could have made. *Highway to Hell* was AC/DC's first platinum album in the States. AC/DC always had a well-deserved reputation as a fierce live band, and when they were ready to hit the road for the *Highway* album, Van Halen, Sammy Hagar, and Foreigner all refused to take them as an opening act, in all likelihood afraid of getting blown off the stage.

The song "Highway to Hell" was often misinterpreted by religious zealots as a pro-Satan song. The song was really about the band being on the road for four years without a break. "When you're sleeping with the singer's sock two inches from your nose, believe me, that's pretty close to hell," said Angus Young.

In January 1980, after the *Highway to Hell* tour ended, AC/DC hardly paused to rest on their laurels. They started prepping another album right away. Scott was writing lyrics, but some friends would later say that he was tired of the fact that there wasn't much room to expand AC/DC's sound or do much different with it, and he was thinking about a solo career.

On February 20, after drinking seven double whiskeys with a friend, Scott was left in a car to sleep it off. He was found dead the next morning. Scott had choked on his vomit. He was thirty-three years old. Several days after his funeral, Scott's friends received Christmas cards from him. They arrived late because he hadn't put enough postage on them.

Angus and Malcolm Young were both very private people and didn't talk much about Scott's death. Malcolm did say to Platt that there were numerous times Scott would disappear after a show and no one could find him until soundcheck the next day. "You know, the thing about Bon was you were never quite sure where he was, but he always turned up," said Malcolm. "We just gotta get used to the fact he's not gonna turn up anymore."

There was too much riding on AC/DC for the band to stop completely, and they didn't waste much time after Scott's death getting back to work. A month later, the band hired Brian Johnson, a native of Newcastle, England, who sang in the band Geordie, and were rehearsing songs for their next album by April 1980.

Recording began in the end of May 1980 in Nassau, Bahamas, at Compass Point Studios. Malcolm later admitted that *Back in Black* was the worst experience he'd ever had recording an album. Dealing with Scott's death was bad enough, but there was a lot of pressure from the label, wondering how the band was going to follow up the success of *Highway to Hell.*

No one could predict how well the album would do, but Platt knew they had a winner. He also knew the band had a hit with "You Shook Me All Night Long," which would become AC/DC's first Top Forty single. "When you're working on a song for hours and hours in the studio, when you finish and go to bed, it's [usually] still going round in your head. If it's still going round in your head the next morning, you know there's something special about it."

When *Back in Black* was finished, Platt took a copy of the album to Atlantic Records in New York. He set up a top-quality tape machine and monitor system in a conference room to play the album for the label executives. After the Atlantic executives heard the album, they remained silent. Finally, one of the head honchos at the label spoke up and said he liked the album. Suddenly, everyone else in the room began buzzing: "Yeah, that's what I was thinking. . . ."

Back in Black was released in July 1980. The album cover was all black, in Scott's memory, with the band's logo and album title embossed in the middle. To date, AC/DC's *Back in Black* has sold 16 million copies, making it the ninth-biggest-selling album of all time.

By the end of 1978, slowly but surely, Led Zeppelin was coming back together and recording a new album. Enduring taunts from Billy Idol and the Clash that they were washed-up dinosaurs, Led Zeppelin had to prove they could still hold their own in the age of punk and new wave.

Jimmy Page took a back seat on the band's next album, *In Through the Out Door,* because he was battling heroin addiction. Robert Plant and John Paul Jones wrote much of the album. Synthesizers were starting to get popular, and many of the songs on the album were keyboard-heavy. *In Through the Out Door* was released in August 1979 and remained at No. 1 on the U.S. charts for seven weeks.

Led Zeppelin next headlined two days at the Knebworth Festival in England beginning on August 4. The band hadn't performed in its mother country since 1975, and it took Plant half the first show to get over his stage fright. But the audience welcomed them back, eliminating any concerns that the band was outdated or a relic of the early '70s.

On the morning of September 24, 1980, John Bonham drank four quadruple screwdrivers before meeting the other band members at rehearsal. No matter how loaded he was, Bonham could always perform, but this time he was so plastered he could barely play. Later, at Jimmy Page's home, he kept drinking, then eventually passed out. He choked on his vomit during his sleep and was found dead the next morning. He was thirty-one.

Led Zeppelin officially announced that the band was no more on December 4, 1980, but the band truly died with Bonham. After Bonham died, Page didn't pick up a guitar for three years. Page's magnificent playing, building mountains out of layers of incredible riffs, would never return to its great standards.

In the '80s, Led Zeppelin finally gained the critical respect they deserved, and they gained a whole new audience of teenage fans discovering their music for the first time. The band was right all along; they knew their music would stand the test of time.

By Black Sabbath's 1976 album, *Technical Ecstasy,* Ozzy Osbourne wasn't happy with the direction the band's music was headed in. Iommi was spending too much time trying to perfect the music. As far as Osbourne was concerned, mistakes made the music sound real, an attitude Led Zeppelin shared. The fans didn't care about how ornate Iommi could make Black Sabbath sound in the studio. They wanted to rock, pure and simple, and the band wasn't delivering for them anymore. Osbourne would later call Iommi "the most boring guitarist since God had crabs."

In 1977, Osbourne left the band after his father died, and was replaced by singer Dave Walker. Walker played live with the band once on the BBC, and shortly afterward was asked to leave when Osbourne decided to come back to the band. Black Sabbath had written some songs with Walker in Osbourne's absence, but he refused to sing them, so they had to write all new material. The band was burned out and struggling to come up with new songs as they limped toward their tenth anniversary. Trying to find the strength to continue, they called their next album *Never Say Die.*

In 1979, Sabbath headed back out onto the road for their *Never Say Die* tour. Van Halen, hot off the success of their first album, was their opening act, and they blew Sabbath off the stage every night with minimal effort. "They just stomped Black Sabbath to death all across the country," says Grover Jackson, founder of Jackson Guitars. "I think that everybody in Sabbath was sort of worn-out and tired, and they were just trying to make some bucks and get through a tour. To pair them with this young bunch of man-eaters from Pasadena was brutal for them."

One night, Tony Iommi was backstage lamenting the fact that Van Halen was stealing the show. He told Osbourne to go into Van Halen's dressing room and yell at them. Osbourne ran into the Van Halen dressing room and began screaming. After a few minutes of ranting and raving, Van Halen asked Osbourne, "Why are you yelling at us?" He couldn't remember. His days in Black Sabbath were numbered.

After Black Sabbath finished the tour, the band members headed back to their homes in Beverly Hills. One day, Iommi pulled Bill Ward aside so they could talk. Iommi was fed up with Osbourne and said that things had to change. Ward was shocked. He knew there were problems in the band but didn't think the singer would have to leave. Ward was the one who ended up giving Osbourne his notice. When he told him they had to have a talk, Osbourne immediately knew what was coming. "It's me, isn't it?" he asked. "Tell me the goddamn truth." Ward deeply regretted firing Osbourne. He didn't want to work with another singer. "It was the end of Black Sabbath," said Ward. "I had no more energy to live the lie. It was over, and I knew it."

Exhausted from being ripped off by their record company, embroiled in lawsuits with their managers, burned out from the massive amounts of drugs and booze they were consuming, Black Sabbath needed a fresh start. Iommi was ready to leave the band and launch a solo career. He was jamming with Ronnie James Dio and wanted to form a band with him. Geezer Butler wanted to come along too. Dio convinced them that they should keep the name Black Sabbath and hire him as the new singer. (Ward would reluctantly stay with the band as well for a short period of time.)

Dio had previously sung for Rainbow, Ritchie Blackmore's band after he left Deep Purple in the mid-1970s. Like Judas Priest's Rob Halford, Dio was considered one of the best singers in the genre. Canceling a gig was never an option for him. One night he had laryngitis and could barely even talk, but when it was showtime, he hit the stage and somehow sang his ass off. Dio was also dictatorial and difficult to work with. Being short made Dio the butt of many jokes; when he sang for Black Sabbath, the roadies sometimes put an orange crate in front of the microphone stand as a joke. When Osbourne became a successful solo artist, every night he had a dwarf come on stage to serve him drinks. He'd tell the audience to "Say hello to Ronnie."

As difficult as Dio was to deal with in a band situation, if you were a fan, there was nothing he wouldn't do for you. Unlike a lot of rock stars who blew off their fans, Dio made himself accessible after every gig and would sometimes spend up to five hours after a show meeting people and signing autographs.

Black Sabbath recorded their first album with Dio, 1980's *Heaven and Hell*, very quickly. The album cover looked like a velvet gothic painting featuring a group of angels smoking and gambling. The managers and former managers were still fighting each other, but the new music the band was writing was so good, no one in the band cared.

Black Sabbath toured Europe first for the *Heaven and Hell* album. They knew the audience would still be there for them, and they were selling out huge venues. When they came to the States, Black Sabbath were surprised to see their audience was still there for them here as well. The band not only had a successful lead-singer transplant but were able to have a hit album and tour in an age when metal was considered on the way out because of the popularity of new wave.

But there were still problems within the band. Bill Ward was falling apart from excessive drinking and missed four gigs on the *Heaven and Hell* tour. Black Sabbath had to find another drummer fast. Whatever gigs the band missed they had to pay for themselves. If they missed many more shows, they would have been wiped out. Vinnie Appice, the younger brother of Vanilla Fudge drummer Carmine Appice, was called in. Vinnie played in Axis, an underrated "power trio" featuring Louisiana blues rock guitarist Danny Johnson. (Ward later got sober in the mid-1980s after losing the drum throne in Black Sabbath and winding up on the streets from alcoholism.)

Since Appice was hired quickly, he had to learn Black Sabbath's live set in a hurry. His first gig with the band was at an outdoor arena in Hawaii. Appice wrote out drum charts he could read onstage so he'd be able to play all the songs. During the song "Black Sabbath," lightning cracked the sky, and it began pouring rain, turning his charts into mush. At the end of the show, he autographed his charts, "This is my first gig—Vinnie Appice," and hurled them into the audience for a lucky fan to catch.

It wasn't the first time something strange happened when the band played the song. When the band played England on the *Heaven and Hell* tour, disaster struck again when they played "Black Sabbath." The band had huge buckets of water they'd fill with dry ice to create fog on stage. A roadie put too much dry ice in one of the buckets, and it blew up, causing a giant explosion of water to crash down on Appice while he was playing. Two minutes later, he felt something burning. A chunk of dry ice had fallen down his pants and was stuck to his ass. He fled the drum riser, and backstage a nurse had to pull down his pants and pry the dry ice off his rear end. For the rest of the gig, Appice had to sit on a pillow.

Black Sabbath's first official live album, *Live Evil,* came out in 1982. During the dubbing, Dio and Iommi accused each other of turning up their own mixes when the other person was out of the room. Today everyone in the band agrees that such a thing never happened, but the paranoia and mistrust between them had grown too strong to continue. The band would end up in separate limos divided by continents: Dio and Appice, the Americans, shared one limo, Iommi and Butler, the Brits, shared another. Soon after Dio would leave Black Sabbath and begin a solo career of his own.

Dio carried a lot of anger from the breakup of Sabbath and was ready to blow everyone away with his new band, simply named Dio. The band put nineteen-year-old Vivian Campbell on the map as a hot guitarist, but Dio's biggest hit was "Rainbow in the Dark," which featured a keyboard riff. Like most metal bands, Dio felt that guitars were the true building blocks of a song, but keyboards were a prominent part of the band as well. "It surprised me that a band like Dio could sound as heavy as it did with the keyboards as prominent as they were," says former Dio keyboard player Claude Schnell.

Dio's first solo album, *Holy Diver,* was a classic '80s metal album. With the success of the "Rainbow in the Dark" single, which got a big boost from a new cable channel called MTV, Dio's solo career took off like a rocket. The band went from opening act to headlining theaters in eight gigs, and were headlining arenas within two months. Every gig on the first tour was over by eleven, but the bus would be rocking with loud music and partying until three in the morning. Dio gained more and more control over his band with every successive album, to the point where everyone in the band would either leave or get fired. But they kicked a lot of ass and had a lot of fun while it lasted.

When Ozzy Osbourne was fired from Black Sabbath, he signed away all rights he had to the band and picked up his last check. He then holed up at the La Park Hotel in Los Angeles for three months. He kept the curtains in his room shut, and drank and snorted blow all alone in the dark. Osbourne thought his life was over. How could he carry on without Black Sabbath?

Sharon Arden, who worked for her father Don when he managed

Black Sabbath, eventually came by to pick up some money from Osbourne. He had spent it all on cocaine before she got there. She yelled at him for blowing the money but was determined to pull him back from out of the muck. She got right to the point: "Get yourself together—I want to manage you." Not only would Sharon Arden launch Osbourne's solo career, but he would always credit her for saving something much more important: his life. No more singing off to the side of the stage for Osbourne. It was time for him to take center stage in his career and life. He and Arden decided to put a new band together and began looking for guitar players.

By the end of the 1970s, the L.A. band Quiet Riot not only hoped they'd get a deal after their rivals Van Halen got signed, "we counted on it," says lead singer Kevin DuBrow. Yet the major-label deal never came. The band auditioned for thirty-two labels, and all thirty-two of them passed. It was clear the band was going in circles. It was also clear that Quiet Riot's guitarist, Randy Rhoads, was too talented to remain a local legend.

Rhoads was considered one of the hottest guitar players in L.A., right alongside Eddie Van Halen. One local fan, Michael Vangerov, was so excited by Randy's playing that when he went to go see Quiet Riot at the Starwood, he'd keep an acoustic guitar in his car. After Quiet Riot ended their set, Vangerov would run out to his car, grab his acoustic, and try to play the riffs he'd just seen on stage.

Quiet Riot and Van Halen ruled the Starwood, but Quiet Riot couldn't get a record deal because, unlike Van Halen, their music wasn't distinctive enough. The record executives told them to write a song just like a current hit on the charts and they would consider signing the band. A month later, Quiet Riot would have the song written, but the label would pass because the hit they tried to emulate was now off the charts. Then the label would tell them, "Now if you could come up with a song like *this . . .*"

When Rhoads got the call that Ozzy Osbourne was looking for guitar players, he asked, "Who's Ozzy Osbourne?" He had never heard of him, nor was he a Black Sabbath fan, and turned down the offer to audition for Osbourne's solo band. Even though Quiet Riot was going nowhere, Rhoads was loyal to DuBrow and didn't want to leave him in the lurch. It was his mother, Delores Rhoads, who finally convinced him to go see Osbourne. She told Randy that even if he didn't get the gig, he needed to be out there meeting people and making connections. With much reluctance, Rhoads went to the audition.

When Rhoads arrived, Osbourne was stoned out of his mind. Rhoads barely had a chance to set up and play before Osbourne told him he had the gig. He came home bewildered, telling his mother, "I don't know what I've got, but I've got something." The next day, Osbourne told a friend he had dreamed that he hired a guitar player. His friend told him he really *had* hired a guitar player. "Oh, God, what have I done?" said Osbourne. "I hope he can play." Once he sobered up enough to really hear Rhoads play, he was floored.

DuBrow was crushed when he found out that Rhoads had landed the Ozzy Osbourne gig. Quiet Riot played their last show with Randy in October 1979. "I put all my eggs into the Randy Rhoads basket," says DuBrow. "I wasn't much of a singer, and he was the greatest guitar player I ever heard. So I had to find some talent pretty quick. I concentrated on my singing and centered my next band around my singing."

Where Osbourne had fronted one of the biggest bands of the '70s, now he was starting over from scratch. But his new band reminded him of the old days of Black Sabbath, when they were still hungry and had something to prove. Osbourne's first two solo albums, *Blizzard of Ozz,* and *Diary of a Madman,* sounded nothing alike, but they were recorded at the same time in England and released a year apart, in 1980 and 1981. Rhoads's guitar playing was miles ahead of anything he'd ever done with Quiet Riot. He would often double- and sometimes even triple-track his solos without leaving a note out of place. Bob Daisley and Lee Kerslake played bass and drums on the album, but after both albums were recorded, Quiet Riot's Rudy Sarzo joined Rhoads in Osbourne's band, and Tommy Aldridge of Black Oak Arkansas took over on drums.

Yet even with two albums of material in the can, Osbourne had trouble getting a record deal. He was turned down by his old label, Warner Bros. He eventually got a one-album deal with Jet Records, a division of CBS, and the label put out *Blizzard* first before committing to put out *Diary of a Madman.*

In Black Sabbath, Osbourne could never adequately explain in musical terms what he wanted to do, and Tony Iommi didn't have the patience to listen to him. He loved working with Rhoads because the guitarist took the time to listen and try to bring Osbourne's ideas to life. He viewed Rhoads not just as a collaborator but as an equal, and they grew closer and closer as friends.

Ozzy's new band went on the road, mainly headlining theaters and small hockey arenas, with Motörhead and Def Leppard opening. Sharon Arden paid for much of the tour out of her own pocket and had to mortgage her home to cover the tour's startup costs. Before the band broke through, there were times they would arrive at the venue and find out they were undersold on tickets and the promoters were threatening to cancel. The band often had to play for free. They saw a lot of hard times, but one of Arden's biggest jobs was to keep everyone upbeat and positive. "I can honestly tell you that if it wasn't for her, the band never would have happened," says Rudy Sarzo. Female managers were an anomaly in the early '80s, but Arden proved that she could play just as tough as the boys. Even though working with Osbourne was her first time managing a band, Arden made it clear she wouldn't be pushed around, and those who crossed her did so at their peril. Once when Arden suspected a promoter was cheating her out of money, she kicked him in the crotch.

Soon the momentum of Osbourne's record and ticket sales began to snowball. The band sold out a show at the Academy of Music in New York, and demand for tickets was so great that they added a second show the same night. The band played the Day on the Green Festival in Oakland, California, on July 4, 1981. As the second band on the bill, they weren't scheduled to do an encore, but by the time they walked all the way back to their trailer, promoter Bill Graham was running after them telling them to get back onstage because the audience was going crazy. Sarzo was halfway undressed and had to throw his clothes back on so he could get back and play one more song.

Osbourne started attracting press attention for his outrageous behavior when he bit the head off a live dove during a marketing meeting for *Blizzard of Ozz* in 1981. Osbourne was then banned from entering the CBS building. Although the incident got a ton of press, the CBS brass were so disgusted that they threatened not to promote the album if he pulled another stunt like that. Obviously, he paid little heed to their warning.

It was in 1982, when the *Diary of a Madman* tour hit Des Moines, Iowa, that the most notorious incident of Osbourne's career took place. Now that he was in charge of his own band, the rule was not to get in his stage space. Bassist Rudy Sarzo had to stay within two or three square feet of the stage. He couldn't go in front of Osbourne, put his foot on the drum riser, or go to the other side of the stage. With his legs practically nailed to the floor, he developed a wild style of headbanging in which his entire upper body would twist and contort. "Half the night I'm looking up; half the night I'm looking down," he says. "I saw a lot of lights, and I saw a lot of the floor."

During the Iowa gig, when Sarzo's headbang was on the downbeat, he saw something rubbery crumpled up on the stage. He motioned to Osbourne to check it out. Someone had tossed a bat on stage. The singer didn't realize it wasn't a toy you'd buy on Halloween, and he picked it up and bit its head off. Once he realized the bat was indeed real, he spat the head out of his mouth, and it landed somewhere behind the barricade. Osbourne was rushed to the hospital, and the road crew scrambled to find the bat so it could be examined for rabies. He felt tremendous dread when his joints began to stiffen up, a sign he probably had the disease. He was then given a painful series of shots. Sharon Arden came to visit him in the hospital. "I love you," she told him. "But you really are a crazy bastard."

Like Alice Cooper and the chicken, Osbourne's bat incident would live on in rock and roll infamy forever. Soon there were outrageous rumors that he tortured animals onstage. Kids would come up to Sarzo backstage and ask him, "Hey, man, is Ozzy really gonna blow up a goat onstage tonight?"

Most people who've been around Ozzy for even a brief period usually come away with a tale of madness. When asked to describe a crazy incident, the musicians who played with him over the years invariably reply, "Name a city." When the band was getting ready to play the Texas Jam, Sarzo was waiting in the airport for Ozzy and Sharon to arrive from England. Sarzo was having a drink in the lounge when he was paged to go to the phone. He was told Osbourne had just shaved his head completely bald, and he had to find a wig and cut it to look like the singer's hair. Sarzo had never cut a wig before and didn't know you had to wet it before you cut it. When Osbourne first put it on, it resembled a helmet. Arden cut it further until it looked like a spiky, punk rock haircut. She wrapped a bandanna around his forehead to hold the wig in place, and Osbourne stepped out on stage.

Right before the band went into its second song, "Crazy Train," Osbourne asked the audience, "You wanna see how fuckin' crazy I am?" He then tore the wig off his head and threw it into the audience. Everyone was in shock. Now in addition to being Osbourne's bassist, Sarzo was assigned to buy a new wig before every show. Osbourne loved fooling the audience and would even put fake blood on top of his head to make it look like he had torn his hair out of his scalp.

While on tour in Hamburg, Germany, the band visited a sex club with tables shaped like penises, and live sex shows. The next night, at a dinner with Sony executives, Osbourne climbed on top of the table, stripped naked, and re-enacted the sex show. He capped his performance by urinating in a carafe of wine. Several minutes later, a waiter entered, took the carafe into the next room, and served it to another table.

When the band toured Europe, they usually stayed in upper-crust hotels where the other guests left their shoes outside of their doors. Osbourne would often steal shoes, take a dump in them, then put them back. Backstage before one European gig, he had to pee and relieved himself out an open window, not realizing that several stories below, his fans were lined up and waiting to get into the show.

With all this craziness and two successful albums under his belt, Osbourne soon established a strong solo career; he became much bigger, and more notorious, than Black Sabbath. Randy Rhoads, though, didn't let his success go to his head. He always remained humble and down-to-earth. With his first royalty payments, Rhoads went out and bought an expensive classical guitar. He spent much of his time on the road taking lessons from teachers he found in the phone book. He was usually better than the teachers and ended up teaching them instead.

Rhoads also remained close to his mother. Where many parents discouraged their children from pursuing careers in music, Delores Rhoads supported her son's guitar playing from day one. Before the *Diary of a Madman* tour took off in December 1981, he took her on a vacation to Mazatlan. "Randy loved his mother more than anyone in the world," says Ace Steele, who was a friend of Rhoads. "She was the one person he knew he could trust."

Rhoads played a polka-dot Flying V, a guitar built for him by Karl Sandoval, who also did custom work for Eddie Van Halen, and a white Les Paul. But wanting a new custom-built guitar, Rhoads went to guitar builder Grover Jackson. Jackson Guitars became one of the most popular guitar companies in the '80s, but before the company was successful, its struggle to succeed mirrored the travails of the bands who played its instruments.

Grover Jackson let a number of promising young players who had no money (including Warren DeMartini of Ratt) go through the factory garbage bins and assemble their own guitars with reject bodies and necks, even though Jackson's family was living hand to mouth. There were weeks they were in danger of going hungry if he didn't sell an instrument out the back door for cash.

"Grover was always very good to the local guitar kids," says Poison guitarist C. C. DeVille. "What he would do was for one-tenth the money you'd buy a guitar for, he would give us parts without the names on them. He'd give us necks without the logo on them, a $150 neck for $40. That's why we all had [Jacksons] in those days! They became the racing-car guitar."

Randy Rhoads walked into Jackson's shop after he finished recording *Blizzard of Ozz,* and they hit it off right away. The two worked on a guitar design from noon to midnight. "We talked about music, we talked about guitars, we talked about everything in the world," recalls Jackson. "That guitar was literally designed that day."

Rhoads was strangely superstitious about guitar building; he didn't want to know too much about how a guitar was made because he liked the mystery of what made a guitar special. He refused to see his guitars until they were finished, and once a guitar was completed, he would take it out of the case every day and look at it, bonding with the instrument before he would play it. The Randy Rhoads Model was tremendously successful once it was available in music stores, and it launched Jackson Guitars.

Rhoads's career was just taking off, and the guitar magazines were showering him with accolades for his incredible playing, but he was growing weary of the music business and wanted to get back to playing classical music, his first love. Randy was planning on leaving the band soon. Rhoads wanted to go back to school and get a doctoral degree in music; his mother was looking at schools he could apply to.

On March 19, 1982, the band's tour bus stopped at a repair shop in Leesburg, right outside their next gig in Orlando, Florida. The band was scheduled to play with UFO and Foreigner the next day. The repair shop was in an airplane hangar adjacent to a landing strip. The bus driver, Andrew Aycock, wanted to remove several of the bunks from the bus to make the band's living accommodations a little more comfortable. Aycock was a pilot. There was an airplane at the compound, and he offered to take the band up in the air while the bus was being worked on. Unbeknownst to anyone in the band, Aycock's pilot's license had been revoked after he crashed a helicopter. A young boy aboard the helicopter had been killed.

Rhoads came onto the tour bus, trying to wake up Rudy Sarzo: "Hey, c'mon, c'mon, get up! Let's go on this plane ride." Sarzo told Rhoads he wanted to stay on the bus until they arrived at the gig. Minutes later, Sarzo was awakened when the private plane Aycock was flying clipped the roof of the bus. After a loud explosion, there was an eerie silence, soon broken by the voices of Osbourne's keyboard player Don Airey, and Jake Duncan, the band's tour manager.

Rudy jumped out of his bunk and opened the door to the front lounge. The seats and the floor were covered in broken glass. He looked through a broken window on his right and saw Duncan on his knees crying and tearing his hair out. "They're gone!" he screamed. "They're gone!" After the plane had clipped the bus, it had smashed through a tree and into a garage that had several cars parked inside. The plane had exploded on impact. All three aboard—Rhoads, Aycock, and Rachel Youngblood, the band's seamstress—were killed. Rhoads was twenty-five.

Rhoads's death altered the lives of everyone in the band. "I suppose when he died, part of me died with him," said Osbourne. "He was the first person that came into my life who gave me hope." As often happens in death, Osbourne felt a tremendous sense of survivor's guilt that haunted him for years. "I feel somewhat responsible, because if he hadn't been with me, he wouldn't have [died]," he said.

Grover Jackson had built two guitars for Rhoads and was working on a third at the time of his death. Uncompleted to this day, the guitar hangs on a wall in his home. "People ask me if I miss Randy as a guitar player," Jackson says. "I miss him as a man." Chet Thompson was a local guitarist who took lessons from Rhoads and later played in the band Hellion. After Rhoads's death, he didn't play guitar for six months. He couldn't bring himself to attend the funeral and still hasn't visited his grave. "I haven't really faced the fact that he died," he said. "I prefer to think he's still out there somewhere playing guitar."

Kevin DuBrow of Quiet Riot got a call at 10 in the morning, which woke him up. He couldn't believe that Rhoads had died and went back to sleep. Several minutes later, he bolted out of bed and turned on the radio. The stations he tuned to were playing Ozzy Osbourne songs. He realized they were playing the songs in Rhoads's memory. DuBrow later checked his watch, and it had stopped at the exact time Rhoads died.

Ten days after the accident, the tour continued. Guitarist Bernie Torme played the first shows but was soon replaced by Night Ranger guitarist Brad Gillis. Osbourne said that if it weren't for Sharon Arden forcing him to continue the tour, he never would have stepped on a stage again. Rhoads's dream had been to play Madison Square Garden. He was killed two weeks before the show.

"The saddest moment, among many, for me was doing Madison Square Garden," says Sarzo. "Randy was really looking forward to that show. By the time we got there, it was like a wake. Everybody in the audience had banners. Having to finish that tour was really tough. We were going to funerals and rehearsing and auditioning people at the same time. It got tougher and tougher to get on that stage." It was especially hard for Sarzo to hear Randy's riffs onstage, then turn around and not see him.

Before Rhoads died, the band was contracted to put out a double live album. Side one would be Osbourne's solo band material; side two would be Black Sabbath songs, which Rhoads hadn't been thrilled about doing. Osbourne had a live album in the can that had been recorded with Rhoads, and former Black Sabbath manager and Jet

Records owner Don Arden tried to force him to put out the album. Osbourne refused, infuriated by even having to consider releasing the album while the wounds of Rhoads's death were still open.

Osbourne owed the label $1.5 million, and Jet wouldn't let him out of his deal until he paid. He could have made a fortune releasing the last known recording of Rhoads right after his death, but he couldn't bear to do it. "The record company had me by the balls," he recalled. "[But] there was no way I was going to let the record company make a whore out of Randy." Osbourne would not release the album without Delores Rhoads's blessing. She granted it in 1987, and *Tribute* became a Top Ten hit.

To fulfill his contractual obligations and free himself from Arden, Osbourne played two nights at the Ritz, performing all Black Sabbath songs, which were recorded and released as the *Speak of the Devil* album. He hadn't sung many of the songs since the 1970s. On a chair illuminated by a desk lamp, Osbourne kept a notebook full of Black Sabbath lyrics that he'd leaf through when he got lost. After his contractual obligations with the label were fulfilled, Sharon—who married Ozzy on July 4, 1982—didn't speak to her father for many years (they recently reconciled).

Randy Rhoads could never truly be replaced, but Osbourne had several fine guitar players in his band after Randy's passing, including Jake E. Lee and Zakk Wylde, who joined the band in 1988. Wylde has played with Osbourne longer than any other guitarist in his solo career, and he also gave the singer a run for the money in the loony-behavior department. One time at a restaurant, Wylde went to the bathroom, rubbed a wine cork up and down the crease of his ass and brought it back to the table. He called the waiter over, told him, "I think there's something wrong with our wine," and asked him to smell the cork. The waiter sniffed it, horrified. "Very sorry! No charge for wine!"

Sharon Osbourne remains Osbourne's wife and one of the toughest and most feared managers in the business. The Osbourne marriage has often been volatile as well: As he put it, "We have full-blown fucking wars, with mortars and cannons going."

Osbourne announced in 1991 that he would retire after his *No More Tears* tour, but several years later he was back in action again. After releasing another solo album in 1995, *Ozzmosis,* he hit the road with his own successful multiband tour called Ozzfest, basically a metal Lolapalooza, that still tours the country every summer. Sharon was also able to reinvent her husband in a big way with the family's own virtual-reality show, *The Osbournes.* Currently the hottest show on television, it is also the highest-rated show in MTV's history. Since renewing their contract with MTV, the tabloids have been writing about Osbourne often, but it seems they are having a hard time finding enough new and interesting dirt on him, considering almost every embarrassing moment of his professional career has already been well-documented.

Osbourne has retained his status as an iconic figure in metal history. His solo career has remained fairly steady throughout the years, with no major drops in popularity. His audience has a wide variety of fans, and they now include people well into their forties who show up to the gigs in faded silk-screened "Ozzy for President" T-shirts. Osbourne now says he'll never retire, and he certainly won't spend all day at home if Sharon has any say about it. "The truth is that all I have is my voice," he said. "Without that, I can't live."

Along with Quiet Riot's *Metal Health,* **Def Leppard**'s *Pyromania* album played a big hand in metal's gaining mainstream acceptance. Pictured here is Def Leppard vocalist Joe Elliott, proudly representing the band's (and metal's) origins with his Union Jack shirt. (Neil Zlozower)

5

"GARY AND BILLY SAT IN THE GAZEBO, BLOWING THE SMOKE FROM THE
SHARED MARIJUANA CIGARETTE INTO THE NIGHT. SITTING IN THE DARK,
ONLY THE GLOW FROM THE TIP OF THE CIGARETTE GAVE THE TWO
TEENAGERS AWAY. THAT AND THE SCRAMBLED, SLAMMING, METAL
SOUNDS OF JUDAS PRIEST THAT FILLED THE GAZEBO LIKE SMOKE FROM
A DAMP BONFIRE. THEIR LYRICS WERE GREAT, MAN, GREAT TO LISTEN
TO WHEN A KID WAS HIGH. THEY TOLD A STORY, MAN. THEY TOLD A
TRUTH. A KID'S REALLY GOTTA LISTEN TO THE LYRICS, 'CAUSE A KID'S
REALLY GOTTA UNDERSTAND THE TRUTH, MAN. AND WHEN YOU'RE
SIXTEEN, THE TRUTH IS WHERE IT'S AT."

—From *Say You Love Satan* by David St. Clair

B Y 1979, THE DISCO CRAZE was wearing out its welcome. Radio
stations across the country started broadcasting "Bee Gees Free Weekends," and Chicago disk jockey Steve Dahl created the "Disco Sucks"
movement, which soon became a popular catchphrase. Dahl held a rally
at Comiskey Park at which thousands of disco records were rounded up,
loaded into a Dumpster, and blown to bits. Thousands of rock fans then
stormed the field, chanting the mantra of "Disco sucks," sending the
message loudly and clearly.

As the 1980s approached, many were waiting to see what the next
big thing would be. For a brief moment, it looked like it would be the
Knack, or so the hype had people believing. The Knack had built up a
strong rep as a live band in the L.A. clubs, and helped start the new-
wave fashion of wearing thin neckties. The band sparked a bidding
war from record companies in 1978, while many hard rock bands who
couldn't get record deals groused about the "skinny tie bands."

The Knack finally landed at Capitol, and their self-titled debut was a
sensation, breaking the record at the time for going gold in less than

two weeks and eventually selling two million copies. Their signature hit, "My Sharona," stayed at No. 1 on the charts for six weeks.

But with the oversaturation of "My Sharona," a backlash against the band quickly developed. "Knuke the Knack" T-shirts started popping up all over Los Angeles. It was clear that the Knack wasn't going to be the next Beatles, and the band burned out like a meteor shortly after headlining Carnegie Hall.

After the dust of disco and the Knack had cleared, it was obvious that the time was right for something new and different in rock and roll. But the heavy metal and hard rock bands of the '70s were now considered dinosaurs on the verge of extinction. With the insurgency of punk, heavy metal and hard rock needed to change if they were to survive into the next decade.

"Rock music was becoming a black hole," says Def Leppard vocalist Joe Elliott. "You'd go see Uriah Heep, you would be inundated with drum solos, bass solos, operatic vocal solos followed by guitar solos. What happened to 'Easy Livin'? Why does it have to be a sixteen-minute epic? Why? Because you can't write songs anymore."

By the early '80s, the British metal bands had to compete with punk to be heard, and for some, it gave their sound much more urgency and directness. "Def Leppard was actually a rock band that was not so much quietly, but rather loudly, embracing of the punk movement to a point," continues Elliott. "Not for what we were playing, but for what they [the punks] were trying to achieve. If you listen to our first album, songs like 'Wasted,' although it comes in a format that's much closer to heavy rock than punk, there's no secret behind the fact that it's a three-minute song with a twenty-second guitar solo."

Iron Maiden's first two albums also weren't far removed from punk, and the band would prove to be important in the development of what later became "speed metal" and "thrash metal." "You listen to those first two Iron Maiden albums, and they're right up there with anything on early Anthrax or Metallica," says Anthrax guitarist Scott Ian.

Like a number of metal bands to follow, Iron Maiden had a mascot.

Theirs was named Eddie, a giant, rotting ghoul with green skin that appeared on their album covers and T-shirts. With the popularity of punk in England, Eddie was originally drawn as a punk with red hair splayed in all directions like a Rorschach test. The creature was designed by an artist named Derek Riggs, who drew all the band's album covers and T-shirt designs. (He wasn't a big metal fan, though—in fact, in later years he would listen to the Spice Girls while drawing his ghastly creations.)

Eddie was the visual link between Iron Maiden albums. With hard rock getting little radio play, and MTV still not on the air, sometimes the only way a fan could discover a new band was finding an album with a cool cover. Finding an Iron Maiden album in a record store—a crusty ghoul with a knife in his hands, stalking the streets of a dreary old gaslit England on the cover—you knew the band didn't sound like the Captain and Tennille. "Sometimes you fell in love with the artwork, never mind the album, and you might buy it for that," says Bill Aucoin.

Even though Iron Maiden and Judas Priest were on major labels (Capitol and Columbia, respectively), their roads to success took many years to travel. Bands had to build their followings the old-fashioned way, by word of mouth and relentless touring. It would take some bands years to even come over to the States. The Scorpions, who hailed from Germany, released their first album, *Lonesome Crow,* in 1973, but didn't tour the United States until 1979. "The established bands [like Judas Priest and Iron Maiden] were just getting on major labels, and they couldn't come over every record," says veteran music journalist Jon Sutherland. "Priest would come to the States, and it took two or three records before they were established."

The underground was quickly becoming a worldwide network of fans spreading the gospel of their favorite bands by word of mouth, phone, and mail. Metalheads even started creating their own self-published magazines, or "fanzines." These were usually photocopied and sold either at gigs or through the mail. Legendary San Francisco underground DJ Ron Quintana and Brian Slagel, founder of Metal Blade

Records in Los Angeles, both started fanzines in July 1981. Quintana says he got the idea to start a fanzine from the punk scene. The metal underground also took the punk ethic of D.I.Y.—Do It Yourself—and applied it to everything: starting a band, doing a fanzine, doing whatever you could do to help. "The punk attitudes that sprung out in 1977 and '78 hit a lot of heavy metal," said Metallica's Lars Ulrich. "A lot of bands found they could do it themselves—record demo tapes, record small independent singles, and tour."

Tape trading was another important tool to promote and push the music further. Fans swapped and sold demos and live tapes of their favorite bands. For the die-hards who traded tapes heavily, "Every day was like Christmas when you'd get packages in the mail," remembers Quintana. " 'Where'd this one come from? Holland! All right! There's some metal bands over there!' " Many great bands never got past the demo stage and remain only in the memories of those who collected their tapes. With no commercial airplay, metal also became a big staple on college radio.

In many countries, buying bootleg albums through the underground, and making bootleg tapes of concerts, was the only way to get ahold of the music. As photographer Alex Solca recalls, the fans in his native Italy were so fanatical that when a metal band played there, you could guarantee it would show up on vinyl within days.

For many fans, metal was an addiction. Says Del James, who wrote about metal and hard rock bands for *RIP Magazine,* "You find out about a cool record, and you want another cool record. And it gets more obscure and more obscure until you're searching the import section for Loudness records, even though they're in Japanese, because it's heavy, and that's all that really mattered back then."

As these records filtered over to America, kids spent hours drawing their favorite heavy metal logos into their schoolbooks. The logos were usually complex and took a long time to draw correctly, but it seemed far more crucial to draw the logo of your favorite band than to learn algebra.

Instead of painting a basket of fruit or a vase full of flowers, Def Leppard lead singer Joe Elliott used to draw rock and roll posters in his high school art class. After drawing posters for Led Zeppelin, Thin Lizzy, David Bowie, and T. Rex, he started making up his own bands and drawing posters for them. One of the names he came up with was Deaf Leopard. In English class, Elliott wrote imaginary reviews of the band he hoped to one day form. He can't quite recall any of the reviews in detail, but, "I'm sure the reviews were fantastic and I was the best musician on the planet."

Elliott joined the band Atomic Mass shortly after it formed in 1977. Immediately, the band decided to change its name to the one Elliott had made up in art class. The band's first drummer, Tony Kenning, suggested making the spelling phonetic: Def Leppard. (Only later did they realize that the name resembled Led Zeppelin.)

The original members of Def Leppard were from Sheffield, England. Like Birmingham, Sheffield was an industrial town. Most of the factories made a range of steel products and cutlery. When world wars I and II hit, the factories switched over to bullets, bombs, and land mines. Growing up in Sheffield meant you were pretty much destined to work for the steel industry in one capacity or another. The members of Def Leppard had other ideas. "I would have taken soccer, bank robbery, anything other than a factory life," says Elliott. "Luckily, we all managed to get out of it before we reached the age of twenty."

Def Leppard played their first show in June 1978, at a local school. They made five pounds. Their second gig was in a grass field with no stage, and they were paid three pounds. When it got dark, several friends aimed their car headlights toward the band so they could be seen. Their third gig was at a bona fide club, the Lemon Club, opening for the Human League, which three years later would have a huge hit with "Don't You Want Me?" None of the bands were paid, but since the admission was free, close to four hundred people showed up.

Having gone from five pounds to three to nothing, Def Leppard realized they had to find another way to build their name. Joe then borrowed 150 pounds from his father to record a three-song EP. They printed picture sleeves, and Joe and his mother stayed up for three nights gluing them together. Def Leppard hoped that music magazines and radio stations would be more impressed with a vinyl release than a demo tape, and they were right.

The first Def Leppard EP came out in January 1979. It could only be ordered by mail, with the orders going through Elliott's parents' house. The EP received a lot of publicity. In *Sounds,* a major British music magazine, critic Geoff Barton announced the arrival of the "New Wave of British Heavy Metal," or NWOBHM, for short. Heavy metal was considered dead, but labels wanted to sign the band. The EP eventually landed on the desk of Cliff Burnstein, who was working A&R for Mercury Records, a division of PolyGram, at the time. Burnstein had signed Rush to the label in the '70s, and he told the British branch of the label to sign Def Leppard.

On August 4, 1979, the members of Def Leppard went to see Led Zeppelin perform the last show they would ever play in England, at Knebworth. As one era was ending for British hard rock bands, a new one was about to begin. The day after the Knebworth gig, the members of Def Leppard drove back to Sheffield and signed their deal with Poly-Gram at drummer Rick Allen's house. Allen's parents had to sign the contract for him because he was only fifteen years old.

Meanwhile, Peter Mensch, who was working for Leber-Krebs management and looking after their client AC/DC, hooked Def Leppard up as the opening act for AC/DC's *Highway to Hell* tour. Mensch would soon become Def Leppard's manager as well.

Def Leppard's first album, *On Through the Night,* was recorded in three weeks and was completed at the dawn of 1980. Tom Allom was the producer. "The first Def Leppard album was a joy," he recalls. "Those guys were so young, but they were all very accomplished as players; there were no passengers in that band at all."

The album was recorded at Ringo Starr's house, where a month later Judas Priest would record *British Steel.* Rick Allen had a lot of fun tearing up Ringo's lawn with his dirt bike. Everyone in Def Leppard still lived at home with his parents, and Allom was a father figure to the band, someone they could confide in. One day, Def Leppard guitarist Steve Clark came up to Allom, and told him nervously, "My girlfriend's coming down on the weekend, but I haven't got any rubbers. Can you help me?" Allom drove Clark to the drugstore and went in to buy condoms while Clark sat waiting in the car. Clark was grateful for Allom's help.

In 1981, Def Leppard recorded their follow-up, *High 'n' Dry.* For the album, the band shot a live concert video of three of the songs from the record: "Let It Go," the title cut, and "Bringin' On the Heartbreak." Sales for *High 'n' Dry* stalled at about 220,000 copies in the States—and then suddenly went gold. The band couldn't figure out why until a friend told them, "There's this new thing out called MTV. It's like a radio station you watch on the telly, and they're playing the video to death."

Music videos first gained popularity in England in the mid-1960s; they usually played on television shows like *Top of the Pops.* When a band couldn't make a live appearance, their record companies would send over a short film of the band that could be played instead. These films usually featured the bands playing live, although the Who, the Beatles, and the Rolling Stones did some of the first "concept videos," which set narratives to the music.

In 1975, director Bruce Gowers directed a video for Queen's "Bohemian Rhapsody." After it aired on the BBC, the song shot to No. 1 in the U.K. and stayed for nine weeks. Russell Mulcahy, who directed clips for Duran Duran and Billy Idol, and David Mallet, who worked with Def Leppard and Queen, both got their start on *Top of the Pops.*

Although music videos had been used for years for promotional purposes, the medium didn't realize its potential until the 1980s with the birth of MTV. (Michael Nesmith of the Monkees directed videos long before MTV and was one of the first to pitch the idea of an all-music network to cable companies.) In America during the 1970s, videos mostly aired on late-night television shows like *The Midnight Special* and *Don Kirshner's Rock Concert*. *Rock Concert* and *Special* both debuted in 1973 and continued until the early 1980s (*Rock Concert* was syndicated to a number of networks; *Special* aired on NBC).

Both *Rock Concert* and *The Midnight Special* differed from *American Bandstand* in that the bands performed live instead of lip-synching, and instead of featuring only popular acts with hits like *Bandstand*, *The Midnight Special* and *Rock Concert* featured a wide variety of artists. For many teenagers across America, watching both shows was a crucial rock and roll ritual every weekend, and it inspired many of them to start playing and form their own bands. "Don Kirshner's shows helped cement the foundation," said former Guns N' Roses guitarist Izzy Stradlin. Although these shows were popular, the market was limited. Both shows usually came on late at night; *The Midnight Special* usually aired after *The Tonight Show*. If a band made a video, they were lucky if it was shown more than once ever on either program.

By January 1981, Warner Communications and American Express approved the creation of an all-music channel, to be called MTV, short for "Music Television." Cable television was still in its infancy, and before MTV's debut, less than 25 percent of U.S. homes had cable. The first night MTV went on the air on August 1, 1981, it had only thirteen advertisers and was connected to only 800,000 homes. The major advertising agencies weren't ready to take a chance on MTV because it wasn't a proven medium, and at first the major labels resisted spending money to make videos—they weren't convinced the channel would last.

But it wasn't long before MTV was available everywhere in the States, and it was a mandatory teenage accessory. The channel that many predicted would collapse within several months soon changed the music business forever. Television and commercial directors were also paying attention, and immediately saw the creative possibilities of music video.

Marty Callner had directed local television in Ohio and Boston before going to work for HBO in 1975. He first saw the video for Kim Carnes's "Bette Davis Eyes," directed by Russell Mulcahy, on the Z Channel, one of the first cable movie networks. Watching the Carnes video, Callner saw experimental filmmaking techniques that weren't being done in any other medium, and it took the boredom out of television. "I knew that MTV was going to revolutionize the way people viewed things and I wanted to be there," he says.

The first video Callner ever made was Twisted Sister's "We're Not Gonna Take It," which immediately established him as a hot video director. He went on to make the videos for Aerosmith, Whitesnake, and Cher that dominated MTV throughout the '80s and early '90s. Callner hit it off with the metal and hard rock bands he would work with because his creative instincts were similar to theirs. He wasn't immediately familiar with the music but felt right at home working with it. "I was a rocker who didn't know he was a rocker," he says.

Comedy and steamy sex would be the cornerstones of Callner's videos. "Comedy's got to have some very basic rules," he says. "There's got to be a setup and a punch." In his 1991 video for Aerosmith's "Sweet Emotion," a young man dials a phone-sex line and fantasizes that he's talking to an incredible model; the punchline is that the woman on the other end of the line is overweight, middle-aged, and ironing clothes.

MTV would even change how music was written. Rickie Lee Jones said she loved MTV so much when it first appeared that she wrote songs and their videos at the same time. While writing Whitesnake's *Slip of the Tongue* album, singer David Coverdale said, "Because of the unbelievable promotional vehicle of MTV, I explored the lyrics maybe twice as much as I would have done before."

Soon everyone in the music business would look to MTV first. If the channel was behind a song first, radio picked it up immediately. Beau Hill discovered how powerful MTV was when he was managing Winger. "Once everyone knew that MTV was in our corner, everything else became so easy," he says. "The label gave us all the tour support we could want. The fact that I had a track record and some hits—it was really amazing how completely and utterly meaningless that was to anybody."

In the late '70s and early '80s, while numerous bands were trying to distance themselves from the term "heavy metal," Judas Priest was a band that would wear it like a badge of honor, even long after the music went out of favor. Ozzy Osbourne called Judas Priest "the last of the Mohicans."

The band took their name from a Bob Dylan song called "The Ballad of Frankie Lee and Judas Priest." Like Black Sabbath, Judas Priest's band members were natives of Birmingham, England. It seemed to be a natural place for heavy metal to grow and develop. "Where we lived, you could always hear the foundry," said guitarist Glenn Tipton. "The big steam hammers. Day after day, when that's pounding, you've got some sort of heavy metal rhythm in you from the word go." While much of the music from the metal bands of the '70s was slow and plodding, Judas Priest's music, with its accelerated pace, helped lay the groundwork for the speed-metal bands of the 1980s.

Judas Priest's early years, however, were a difficult struggle. While recording one of their first albums, the band slept in their van in London's Notting Hill, then a bad neighborhood. During one of Judas Priest's earliest tours of Europe, the band ran out of money and were stuck in the freezing cold of Germany and Holland during the winter, cleaning their teeth with snow.

Guitarist K. K. Downing had endured a troubled adolescence, and his parents refused to accept his dream of being a musician. "I suppose it was my drug in a way," he said. "I went through everything any young junkie goes through: getting kicked out of the house, not wanting to work, not having any money." Even years later, when the band had a platinum album, Downing's parents didn't approve of his career choice.

In 1973, Judas Priest's original singer, Alan Atkins, left the band, and

Rob Halford was hired to replace him. He would go on to be one of the best singers in the metal genre. Halford knew he was gay before he turned thirteen, and it was hard for him to come to terms with it. "I think I was angry at myself," he said. "I thought that I was sexually dysfunctional, that I didn't fit in because I was still the gay man in an exclusively straight rock world." When Judas Priest became successful and started touring regularly, Halford felt isolated while on the road. When everyone else went to strip clubs and were banging groupies, he'd usually go back to his room alone. The other members of Judas Priest knew their frontman was gay pretty much from the beginning. It was never a problem among them until the '90s, when Halford wanted to come out of the closet. The rest of the band protested, fearing it would hurt his image as a tough heavy metal singer. (Halford didn't officially come out until long after he had left the band and was pursuing a solo career.)

In 1978, Halford began shopping for leather and studs at gay and underground S&M stores. It was a perfect manifestation of the music Judas Priest was playing: tough, angry, aggressive, and extreme. Halford's look blatantly expressed his sexuality without him ever saying it. Eventually countless metal bands and fans adopted Halford's leather-and-studs look, though few realized that it had its roots in the gay community. "Rob was very instrumental in laying down laws and codes for what heavy metal bands should wear at that point in time," said Glenn Tipton. When Halford finally came out, no one was surprised. His homosexuality was one of the worst-kept secrets in heavy metal, and in hindsight it seemed obvious.

After a slow and difficult climb, Judas Priest's breakthrough in America would come with the *Hell Bent for Leather* album in 1979.* For their first appearance on *Top of the Pops,* Judas Priest performed "Take On the World." Donnie and Marie Osmond appeared on the same episode. The Osmonds were appalled by Halford lashing his whip onstage and said if he didn't put it away they weren't going to perform.

---

* In the U.K. the album was released in 1978 under the title *Killing Machine.*

It was during the *Hell Bent For Leather* tour that Halford began riding a motorcycle onstage. The band made an endorsement deal with Harley-Davidson when the company needed a boost, and Halford's deal for the Harley was sealed with a dollar. He loved his bike. "By definition, Harley-Davidsons work well within the big picture of rock and roll," he said. "They're loud, smelly, they piss people off."

Judas Priest finally broke through in the States with their 1980 *British Steel* album. The album cover featured the band's logo emblazoned on a razor blade; the title was a proud proclamation of metal's English origins. *British Steel* was produced by Tom Allom shortly after finishing Def Leppard's debut, *On Through the Night*. *British Steel* took twenty-eight days to record and, as with the first Leppard album, was recorded at Ringo Starr's home in England.

British Steel featured several Judas Priest classics, including "Breaking the Law" and "Living After Midnight." It was the band's first album to break the Top Forty in the States, and would eventually go platinum. Judas Priest would peak in 1982 with their *Screaming for Vengeance* album, which included the radio and MTV hit "You've Got Another Thing Comin'." Tom Allom continued to work with Judas Priest for over a decade and loved the band and what they stood for. "To me, heavy metal is about the unreal and the unobtainable," says Allom. "It became an aspiration to live up to the world of heavy metal, which nobody can do. It's always bigger than [life]; by definition, it's bigger than big. That's why you have to strive to make it sound impossibly large."

Where the British bands had finally found success in America, a number of metal bands based in the Los Angeles area were struggling to get noticed. According to journalist Jon Sutherland, it was Brian Slagel who came to the rescue. Slagel was just a kid, "a mama's boy" who still lived at home and was a die-hard metal fan. He worked at a store called Oz Records in Woodland Hills, California, in the San Fernando Valley in Los Angeles. The store is now a travel agency, but at the time it was a heavy metal mecca. It sold mostly obscure imports, especially from the New Wave of British Heavy Metal bands.

Slagel had always wanted to start his own record label, and he haunted the clubs around Los Angeles, looking for bands to sign. He told the musicians he met that if they gave him a demo he'd put it on a compilation album he was planning to call *Metal Massacre* and get into stores. Slagel didn't even have contracts for the album. Many of the bands he approached were thrilled just to have the opportunity to put their music on vinyl: "Oh wow! If we give you our demo, will you put it on there?" One of the musicians who convinced Slagel to save a spot on the album was a young drummer named Lars Ulrich.

Ulrich was born in Copenhagen, Denmark. His father, Torben Ulrich, was a professional tennis player and considered a rebel in the conservative world of tennis because he had long hippie hair and a Rasputin beard. "To this day, my dad has got longer hair than I do," said Ulrich. "He's got a longer beard than the guys in ZZ Top."

Because of his father's tennis career, Ulrich's family traveled often. He had already been around the world long before he toured as a rock star. Ulrich's parents used to host loud parties while he was growing up, "a bunch of people drinking and roaring," he recalled. "I always had to wake myself up in the morning and bike myself to school. I'd wake up at 7:30, go downstairs, and the front door would be open—six hundred beers in the kitchen and living room, and nobody in the house. So I'd close the doors, make breakfast, and go to school." Ulrich himself started drinking at an early age. "If you look like you have pubic hair [in Denmark], you can get away with drinking."

In August 1980, the Ulrich family moved to Newport Beach, California, just south of Los Angeles. Lars was always social and outgoing, and was convinced he was a star before he could play the drums. Brian Slagel met Ulrich through another local metal fan, John Kornarens. Kornarens had met Ulrich in the parking lot of the Country Club, a rock club in the San Fernando Valley, during a Michael Schenker show. He noticed that Ulrich had a Saxon tour shirt on, a NWOBHM band he didn't think anyone in Los Angeles knew about. Like many metal fans, the shirts they wore told them all they needed to know about each other, and they became friends. Kornarens, Slagel, and Ulrich became a metal troika who scoured stores like Moby Disc, Aarons, Poo Bahs, and Oz Records, all of which sold mainly metal records and imports. Like many metal fans, Ulrich was competitive as to who got the coolest new album in the underground first. He kept telling his friends he was going to put a band together, but few believed it would ever happen.

In 1981, Slagel started a fanzine that he named *The New Heavy Metal Revue,* and he and Kornarens soon started trolling the clubs looking for bands to be on their *Metal Massacre* compilation album. Ulrich caught wind of the project and, after talking with Slagel, landed a spot on the album. The only problem was that Ulrich didn't have a band together yet.

He had met guitarist and singer James Hetfield earlier through an ad in the *Recycler,* a local classified newspaper. The two seemed destined to meet. They were the only two musicians placing ads in the *Recycler* who wanted to start a metal band. Ulrich's audition was a disaster. He had a beat-up drum kit with one cymbal that kept falling over. Every time it crashed to the ground, Ulrich had to stop playing, run around the kit, and pick it up. Hetfield began looking elsewhere for a drummer.

But when the *Metal Massacre* opportunity arose, Ulrich called Hetfield again, and they quickly wrote the song "Hit the Lights" for the album. Since they didn't have a lead guitarist, they went to a guitarist named Lloyd Grant and hauled a four-track recorder into his living room. He laid down a mean solo—right before the album was due to be mixed at Bijou Studios in North Hollywood.

Ulrich was due at the studio at three o'clock. Slagel and Kornarens already had all the tapes from the other bands, including Ratt, Malice, and Steeler. Metallica's was the only one missing. Just then they saw Ulrich running up the street, out of breath. Slagel asked him, "Did you bring the fifty bucks?" Slagel needed $50 to transfer Metallica's cassette to a reel-to-reel tape. Every other band had turned in their song on reel-to-reel, except Metallica, who were on a tight budget.

"Noooo, I thought you were gonna pay for it," said Ulrich. He then turned to Kornarens. "You *gotta* have fifty bucks." Kornarens pulled out his wallet and had exactly $52. The song made it onto the album, and from then on he would be known as John "Fifty Bucks" Kornarens.

The *Metal Massacre* album was released on June 14, 1982. According to Kornarens, it cost $2,400, half of which he financed himself. The first pressing was supposed to be only 2,000 copies, but strong demand pushed it up to 4,500. Seven out of the ten bands on the *Metal Massacre* album would eventually be signed to major and independent labels, but the standout track was Metallica's "Hit the Lights."

Ulrich's friend Ron Quintana, the underground DJ and tape trader from San Francisco, came up with the band's name. When Quintana was starting his fanzine, he asked Lars which name would be cooler, Metallica or Metal Mania. Ulrich told him Metal Mania was definitely the cooler name—he wanted Metallica for himself.

Some believe that if Ulrich hadn't been given the chance to get on *Metal Massacre*, Metallica might never have formed. "I think the idea to form a band was already in Lars's head," says Kornarens. "But I think when *Metal Massacre* came up, Lars saw it as an opportunity to get something out. In my mind, it was the catalyst that got things going quickly." It also brought Ulrich and Hetfield together.

The two musicians couldn't have had more different upbringings. Like many band partnerships, they were polar opposites as people. While Ulrich grew up in an affluent family who gave him almost unlimited freedom, Hetfield's family was restrictive and working-class (his father owned a trucking company). But metal was their bond, and it would hold them together for the next twenty years.

Hetfield grew up in a strict Christian Science home in Downey, California. He wasn't allowed to go to doctors, and was excused from health class in school. Hetfield's father left the family when he was beginning junior high school. "My mom needed to be home, or I'd have killed my sister," he said. "We beat the living hell out of each other." Raising a family by herself, "my mom worried a lot," he continues. "And that made her sick. She hid it from us. All of a sudden, she's in the hospital, then all of a sudden, she's gone." After his mother died, Hetfield went to live with his stepbrother. Growing up, he was guarded and usually kept to himself.

Metallica was heavily influenced by the NWOBHM bands. They didn't copy other bands' riffs verbatim but would often figure out how a song was structured then arrange their own songs accordingly. "Seek and Destroy" was built on a song by the band Diamond Head called "Dead Reckoning," and "One" borrowed the feel of Venom's dirgy "Buried Alive." John Kornarens always thought Metallica sounded like a cross between Motörhead and Diamond Head, and as Hetfield once said, "We just put the two heads together." When Metallica were playing their first club shows, they did covers of their favorite bands, mixed with originals, and since crowds in L.A. still weren't familiar with bands like Diamond Head, no one was the wiser.

Metallica's lineup solidified when Dave Mustaine joined as lead guitarist and Ron McGovney came in on bass. Hetfield was a tight rhythm player, and like his hero, Tony Iommi, he was an endless fountain of heavy riffs. He once said he didn't like to play lead guitar because "it interferes with my drinking."

In the summer of 1982, Metallica recorded a demo entitled *No Life Till Leather.* Copies of it eventually circulated around the world; it was one of the demos that helped launch the underground tape-trading craze. K. J. Doughton, then living in Oregon, got a copy of the demo and flipped. He and Ulrich became friends, and Doughton later started the band's fan club, dubbings hundreds of copies of the *Leather* demo for the band. Ron Quintana also traded and sold copies of the *Leather* demo as well as Metallica live tapes.

At first, Metallica wasn't happy about Quintana selling their tapes, but they eventually relaxed about it. "Mild bootlegging does not detract from a band's revenues," said Quintana. "In fact, if anything, it enhances it by helping the band's popularity snowball faster than if there is not enough merchandise available." Through tape trading, Metallica built a strong underground following before they ever released an album.

Back in Los Angeles, however, Metallica were still persona non grata. The rock clubs there wouldn't book them because they thought they were a punk band, and the punk clubs wouldn't book them because they had long hair. Over and over, all Metallica would hear was they played too fast, they played too loud—even that they were too heavy, if such a thing was possible. The hair bands that ruled the clubs at the time thought Metallica were a joke (Metallica's feelings toward them were mutual) and condescended to them. As the L.A. music scene was entering an age of Aqua Net and mascara, Metallica just didn't fit in.

At the urging of Quintana, Metallica drove to San Francisco to play a show in September 1982 with a Van Halen clone band from L.A. called Hans Naughty. Metallica, who had been met with absolute indifference by Los Angeles audiences, was welcomed with open arms by the Bay Area crowd, who already knew the band through tape trading. When Hans Naughty came onstage after Metallica, the audience turned their backs for the duration of their set. Eventually, fans started sewing Metallica patches onto the backs of their Levi's jackets, which acts deemed unworthy were forced to look at while they played.

At the end of 1982, the band replaced bassist Ron McGovney with Cliff Burton. Lars and James had seen Burton performing one night in a band called Trauma and were so blown away that they practically begged Burton to join Metallica. He agreed, on the condition that the band relocate to San Francisco. With little going for them in Los Angeles, Ulrich and Hetfield gladly left. Burton may have resembled a hippie with his huge bell-bottoms and long, red hair parted down the middle, but he had the attitude of a punk. Burton also had a gigantic middle finger, and when he flipped off a photographer, it took up practically half the picture. He played bass through a wah-wah pedal, and it sounded so distorted and wild that audience members would often mistake him for a guitar player. Yet Burton was a schooled musician. As frantic as his playing was, it was also incredibly melodic.

About the same time that Brian Slagel was working at Oz Records in Los Angeles, Jon Zazula was released from a halfway house in New Jersey on a charge of conspiracy to commit wire fraud. With his last $180, he started a record store called Metal Heaven, setting up shop in a South New Jersey flea market.

Anthrax guitarist Scott Ian was a frequent visitor to Metal Heaven. "We would make our pilgrimages there on the weekends to check out all the new stuff that Jonny Z would get from England," he says. "He was the only one really getting that stuff, so he was really on the edge of it. If anything, he was *ahead* of it, because he would get stuff we'd never even heard of. We couldn't believe it—every week we could go down there and get [an album] that was better than the record we got last week."

One day, Ian came into the store, and Jonny Z told him, "I've got this band from San Francisco I want you to hear. They're called Metallica." Zazula had been playing the tape religiously for three days. Within seconds the music was flooding the store. Ian thought, "Wow, this is insane." It was the fastest music Ian had heard outside of hardcore punk.

"It was totally cool hearing that there was this band out in San Francisco that was kind of on the same wavelength of what we were doing," says Ian. "Anthrax were doing our own thing, but it just never seemed like it was gonna work, because we didn't sound like any other band or anything that was around in New York. And then all of a sudden, there's a band out of San Francisco that had their own thing too. It made me feel like maybe there's something going on here."

Jonny Z and his wife Marsha shopped Metallica's demo around to record labels in New York. No one was interested in signing them, so the Zazulas decided to start their own label, which they called Megaforce. Metallica headed for New Jersey in April 1983 to rehearse and record their debut album. At first, the band members lived at the Zazulas' house, which would later become a flophouse for countless bands and musicians. Sometimes the Zazulas would find musicians sleeping in their beds, reeking from lack of bathing. "That's why my kids are six years apart," said Marsha. "They were raised between Metallica and Anthrax."

Eventually the Zazulas kicked Metallica out for raiding the family liquor cabinet and drinking their wedding champagne. The band moved into the building where they rehearsed, located in a rundown section of Queens, New York. There was no hot water, and the band members didn't shower more than once a week. They could barely afford food and sometimes ate raw hot dogs.

It soon became clear to the rest of Metallica that Dave Mustaine would have to be let go. His drinking was out of control, and considering how much the rest of the band drank, that was really saying something. Bad blood had also been brewing between Mustaine and Hetfield for some time, before they even moved out to the East Coast. They once got into a fistfight, which Mustaine believed eventually hastened his exit from the band. According to his version of the fight, Hetfield kicked Mustaine's dog, and he retaliated by punching Hetfield in the mouth. According to bassist Ron McGovney, the fight didn't end there. McGovney was getting out of the shower when he saw Mustaine clock Hetfield in the mouth. McGovney jumped on Mustaine's back, trying to break up the fight, and Mustaine flipped him onto a coffee table. Hetfield screamed, "You're out of the fucking band! Get the fuck out of here!" and Mustaine took off in a huff. The next day, he returned in tears, pleading not to be fired.

Right before they went into the studio to record their first album, Metallica asked Kirk Hammett to fly out to New Jersey to audition for the band. Hammett was from San Francisco, where he had formed the band Exodus and become friendly with the members of Metallica. Hammett's bandmates were not happy to hear he was auditioning for another band and told him that they wouldn't take him back.

As Hammett was flying in, the band still hadn't told Mustaine he was out, and they had to do it fast, so they woke him up one morning and told him he was fired. Anthrax was rehearsing in the same building that day. Recalls Greg D'Angelo, who was playing drums in Anthrax at the time, "We were there rehearsing. They came down, hung out in our room for a couple of minutes, went upstairs, kicked Dave out, then came right back down." Mustaine asked what time his plane was leaving, and they handed him a Greyhound bus ticket. It took him three days to get back to Los Angeles. Mustaine remained bitter for many years. He vowed to form a new band that would "kick Metallica's ass" and started forming Megadeth.

If Hammett didn't work out, Metallica had no money to send him home. Once he plugged in and ripped into a lead, the band was relieved: He would work out just fine. Hammett and Hetfield bonded because they both came from dysfunctional families. Hammett's father had a drinking problem and physically abused him and his mother. While living at their rehearsal space, Metallica had nothing to do except play all day and make their music tighter and stronger. "None of us were tied down by other obligations, like work or school or marriage," said Hammett. "So what else were we going to do but this?"

Metallica called their first album *Kill 'Em All,* and it was released in 1983. *Kill 'Em All* is what they wanted to do to the record distributors who said no to their original title, *Metal Up Your Ass. Easter's Cancelled: The Body's Been Found* was another title they considered.

Kill 'Em All remains the rawest album of Metallica's career; it's a tough and abrasive affair. Metallica has been dogged by accusations of selling out throughout their career, and surprisingly, those taunts started with *Kill 'Em All,* the band's most uncommercial effort. "At first, a lot of people [in the scene] didn't like the album," says Harold Oimen, one of the band's first photographers. "They thought it was too polished, believe it or not, compared to the demo. Now, thinking that *Kill 'Em All* is too polished is just hilarious."

Metallica embarked on a tour with the band Raven to promote the album. They also played in Europe, opening for Venom. Both Raven and Venom were heavily influential New Wave of British Heavy Metal bands (and both bands were from Newcastle, England). The pioneers of a musical genre often don't get their due, and it was ironic that Metallica, an American band heavily influenced by the British New Wave, would go on to great heights while Raven and Venom foundered.

When the *Kill 'Em All* tour returned to New York in 1984, Michael Alago made sure he was there. Alago had been hired as an A&R executive at Elektra Records the year before. He loved *Kill 'Em All* and was determined to sign the band to Elektra. The band played the Roseland Ballroom with Raven and Anthrax, and Alago brought along Elektra chairman Bob Krasnow and Mike Bone, head of radio for the label.

Krasnow always hated heavy metal, but that night it was obvious the audience loved the band. Bone was impressed by the fact that Metallica T-shirts sold out at the merchandise booth. Alago told the band after the show to come to his office the next day so they could talk about signing a deal. "Is there gonna be lots of beer there?" asked Cliff. (On the *Kill 'Em All* tour, Metallica had a typewritten rider that demanded forty-eight beers backstage after each show, a dozen per member, "preferably Heineken or Carlsberg.")

Even if an A&R executive wasn't a fan of heavy metal, if the crowd went nuts for a band it wasn't difficult to figure out they could potentially sell records. To help the press understand Metallica, their publicists used to bring journalists to their gigs. With the whole floor turning into one giant mosh pit, and the heat from the pit soaking the walls with sweat, writers immediately understood what the band was all about.

Metallica would indeed sign with Elektra, and they would leave behind Jonny Z and sign with new management as well. Q-Prime was formed by Cliff Burnstein and Peter Mensch, who became friends in 1974. At the time, Burnstein was working promotion at Mercury and signed Rush to the label that year. Mensch was working at Leber-Krebs, who managed Aerosmith. Their paths crossed again in 1979, when Mensch started managing AC/DC under the Leber-Krebs umbrella.

Later that year, Mensch moved to London, where he was managing Def Leppard. In 1980, Burnstein left Mercury to work at Leber-Krebs alongside Mensch. AC/DC fired Mensch in 1981, and soon both he and Burnstein left Leber-Krebs over monies AC/DC owed them on commissions (they took Leber-Krebs to court and won the commission money they were owed). The only band that stayed loyal to Burnstein and Mensch was Def Leppard. In 1982, the pair decided to join forces and form their own management company, which became Q-Prime.

Burstein and Mensch were looking to sign an indie metal band and went out and bought copies of twenty albums from new bands. The only one they liked was Metallica. When they heard the as-yet-unreleased *Ride the Lightning* album, they were floored. They realized the band had made a huge leap since *Kill 'Em All,* and with *Ride the Lightning,* it was as if they could do anything within the metal genre.

Taking another nod from the punk scene, Metallica's lyrics became more politically aware. Once Hetfield and Ulrich could afford a TV set, they watched the news religiously; later they called the years they wrote these songs "the CNN years." The song "Ride the Lightning" was about capital punishment and someone innocent being executed by mistake. "For Whom the Bell Tolls" was about the atrocities of war; the massive, chiming bell at the beginning of the song is reputed to be a doorbell.

Hetfield wrote "Fade to Black," a song about suicide, when his favorite Marshall amp was stolen on their first tour (it may not seem like anything worth killing yourself over, but Hetfield said, "It was my favorite amp, man!"). When the song became popular, it was attacked by anti-metal zealots who thought it was pro-suicide. Meanwhile, the band got countless letters from fans telling them the song had saved their lives.

"Fade to Black" was a ballad, which at first alienated a lot of Metallica's die-hard fans, but the band was sure of itself and wasn't afraid to take risks. Metallica had an unusual degree of control over their music, and the label didn't interfere. "It was having absolute blind faith in their vision," says Michael Alago. "And knowing that if we left them to their own devices, it was just gonna come out correct, because they were that smart and that clear about what they wanted to do."

"Metallica knew where they wanted to go," says publicist Byron Hontas, who worked on the *Ride the Lightning* and *Master of Puppets* albums when he was at Elektra. "They had their own direction musically. They didn't want to do makeup; black was their thing. Their music was extremely aggressive, and people didn't know how to take it. In the first publicity photo we had of them, Cliff wore a FUCK YOU T-shirt. The people at Elektra didn't know how to deal with that."

The fans felt a close bond with Metallica and were possessive of them. They weren't larger-than-life icons whom you needed ten backstage passes to get close to. The fans looked onstage and saw themselves. Metallica wore basic T-shirts and jeans on stage, and had no "image" to speak of. They made their music the No. 1 focus instead of doing their hair and getting laid. In an attempt to be taken seriously, many of the image-conscious hair bands that came later in the 1980s, like Poison, would eventually follow Metallica's example and dress down considerably.

When Hontas worked for Metallica, they always stayed late after the gigs to meet their fans, and held "meet and greets" after every show. "Metallica takes care of their fans better than any band," he says. "That's all a fan wants, to feel like they're part of it and close to a band." Metallica knew the easiest way to lose their fans was to blow them off. Hetfield remembered how it felt when he'd wait outside a concert for hours, and instead of signing autographs, the rock star he wanted to meet would get in his limo and leave everyone in the dust.

At first Metallica was uncomfortable with the trappings of success. While on tour for the *Master of Puppets* album in 1986, they resented having to go to a record signing in a limo, and considered having it stop a block away from the store so it would look as if they had walked there.

"In the beginning, they didn't want the limos," says Hontas. "They didn't want to look pretentious. Even after *Master of Puppets* came out, if you told them after the next record they'd be performing on the Grammies, they would have said 'Fuuccckkk you!' " At the peak of the band's success, Lars Ulrich said, "If you had told me ten years ago when we put out *Kill 'Em All* that in 1992 we'd have a record that sold almost nine million copies worldwide, I'd ask what kind of drugs you were on and if you could share with me."

Over the next few years, as metal and hard rock would become clogged with hairspray and makeup, Metallica would be one band the kids could always believe in and return to. Their fans had faith that Metallica would always stick to their guns. Manager Cliff Burnstein once proclaimed to *Spin,* "If one of them gets a haircut, I'll kill myself."

Def Leppard entered the studio in March 1982 to record their third album, *Pyromania.* They wouldn't finish until Christmas week, nine months later. Mutt Lange, who produced the previous album, *High 'n' Dry,* was behind the boards again. Mutt was a strong driving force in the direction Def Leppard went with on *Pyromania,* and making the record proved to be a learning experience for everyone involved. "We wanted it to be a commercial-sounding album," says Joe Elliott. "We were up for the challenge in trying to make a crossover record."

There was a lot of pressure on the band while they recorded *Pyromania.* By the time the album was finished, the band had spent so much time in the studio that they were close to a million dollars in debt. Guitarist Pete Willis had been fired for excessive drinking and replaced by Phil Collen. During the recording of the album, the band handled the pressure well, barring a few exceptions. Elliott recalled a "ten-minute drumstick throwing session" and a twenty-minute period where he was slumped on the ground crying after doing a few too many takes. "We were just too interested in getting the record done," says Elliott. "Of course, when it was finished, we all thought it was the best thing ever made. Obnoxiously, as youthful exuberance goes, we thought, if people don't buy this, they must be dumb. Or, if any rock fan hears this, it's gonna blow their heads off. You have to believe in things like that."

The label figured that by the third album, the band would hit its stride. Of course, no one had any idea *Pyromania* would be as big as it was, "other than Cliff Burnstein and Mutt Lange," says Jim Lewis, vice president of marketing at PolyGram at the time. " 'Photograph' was the first single. It was one of the first big videos [on MTV], and it just exploded." According to Lewis, the album went double platinum on the success of "Photograph" alone.

Def Leppard started the *Pyromania* tour in March 1983, a year after they had entered the studio. They opened for Billy Squier, who had a big album in 1981 with *Don't Say No,* in Atlanta, but "Photograph" was already a hit on the radio, and they outsold Squier on T-shirts eight to one. By June, they sold out two nights at Cobo Hall in Detroit, and every show they did from June to September was sold out. The band finished at Jack Murphy Stadium in San Diego that September, headlining over Mötley Crüe, Uriah Heep, and Eddie Money.

Pyromania was one of the most successful albums of the '80s, selling nine million copies in the United States. It was the No. 2 album of the year in 1983. "It was only Michael Jackson keeping it off the No. 1 spot," says Joe Elliott, "and that was a hell of an *only!*"

Pyromania also turned out to be an influential album for many '80s bands, with its dense production, multiple-overdubs, and vocal harmonies inspired by Queen. It was also a crucial album for breaking the heavy metal/hard rock market open to the mainstream. "Because of Quiet Riot, L.A. exploded," says former Dokken bassist Jeff Pilson, "but because of Def Leppard, the world was exploding."

When the *Metal Health* album hit the top of the charts in 1983, it opened the floodgates for countless metal and hard rock bands from Los Angeles. The members of **Quiet Riot,** clockwise from top left: Rudy Sarzo, Frankie Banalli, Kevin DuBrow, and Carlos Cavazo. (Neil Zlozower)

6

"I HAD NEVER HEARD ANYBODY CALLED 'DUDE' BEFORE I MET TOMMY AND VINCE."

—Nikki Sixx

THE STARWOOD FINALLY CLOSED its doors in 1982. Its owner, Eddie Nash, also owned thirty liquor licenses around town, which made him a multimillionaire. But in 1982 he was dogged with financial problems, a crushing cocaine freebasing habit that kept him a virtual recluse in his mansion, and an impending murder investigation. Nash was a porn groupie and close friend of legendary porn star John Holmes, who also had a major freebasing habit.

On June 29, 1981, several of Holmes's friends who lived in Laurel Canyon robbed Nash's mansion in order to make off with a large quantity of cash and drugs. On July 1, the four robbers were found bludgeoned to death in their Laurel Canyon home. The crime was so grisly that it was compared to the Manson slayings. Nash was the prime suspect in the murders, though he was never convicted and the crime remains unsolved.

As Nash's fortunes plummeted, so did the Starwood's. When the club came to an end, so did an era for many people who frequented it. "I'm really glad that I got to go there and experience it," says Steve Mercer, a Starwood regular. "I kind of feel sorry for the kids who will never know what the Starwood was like. You were away from the rest of the world; you'd walk into Fantasyland, and there's a great band going." "It was good to be part of the family there," says John Arnold, who worked the soundboard at the Starwood in the 1970s. "I knew it was significant at the time even though I had relatively no reference of where we were in time."

Mötley Crüe was one of the last bands to play the Starwood before it closed. Drummer Tommy Lee had made a name for himself in a band

One of the most notorious bands to come out of Los Angeles in the 1980s, **Mötley Crüe**, the brainchild of bassist/chief songwriter Nikki Sixx, were living examples of the decadent rock and roll life, which they took to dangerous extremes. Left to right: Mick Mars, Sixx, Vince Neil, and Tommy Lee. (Neil Zlozower)

called Suite 19, which along with Quiet Riot were the biggest draws at the Starwood in the late '70s. Suite 19 drew so many fans that the band played almost every night of the week and were able to make a decent living just playing gigs.

Lee's mother was a former beauty queen from Greece. His father proposed to her the first time they met, and they were married within five days (perhaps trying to beat that record, Lee would outdo his father by marrying Pamela Anderson in four days). Lee's father supported his son's music and went to every one of his local shows. He built a soundproofed rehearsal room for Tommy in the family garage. When Lee was in Suite 19, the band would practice there up to nine hours a day.

After Suite 19 broke up, their guitarist, Greg Leon, helped introduce Lee to bassist Nikki Sixx, and they immediately hit it off. "Nikki had auditioned for Suite 19 twice, but we didn't hire him," says Leon. "He had the greatest image, was the nicest guy, but I was looking for more of a musician at the time. I think we can laugh about it now, but I remember in one audition I had to tune his bass for him."

Sixx was born Frank Ferrano, in San Jose, California. Both his parents were musicians, but his father ran out on the family when Frank was three. At the age of sixteen, Frank tried to reconnect with his father. He located him through directory assistance and called him one night. "I don't have a son," he told Frank. "Go fuck yourself!" he screamed back. His father said, "Don't ever call me again," before hanging up. It was the last time they ever spoke. Saddened and bitter that his father had abandoned him, he changed his name to Nikki Sixx, and moved down to Los Angeles in 1975.

Sixx was the architect of Mötley Crüe and had a shrewd business mind. In 1979 he had formed the band London and was on the verge of signing a major deal a year later when lead singer Nigel Benjamin quit the band. Sixx was furious. According to one source who knew him at the time, the bassist vowed for his next band, "I'm gonna get three slugs that are young and stupid or old and burned-out, and they'll do whatever I tell them."

Through a classified ad in *The Recycler,* he found guitarist Mick Mars (real name: Bob Deal), who had attended the same Indiana high school as eventual vice president Dan Quayle. Mars had been playing in bands for years, going nowhere. This would finally be his big break.

Lee, Sixx, and Mars went to the Starwood one night to have a drink and saw Vince Neil performing in a club band called Rock Candy. Mick told Nikki, "I don't care if he can sing—he looks really good. He'll make it. He'll make all four of us right."

Neil's main priorities were getting paid and getting laid. "All Vince cares about is pussy," said the Dust Brothers, who produced his 1995 solo album. "Making records for him was just a vehicle for getting pussy and getting money to buy pussy." Neil wanted to be like Los Angeles Lakers owner Jerry Buss or Hugh Hefner when he got old: living in a big mansion with plenty of money and young chicks around. Despite the band's claims that they were the best of friends, neither Lee nor Sixx got along with Neil. Lee beat Neil up on a number of occasions and once even broke his nose in a fight.

With the exception of Tommy Lee, none of the members of Mötley Crüe were great musicians. But the point of the band was to be a strong unit rather than a gang of virtuoso players. And Sixx was smart enough to realize that the song was king. He wanted heavy music with melodies and hooks. "I didn't want to go completely over-the-top heavy metal and have garbage songs. I wanted to have really catchy tunes, because that's what I'd always liked when I was listening to bands like Sweet and Slade."

Sweet was a wildly popular British band from the glitter/glam period of the '70s. They combined great melodies with heavy guitars—exactly the kind of metallic pop music Sixx liked to write. When Sweet headlined the Santa Monica Civic Auditorium in 1975, most of the audience was fourteen-year-old girls, chaperoned by their mothers. During the drum solo, two giant movie screens dropped down, showing XXX-rated porno films. An exodus of mothers dragged their teenage daughters into the lobby with their hands over their eyes. Just as some of the mothers felt safe enough to bring their daughters back into the show, they were horrified again when a giant papier-mâché penis came down from the ceiling, shooting confetti all over the audience.

Mötley Crüe officially became a band on January 17, 1981, and played their first gig in a Pasadena deli called Pookie's. The dressing room was a broom closet. Four people showed up, along with eight members of the band's family, who got in for free. The band would have made 100 percent on the $12 door but ran up a $30 bar tab.

Except for Neil, who dyed his hair stark white, the other band members wore their hair jet-black and sprayed thick and spiky with the strongest hair-spray they could get their hands on. When Sixx was preparing to go out on the town, he'd bend over and let his hair fall to the floor. He'd then spray it with Aqua Net so when he stood up straight, so did his hair. Whitesnake vocalist David Coverdale once explained that the reason why so many '80s bands had huge hair was so that fans in the nosebleed seats could still see something. Whitesnake had a three-tiered follicular system: There were "arena" and "stadium" levels for live shows, and the hair would come down to "lobby" for personal appearances.

Mötley Crüe first started developing their look when playing in small clubs. For little to no money, they were able to put on wild and extreme stage shows. Sixx used to pour rubbing alcohol on his leather pants and light himself on fire; he quit the stunt when he singed off all his leg hair. The band constructed their stage costumes out of primer cord, duct tape, and parachute nylon. By 1985, they were spending $20,000 on their costumes alone, and what they first learned about putting on a good show in the clubs translated perfectly into the big arenas.

The members of Mötley Crüe lived in an apartment on Clark Street, right off Sunset Boulevard behind the Whisky, in Hollywood. When the band played at the Whisky, they'd invite everyone in the audience to party at their place afterward, and usually hundreds of people followed them around the corner. David Lee Roth and the Scorpions were regulars at their apartment, which Tommy dubbed "the Crib." Drugs were usually easy to score because almost everyone who lived in their building was a dealer.

In the early 1980s, the punk scene was going full force in L.A., and surprisingly, "Some of the [punks] liked Mötley Crüe because they were a new band and a new sound," says Cletus Nelson, a fan and observer from the period. "Their hair was so high, the punks could relate to them. They looked like no band before them."

With the Starwood gone and the Whisky closing for several years in the '80s due to the violence of the punk scene, the metal bands had to find a new place to play. Doug Weston, owner of the Troubadour, once one of the premier clubs in Los Angeles, the place where Elton John made his L.A. debut, was facing financial ruin and had to take on a partner named Ed Karayan. Karayan started booking heavy metal bands, and soon the Troubadour became an L.A. metal haven.

At the time, punk and metal were still natural enemies in many corners. On Santa Monica Boulevard in Hollywood, not far from the Troubadour, was a famous wiener stand called Oki Dog, where punks would congregate. One night, one of the Oki Dog regulars was overheard calling Mötley Crüe a bunch of women. Word soon got back to the band. Sixx and Lee, drunk, with their hair stacked up to the sky, roared up in their car and jumped out to confront the offender. "We heard you called us a bunch of women." With the pair towering over him, he quickly backed down and apologized, explaining that he was drunk when he said it.

Mötley Crüe's first album, *Too Fast for Love,* was initially released on their own label, Leathur Records, in 1981. The band signed a management deal with Allan Coffman. Coffman was involved in real estate, developing tract homes and Mötley Crüe eventually had a bitter falling-out with him. It was clear to many close to the band that Coffman had never managed a band before, and some felt the band wouldn't be taken seriously and be able to go to the next level with him handling their affairs.

Despite the fact that new wave was all the rage at the time, a number of people saw Mötley Crüe's potential. Photographer Barry Levine was an early supporter of the band and tried to help them in numerous ways: shooting their photos, designing and building their stage set, even helping with their choreography. He also set up two showcase gigs for them at the Santa Monica Civic for potential managers to check out the band.

Hernando Courtright tried to get the band signed at A&M Records. But A&M, which boasted new wave heavyweights the Police and Joe Jackson, felt that signing a metal band was beneath them and passed. Courtright knew Mötley Crüe weren't great musicians—but that the band was going to be big. "They were like fast food," says Courtright. "I was a big Kiss fan, and this was my kind of music. It was obvious they were going to put it together, and it was going to happen." Clearly, the only problem that stood in their way was the booze and the drugs. "They had a vision of what they wanted—there was no doubt about that—but it was very hazy."

Courtright was friendly with Doug Thaler, a booking agent who was working for David Krebs at Leber-Krebs management. Thaler was forming an association with Doc McGhee (who went on to manage Bon Jovi and the Scorpions), and they began managing bands together. When Thaler visited Courtright in his office, there were stacks of Mötley Crüe's self-released first album on the floor. "You should check this out," he told Thaler. "This is really gonna do something. It's happening in L.A. right now." Thaler and McGhee both went to see Mötley Crüe, and soon they were managing the band as well.

Courtright's wife Doreen tried to get Mötley Crüe signed to Epic Records, where she worked in the publicity department. She knew producer Tom Werman, who was now working with obscure pop bands like the Producers. Doreen felt that Werman should stay true to what he really loved, which was rock and roll, and knew that Mötley Crüe was right up his alley.

She convinced Werman to see the band perform. He called her the next day and said, "You have got to be out of your mind. They were terrible—they couldn't play." Doreen reminded Werman she never said they could play, only that he'd sell a ton of records with them. "I didn't realize what they could be," Werman now admits.

Werman soon left his job as an A&R executive at Elektra to return to producing. Before he left, his assistant Tom Zutaut (who would later sign Guns N' Roses to Geffen) succeeded in signing Mötley Crüe to Elektra. Zutaut wanted to sign the band after he saw their fans go nuts for them at the Whisky. "You don't need ears to be a talent scout," he said. "You need eyes."

In May 1983, Werman, Zutaut, and Bruce Lundvall, then second-in-command at Elektra Records, were having lunch with Bob Krasnow in Beverly Hills. Krasnow said, "The first thing I want to do is drop Mötley Crüe. They're an embarrassment. I don't want that kind of music on this label."

"But Bob, who's going to pay the bills?" Werman asked. He then suggested to Krasnow, as diplomatically as possible, that he should take care of the music he liked and let the rock and roll guys take care of the meat and potatoes. At the time, the label was having financial difficulties. Elektra had a lot of vintage acts like the Doors and Judy Collins, but they clearly needed new blood. After Mötley Crüe became successful in spite of the initial doubts, Sixx would scoff, "The record companies don't know what the fuck they're doing. They sit behind their oak desks with their red-haired secretaries, snorting lines and taking quaaludes and trying to dictate what the music industry's all about."

Werman may have been hesitant to work with Mötley Crüe at first, but once in the studio with the band to record their second album, *Shout at the Devil,* he found he loved working with them. Like many hard rock and metal bands, Mötley had a gang mentality: us against the world. "It was like fuck everybody, fuck everything," says Werman. "They were just completely irreverent. For a nice Jewish boy from Boston, it was like hanging out with the mob." The band was young, hungry, and furious, with nothing to lose.

The songs on the *Shout at the Devil* album were a perfect reflection of the band's attitude—angry, mean, and aggressive. Mick Mars's guitar sound was thick as fog with distortion and had all the subtlety of a lead pipe crashing into someone's skull. Tommy Lee completed his drum tracks with the enthusiasm of a child unwrapping his presents at Christmas. He had the timing of a metronome and would throw his entire body into every hit. Nikki Sixx was a mediocre bass player, and it would take him four to five hours to record the bass line of each song. Sixx had to record the song "Red Hot" in a cast after breaking his arm while driving intoxicated. Werman joked that since he wasn't a good bassist, it didn't really make much of a difference. At first, Sixx wanted to prove he was in charge and disagreed with most of Werman's suggestions. But later, during a band meeting, Lee tried to reel Sixx in, saying, "Listen, if this guy's going to produce our album, I think we should hear what he has to say."

Shout at the Devil was completed in six weeks at a cost of approximately $70,000 and was released in September 1983. Doc McGhee had money and promised the band that whatever the label wouldn't pay for, he'd take care of. Mötley Crüe wanted a gatefold sleeve that opened to show four intense Barry Levine photos of the band. Elektra didn't want to pay for a gatefold sleeve, considering they didn't want the band on the label at all, so McGhee paid for the expensive production of the cover himself.

A month after the album's release, Werman was playing golf at Pebble Beach when he got a call from Zutaut. "We have a hit," he said. The album took off so fast that Krasnow hadn't had a chance to drop the band. *Shout at the Devil* started selling 100,000 units a week right out of the gate and went on to sell more than three million copies. In the '70s, kids used to dress up like their favorite members of Kiss on Halloween. When Sixx saw kids dressing up as Mötley Crüe that year, he knew the band had made it.

Mötley Crüe's reputation for sex, drugs, and decadence was well-known, especially since the band didn't make much effort to hide it. Indeed, the band loved to play up their sex-and-drugs escapades in the press. Still, some people couldn't help but wonder if their wild antics were genuine. "Is Mötley Crüe's Bad Image for Real?" asked a *Los Angeles Times* feature on the band. Writer Dennis Hunt pointed out there were already a lot of skeptics who felt that the band's image was a bunch of hype. Bryn Bridenthal, then a publicist at Elektra Records, confessed to one reporter that Mötley Crüe were "cute, naïve, nice guys. You're not going to tell anyone, are you? I mean, if you want a gang bang, they'll give you a gang bang."

Hunt found Sixx to be shy and polite in person, which is what fueled his skepticism. Underneath his bad-boy exterior, Sixx briefly revealed a painful area of his past: the fact that his father abandoned him. But he stopped himself quickly, saying, "I don't like to look back. It's too depressing." Hunt did guess correctly that Sixx was a shrewd manipulator of the press and knew what the fans wanted to read. Genuine or not, other metal and hard rock bands tried to outdo Mötley Crüe's excesses on every level. Bill Holdship, the former editor of *BAM* magazine, a rock journal distributed free in record stores, went on tour with Dokken for several days in the mid-1980s. The band tried hard to live up to Mötley Crüe's reputation. The band members made sure Holdship knew when they were getting blow jobs on the bus, and convinced two groupies to take off their tops in front of him so he'd put it in his story. One of the band members even grabbed Holdship's hand and placed it on one of the girl's breasts, telling him, "Come on, Bill, have a good time."

"There was a lot of pressure around you to emulate what a rock star is supposed to be," says former Dokken guitarist George Lynch. "That stereotype was alive and well then. I was pretty weak-spirited. I'm ashamed of myself that I followed along so easily."

Although everything was going Mötley Crüe's way, Nikki Sixx had an ugly secret. He was addicted to heroin, and his habit was catching up with him. He would often binge for days with Robbin Crosby of the band Ratt, who was also hiding a habit. In late November of 1984, Sixx, Crosby, and Neil Zlozower went to the Caribbean for a vacation. Sixx later said he was so stoned that he had to be carried onto the plane. Zlozower came home after a week, while Sixx and Crosby stayed on the island.

When Zlozower's girlfriend picked him up at the airport, she looked shell-shocked. She told him that while he was away, Vince Neil had been in an accident and someone was killed. Sixx still hadn't heard about the accident, because the island he was on didn't have television or phones. At a stopover in Florida on the way back to Los Angeles, someone approached him at the airport.

"Hey, aren't you in that band of the singer that killed someone?"

"What?"

"Yeah, Mötley Crüe. I heard the lead singer got into a car accident and killed someone."

At approximately 6:30 P.M. on December 8, 1984, after partying for days at Vince Neil's Redondo Beach house, Neil went on a beer run with Nicholas "Razzle" Dingley, drummer of the Finnish band Hanoi Rocks. Neil was driving sixty-five miles an hour on residential streets when his car skidded and swerved into an oncoming vehicle. The driver of the other car was rushed to the hospital with both her legs and an arm broken. She remained in a coma until the end of the month and would suffer permanent brain damage.

Neil's blood alcohol level was .017, almost twice the legal limit. Except for several cracked ribs and a few scrapes, he was virtually unharmed, but Dingley was killed in the crash.

Mötley Crüe was already successful, but Hanoi Rocks was on the verge of breaking. The accident happened right before the band was to play the Roxy in their Los Angeles debut. There was little question that the accident derailed the band from a promising future. "I believe that [lead singer] Michael Monroe was a total innovator," says John Kalodner. "They were the [creators] of a whole new style."

The members of Hanoi Rocks never got over Dingley's death; they swore there would be no band without him. It is believed that Tom Zutaut at one point tried to get Hanoi Rocks to re-form, offering a substantial amount of money, but the band still refused. According to Monroe, Nikki Sixx later had the chutzpah to ask him if he was interested in starting a new band when Neil was facing seven years in prison for manslaughter. Neil always had a devil-may-care, throw-caution-to-the-wind attitude. After the accident, Werman could see the grief and the burden of guilt in his face.

A year after the accident, in 1985, Neil was sentenced to thirty days in jail and two hundred hours of community service. He would also pay $2.6 million to the victims' families. There was a cry of outrage that Neil got off so lightly. It wasn't widely reported, but Neil had been found guilty of another drunk driving charge before the fatal crash.

"[Then-D.A.] Ira Reiner had a complete and total hard-on for Vince Neil and really wanted to put him away," says Charrie Foglio, who was working for Doc McGhee at the time. It was no coincidence that drunk-driving laws would get much tougher in Los Angeles after Neil's verdict.

Doc McGhee would later say, "My biggest regret as a manager is that I let Vince think he could get away with murder. . . . In Vince's mind, he thought he was above the law. And walking away from that disaster with a few weeks in a luxury jail and a $12,000 Rolex certainly didn't teach him otherwise."

Theatre of Pain, the follow-up to *Shout at the Devil,* was released in 1985. It was a bizarre quasi-concept album that nobody quite understood. The songs weren't very strong, but when Werman heard the ballad "Home Sweet Home," he could see Bic lighters flicking on in arenas all across the country. It would become one of Mötley Crüe's biggest hits, a live staple throughout their career. It was MTV's most-requested video for four months.

The tragedy of Neil's accident cast a shadow over the band. Sixx fell deeply into heroin addiction, which made *Pain* a difficult album to record. One day Sixx brought two shopping bags full of candy bars to the studio to eat, needing the sugar rush because he was strung out. Cocaine was a status symbol for rock stars in the 1980s: Either you were selling enough records to afford it, or you were important enough to get it dropped into your pocket for free. Cocaine was easy to conceal, and there was no shame doing it in the open. For hangers-on, it was the easiest way to hook up with a musician. Most people didn't equate being rich and successful with heroin; it was usually associated with people on skid row. Heroin was an unspeakable taboo, even within the anything-goes culture of rock and roll. Neil's accident should have been a strong warning to the band, but the members of Mötley Crüe didn't feel any need to clean up their acts—and continued to drink and drug their way toward oblivion.

By 1982, Quiet Riot had moved far away from their glitter-rock roots. At a pivotal Troubadour show in 1982, lead singer Kevin DuBrow came out onstage wearing leopard-patterned spandex and a chrome-studded belt, sprinkling his stage raps with references to headbangers. The song "No More Booze" was now called "Metal Health." "We took advantage of the term *heavy metal* for our album," said DuBrow. "When we titled it *Metal Health*, we knew it was coming back."

The new-model Quiet Riot included Carlos Cavazo on guitar and drummer Frankie Banali, and bassist Rudy Sarzo was now back in the fold after leaving Ozzy Osbourne's band. The band showcased at the Roxy after signing a deal with Pasha Records in September 1982. To emphasize the point of their newfound metaldom, the band played at ear-splitting levels in the tiny club. A local fan ran into Don Dokken in the lobby, who was so overwhelmed by the volume that he moaned, "I'm getting vertigo—I'm outta here!"

Spencer Proffer produced *Metal Health*. Three of the original songs the band recorded didn't generate his enthusiasm, and he decided the band should record a cover to hedge their bets. The first time Proffer heard Kevin DuBrow's voice, he thought he sounded like Noddy Holder of the English pub-rock band Slade. Proffer suggested they record one of Slade's songs, "Cum on Feel the Noize," a No. 1 U.K. hit in 1973. He didn't think the American public would recognize the song as a cover. Quiet Riot wasn't thrilled about covering the song and screwed up their performance on purpose, hoping the recording wouldn't make it on the album. "I still don't like the song very much, to be honest with you," says DuBrow. While Quiet Riot were recording the song, DuBrow made funny faces at Frankie Banali while he was playing his drum parts so he'd laugh and screw them up. Fed up, Proffer told the singer to leave the studio. When it came time for DuBrow to lay down his vocals, Banali told him to "Sing it like shit so they'll never use it." DuBrow put in such a weak performance that his vocals had to be doubled.

The *Metal Health* album cost about $35,000 and was recorded in a month. After its release in March 1983, Quiet Riot hopped in a Winnebago and drove to Duluth, Minnesota, where they opened for the

Scorpions. The band then played with ZZ Top on their *Eliminator* tour. ZZ Top's audience, full of beer drinkers and hell raisers, was one of the toughest to open for at the time (picture a lot of mangy beards, beer bellies, and Confederate-flag belt buckles). The Melvins' Buzz Osborne once recalled a ZZ Top concert as having "One of the scariest audiences imaginable. If they stacked up all the warrants due in that place . . ."

One of the biggest breaks for Quiet Riot came when they were added to the bill for the US Festival, which remains one of the largest concerts ever staged. Steve Wozniak, one of the founders of Apple Computer, organized the event, which cost him $18 million to put on. Says one source that worked at the festival, "One of the richest guys in America threw the concert just so he could get backstage." Even though they put on a terrible performance at the festival, Van Halen made the record books for being paid the most for a single perfomance—$1.5 million, or $17,000 a minute.

Quiet Riot opened "Heavy Metal Sunday," on May 29, 1983. As they left their hotel at 10 A.M. to go to the show, they ran into the members of Van Halen looking haggard and hung over, coming in to crash from a night of partying. Quiet Riot went on at 11:45. Over 300,000 people had come to the festival. "There were so many people [in the audience] that the curve of the earth hid you from seeing them all," says DuBrow. He was nervous the entire set; it was the last time he ever had stage fright. The "ego-ramps," the long planks in between the stage and the crowd barrier on which the singer walks to get closer to the audience, were roped off for David Lee Roth; no other performer was allowed to go near them. But DuBrow was so hyped as the crowd pumped their fists to "Metal Health" that he jumped right onto the ramps and led the crowd in a fist-pounding frenzy. One review of their performance read: "A local club band six months ago, Quiet Riot, with hardly any time to prepare, play their best set ever."

After playing the US Festival, Quiet Riot went on the road with multiplatinum quintet Loverboy, and DuBrow felt the tour did more to expand his band's audience than any previous road jaunt. Playing with

Iron Maiden or the Scorpions was like preaching to the converted, but on the Loverboy tour, Quiet Riot played in front of a Top Forty audience and won them over.

When a headliner feels threatened by an opening act, the headliner will often take away their drum riser, reduce the stage space they can use, refuse to give them a soundcheck, or screw up their sound at the mixing board (unplugging the guitar player's amp so he thinks his gear is breaking down is an old trick that devious headliners like to pull). As DuBrow recalls, "Loverboy kept taking stuff away from us, because we kept smokin' 'em. They took the drum riser, lights, sound—it didn't make any difference, we still smoked."

MTV started playing the video for "Cum on Feel the Noize" in August 1983. The clip was added to a program called *Friday Night Video Fights,* for which MTV played two videos and the fans voted which one they liked best. "Cum" clobbered videos from the Rolling Stones, the Doors, and Journey. The band was quickly discovering what an effective promotional tool MTV could be as it introduced them to markets normally difficult for metal bands to reach. "I've been approached by lots of people who say they had never heard of Quiet Riot until MTV," said Carlos Cavazo at the time. "In the past, bands depended on radio airplay, concert tours, and magazine coverage," said DuBrow in 1985. "Now in one fell swoop, you can project yourself into millions of homes across the nation. It would take you six months on the road to reach that many people."

Quiet Riot was so busy touring the country that they didn't have time to stop and see how well the *Metal Health* album was doing until November 26, 1983, when they were opening for Black Sabbath on their *Born Again* tour in Rockford, Illinois. Backstage after the show, the members of Quiet Riot were informed that *Metal Health* was the No. 1 album in the country. The members of Black Sabbath presented Quiet Riot with bottles of Dom Perignon to celebrate. DuBrow then felt a combination of euphoria and panic: How are we gonna get another No. 1 record? Something told him it was going to be downhill from there.

For the time being, however, Quiet Riot were still cruising. *Metal Health* sold three million copies by November 1983, another million by January 1984, and a million more by March. A great irony in Quiet Riot's success was that the song they had to be dragged kicking and screaming to record, "Cum on Feel the Noize," became their biggest single, peaking at No. 5 on the charts.

Quiet Riot's tremendous success opened the floodgates for a second wave of L.A. bands in 1984. Soon every label would want a metal band, fast, and L.A. became the city everyone looked to as the hotbed of activity. The majors started signing metal bands in droves, and it was a music-industry feeding frenzy not unlike the Seattle explosion of the '90s. Every major label had at least one metal band, and Ratt, Great White, Dokken, Armored Saint, Black 'N Blue, and W.A.S.P. would all score major-label deals.

Out of all the L.A. bands signed in the early 1980s, Armored Saint would turn out to be one of the best despite being consistently underrated and overlooked. Armored Saint are a favorite of baseball superstar Mike Piazza, one of the biggest metalheads in professional sports. Piazza has every Armored Saint album in his collection and once said their music "gave me a mental edge to be relentless. It would drive me even harder."

The members of Armored Saint were close friends even before they formed a band in 1982. Singer John Bush, bassist Joey Vera, and drummer Gonzo first met in elementary school growing up in East L.A., and would be joined in the band by Gonzo's brother, guitarist Phil Sandoval, and guitarist Dave Pritchard. At the time the band started, sword-and-sorcery movies were very popular. One night, they all got stoned and went to see the film *Excalibur,* about King Arthur. After seeing the film, Gonzo came up with the name Armored Saint. The band dressed in homemade medieval costumes. They painted elbow and kneepads black and silver to resemble armor, unscrewed aluminum reflectors off telephone poles to wear, and bought plastic toy swords and breastplates.

Joey Vera had played with Tommy Lee prior to joining Armored Saint in a band called Sapphire. After Vera joined Armored Saint and Lee joined Mötley Crüe, they remained friends. When Armored Saint played a gig at a ski lodge in Mount Baldy, near Los Angeles, Lee came up with his sister, Athena. Lee and Vera later left the show to go to a party down the hill. Everyone was drunk, and Vera had passed out in the back of the 280Z Lee was driving. Lee was driving too fast, and coming off an off-ramp, the car rolled four times down a ravine. Vera went through the hatchback windshield, and his thumb was almost torn off his right hand.

The car Lee had wrecked was not his, but the girl he borrowed it from had insurance. With the insurance money, Vera was able to pay his medical bills, and with the leftover money, Armored Saint was able to record a demo. But the band didn't have to shop the tape; the labels were coming to them without it. With the frenzy to sign L.A. bands in full force, Armored Saint landed at Chrysalis Records.

Armored Saint didn't follow the commercial trends of what was happening in L.A.—their sound was traditional heavy metal. Instead of trying to turn L.A. into a beauty parlor like the hair bands would eventually accomplish, Armored Saint would have loved nothing more than to turn L.A. into another England. They were following the New Wave of British Heavy Metal very closely and, like Metallica, wanted to do a similar version of that sound in the States.

Armored Saint were very close to Metallica, and the bands would tour together several times. Metallica even asked John Bush to sing for the band right before they recorded the *Kill 'Em All* album in 1982. James Hetfield wasn't 100 percent convinced he wanted to sing, and Metallica knew Bush was a great singer. Bush turned down the offer, a decision he doesn't regret. At the time Metallica asked him to join, Armored Saint was getting big in L.A. and was building a strong buzz. Metallica was going nowhere and was about to leave for the Bay Area. Bush wasn't going to leave his friends to join another band that wasn't doing well at the time. "It just wasn't meant to be," he says.

Armored Saint got a lot of MTV play with the single "Can U Deliver" but Chrysalis didn't know how to market the band. They wanted the band to be the next Def Leppard and tried to market Armored Saint to radio, when they were really a touring band. It was all about data: Where was the band on the charts? Where were they with MTV? They could have built a strong following in Europe, but Armored Saint didn't make it over there until 1989.

While touring with Metallica, Armored Saint saw how they were breaking through without costumes. When the tour hit San Francisco, Lars Ulrich pulled Joey aside at four in the morning while everyone was getting hammered and told him, "Hey, don't take this the wrong way, man, but you guys don't need to wear those [costumes]. Just be who you are. You're a great band; you don't need that."

With Alice Cooper still several years away from having a modest comeback, and Kiss taking off their makeup and attempting to revive their careers without it, some L.A. bands were trying to follow in their footsteps and establish themselves as the new shock-rock kings. W.A.S.P., who was signed to Capitol, was one of those bands. The band had made its name at the Troubadour with a stage show reminiscent of Alice Cooper and Kiss. Their costumes featured buzzsaw blades attached to their wrists and crotches, bought for the band by guitarist Chris Holmes's mother.

Inspired by the film *The Road Warrior,* W.A.S.P. wore black leather pants with the cheeks cut out (an idea borrowed from David Lee Roth). The pants were far from practical; one night Holmes slid on stage and got a bad case of splinters. Behind the drums was a gigantic steel W.A.S.P. logo that shot flames into the air. The band turned the flames up so high that they reached the Troubadour ceiling and the spiders that nested there would flee to the corners for safety. The band also threw raw meat into the audience; eventually fans brought their own meat to the shows to throw back at the band. One night Holmes was knocked unconscious by a flying rump roast.

W.A.S.P. lead singer and bassist Blackie Lawless, whose real name was Steve Duran, had been on the fringes of the L.A. scene for years. He made a name for himself replacing Johnny Thunders in the Malcolm McLaren–era New York Dolls. They toured for several weeks before breaking up in Florida in 1975.

Lawless then started a band with Dolls bassist Arthur Kane that they called Killer Kane. They lasted only a handful of gigs and played their last show at the Starwood. That night, Arthur Kane was so out of it that when the final song ended and the rest of the band left, he remained playing onstage for another twenty minutes. A roadie finally picked him up and carried him off.

Lawless continued to form bands, including Circus Circus and Sister. Nikki Sixx looked up to him when he first moved to L.A., and Mötley Crüe ended up using the pentagram banners and mannequin props Sister had used.

In 1982, Lawless was putting together another band. Rik Fox, who played bass for local bands such as Steeler and Sin, was briefly a member. It was his idea to call the band W.A.S.P., an acronym for "We Are Sexually Perverted."

Chris Holmes joined the band in 1983. Blackie phoned the day Holmes was released from jail on his fifth DUI and invited him to join the band. (Holmes had his boss lay him off so that he could collect unemployment in jail.) Holmes was the Dennis Hopper of heavy metal, a crazed wild man whose stories are numerous and legendary. One night at an industry party, when the line to the bathroom was too long, Holmes climbed onto the ledge of the building and urinated onto the cars below. Once he was dragged back inside, Lawless scolded him in the corner like a child. Holmes had played with Lawless in Sister and didn't want to have anything to do with him again. Lawless was a notorious tyrant; his bookshelves were lined with books on how to intimidate people. Even Gene Simmons found Lawless's ego trips ridiculous. When W.A.S.P. opened for Kiss in 1985, their stage show featured giant replicas of the band's heads that floated high above the stage. Simmons looked at Lawless's head and remarked, "Yep, that's about the size of it."

Lawless promised Holmes that they'd have a record deal in nine months. He made good on his promise with the help of Rod Smallwood, W.A.S.P.'s manager. Smallwood also handled Iron Maiden, who were then signed with Capitol. According to Holmes, Smallwood threatened to pull Iron Maiden off the label if the record company didn't sign W.A.S.P. Ric Browde was one of the producers on the first W.A.S.P. album. Lawless assured Browde that he had $50,000 to record the album, but he really had only $1,500, which he took to Las Vegas and blew on roulette. W.A.S.P.'s self-titled debut album was released in 1984.

W.A.S.P. co-headlined a tour with Metallica, with Armored Saint opening, in the beginning of 1985. Lawless had a knack for making enemies among his fellow metal bands as well as alienating even his staunchest fans. When the tour arrived in Boston, there weren't enough dressing rooms, so Metallica had to change outside in a garden shed in the dead of winter. When Lars Ulrich came backstage and asked to borrow one of the heaters (there were several lying around), Lawless ordered him out of his dressing room.

"Blackie would go out of his way not to be friendly," says Joey Vera. "He didn't even want to deal with fans. We always felt there was a connection with the fans; you can't be disconnected from it. He would not make any effort to do anything with fans, and I thought that was so fucked up. It was totally against what Metallica and us believed in." When the tour hit Canada, Lawless insisted that W.A.S.P. headline the gigs, because they had sold more records there. Because of his arrogance, Lawless ultimately granted Metallica a huge favor—they blew W.A.S.P. off the stage every night.

Elektra Records already had two strong metal acts in their stable with Metallica and Mötley Crüe when they added Dokken to their roster in 1983. Lead singer Don Dokken and lead guitarist George Lynch had been in L.A. bands throughout the '70s. With the major labels not interested in signing metal and hard rock in 1980 and 1981, Dokken secured a publishing deal in Europe and made their first album with the money they were advanced.

The band flew to Europe on inexpensive charter flights, carrying their instruments on as baggage. Their first album was recorded in eighteen days in 1981. The band rehearsed in a wine cellar. It was so damp in their rehearsal space that mold formed in the drums and amps, but this actually gave their instruments a unique sound, so they kept the mold while they recorded.

Although Dokken toured Europe twice and reportedly sold 30,000 copies of their debut album overseas, they still couldn't get a deal in the States. Elektra strongly considered signing them, but apparently the label was still unsure about signing heavy metal acts. Waiting for Elektra to make up its mind was an emotional roller coaster for the band, especially after working so hard to establish their name in Europe. But with Mötley Crüe gathering steam, Tom Zutaut had earned his stripes as an A&R executive and had the power to sign Dokken to the label. Their first album, now titled *Breaking the Chains,* was finally released Stateside in 1983.

Dokken had a lot of promise as a band. They had one of those razor-sharp logos that fans spent hours drawing on the cover of their history books. George Lynch was getting a lot of attention in the guitar magazines and, along with Ratt's Warren DeMartini, had the potential to become one of the next guitar gods. His playing was fluid and intense, and he really knew how to make a note scream. In fact, Lynch's playing made him the star of Dokken. The guitarist becoming the star of a metal band can often cause problems, but former bassist Jeff Pilson says it wasn't an issue. "The plan all along was to push George," he says. "Don's the sort of person who likes to use strengths."

The problem was that Don Dokken and Lynch had one of the most volatile lead singer/lead guitarist combinations in history, and they both fought constantly. "[We were] like a husband and wife who hate each other but stay together for the kid," said Don Dokken. "Our music is the kid." Dokken and Lynch could never be in the studio at the same time. When the band recorded their *Back for the Attack* album in 1987, producer Neil Kernon scheduled Lynch's studio time during the day, Dokken's at night. The two even recorded some of the tracks in separate states.

Dokken also seemed to be plagued by bad timing and accidents. "We had so many mishaps," says Lynch. "Don throwin' his mike up, getting it lost in the lights, the mike comin' back down hitting him in the head, knockin' him out onstage, knockin' his wig off." (Dokken has denied he's ever worn a wig but has admitted to having transplants and extensions.) One night onstage, Lynch spread his legs while playing guitar, and his skin-tight pants split down the crotch. He was able to hide his exposed genitals behind his guitar for a while, but he was in the midst of a long song and couldn't stop playing. A roadie ran onstage with a roll of duct tape, crouched behind Lynch, and taped his pants back up while he was still playing. It was painful when the tape came off. "I lost a little hair there," he recalls. When Marty Callner directed the video for Dokken's single "Just Got Lucky," Lynch's guitar solo was shot on a live volcano. It began erupting, and the rock beneath Lynch's feet got so hot that his shoes melted. A helicopter got him out of there just in time.

Dokken's second album, *Tooth and Nail,* was released in September 1984. Dokken's ace in the hole was Q-Prime, the management team that also handled Metallica and Def Leppard. Burnstein and Mensch believed their bands should have a strong touring ethic, and they set Dokken up with many prime opening spots. "There was a great model for building the band, and I think Cliff and the record company definitely have to take credit for that," says Lynch. "This is how we're gonna build this band, we got MTV in our pocket, we got these tours lined up, we're gonna put it all together and build it up by constantly playing live instead of the quick fix and fizzling out right away. I'm glad we did it that way—we had more staying power."

Tooth and Nail was Dokken's best album, showcasing the band at the peak of their abilities. "We were very hungry and very focused," says Pilson. "None of the rock-star trappings had set in yet." Tom Werman produced the album. He didn't get along with Lynch during the recording but felt he was, "one of the best guitar players I've ever seen."

Back in 1979, Don Dokken had written a power ballad called "Alone Again." Producer Michael Wagener was a friend of Dokken, and when the singer played it for him, he knew on first listen that it was a hit. For years Wagener encouraged Dokken to record it, but Lynch and drummer Mick Brown resisted recording the song, and Burnstein felt it "didn't deliver the goods." Dokken finally persevered and was able to get the song on the *Tooth and Nail* album. Once the album was finished, Elektra wasn't fond of the song either and didn't support it as a single. The band had to pay for the "Alone Again" video, which cost $19,000. Even though the song didn't chart, it went on to become one of the band's biggest MTV hits. "I gotta give a lot of credit to Don for fighting extra hard," says Pilson.

The "power ballad" was usually a soft song with heavy guitars, and heavy on the schmaltz. The style would become a dilemma for many '80s metal bands. One member, often the singer, would want to record a power ballad, perhaps to impress female listeners with his "sensitive" side. The other members usually wanted to stay hard and heavy to avoid potentially alienating their core audience. When a metal band wanted to do a ballad, the guitarist would make sure the song had heavy riffs and a hot solo, so it wouldn't be completely fluffy.

As much as some musicians within bands hated them, the power ballads were often the biggest hits, the tracks radio was most receptive to. The biggest hits Werman produced for Kix, L.A. Guns, and Dokken were power ballads. "You know that collection of power ballads they advertise on late-night TV? I've got about six songs on that disc!"

Dokken were clearly a talented band, but they never had a definable image and followed a lot of trends. "Other bands were wearing bandannas—we're gonna wear bandannas too," recalled Lynch. "What kind of hairspray is Mötley Crüe using? Aqua Net pink? Extra superhold? Right. Gotta get two cases of that for the road."

For Dokken's third album, *Under Lock and Key,* released in 1985, the band invested in expensive stage costumes that cost $3,000 each. Lynch called them "the clown outfits." He knew the costumes were a mistake, and so did Q-Prime, who told Dokken that the band should wear everyday clothes on stage and let the music speak for itself. The singer wouldn't hear any of it.

Lynch hated the costumes so much that he almost didn't show up for the *Lock and Key* photo session. Cliff Burnstein got on the phone and said, "George, just do it. Just show up and be there." Lynch made it to the session. A decade later, Don Dokken admitted that he too was embarrassed about wearing the costumes.

Dokken was a band stuck between art and commerce. They longed for a big hit record like Mötley Crüe, but Lynch felt an album should be an album, not just a string of singles. (He also wanted the music to progress to where he could solo longer.) As the band was preparing for their fourth album, it was a crucial point for Dokken. It remained to be seen if they would have a big breakthrough commercially or if their internal tensions would finally cause the band to unravel.

With the explosion of MTV, bands needed a stronger visual presentation to accentuate their music. Much of metal fashion was influenced by the movies. Paul Stanley wore sweatshirts with torn collars à la Jennifer Beals in *Flashdance;* Quiet Riot bassist Rudy Sarzo wore leg warmers.

Many bands wore multi-patterned spandex: checkerboards and stripes and kamikaze suns. Mötley Crüe's stage set for the *Shout at the Devil* tour was inspired by the 1981 film *Escape From New York*, and bands borrowed costume ideas from *The Road Warrior* as well.

While most '80s metal bands didn't wear full-face makeup like Kiss, they still protected their offstage personas zealously. Bon Jovi and Mötley Crüe would not allow photographers to shoot them unshaven or in everyday clothes. "We can't be [photographed] when I'm in sweatpants," said Tommy Lee in 1985. "People pay a lot of money for you to look like a motherfucker and kick ass on stage. Why show what you're really like offstage? I get off the bus, my hair's messy. Until I get in the shower, put on my makeup, and I'm dressed to the tens, I don't wanna be seen."

Video could make a stage look infinitely huge and expectations from the fans grew accordingly; they had to see a similar spectacle in concert as well. With the potential dangers of pyro effects, a show had to run like clockwork to avoid accidents and mishaps. Often, a concert had to be the same way every night, leaving no room for spontaneity.

Judas Priest were probably the first to popularize one favorite metal stage set. They had giant walls of Marshall cabinets that towered over them like monoliths. Most of the amps were "dummies"—cabinets with no electronics inside them. But it was a powerful image, and a great optical and aural illusion. Seeing the wall of amps convinced you that the concert was louder than it really was.

With the foundation Kiss had built in the '70s, tours were now far more expensive to produce, often costing millions of dollars. It would usually take a number of semis to haul all the equipment from state to state, and how many trucks you needed to lug everything around soon became a strange bragging right.

Anthrax came from the Iron Maiden sensibility that with every tour there should be a whole new stage show that was bigger and better than the last. "That's where we spent insane amounts of money," says Scott Ian. "We probably could have had a million dollars in the bank for all the money we spent shipping stuff."

When tour costs went through the roof in the '80s, the only thing that kept bands from being wiped out financially was merchandising sales, a practice for which they had Kiss to thank. When Dio's production costs spiraled up into the seven-figure range for the *Last in Line* tour, they were able to underwrite the entire tour with merchandise money.

Fans bought T-shirts like crazy throughout the '80s. "It became just as important to get the T-shirt as it was to actually have gone to the show," said David Lee Roth. "It totally spoke of who you were and where you were going. You saw somebody with a Black Sabbath T-shirt, you knew exactly who that person was." Cliff Burnstein put it best when he said, "A kid puts on a Judas Priest or an Iron Maiden or a Motörhead shirt and it makes a statement. Hall and Oates don't make a statement."

By 1984, metal and pop were coming together in a big way. Metal had always been an album format; bands like Iron Maiden and Judas Priest didn't sell records on the strength of hit singles. The '80s metal bands were starting to break through onto radio and MTV with singles. Now they were sharing the Top Ten with such acts as Bruce Springsteen and Madonna.

The bands that were signed in the metal explosion were playing great pop with heavy guitars. Usually when a pop band used heavy guitars on a single, it sounded contrived and phony. Now bands with their roots in true heavy metal were writing hit singles, and it was an irresistible combination.

"As much flak as the '80s metal scene gets, the reality of it is there was some good songwriting in there," says Jeff Pilson. "And one of the things the songwriters did, Dokken included, was we would make [our songs] concise, not to be radio-friendly, but just because that's the evolution of the music. You're always trying to find the most simple way of saying what you need to say. I think that was a by-product more than a conscious thing. Certainly it became conscious [later], and that's what killed the scene."

Robbin Crosby of Ratt once said that even someone's mother could walk away humming one of the band's songs. Of course, this went against the popular belief that the minute your parents could appreciate the music you loved, it wasn't cool anymore. Ratt were even pleased they could play on the same bill with pop bands like The Cars and Huey Lewis and the News.

Ratt, along with Twisted Sister, were Atlantic Records's big metal signings of 1983. Ratt vocalist Stephen Pearcy started the band in San Diego under the name Mickey Ratt. In the '70s, he used to drive up to L.A. to see Van Halen play empty clubs and, eventually, moved there in 1980 hoping for his own success.

Like most two-guitar bands, one player, Warren DeMartini, was the flashy whiz kid, and Robbin Crosby played in a simpler style. Quiet and reserved, DeMartini was by far the most respected musician of the band. Crosby was a gentle giant at 6'5". He had once considered a career in baseball before joining Ratt and, with his handsome, rugged looks, could have been a movie star. Many considered Pearcy and DiMartini the musical core of the band, but Crosby was a good songwriter as well, and most of Ratt's hits were collaborative efforts. Pearcy was a terrible singer and not much of a performer onstage, but following the Van Halen formula, he took care of the costumes and the show. Like Vince Neil, Pearcy was the most sexually driven of the group. His top priorities were the three Ps: pussy, partying, and paycheck.

Pearcy later said he had more fun struggling to get a record deal than when the band made it big. While Ratt was getting started, he shared a one-bedroom apartment with DeMartini and Crosby that they called Ratt Mansion West. When they were able to afford a good meal and beer, they felt successful, and Pearcy figured it would always be that way. The members of Ratt were also close friends with Mötley Crüe and formed a hard-partying clique dubbed the Gladiators. Sixx was nicknamed "Fearless Leader," Pearcy was "Field Marshal," and Crosby was "King."

Marshall Berle first saw Ratt play at the Whisky. He was impressed enough to get them financial backing and then put them in the studio to record an EP, which took three days and $10,000 to record. It was released through Berle's label, Time Coast, in April 1983. Like the New Wave of British Heavy Metal bands, many L.A. bands were doing their own records first, which showed the majors that with a bigger push and more money, they could go even further. Ten thousand dollars wasn't a lot of money to record anything, but Ratt's EP was hard and raw, and captured their energy perfectly.

KLOS and KMET (nicknamed "the Mighty Met") were two rival FM stations in L.A. If one station was playing a local band, the other wouldn't touch them. But "You Think You're Tough," a song from Ratt's EP, was so strong that both stations played it. Thirty out of 40 AOR (Album Oriented Rock) stations, mostly on the West Coast and Texas, added the EP to their rotations, and it sold more than 30,000 copies.

Ratt played an industry showcase on July 27, 1983, at the Beverly Theater. The opening act never showed up, and the crowd became restless and irritated. Ratt was nervous: They knew that representatives from the major labels would be in the audience. As they finished their set, Ratt thought it was the worst gig they had ever played, so they were surprised when Doug Morris came up to them backstage and offered them a deal with Atlantic.

Ratt's debut LP, *Out of the Cellar,* was produced by newcomer Beau Hill. Ratt wanted Tom Allom so they could get a really heavy sound, but Berle and Morris told them to shut up and do what Hill told them.

Hill liked Ratt but felt their arrangements didn't capitalize on the hooks of their songs enough, so he helped the band restructure them. Hill's contributions to Ratt's sound were crucial to the band's success. The backward echo that helped make the chorus of "Round and Round" memorable was his idea, and Hill sang background vocals as well. He contributed to Ratt's songwriting, and, a few years later, wrote Ratt's hit "Way Cool Jr." off Warren DeMartini's bluesy guitar riff.

Ratt were on a tight schedule and budget. Berle didn't like his bands to waste time in the studio, and Hill was of the same school of thought. He ran a tight ship, and if the band wanted to screw around and have fun, they had to do it somewhere where it didn't cost $250 an hour. "There were none of the fun rock and roll stories of catered sushi dinners, strippers coming in limousines, and stuff like that," he says. Hill figured that if he didn't live and breathe the album twenty-four hours a day, it wouldn't come in on time or on budget, which would have reflected badly on him as a first-time producer and hurt his career before it even started. So Hill lived at the studio, using the upstairs shower and sleeping on the couch, because he couldn't afford to stay at the nearby Holiday Inn anymore.

Out of the Cellar was finished in twenty-eight days for around $60,000 and would turn out to be Ratt's finest hour. With a crisp guitar sound, great songs, and just the right mix of heavy and hooks, it was a pop metal classic. The guitar riffs in songs like "Round and Round" followed the vocal melodies, which made the songs instantly catchy and memorable. They had "the melody in their rhythm," said DeMartini. "The songs hum themselves."

Berle brought his "Uncle Miltie" onto the set of Ratt's video for "Round and Round." Milton Berle played two roles in the clip—one in regular clothes, the other in drag. The *Out of the Cellar* album came out about six weeks before the "Round and Round" video debuted on MTV. The label was having trouble getting radio play for "Round and Round," and the video saved the day. It helped drive MTV's ratings through the roof, and MTV did the same with Ratt's record sales. *Out of the Cellar* would stay on the charts for over a year and sell more than three million copies. "MTV can take the majority of credit for making Ratt go platinum," says Marshall Berle. "That's what really drove their sales. The medium and the talent were there; it was waiting for each other to meet."

Ratt soon took off for the road. Like Mötley Crüe, they lined their bus with bras and panties that swayed in the breeze. On the destination scroll at the front of the bus (usually listing a city) was the command

"Show Your Tits." They played their first big arena show in San Antonio, opening for ZZ Top. That night, Ratt bassist Juan Croucier was at the bottom of the steps waiting to go on. The minute the lights went down, and the crowd began to roar, it was like he was playing his first gig all over again. Walking up the steps, he kept repeating certain mantras in his head, resorting to every professional instinct he had not to get overwhelmed by everything.

Ratt alternated between opening for other bands and headlining theaters and clubs. They were slated to open for the band Alcatrazz, which featured guitarist Yngwie Malmsteen, at the Hollywood Palladium in February 1984. The bands flipped a coin to see who would headline the show; Ratt won. The band also headlined a tour with the band Fastway, which had a hit with the song "Say What You Will," and Mama's Boys, a terrific Irish metal group with a fiddle player.

Ratt later opened arenas for Ozzy Osbourne and Billy Squier when Squier's popularity was waning and he needed a strong opening act. Squier's managers tried to tell Ratt what they could and couldn't do during their set. Berle told Squier's people to go fuck themselves, and they backed down immediately—Ratt was saving their asses on tour. That's when Berle knew that the band was really getting somewhere.

Ratt was so crazed playing gigs that they hardly realized the *Out of the Cellar* album and "Round and Round" single had finally become successful. It wasn't until they got back home to L.A. that their friends told them, "Hey man, haven't you heard? You're on the radio every day." Ratt had played more than two hundred shows in fourteen months. At one point, they played twenty-one gigs in twenty-one days. They played clubs on their days off. Members of their road crew came to the band in tears, pleading, "I can't handle this anymore—I gotta go home!" But Ratt was so hungry to prove themselves that they could have easily toured another ten months.

As Ratt were gaining mainstream success, they started to distance themselves from their heavy metal roots. In fact, many of the '80s bands that were successful as a result of the heavy metal flood didn't want to be associated with the term. "We don't have that offensive leather-and-studs look," Pearcy said. "We're not afraid to admit that we're into fashion. We like to look good; we're not trying to scare anybody."

One reason why Ratt would falter early was that many were turned off by Pearcy's arrogance. He once claimed in an interview that the only bands that could compete with Ratt were the Rolling Stones and Led Zeppelin. Pearcy constantly fought with Croucier because he wanted the bassist to tone down his stage act. Even in the club days, Pearcy used to draw lines on the stage with duct tape that Croucier was not allowed to cross. It was common knowledge that Pearcy stuffed his spandex pants with socks. He later had an opportunity to set the record straight on what was below the belt when he posed for *Playgirl*, yet he declined to reveal all.

Ratt followed *Out of the Cellar* in 1985 with *Invasion of Your Privacy*. The album sold two and a half million copies. The band's fears of following in Quiet Riot's footsteps as one-hit wonders didn't come true, but they would never again capture the excitement of *Out of the Cellar*.

Ratt's third album, *Dancing Undercover*, released in 1986, was rushed because Berle had booked $50,000 of studio time, and the band was under pressure to write songs quickly. After the album was recorded, Beau Hill told Robbin Crosby, "You know something? We do not have a single on this record. We have recorded a complete piece of shit." They decided to write a single right there, and came up with "Dance," which became the standout track. The band went right back into the studio and recorded the song as quickly as they could to get it on the album. Once *Dancing Undercover* was released, it would only break the Top Thirty. The album was largely viewed as a disappointment, even though it eventually went platinum.

"All the bands I've ever worked with, the first shot was always [the best]," reflects Berle. "In the beginning, the recordings went very quickly. As the band grew in stature, so did other things that would eventually slow the process down."

Many of the metal and hard rock bands signed in 1982 and 1983 peaked with their first record. When recording their debuts, a lot of bands are excited just to be making a record. They're hungry and have something to prove. And with new acts, there usually isn't a lot of time or money to record, which can work in a band's favor because it captures their raw energy on tape.

Of course, if the album winds up a hit, everyone wants to repeat the trick. Some bands begin analyzing every detail, and they end up micromanaging themselves, which is why follow-up albums often sound stiff and lack spontaneity. Some bands practically kill themselves trying to recreate the magic of a debut (Guns N' Roses come to mind).

Many of the L.A. bands who got snatched up by the majors usually had years to develop their music before they were signed. Once a band came off the road from their first major tour, the labels would demand another album as soon as possible, while the momentum was still rolling in the band's favor. Musicians like to say that a band has five years to write their first record and two weeks to write the next one. But according to former Dio keyboardist Claude Schnell, a band's debut album takes even longer than that to come together. "The first effort of an artist generally represents a lifetime of preparation," he says. "Everything you've ever done—all the music, riffs, whatever you've accumulated in your toolbox—you have at your disposal to create your first album and blow everyone's socks off.

"However, by the time you're done recording it and touring to support it, next thing you know you're back in the studio. You have virtually no time to replenish yourself. Now you have to come up with all the best tricks you can, and do them better, because everyone expects the second effort to be better than the first. And more often than not, that doesn't happen, because you don't have the time or the life resources at your disposal that you had the first time out."

Pop artists live and die by the single, and bands like Ratt and Quiet Riot had crossover success because of hit singles. But it also trapped them when their labels kept asking, "Where's the next 'Round and

Round'?" or "Where's the next 'Cum on Feel the Noize'?" As *Circus* magazine noted toward the end of Ratt's career in 1989, "Ratt's biggest problem is that they've spent a career trying to live up to (or should that be live down?) the success of 'Round and Round.' They make good solid albums, not singles."

Quiet Riot may have been on top of the world with the breakthrough of the *Metal Health* album, but rather than enjoy his success, Kevin DuBrow was angry that the bands signed in Quiet Riot's wake wouldn't acknowledge their success helped them get signed. DuBrow was also angry that his band had signed away all of their publishing rights to their producer, Spencer Proffer. As DuBrow and Proffer have confirmed, the band did have legal counsel, and DuBrow admits the band knew they were signing a bad deal.

In the 1970s, it usually took a band several albums to break. Quiet Riot figured they'd become successful by the third album, which was when their deal with Proffer would end. They never counted on their first album being their biggest success. Skid Row also signed away their publishing to Jon Bon Jovi, with their deal also ending on the third album, "which sold about ten copies," jokes former Skid Row drummer Rob Affuso.

As it turns out, a lot of metal musicians were screwed out of their royalties, which is one reason why a lot of '80s artists are now broke. When a high-profile gig came along, many struggling and naïve musicians took whatever was offered to them, no matter how unfair the terms. If they didn't accept those terms, there were hundreds of others who would. Years after the band Winger had sold millions of albums, guitarist Reb Beach confessed, "I'm certainly not set financially. I didn't sign the best contract. Back then, it was, 'Sign this or we'll get another guitar player.'"

DuBrow was pissed off that Quiet Riot had signed a bad deal, and that they weren't getting the respect he felt they were due. He decided to take his grievances to the press, which hastened the band's downfall. It all started when writer Marc Shapiro interviewed DuBrow for *Hit Parader* magazine. DuBrow was hung over and grumpy when Shapiro asked him what he thought of the explosion of L.A. bands signed in the wake of Quiet Riot's success. DuBrow groused, "If hair was gold, they'd all be millionaires. They can't fuckin' play," as he rattled off the names of a number of L.A. bands. DuBrow continued to shoot off his mouth in interview after interview.

The letters sections of metal magazines started to overflow with DuBrow hate mail, and Quiet Riot began losing fans in droves. "The bands I put down should have thanked me," he says. "I turned our fans against us and toward them. These people all became friends in their common dislike for me. By fucking my career up, I helped them all sell more units!"

Quiet Riot released the follow-up to *Metal Health,* the aptly titled *Condition Critical,* in 1984. The album was rushed to capitalize on the success of *Health,* and as a result, many of the songs were leftovers that didn't make it on the first album. Quiet Riot then hit the road and tried to compete with Van Halen's giant *1984* tour, bringing as much stage equipment and lights as they could.

Quiet Riot was booked to play arenas, but they weren't selling them out, so the shows had to be scaled down considerably. Their show was supposed to begin with elevators pushing each band member up to the stage. The elevators kept breaking down, and the band members had to climb out of the holes before the lights came up.

Even though *Condition Critical* sold 1.5 million copies, it was considered a major disappointment. The album was later dubbed by one writer as a "platinum failure." When Rudy Sarzo opened an issue of *Hit Parader* and the centerfold was a dartboard of DuBrow, he knew it was time to leave. He quit soon after the tour.

The band's third album, *QR III,* came out in 1986. Their manager, Warren Entner, pulled DuBrow aside and told him he had to put a leash on his mouth or it would kill his career. "You can't walk on water," Entner reminded him. "Yeah, but I can take a few steps," said DuBrow.

QR III sold poorly, and the resulting tour was a disaster. Keel, another band signed to a major label, MCA, after the success of *Metal Health,* opened the *QR III* tour. The tour pulled into Pittsburgh and when Keel guitarist Marc Ferrari entered the arena, he noticed something was wrong. Usually with an arena show, the few hundred seats behind the stage aren't sold and are blocked off by a curtain. But the roadies were setting up the stage to face those seats. Ferrari figured the road crew didn't know what they were doing. Then he realized that Quiet Riot hadn't sold enough tickets and would be playing to the seats behind the stage while the rest of the arena remained empty.

By the end of the *QR III* tour, the rest of Quiet Riot was fed up with DuBrow. They played their last show with him in Hawaii on December 7, 1986, the anniversary of the attack on Pearl Harbor. Afterward the rest of the band secretly changed their airline flights back home so they could leave early, and slipped a new plane ticket underneath DuBrow's door. He was officially fired soon after.

Paul Shortino, who sang for the L.A. band Rough Cutt, replaced DuBrow. Shortino had a smoky, bluesy vocal style, and the album he recorded with them, simply titled *Quiet Riot,* was supposed to be a return to form. The album featured some good tunes, Cavazo played better than ever, and no one was listening. Kevin DuBrow had soured Quiet Riot's fans from listening to the music, no matter how good it was. "It's one thing hurting yourself, but I hurt the rest of the band, who were three really good friends of mine," he says. "That was the worst part about it, and something I regret more than anything else."

By 1997, Quiet Riot had completely re-formed the *Metal Health* lineup with Carazo, Sarzo, and Banali. When Sarzo rejoined the band, it was the first time he'd spoken to Dubrow in thirteen years. In 1999, DuBrow made news for failing to pay a settlement to a woman who claimed she had suffered injuries at a Quiet Riot show. DuBrow pleaded to a judge that he couldn't pay off the judgment, which was over $100,000, because he was completely broke and living with his mother. He also claimed he hadn't received a royalty check since 1987.

As for all the bands he bad-mouthed, DuBrow now realizes he should have just said that they were great and left it at that. "I think if I had had somebody to slap me in the head and talk to me in a way I could understand, it would have saved me the trouble."

In the 1980s, young kids learning to play guitar looked at a picture like this and dreamed of the day when they could rip up the frets like former Dokken guitarist **George Lynch,** one of the hottest players to come out of the L.A. scene. (John Harrell)

"EVERY NIGHT, SAMMY HAGAR'S GOTTA SING 'JUMP,' AND I WILL NEVER SING A SAMMY HAGAR SONG."

—David Lee Roth after leaving Van Halen

T O ANYONE NOT IN Van Halen's inner circle, David Lee Roth's exit from the band was a shocking event. Yet the truth is that it's amazing the band didn't disintegrate long before he left.

As early as 1980, Eddie Van Halen was ready to pull the plug on Van Halen so he could pursue a solo career. According to one report, he began writing music for a solo album. When Roth learned of Eddie's plans, he came up with lyrics as quickly as he could. The resulting album was *Fair Warning*. (According to Alex Van Halen, he was the one who convinced Eddie to stick it out.)

Recording *Fair Warning* was a difficult process. Eddie had to sneak into the studio at 4 A.M. every morning to get what he wanted on the album. For one song on the album, "Push Comes to Shove," Eddie played the guitar solo more than twenty times. Producer Ted Templeman kept saying, "No, it's not good enough." Finally, the session was called off for the day. Later that night, Eddie came back to the studio and recorded the exact same solo Templeman had kept rejecting. The next day, the producer gave it a listen and told Eddie, "That's great."

Fair Warning turned out to be one of Van Halen's angriest and most aggressive records, and tracks like "Push Comes to Shove" and "One Foot Out the Door" only hinted at the turmoil within. Even Eddie's guitar solos sounded pissed-off. Warner Bros. didn't release any singles from the album when it came out in May 1981 because the material was too dark, although "Unchained" became a hit on rock radio. Years after its release, *Fair Warning* is a lost classic among Van Halen fans, and several alternative-rock stars, such as Billy Corgan of Smashing Pumpkins, have cited it as one of their favorite Van Halen albums.

As much as Roth and Eddie didn't get along, in all likelihood they were probably scared that they wouldn't get anywhere without each other. When Gene Simmons first tried to get Van Halen a record deal in the '70s, Roth kept Eddie away from Simmons as much as possible. Apparently, Simmons wanted Eddie to join Kiss, and Roth was terrified at the prospect of losing the golden guitarist right as Van Halen was on the verge of breaking through.

As Eddie's legend as a guitarist grew, Roth also tried to prevent him from performing on other people's albums. In April 1983, Eddie recorded two tracks with Queen guitarist Brian May for a side project called *Star Fleet Project,* and he performed a solo on pop singer Nicolette Larson's 1978 debut (Ted Templeman produced her album).

One day in 1982, Eddie got a call from Quincy Jones, who was producing the new Michael Jackson album and asked Eddie to come down to the studio and play a solo for a song called "Beat It." At the time, Roth was out of town on an excursion with a group of adventure-seekers he organized called the Jungle Studs. Eddie agreed to come down to the studio, and nailed the solo in two takes, a job he did for free. Who would know? Little did anyone suspect that the album he contributed to, *Thriller,* would become the biggest-selling album in history. Years after the fact, Roth claimed that if he had known about the Michael Jackson session, he wouldn't have had a problem with Eddie playing on it because he respected Quincy Jones. "Don't waste it on Gene Simmons or Nicolette Larson," he wrote in his autobiography. Roth wasn't impressed with the guitarist's performance on the *Thriller* album regardless. "What did Edward do with Michael Jackson?" he asked. "He played the same solo he's been playing in this band for ten years. Big fucking deal!"

Van Halen's last album with Roth, *1984,* was an unprecedented triumph for the band. Ed had written the song "Jump" back in 1980 and wanted to record it then, but Roth told him repeatedly, "You're a guitar hero—no one wants to hear you play keyboards." But Eddie believed in the song and persevered.

When Eddie was writing the *1984* album, he lied to the band, telling them he had writer's block. He claimed the only song he could come up with was "Jump," which forced them to include it on the album. "Jump" became the band's only No. 1 single and spent five weeks at the top of the charts. *1984* was a huge smash and ultimately sold more than seven million copies.

With the success of *1984* and the "Jump" single, Van Halen hit the road. When Roth entered the tour bus, if he discovered there were too many blondes on board, he'd order them off—he didn't want to compete with anyone else's hair. Supposedly, bands with blond singers were banned from opening for Van Halen. Twisted Sister's Dee Snider even considered dying his hair for the slot. Autograph, whose singer was a redhead, was picked as the opening act.

Roth also dictated that no wives were allowed on tour, though Eddie had been married to actress Valerie Bertinelli for three years. They met backstage at a gig in 1980 and married a year later. But Roth wanted Van Halen to keep up their playboy bachelor image. When *Life* magazine went on tour with the band for a feature story, Roth insisted that Bertinelli not accompany them. She stayed home, hurt by the snub. Roth often took cheap shots at Bertinelli in the press and compared her to David St. Hubbins's fictional Yoko-esque girlfriend in *This Is Spinal Tap*. According to Eddie, when Bertinelli came backstage to meet him for the first time, Roth hit on her first but was rebuffed. Eddie also thought that Roth was jealous that he was dating an actress. Another possible explanation for Roth's dislike of Bertinelli is that she encouraged her husband to stand up to him. Roth bullied Eddie a lot, and Bertinelli felt he wanted to keep Eddie miserable so he could control him—not an unreasonable suspicion.

After the *1984* tour, Roth put together a solo EP called *Crazy From the Heat*. The record was all cover tunes, which Roth loved to sing, and his video for "Just a Gigolo / I Ain't Got Nobody" became a huge hit on MTV. When Van Halen played the Monsters of Rock festival in 1984, Roth spent a lot of time with Dio keyboardist Claude Schnell. Schnell thought David was trying to put as much on his plate as possible. He never got the impression that Roth was going to jump ship. "He either didn't anticipate the success of the EP, or that it would cause the rift in the band that it did," says Schnell.

Schnell felt a breakup with Van Halen was not only something Roth didn't foresee but something he didn't want. "I think David [is] a modest guy, if you can believe that. I don't think he considered himself a tremendous singer . . . and I think he knew damn well that his success [rested] on the shoulders of Van Halen, not the other way around.

"When a band is at a stage that Van Halen was at that point, when a band has a No. 1 hit and a No. 1 album, egos are running wild. And a band's frontman typically has the biggest ego. There's no greater untapped resource than the ego of a musician, and typically this is true of frontmen. But in Van Halen, who was the frontman? David or Eddie?"

While the Los Angeles area was becoming known as a hotbed for metal, bands on the East Coast were being offered major-label deals as well. Twisted Sister was one of several New York bands that inked deals during the L.A. metal explosion of 1983. Atlantic (who had also signed Ratt) picked up Zebra and Twisted Sister, both from Long Island. Twisted Sister had spent much of the 1970s slugging it out as a top draw in the Long Island clubs. Most record labels passed on them more than once; in fact, Atlantic had previously rejected their demos five times. Lead singer Dee Snider had a tattoo on his arm that read, *"Illegitimus non carborundum est,"* Latin for, "Never let the bastards get you down." It was this mentality that kept the band going during the tough times and finally brought them success.

Twisted Sister's look was heavily influenced by the 1979 film *The Warriors,* about New York street gangs trying to take over the city. (One of the gangs, the Baseball Furies, even wore makeup like Kiss.) With his long mane of blond curly hair and heavy stage makeup, Snider was an imposing figure on stage. He never took any crap from the audience either. He'd brawl at the drop of a dime and give you nine cents change. If anyone heckled the band, he'd jump off stage and beat up the offender. He became famous in August 1982 for saying he'd take on all 30,000 fans at the Reading Festival in England if they didn't stop throwing things at the band. It earned Twisted Sister instant respect in England.

Snider had a mouth that would embarrass a longshoreman. If you came to a Twisted Sister show and weren't ready to rock, there was hell to pay. In their club days, Snider would single out people in the audience who clearly weren't enjoying the show, put the spotlight on them, and cuss them out. At one show, Snider swore at the entire balcony section for several minutes because they wouldn't get on their feet for the band like the fans in front of the stage. After the show, the manager informed him it was the handicapped section.

On the other hand, there was nothing Snider wouldn't do for the fans who supported Twisted Sister. At a club show in Long Island, bassist Mark Mendoza walked past a line of fans waiting to get in. Snider stopped him dead in his tracks. Why didn't he sign any autographs? Why didn't he give out any backstage passes? Snider told Mendoza that if he didn't get back to the fans and spend time with them immediately, he'd be fired after the show. Even years after the band's demise, Snider always made time for his fans.

The band's first album for Atlantic, 1983's *You Can't Stop Rock 'n' Roll*, featured solid songs, including the title cut and the anthem "The Kids Are Back," but the record didn't break through commercially. It wasn't until 1984's *Stay Hungry*, which featured "We're Not Gonna Take It," that the band finally smashed into the big time, albeit with a heavy assist from MTV. When Marty Callner decided to start directing music videos, he met with Atlantic's Ahmet Ertegun, who offered Callner several bands, including INXS, but Callner chose to work with Twisted Sister.

Twisted Sister's songs were anthems for the underdog, and the "We're Not Gonna Take It" video, perfectly, as well as hilariously, embodied their struggle. It was something millions of teenagers could relate to— an abusive father screaming at his kid. This was a scenario that Snider recreated from his own youth. "My father was not the most sensitive guy in the world," he says. "He caused my brother to have an ulcer at eleven years old, then gave him worry beads for his birthday."

The kid in the video for "We're Not Gonna Take It" eventually transforms into Dee Snider, who takes revenge on the father, physically abusing him throughout the song and blowing him out the window by striking a power chord on his guitar. "We're Not Gonna Take It" was cited by the Parents Music Resource Center as one of the most violent videos on MTV, though the violence was taken directly from Wile E. Coyote cartoons. Although the song never made it to the Top Ten, it's still remembered nearly twenty years after its release, thanks to the power of MTV. Without question, it is one of the decade's most memorable videos; scenes usually pop up on 1980s retro specials.

"If ever there was a video band, [Twisted Sister] was it," says Callner. "They couldn't play too well, they weren't really good looking, [and] they were about to get dropped [from their label]. With the video, they sold three and a half million records. It was extraordinary."

Yet Twisted Sister was not the overnight sensation their massive exposure on MTV would lead one to believe. It took them six years of playing clubs before they signed with Atlantic and another two years before they broke. They just happened to break *big.* "I'm always tickled when people tell me our success was luck," says Snider. "Eight years, over two thousand live shows before you got a deal . . . that's not luck. That's never say die, refusing to give up, and refusing to accept any negative vibes."

Twisted Sister rapidly became a pop-culture phenomenon. In 1985, Snider was given the honor of being the first metal musician to present a Grammy Award. But with all the media attention focused on Snider, many of the band's original fans believed he'd "gone Hollywood." Snider thought he was an average guy who was enjoying his newfound fame. "I was viewed as selling out and going mainstream," he said, "whereas I viewed it as the ugly guy fucking the beautiful *Playboy* model." MTV usually rejected bands for being unattractive, so Snider considered it a major victory that an unattractive band like Twisted Sister could thrive on the network. He felt the band "pioneered ugly way before it was in vogue."

Snider was a true metal fan, and he was always eager to support the cause. He couldn't stand the new wave bands that were all over MTV in the 1980s, and continually insulted them in his usual foulmouthed style. "All those bands, fuckin' Boy George, Wham! I used to slam the shit out of them," he says. But Snider rarely took swipes at other metal bands. "You work too hard, and everybody's trying. It's tough enough out there without taking shots from your brethren."

In 1985, Twisted Sister followed up *Stay Hungry* with *Come Out and Play*, a title taken from a line in *The Warriors*. *Play* cost more than $300,000 to record. The album featured an expensive pop-up cover, with Snider coming out of a manhole. The first single, a cover of "Leader of the Pack," didn't fare well, so the label stopped promoting it, and the album ultimately tanked. The tour for *Come Out and Play* was canceled after only eighteen shows.

With Dee Snider's overexposure in the press and on MTV, Twisted Sister had lost credibility with their fans. Just as when Alice Cooper began appearing in public without makeup and playing golf with Groucho Marx, metal fans were disappointed to see that Snider wasn't the monster he appeared to be onstage. "I went from being scary to being cute," he says. "I was getting fan letters from girls in *16 Magazine* saying my favorite bands are Duran Duran, Kajagoogoo, and Twisted Sister. I'm goin', Uh oh. Problem here, major problem."

Metal's hardcore underground fans always work hard to promote their favorite bands, telling anyone who'd listen how great they are, and hoping and praying that the bands becomes the successes they deserve to be. But these are usually the first fans to abandon ship when the band finally does become successful; their favorite band is often about more than just the music. Many of the teenagers who listened to heavy metal throughout the '70s and '80s didn't fit in at school, didn't have a good home life, couldn't figure out their place in the grand scheme of things.

The music helped them through difficult times and made them feel as if they weren't the only ones feeling this way. So when a metal band became popular with the jocks and cheerleaders, or became too commercial, or changed too drastically, many of those fans felt as though they had been stabbed in the back.

Dee Snider understood the point of view of the die-hard fans. "All of the sudden, when the band breaks, you feel like something is taken from you," he said. "Suddenly you've been violated in some strange way. I did it with AC/DC! I did it with Queen! I'd done it to my bands, and then the fans did it to me!" (James Hetfield once joked that when Metallica's "Black" album became a crossover smash, he stopped listening to it.)

Twisted Sister broke up in 1987, after their fourth album, *Love Is for Suckers,* was all but dead on arrival in stores. After the band's demise, Snider found himself deeply in debt and didn't leave his house for a year. It took a lot of therapy and his family's support to finally bring Snider out of his depression. "As crazy as things got on the high side or the low side, I've always had my family to return to," says Snider, who has been with his wife Suzette since high school. "I had my first kid pretty young, but it's kinda cool, 'cause now we go to see Pantera and Nine Inch Nails together, and it's righteous! It's also kept me very level and focused."

The wounds from Twisted Sister's breakup took a long time to heal. (Only recently, after twelve years of animosity, have the band members been speaking to each other again.) Snider eventually began working on a solo career. His first band, Desperado, snagged a deal with Elektra, but a day before Snider was set to shoot the first video, the label pulled the plug and shelved the album. He spent a year in court to get out of his contract. He wanted to use several of the songs he wrote for Desperado with his new band, Widowmaker, but was forced to pay Elektra $40,000 each to use them.

Unlike many '80s musicians, Snider says he's not ashamed of his past. But, he says, the past has a way of coming back to haunt you. "I don't wanna bury it, but I am trying to distance myself from it. The '90s is the first decade I've seen where people have made a clean break from the last decade. I don't remember anybody trying to reject the '60s wholesale, same thing with the '70s. I'm constantly dealing with the fact that I'm an '80s artist and I'm trying to say, I'm not an '80s artist—I'm an artist."

Little by little, it has become cool to admit you were a Twisted Sister fan. At Woodstock '94, Green Day teased the crowd with "We're Not Gonna Take It." Snider relished the fact that all 400,000 fans in attendance still remembered the words and sang along. He is proud of what Twisted Sister accomplished when they were together.

"I'm sure there's a picture or two of me wearing something that might look a little embarrassing in twenty years, but I like to think that I'll probably just laugh, as I laugh now." One day, Snider's youngest son saw a picture of his old man in full stage makeup. "Look, Mommy," he said. "There's Daddy when he used to be a monster."

The explosion of metal and hard rock in the 1980s brought a plethora of young guitarists who wanted to play the hottest new instruments. The new guitar companies that manufactured these "hot-rod guitars" threatened to put the classic guitar companies, such as Gibson and Fender, out of business. Jackson, B. C. Rich, and Kramer were three companies that seemed to come out of nowhere to dominate the industry. Their instruments were considered the new "dream guitars" of the '80s. B. C. Rich, which designed such radical guitar models as the Warlock and the Mockingbird, was used by guitarists Joe Perry and Rick Derringer throughout the 1970s, and were now being used by Mötley Crüe, W.A.S.P., and many other '80s bands. Eddie Van Halen endorsed Kramer guitars, boosting annual sales from $1 million to $15 million within several years. Having Van Halen endorse your guitar was "instant credibility that would take other companies years to achieve," according to Henry Vaccaro, former chairman of the board of Kramer.

Having a hot guitarist playing your instrument was just as important as a basketball star wearing your shoes. Musicians knew they could get a lot of free gear from these companies, and many took it by the truckload. These players were often known as "guitar whores" by the guitar-making community. Dean Zelinsky, the founder of Dean Guitars, another popular hot-rod guitar company, observed that the guitar-whore phenomenon became so bad that he'd see a musician using his guitar on one page of a magazine, turn a few pages, and see the same musician endorsing someone else's guitar. Zelinsky preferred using scantily clad women in his ads. "You played the guitar so you could get laid," he said. "We found out that a hot chick sold more guitars than a hot rock star."

Countless fine guitarists came out of the hard rock and metal genre, and many are remembered by only their fans and fellow musicians. Only a handful of guitarists, like Eddie Van Halen, were truly revolutionary. Yngwie Malmsteen was one guitarist who, when he broke on the scene in the 1980s, had the potential to rewrite history as well.

Malmsteen was born in Sweden (he claimed his first name means "young Viking chief"). As his legend goes, he was seven years old when he saw the news of Jimi Hendrix's death on September 18, 1970. That same day he picked up a guitar and began playing. He played until his fingers ached, then reinforced them with Band-Aids and kept playing.

Malmsteen was also obsessed with classical music from an early age. He worshipped J. S. Bach and Niccolò Paganini, a violinist born in Genoa, Italy, in 1782. Paganini's music was startlingly challenging and innovative, even by today's standards, and Malmsteen wanted to follow in his footsteps. "What this guy does with a violin in the Caprice No. 24—that's extreme," said Malmsteen. "There's no guitar player in the world who can do that. His way of playing the violin was kind of the way I wanted to play guitar."

Not only was Malmsteen's playing innovative—it was incredibly fast, clean, and precise. He would play arpeggios, chords played one note at a time. He knew his way around the instrument and taught himself countless "broken chords," as he called them, all over the neck in every key. He was also one of the first musicians to use a picking technique called "sweep picking." Often when guitarists play fast, it's done with "alternate picking" or picking up and down one note at a time. With a single upstroke or downstroke of his pick, Malmsteen could hit several notes in sequence. With a surgeon's precision and with minimal pick movement, he could glide through a wide succession of notes very quickly.

Malmsteen's playing was also incredibly musical. The true test of his skill could be appreciated when his music was slowed down. Other 1980s guitarists who tried to play fast like him sounded terrible when slowed down, their licks making no musical sense. All of Malmsteen's solos made sense whether played slowly or at blinding speed.

With a strong taste for classical music, Malmsteen didn't care much for other rock guitarists, with the exception of players like Jimi Hendrix and Ritchie Blackmore, and he angered a lot of people when he said so in interviews. With his poofy hair and stuffy demeanor, he often came across like a classical musician stuck in a heavy metal time warp.

Malmsteen moved to America in 1982, when he was nineteen. Often a really hot guitar player could carry an average metal band, and this was the case when he joined Steeler. The band had a huge L.A. following, mostly because of Malmsteen. The band was merely a stepping-stone for him to establish himself. He next joined a band named Alcatrazz, only to quit before they recorded their second album (he was replaced by Steve Vai). By the time he formed a solo band in 1984, Yngwie Malmsteen's Rising Force, he had made the cover of *Guitar Player,* at the age of twenty-one. Just as Eric Clapton's fans named him the new guitar messiah two decades before, Malmsteen's fans wore T-shirts to his gigs that read: "Yngwie is God."

Because of Malmsteen's popularity, many guitar players rushed to learn music theory and develop advanced techniques. But instead of creating their own style of music, they simply tried to play faster than their idol. Players practiced his licks endlessly, but few were able to produce any significant innovations on his technique. This copycat phenomenon only fed Malmsteen's growing contempt for his fellow metal musicians.

Besides his musical prowess, Malmsteen was also known for his gigantic ego, which couldn't be measured with existing technology. His arrogance and rock-star temper tantrums are legendary. When he played a club in Phoenix Arizona, called the Mason Jar, a large pole was several feet away from the stage, and Malmsteen said, "The pole's gotta go, or I don't play." The pole didn't go—it held up the ceiling. Another time, at a concert to raise money for charity, Malmsteen ordered the band Faster Pussycat out of the venue's only dressing room, forcing the band to change in a laundry room. Malmsteen played only one song that night. Joe Lynn Turner, the guitarist's lead singer in the late 1980s, said, "Malmsteen and I broke up over religious reasons. He thought he was God, and I didn't agree."

Journalist Steve Rosen wrote a positive story on Malmsteem for *Guitar World* magazine in 1984. The magazine's editors titled the article "The God With a Chip on His Shoulder." Malmsteen was furious about the title and took it out on Rosen one night soon after at a party, verbally abusing him. With one punch, the small and usually timid Rosen knocked the guitarist to the floor. The next day, Rosen's answering machine was full of people congratulating him.

Malmsteen's luck took a much graver turn in 1987, when he was in a car accident that almost killed him. The accident left him with brain and nerve damage, and he was lucky to come out of it alive, let alone be able to play guitar again. In later years, he was arrested for allegedly abusing his girlfriend (the charges were later dismissed) and was forced to file for bankruptcy.

Malmsteen would enjoy a strong following in Japan and other foreign territories well into the '90s, but he never was able to break into the U.S. market in a big way. Billy Sheehan, whose band Talas opened for Malmsteen, says: "Unfortunately, as bad of a reputation as Yngwie has, his reputation is worse than he really [is]. The tragedy of the whole thing is he was probably one of the best [guitarists] there ever was, and due to whatever personality conflicts [people had with him], he lost whatever credit he could've gotten. A lot of musicians took a lot of [techniques] from him. He came out with about five or six major new guitar moves that were stolen by everybody that he never got credit for."

Sheehan felt that Malmsteem reinvented the guitar rule book to the same extent as Eddie Van Halen did. "Unfortunately, he didn't have the vehicle of Van Halen. He didn't have the personality of Eddie, the salesmanship of Dave, and the songs of Van Halen. If he would have, it would have been a different story."

Right as Malmsteen's career was peaking, Sheehan's career was on the verge of a breakthrough. He had been struggling in the clubs in his native Buffalo for over ten years with his band Talas. Sheehan put all the money he made into his gear. For years he drove around in a Pinto with the tiny emergency spare tire intended to be used only until you made it to the nearest gas station.

But in a single day, Sheehan's luck changed completely. Talas finally got an offer from Gold Mountain Entertainment, which had major distribution (Danny Goldberg, who went on to manage Nirvana, ran the label). Then the music department at William Morris called, wanting to represent the band. The next time the phone rang, it was David Lee Roth's office. Talas was about to go on tour, opening for Yngwie Malmsteen's Rising Force. Roth wanted to see Sheehan as soon as he arrived in Los Angeles.

The day before Sheehan was to leave for Los Angeles, he called Eddie Van Halen. Van Halen often toured with unsigned bands, and Talas opened forty shows on Van Halen's tour for the *Women and Children First* album in 1980. Ironically, Eddie even considered replacing bassist Michael Anthony with Sheehan. Sheehan and Eddie remained friends and stayed in contact with each other. Sheehan thought it was a little strange that Roth called him but didn't think much of it.

Sheehan told Eddie that Talas was going to be in town and invited him to the show, at the Hollywood Palladium. "I don't know if I can make it, but I'll try," said Eddie.

"You know, Dave called."

"What? You're kidding."

"No, I'm not."

"Okay . . . I gotta tell you—don't tell anybody, right? We fired the fucker."

Sheehan couldn't believe it.

"Hey, do me a favor," said Eddie. "After you have a meeting with him, call me up. We wanna find out what he's doing now."

Although Eddie told Sheehan that they had fired Roth, the band publicly announced that Roth had quit. "They changed it because they figured they'd lose face with their fans if they said he was fired," says Sheehan. "But then again, maybe he *did* quit. Who knows? The truth lies somewhere in between in situations like that." Often in band breakups, the exact details are unclear, even to the principles involved.

Once word got out that Roth had left the band, the fans were shocked. Van Halen were one of the greatest party bands in the universe, and the fact that Roth and the rest of the band hated each other was kept well hidden from the public.

"The audience loves to see pain up there," said Roth. "But [they] don't know where it's coming from. They have no idea that between the band members it can be miserable. . . .

"People ask, 'Was it fun, Dave?' It was never fun. I'm one of those people who's not happy unless he's miserable. We were all that way at the time. Furious. That's why the celebrations took on a highly dialed-up tone. It was the only release for that fury. On the stage and in the studio it was absolutely explosive."

The day Sheehan arrived in Los Angeles, June 4, 1985, he visited David Lee Roth's mansion in Pasadena. Roth told him that he had quit Van Halen and wanted Sheehan to be his partner in a new band. Sheehan was faced with the most difficult decision of his life. It was the first night of the Talas tour; everyone in the band was pumped up knowing they were about to get signed. But Roth had offered Sheehan the gig of a lifetime. When he got back to the hotel, Sheehan realized that if he called Eddie and told him about his meeting with Roth, he'd violate the deal he had just made with Roth. He didn't call Eddie back. Sheehan decided to join David's solo band and never looked back.

Only a handful of guitar players were considered for Roth's new band, including former Billy Idol guitarist Steve Stevens. Steve Vai, whom Sheehan recommended, eventually got the job. Vai had attended the prestigious Berklee School of Music in Boston when he was a teenager. He joined Frank Zappa's band at the age of twenty, was able to handle Zappa's complex musical arrangements and demands. Vai eventually replaced Yngwie Malmsteen in Alcatrazz, another situation that would have terrified most guitarists.

Vai probably forgot more about music theory than many musicians ever learned; Sheehan was completely self-taught. He learned to play by ear, practicing endlessly to absorb everything he could. As Sheehan once put it, "Steve will say, 'It's that E demented, cemented, fermented chord,' and I say, 'Oh, you mean this,' and I play a chord that I saw Jimi Hendrix do in the *Woodstock* movie."

After auditioning more than two hundred drummers, Roth settled on Greg Bissonette, one of the hottest session musicians around, and now had the best band he could possibly put together. There was no question he wanted to leave Van Halen in the dust.

The general consensus within the music industry was that Van Halen would go down the toilet without Roth. "I'm bummed for Van Halen now that they've thrown everything away," Sheehan said at the time. Most of the people who had been part of the Van Halen organization decided to jump ship and work for Roth as a solo artist. Eddie didn't get along with Ted Templeman anymore, so Roth asked him to produce his first full-blown solo effort. Eddie even lost Rudy Leiren, who had been his guitar technician since 1973.

With his new band gaining momentum, Roth told *Circus* magazine that he'd never go back to Van Halen. "No, there's no chance we'll ever get back together. Too much shit has come down, and you know, once you leave, you can never go home again."

After the breakup, Eddie Van Halen had no idea what to do. At a National Association of Music Merchants convention with Ted Nugent, Eddie suddenly began crying over Roth leaving. Not known for his sensitivity in delicate situations, Nugent said, "I oughta pull out my gun and shoot you right now." Nugent told Eddie to get a new singer and snap out of it. He tried to convince him that Van Halen would continue without Roth, that Eddie was the star, that *he* was the one the fans were coming to see.

At first, after Roth's departure, Eddie considered doing a solo album that would feature a different singer on each song. But once Eddie was introduced to Sammy Hagar, they hit if off right away. Hagar had sung with the band Montrose, who played the stadium festival circuit regularly in the '70s and were known for the AOR radio hits "Bad Motor Scooter" and "Rock Candy."

Hagar had a big, strong voice with an ego to match. He and Eddie quickly became best friends, and Hagar would soon buy a house two doors down from Eddie in Malibu. For the first time in a long time, Van Halen had fun in the recording studio and new songs were written quickly, keeping the vibe fresh. Van Halen would call their next album *5150*, the police code for the criminally insane.

Although the new music sounded great, Warner Bros. wasn't convinced that Van Halen would fly without Roth. Lenny Waronker, then president of the label, even wanted them to drop the name Van Halen. Eddie refused. There were also legal complications with Hagar—he had a solo deal with Geffen Records and still owed them albums on his contract. David Geffen did not want Hagar to leave, since he was one of the only hit artists on the struggling label. A bitter feud resulted between Geffen and Warner Bros. chairman Mo Ostin over the Hagar custody battle.

Van Halen was so desperate to play with Hagar that they briefly considered calling themselves *Sammy Hagar*, effectively becoming his backup band, which would release everyone from their contractual restraints. A compromise was eventually reached. Sammy was free to go to Van

Halen on the conditions that he would deliver three more solo albums to Geffen and that the label would get a hefty sales percentage of the *5150* album.

Meanwhile, with his new band in place, Roth was ready to show the world what he could do. Roth called his solo album *Eat 'Em and Smile,* a title that, of course, was open to multiple interpretations. Most felt it was a knock against his former band, which Roth denied, saying he saw the phrase on a watermelon sticker. When *Guitar World* reviewed *5150* and *Eat 'Em* in the same issue, the accompanying cartoon showed a bare-chested Roth at a dinner table chomping on Eddie's striped guitar.

Ted Templeman produced the *Eat 'Em and Smile* album, and it was not a meticulous process. Like the early Van Halen days, Roth and his new band went for raw energy. Templeman didn't want to overproduce the album, and the band had to go into the studio and deliver right on the spot. As Steve Vai recalls, "When I listen to those tracks now, I think, 'Jeez, man, I was able to do that in one take, the whole song.' And I'm very proud of that." *Eat 'Em and Smile* took about a month to record and ran thirty-three minutes long. Roth clearly wanted his debut effort to be fast and in-your-face. The songs on the album were written to be numbers in what was to be Roth's feature-film debut, a musical called *Crazy From the Heat.* With MTV bringing out a new level of ham in many rock stars, several bands, including Twisted Sister, considered making films. Roth was a natural for the silver screen, and as his career was at its peak, a film with him starring could have been a big hit. A month before *Crazy* was to commence principal photography, CBS Pictures, the company financing the film, shut down. Roth sued CBS Pictures and won, then shopped the project to other companies. But he balked at having the script rewritten or having to make another movie first as a test, and after over a year of preparation, his hopes of becoming a movie star were dashed.

Van Halen's *5150* would come out first, on March 24, 1986. *Eat 'Em and Smile* came out on July 4. Everyone was waiting to see which would fare better. Both albums were chops-heavy, and Steve Vai and Billy

Sheehan both made the covers of *Guitar Player* and *Guitar World* (Sheehan was one of the few bassists to ever make the cover of *Guitar Player*).

Both Sheehan and Vai kept pretty dry during the Van Halen/Roth pissing contest. "I wasn't trying to compete with Edward," says Vai. "I adored the guy. He did more for rock guitar playing than anybody. I loved the way he played, and I liked him as a person. Unfortunately, because of the situation, I could never communicate those things to him."

As Van Halen prepared to head out on the road that March, there were some notable changes. The band would perform only four old Van Halen songs each night at most, including "You Really Got Me," "Panama," and "Ain't Talkin' 'Bout Love." In what was no doubt a response to Roth's taunt about having to play "Jump" every night, Van Halen played the song only a handful of times during the tour. And to make sure they weren't making it easy on themselves, the band would shoot no videos for *5150*. Eddie Van Halen wanted the music to stand on its own without a flashy video drawing attention away from it.

5150 went to No. 1 on the charts, the band's first No. 1 album, and the tour was a sold-out success. *5150* sold more than five million copies. *Eat 'Em and Smile* peaked at No. 4 and went platinum.

After *5150* topped the charts, Eddie said, "It shows me that music overpowers bullshit. Dave and I wrote a lot of good stuff and made a lot of good music together, but I guess the clowning and the show-biz part of it only works and helps so much. What's on that tape is what counts. Bottom line. And our going to No. 1 proves that."

As the press war between Roth and Van Halen became increasingly vicious, the band asked Hagar not to bash Roth onstage. But one night a pro-Roth banner was thrown onstage, and Hagar burned it with a cigarette lighter. He threw the flaming banner behind Eddie's amp line, and it landed on his new guitar technician. The die-hard Van Halen fans were not coping well with the loss of Roth, and Hagar-bashing became popular. Howard Stern called him "Hagar the horrible."

Yet Van Halen with Sammy Hagar continued its streak of every album going at least platinum. Along with AC/DC, the band would manage one of hard rock's few successful lead-singer transplants. There would be no worry of Roth coming back—Van Halen was doing just fine without him.

On the first night of the *Eat 'Em and Smile* tour, in Huntsville, Alabama, Vai was scared to death. All eyes were on him because he was widely seen as Eddie Van Halen's replacement. Roth told Vai to imagine that the anxiety he was feeling was a drug and he was getting off on it. Once the band stepped onstage and ripped into the first song, the Van Halen classic "On Fire," the audience immediately embraced them.

"The audience was screaming so loud, I thought someone was playing a joke on me," says Vai. "The pitch of the audience was so intense, I thought it was being broadcast into my ears from the speakers. There was one point where Billy and I looked at each other, and we just started crying. It was what you always thought or hoped being a rock star would be." Later in the evening, a crew brought out a giant video camera. Roth told the audience, "You're all gonna be in our new video!" and everyone went crazy. There was no film in the camera; Roth did it every night to hype up the crowd.

The band's set list usually contained numerous Van Halen songs, including "On Fire," "Panama," "Pretty Woman," "Unchained," "Ice Cream Man," "Hot for Teacher," and "You Really Got Me." "Jump," the song Roth swore he'd never sing again, was played every night of the tour.

Vai and Sheehan could deliver incredible musicianship every night, and fans lucky enough to attend the *Eat 'Em and Smile* tour witnessed something special. "You couldn't see a better combination than what you saw up on that stage; there wasn't a slacker among them," says Billy Sheehan's personal manager, Mike Fahley. "Roth had assembled a great, great band. They delivered on record, and they delivered on tour. To this day, people [are still] talking about those shows."

"It was a fantastic band, and it was a fantastic time to be doing what we were doing," says Vai. "We were young, we could wear wild clothes, we did costume changes all night, we could do crazy things with our hair, and we could play the shit out of our instruments. That's the thing that I miss in today's music. I just don't see that anymore." Great chemistry is one of the most difficult things for any band to achieve. Successful combinations like Van Halen are one in a million, but with Roth's solo band, he came close to repeating the trick. It was not to last long.

In 1988, Roth followed up *Eat 'Em and Smile* with *Skyscraper,* a departure from his first album. *Skyscraper* was slick and polished. Every detail and nuance was micromanaged, stifling the reckless abandon of the first album. Sheehan hated the *Skyscraper* album. He was one of the most talented bass players in rock but was given few opportunities to shine on the album. He left the band soon after the album was finished; Vai followed him after the tour.

By this time, Roth no longer looked like the young rock stud he had been in Van Halen's glory days. He had gained weight and was losing his hair. The rule became that when working for Roth, there were three things you never mentioned around him, at the risk of being fired: his movie career, his hairline, and Van Halen. Where Roth's solo career had once seemed limitless, now leaving Van Halen landed him on the "Bad Career Move" list in *People* magazine, along with David Caruso of *NYPD Blue* and Mike Tyson. Roth's entry read: "With the inevitable split in '85, Eddie got custody of the career."

Sheehan now believes that if David Lee Roth's first solo band had stayed together and remained true to its original vision, the music scene wouldn't be what it is today. Vai feels that no matter what happened to the band, Kurt Cobain and Eddie Vedder would have come along to lead the rebellion against the 1980s, but Roth's band would still be in good shape. "We'd be selling out the Sahara Desert right now," he says.

After Sheehan and Vai left his band, Roth was never able to get his solo career back on track. Unable to reinvent himself, his schtick, which had seemed so fresh and fun, became a wrenching self-parody. Roth even played Las Vegas for two weeks in 1995; some in the audience booed him when he took verbal swats at Van Halen onstage. Roth needed an audience to entertain, and without one he was lost.

"I really think David Lee Roth suffered in the quiet moments when he was alone," says John McBurnie, the longtime doorman at the famous Rainbow Bar and Grill on Sunset Boulevard. Roth was a Rainbow regular and was rarely alone there. But if his friends hadn't arrived yet or had left the table to say hello to someone else, Roth's usual happy façade would fade into sadness. "Then when he'd make eye contact with somebody, he'd just light up. The closer you walked toward him, he just got brighter and brighter."

Along with the resurgence of heavy metal in the mid-1980s, the Rainbow Bar and Grill was enjoying a rebirth as well. A true rock and roll restaurant if there ever was one, the Rainbow was such a wild scene in its heyday that, as one regular put it, "You walked in the place, you got VD."

The Rainbow was owned and operated by Mario Maglieri. As a teenager, Maglieri had made deliveries for a Chicago brewery that was once owned by Al Capone. At various times in his life, he worked as a plumber, court bailiff, and saloon owner. Maglieri met up with Elmer Valentine, a retired policeman, in 1963, when Valentine came out to California to open the Whisky. Mario became the manager and eventually Elmer's partner at the club (Maglieri currently owns the Whisky).

The restaurant that became the Rainbow opened in the mid-1930s under the name Villa Nova. It was supposedly the first restaurant to open on Sunset Boulevard and was most famous as the location where Joe DiMaggio and Marilyn Monroe met on a blind date. It officially reopened as the Rainbow Bar and Grill in 1972, with Mick Jagger's birthday party a key event to kick things off.

It didn't take the Rainbow long to gain its rock and roll reputation. When Led Zeppelin came to L.A. on tour in the early 1970s, they realized, judging by the selection of girls at the Whisky, that their old hang-out wasn't happening anymore. So the members of Led Zeppelin went up the street to the Rainbow and kept going there for years. Zeppelin's tour manager, Richard Cole, often phoned the Rainbow from the Star-ship to reserve their favorite tables. If the band was in town for the week, no one was allowed to sit at the table until the band arrived.

Former Guns N' Roses guitarist Slash first started sneaking into the Rainbow as a teenager. He made fake IDs in his graphic arts class for himself and Steven Adler, who eventually joined Slash in Guns N' Roses. Adler got in fine with his ID, but Slash was turned away at the door. Realizing it was Ladies Night, Slash went home and put on his mother's clothes. He wore a dress and tucked his long hair up into a hat. The disguise worked, and once he was allowed entry, Slash thought about hitting on Steven to see if he'd try to pick him up. But when he realized Steven had already gone home with a girl, and that he was standing in the middle of the Rainbow in drag, Slash fled. The walk up the Strip afterward was terrifying. Every time a passing car honked it's horn, he practically had a heart attack. By the time Slash reached his car, he had torn off all his clothes except for a pair of shorts he had on underneath the dress. (When Guns N' Roses had their breakthrough years later, the DJ at the upstairs bar would play "Sweet Child O' Mine" to signal last call.)

Throughout the 1980s, the Rainbow was where a conquering rock star would go after a sold-out show at the Forum to celebrate and get laid. Table 14, in front of the fireplace (where Maglieri still eats with his wife), is the big-shot table. Table 6, in a quiet corner of the restaurant, was Guns N' Roses' favorite table because it could fit the entire band and plenty of girls.

If you were a struggling musician and hadn't made it yet, the Rain-bow was a great place to pretend you were somebody. For most of the '80s, half the patrons could have passed for Vince Neil. "I'm in a band," whether you were actually in one or not, was a popular pickup line.

"Around 11 o'clock, the place would be mobbed with every cartoon character in heavy metal," recalls Byron Hontas, who was a Rainbow regular. "Those who make it happen, those who think they make it happen, and those who wonder what happened!" If you ran up to David Lee Roth breathlessly asking for an autograph, it was clear you didn't belong. Everybody at the Rainbow had to be as cool as Roth was.

In 1985, journalist Lonn Friend received his introduction to the world of heavy metal when he was assigned to write about the Rainbow for *Hustler* magazine. With tape recorder in hand, Friend interviewed numerous hard rock slobs who spoke freely about the sex and debauchery inside the restaurant. One patron spoke of getting a blow job on the crowded dance floor upstairs ("No one cared, I dug it"); another talked about walking into the bathroom and seeing a girl snorting cocaine off the paper-towel dispenser ("Now that's the Rainbow for ya"); the *Hustler* article never made Friend unpopular at the Rainbow; in fact, it increased business.

There are many legends about the Rainbow, and most of them are true. There is a drawer full of watches and jewelry taken from rock and roll yo-yos unable to pay their checks; "I just gave a watch to a waitress the other day," says Maglieri. At one point, the restaurant started using shorter tablecloths because there were too many blow jobs going on underneath the tables. They also had to take out the phone booth from upstairs because too many people were having sex in it. A common scene would have a line of people angrily banging on the door to use the phone while people were having sex inside. "I was in there a few times myself," says John McBurnie.

Maglieri is surprisingly nonchalant about the craziness that still happens at the Rainbow. "We let 'em do what they want here," he says. "We don't like people causing problems, but if they wanna make love in the booth or whatever, we don't bother 'em, you know?"

The wild sexual antics that accompanied many metal bands in the '80s were in many ways the last gasp of the sexual revolution. The specter of

AIDS was already casting its shadow over the music industry. Throughout the 1970s, the clap and crabs were a band's biggest problems. At the end of a tour, band members and crew would usually pile out of the bus into a clinic for a shot and a bottle of A200 anti-crab shampoo. But even syphilis could be deadly if it went untreated. Chris Holmes from W.A.S.P. didn't even realize he was infected until he was told that a woman on her deathbed in San Francisco mentioned his name. When he learned he had the advanced stage of the disease, Holmes had to get injections of over 2.5 million units of penicillin, and when he performed on stage with his bottomless pants, the Band-Aids were visible.

Some bands in the '80s would make it a point to avoid women who performed oral sex on the roadies to get backstage. On Mötley Crüe's *Shout at the Devil* tour, any girl who had been with a roadie was given a laminated backstage pass with "PSP" on it, for "Pre-Show Pussy." The band then avoided these girls. The cover of the band's *Theatre of Pain* album had twin masks of comedy and tragedy. Girls the band members wanted for themselves were given passes bearing a comedy mask. The PSP girls were given passes with a tragedy mask.

David Lee Roth wrote in his autobiography that he stayed away from girls who were blatant groupies. If a woman started the conversation with "Let's go upstairs and fuck," Roth skipped her. "Why fool around?" he reasoned. "Medically, it made a lot more sense." As Warrant's Jerry Dixon recalls, the girls you had to worry about were the ones who stepped on the bus and said: "This looks like a 1989 raise-roof ten. Is this a twelve or a six bunker?"

According to Julia Nine, a former groupie, most groupies were under the spell of the Prince Charming fantasy: marry a rock star, live happily ever after. "These are girls who want to travel, see the world, and live the ultimate exciting life," she says. "A band passing through town on tour was the easiest way out of [their] small-town lives."

Nine found coming from a dysfunctional family to be another common denominator among groupies. "I left home at age sixteen because of family problems, and I've met a lot of others like me," she says.

"Seems we're unfortunately related to the kind of people who make great *Jerry Springer* panelists. When asked to describe my relatives, I sum it up by asking, 'Have you ever seen the movie *Deliverance?*' "

With home video technology becoming popular, some musicians made videos of their sexual exploits. These tapes were traded among their friends like baseball cards. Many bands even installed hidden cameras on their tour buses. Not only would the women not know they were being videotaped—they didn't know the rest of the band and the road crew were watching from a TV monitor at the front of the bus. If the woman asked why the guys at the front of the bus were cheering, the guy she was with would usually say, "Oh, there's a football game on TV." Recently George Lynch admitted that Dokken was one of the bands with hidden cameras on their bus. "May those tapes never resurface!" he said.

The rock and roll life, as most musicians have found out, is often not conducive to long-term relationships and marriage. Even before Slash got married, he was wary of the implications matrimony held. "I thought marriage was just another contract—like I need one," he says. "You don't fulfill your contractual obligations, she can take you to the cleaners, same as a record company." Slash said that he "tried to be married" for the four years he was with his wife Renee Suran. Once he was back out on the road, he would book four or five separate hotel rooms, with a different girl in every room, unbeknownst to one another, and go from room to room all night. "I'd explain, 'Oh, I gotta go for one second. There's a band interview—I'll be right back,' " said Slash.

At the height of metal's popularity, one comedian saw the music and its performers as satiric fruit ripe for picking. Well-known as Michael "Meathead" Stivic on *All in the Family,* Rob Reiner was ready to reinvent himself as a film director, and *This Is Spinal Tap* was his debut.

The film was a "mockumentary"—a fictitious story that was supposed to look like a documentary with interviews, "real" concert footage, and backstage shenanigans. Reiner appeared in the film as Marty DiBergi, a documentary filmmaker who is chronicling the attempted comeback of a has-been English metal band named Spiñal Tap.

It took Reiner four and a half years to sell the concept for *This Is Spiñal Tap.* He showed a twenty-minute reel to studio executives, but most didn't understand the concept or find the idea funny. Reiner finally sold the film to Avco Embassy, which had been bought by a group of investors including Norman Lear, the man who gave Rob his big break on *All in the Family.*

The comedians who portrayed the members of Spiñal Tap were Michael McKean, the lanky blonde who played Lenny on *Laverne and Shirley,* Christopher Guest, a writer on *Saturday Night Live,* and political satirist Harry Shearer, who went on to perform many of the voices on the *The Simpsons.* Guest's character, lead guitarist Nigel Tufnel, was obviously inspired by legendary guitarist Jeff Beck. He had the same hairstyle and in one scene is reading a racing magazine (Beck is an auto enthusiast).

This Is Spiñal Tap was shot in five weeks on a $2.2 million budget. Most of the film was reportedly improvised—there was no screenplay, just a twenty-page outline. Few scenes required more than a few takes. *Spiñal Tap* then took over ten months to edit, cut down from more than fifty hours of film. Once the film was complete, Embassy issued press kits featuring fake band bios and lyric sheets. PolyGram even honored Spiñal Tap with a platinum award for a million albums returned instead of a million records sold.

This Is Spiñal Tap was first previewed in a Dallas shopping mall. Only a handful of people in the audience laughed at the film. One moviegoer said to Reiner, "Jesus, what is this? These guys aren't any good. Why didn't they make a film about Van Halen or Def Leppard?" Critics thought differently—*Spiñal Tap* opened to rave reviews on March 2, 1984. *Los Angeles Magazine* called the film "The funniest rock and roll movie ever made. They're a lot better than Mötley Crüe and a lot funnier, too." *New York* magazine noted the film was so accurate that "it almost becomes the thing it satirizes."

The reaction to the film in the heavy metal community was complete shock. On first viewing, few musicians found it funny at all. The first time Eddie Van Halen saw the film, everyone in the theater was laughing while he sat thinking, This isn't funny. "Everything in that movie had happened to me," Eddie recalled. "No one showing up to things, the Air Force base gigs, the guy who couldn't get out of his pod." The first time Dokken's George Lynch saw the film, he said, "That's us! How'd they make a movie about us?"

Steven Tyler almost couldn't watch the whole film. At the time of *Spinal Tap*'s release, Aerosmith was on its last legs. Their latest album, *Rock in a Hard Place,* had Stonehenge on the cover, and here was this joke band with a stage set that looked just like their album cover. "That movie was way too close, way too real," said Tyler. "I took *Spinal Tap* real personal." As Harry Shearer put it, "The closer we got to the real thing, the closer the real thing dared to get to us. Reality was calling our bluff at every step."

Black Sabbath was touring the States at the same time the movie opened, and for them it was truly life imitating parody. Their set was a replica of Stonehenge, and the band had hired a dwarf to appear on stage in a devil costume. Their Stonehenge set was so big that they couldn't fit many of the pieces onstage. Vocalist Ian Gillan had recently joined the band and was still trying to learn the lyrics to Black Sabbath's songs, so he wrote them out on legal pads and taped them to the monitors. But during one show he ran into trouble when a massive dry-ice fog hit the stage and he couldn't see his cheat sheets. Gillan had to get on his knees and wave the smoke away with his hands for the entire show so he could read the lyrics.

In fact, most musicians could recall incidents in their careers that resembled scenes in the film. The stage set for Dio's *Last in Line* tour featured a giant pyramid. During the opening song, the top of the pyramid was supposed to open up, dry-ice fog would float out, and drummer Vinnie Appice was supposed to appear through the mist. One night the top of the pyramid got stuck, trapping Vinnie inside with little room to breathe. While the band played on, two members of the road crew frantically tried to pry open the top of the pyramid. Once they did, the song was over.

Practically every metal band could relate to the scene where Spiñal Tap couldn't find their way to the stage. Many of the theaters that metal bands played in throughout the '80s were old vaudeville venues with endless hallways and doors. Quiet Riot found that the trick was to keep opening doors until they finally found the stage. When Great White opened for Whitesnake in Liverpool, England, someone locked them in their dressing room from the outside. When they were announced to go on, the band was running around like rats in their dressing room, frantically trying to escape.

Another hilarious scene in *Spiñal Tap* features the band playing at an Air Force base as radio signals start coming through the wireless pickup on Nigel Tufnel's guitar. During one Danzig show, guitarist John Christ was trying to build a slow, eerie mood on his guitar, when all of a sudden through his amp he heard: "Breaker one nine! Breaker one nine!"

This Is Spiñal Tap became a sore spot for many metal bands who took themselves too seriously. One of the easiest ways to piss off a pretentious rock star was to say that his band resembled—or, better yet, was funnier than—Spiñal Tap. As George Lynch put it, the harder a band tried to take themselves seriously and not get laughed at, the more they resembled Spiñal Tap.

This Is Spiñal Tap didn't fare well at the box office, but the film went on to become a huge cult favorite. It was also the beginning of Rob Reiner's long and successful directing career. He later went on to direct such hit films as *The Princess Bride* and *Misery*.

When *This Is Spiñal Tap* was released on DVD in the year 2000, Michael McKean, granting an interview in his David St. Hubbins character, called the film "a hatchet job," and blamed Marty DiBergi for making them look stupid. He didn't show "the innumerable times" Spiñal Tap actually *found* the stage, or when the stage props *did* work. St. Hubbins said DiBergi refused to show that side of the band because he had an agenda, "and I think the agenda was that he wasn't getting as many women as the band."

The critics were right about *This Is Spiñal Tap*. Reiner made not only the most hilarious movie about rock and roll but the most accurate one. "I've seen rock bands cry watching *Spiñal Tap*," said Monster Magnet's Dave Wyndorf. "Not laugh—cry. That's how real it is."

With the 1980 election of Ronald Reagan, the nation had swung hard to the right, and the government tried to drag morals and standards back to the 1950s. The Parents Music Resource Center (PMRC) was formed in the spring of 1985. Susan Baker, wife of Treasury Secretary James Baker, and Tipper Gore, wife of Senator Al Gore, founded the organization. Seventeen out of the twenty members of the PMRC were married to politicians.

Prince actually started the entire brouhaha. Tipper Gore was shocked when she found her eleven-year-old daughter Karenna listening to the *Purple Rain* album, which included a song called "Darling Nikki" that spoke of a woman "masturbating with a magazine." Baker and Gore decided that rock music had gone too far; President Reagan went so far as to say that rock lyrics didn't qualify as free speech. "The First Amendment has been twisted into a pretext for license," he said. The PMRC, of course, insisted that censorship was not their goal—protecting the tender ears of children was the reason they wanted to put a leash on the music.

The PMRC sent a letter to the Recording Industry Association of America (RIAA) on May 31, 1985, proposing the following ratings for album lyrics: X for sex, D/A for drugs and alcohol, O for occult, and V for violence. The PMRC advocated plain brown wrappers to go over album covers they found distasteful, and they wanted record labels to "reevaluate contracts" with artists who "engage in questionable onstage behavior." The RIAA responded to the PMRC by saying they would begin to sticker albums. The stickers would be standardized, but each label would have the choice of what bands would get the stickers. Those were the only demands the RIAA would accede to.

Frank Zappa was disgusted that the RIAA had caved in. Labeling records was the first step to censorship, he reasoned. It would put a "scarlet letter" on an album, causing retailers not to carry it and radio stations not to play it. Zappa famously referred to the PMRC as an "ill-conceived housewife hobby project" and called Gore a "cultural terrorist."

The PMRC wrote up a list of bands they found offensive, including Def Leppard, Mötley Crüe, Black Sabbath, and Venom. Pop artists such as Prince, Sheena Easton, and Cyndi Lauper also made the list. Twisted Sister was criticized for the violence in their video for "We're Not Gonna Take It." Baker said that Madonna had to be stopped, because she was showing young girls "how to be a porn queen in heat." AC/DC came under fire from the PMRC for songs like "Shoot to Thrill" and "Let Me Put My Love Into You." Not even the Captain and Tennille were safe to listen to; they made the list for their song "Do That to Me One More Time."

The PMRC held hearings before Congress on September 19, 1985. Only three musicians came forth to testify on behalf of the First Amendment: Frank Zappa, Dee Snider, and John Denver. It was certainly a diverse group of musicians, but Denver was vehemently against censorship. His song "Rocky Mountain High" had been banned by radio stations that thought the song was pro-drug.

During the hearings, certain lyrics, such as the Mentors' "Golden Showers"—with the immortal line, "Bend up and smell my anal vapor / your face is my toilet paper"—were read aloud. When the W.A.S.P. single "Animal (Fuck Like a Beast)" was brought up, Susan Baker couldn't bring herself to say the word "fuck"—she had to spell it out.

Snider then testified, decked out in a Twisted Sister T-shirt that read

"Play It Loud Mutha," torn jeans, and a sleeveless denim jacket. He said he was a proud family man with a young son, he didn't drink or do drugs, and was a Christian. Snider told the committee that every parent had to be responsible for what his or her children listened to and watched. One senator told Snider that many parents didn't have time to do that, a statement the singer found completely unacceptable. Most kids buy only one album a week, Snider said, and it wasn't too much to ask a parent to listen to an album a week.

Zappa said during his speech, "While the wife of the Secretary of the Treasury recites 'Gonna drive my love inside you ... ' [a lyric from "Golden Showers"], and Senator Gore's wife talks about 'bondage' and 'oral sex at gunpoint' [referring to Judas Priest's "Eat Me Alive"], on the CBS Evening News, people in high places work on a tax bill that is so ridiculous, the only way to sneak it through is to keep the public's mind on something else: 'porn rock.' "

Dee Snider was the only heavy metal musician to testify against the PMRC, and it's puzzling why more metal musicians didn't fight the group. Many metal bands wore "Fuck Censorship" T-shirts on stage, used the word "fuck" in their lyrics so they could sell more records, and railed against the PMRC in interviews, but they ultimately didn't do anything significant to fight for free speech.

By 1986, the PMRC furor had largely died down. Tipper's husband Al eventually became vice president in 1992, and Zappa reconciled with Gore before he passed away in 1993. The PMRC still exists today and is run by Barbara Wyatt. Wyatt told the Los Angeles Times recently that she wished Gore were more involved in the PMRC. "It's a shame," she said. "She has the bully pulpit now, and she could make a big difference. But much of [Al Gore's donation] money comes from the entertainment world, frankly, so I don't see that happening."

Looking back on the PMRC, it's clear how ridiculous their crusade was. Many of the metal bands that the organization once considered dangerous or threatening now appear comical and silly. The PMRC also increased sales of controversial groups. Hardly anyone had heard of the

Mentors until the PMRC put them on their list, but after all the publicity the band received from the PMRC hearings, their record sales doubled. When the government didn't have heavy metal to kick around anymore in the '90s, it would try to censor rap music and violent films. Perhaps Zappa summed it up best when he said, "There is no conclusive evidence to support the claim that exposure to any form of music will cause the listener to commit a crime or damn his soul to hell."

Through the first half of the 1980s, metal and hard rock had a successful run in the mainstream, but halfway through the decade many people, especially in the media, had passed it off as a fad and began to turn away from it. In January 1985, MTV cut back on its metal videos by almost 75 percent. The popular Los Angeles hard rock radio station KMET cut almost all their metal programming. The station's program director, George Harris, said the music had too narrow an appeal and "turns off too many listeners." KMET focused on the bands the baby boom generation was nostalgic for, like the Rolling Stones and Steely Dan—what would later be termed "classic rock," which would be all some L.A. stations would play in the future.

Largely because of MTV, and radio's lack of support, ticket and record sales for metal bands were also down. Now record labels and musicians alike were nervous about selling a record without the support of MTV. Dokken had built up a lot of momentum from touring and by the time they made a video for "Just Got Lucky," it looked to be their biggest single yet. But when MTV pulled the plug on metal, the single was dead. Armored Saint didn't even bother making a video for their 1985 *Delirious Nomad* album, because they knew MTV wouldn't play it. The album sold poorly.

MTV was a double-edged sword. When the network was playing metal in "heavy rotation," an unfortunate side effect was that bands became overexposed and the fans would burn out on them quickly. But when the network supported them, MTV had given these bands the biggest jump-start they could ever hope for, and more success than they could have ever dreamed of. "MTV had a profound effect on Dokken's success," says George Lynch. "We couldn't have done it without them." Says Rudy Sarzo, "Without MTV, the whole '80s scene wouldn't have been as big. After MTV, artists were expected to have a platinum or multi-platinum success with their first record. In the old days, it took two or three albums, at least."

At first considered too raw and abrasive for mainstream acceptance, **Metallica** always did things their way and ultimately changed metal in the process. Pictured above are lead singer/guitarist James Hetfield and lead guitarist Kirk Hammett, playing the Long Beach Arena in 1986, where they were the opening act for Ozzy Osbourne. (Neil Zlozower)

8

"I KNOW OUR MUSIC HAS THE TENDENCY TO INCITE PEOPLE TO RIOT, BUT THAT'S NOT DONE INTENTIONALLY. I USE THE MUSIC AS A RELEASE TOO. HAVE YOU EVER HEARD ME SING?"

—Slayer lead singer Tom Araya

IN 1986, METALLICA SCORED their biggest success to date with their *Master of Puppets* album. The album hit the Top Thirty in April 1986 with practically zero airplay on radio or MTV. Many in the music industry couldn't believe it. A band that made it without videos? "MTV wasn't our concern," says Michael Alago, the A&R executive who signed Metallica to Elektra. "Our concern was getting the band out on the road and doing as many gigs as possible. I don't think MTV was ever totally accepting of metal on a grand scale. With a lot of the underground bands, it was all about touring, press, and word of mouth."

Touring and word of mouth was always the M.O. for many of the British metal bands as well, but by 1986, most of these bands had peaked or were content to rest on their laurels and churn out music that their fans had come to expect. After the *Powerslave* tour ended in 1985, Iron Maiden lead singer Bruce Dickinson felt the band had done all they could with their sound. He wanted the band to make a radical departure, one they would always be remembered for. He had always hoped Iron Maiden would make a masterpiece like Led Zeppelin's fourth album or *Physical Graffiti*.

Dickinson had written a number of acoustic songs. Led Zeppelin's third album had an all-acoustic side, proving that a rock band could still be heavy without electric guitars. Doing an all-acoustic album would have been a radical move for Iron Maiden in 1986, years before the "unplugged" craze. Many of their fans probably would have a hard time accepting this new musical direction, just as fans did with *Led Zep-*

pelin III, but without advancing Iron Maiden's music further, Dickinson felt the band would "stagnate and just drift away."

Instead, their next album, 1986's *Somewhere in Time,* stayed with the usual Iron Maiden formula and none of Dickinson's acoustic songs were used. Likewise, most of guitarist Adrian Smith's songs, which were more commercial and could have had crossover appeal, were also passed on by bassist Steve Harris, who called the shots in the band, and producer Martin Birch. "Neither Steve nor I envisioned the band as anything other than what they were," said Birch. (The band did have a hit with one Smith composition, "Wasted Years," a song that fit in with Iron Maiden's formula.)

"I felt the time was right for us to do something audacious, something vast and daring," said Dickinson. "And I didn't feel that we did that with *Somewhere in Time.* We just made another Iron Maiden album." Both Dickinson and Smith would leave the band several albums later, when the band did in fact stagnate, and sounded tired and dated.

By 1986, even Judas Priest were moving in a more commercial direction with their *Turbo* album, forsaking their leather and spikes for long Bon Jovi cloaks and fluffy hair. As the classic English metal bands peaked, a new, vicious form of heavy metal was beginning to take over. As Metallica led the way with their commercial breakthrough with *Master of Puppets,* a number of bands that played their metal harder, faster, and angrier than the rest would be signed by major labels. Their violent new brand of music was called "speed metal" or "thrash metal." Just as every major label wanted to sign a metal band in 1983 after the success of Quiet Riot, in the wake of Metallica's success, the majors wanted speed metal bands. Several bands, including Megadeth, Anthrax, and Slayer, had the potential to take metal to the next level.

It is unclear exactly when the terms "speed metal" and "thrash metal" took hold, but they were used to describe music that was much heavier and faster than traditional metal. The beginnings of what became speed and thrash metal can be traced, as with all things heavy, back to England. Though they haven't achieved widespread commercial success, Motörhead, led by rough-and-tumble singer/bassist Ian "Lemmy" Kilmister, is one of the most revered underground metal bands and one of the most influential in the speed metal movement. Lemmy, who got his nickname because he was constantly borrowing money (as in, "Lemme a fiver"), started out as a roadie for Jimi Hendrix and went on to play in the space-rock band Hawkwind. After he was fired for "doing the wrong drugs," as he put it, he formed Motörhead in 1975.

In the first press-release bio of Motörhead, they claimed that if they moved next door to you, your lawn would die. Lemmy is also reputed to have said that the band knows only three chords but knows how to arrange them well. Motörhead's signature song, "Ace of Spades," is about the band playing poker in their tour van while it was barreling down the highways of Europe at 100 miles an hour.

Even though Motörhead is considered the godfather of speed metal, to call them a speed metal band does not do the band justice. Motörhead always had their own unique sound. Says writer Jon Sutherland, "They're the bravest, dumbest, smartest . . . you can't define them other than saying they are Motörhead." Motörhead was always first and foremost a people's band. When Lemmy went to the Rainbow Bar and Grill, he'd take lyrics he was working on to patrons around the restaurant to solicit their opinions. Often their suggestions made it into the songs.

Motörhead has been trying to crack the U.S. market its entire career but has never had a gold or platinum album in the United States. Its members may never have huge bank accounts, but they will always have the respect and admiration of the metal community. You couldn't count how many true metalheads wore Motörhead patches on the back of their denim jackets to concerts.

If Lemmy had a dollar for every Motörhead patch sold, he'd surely be living in a palatial mansion by now. Now in his mid-fifties, Lemmy will likely spend the rest of his life touring, which is probably fine with him.

Despite his crude and rough exterior, Lemmy is extremely intelligent and well-read. When Motörhead opened for Ozzy Osbourne in 1981, Lemmy brought few clothes but an entire suitcase full of books. He remains a history buff, especially about World War II.

Motörhead laid much of the groundwork for the bands that came after them. They were a tremendous influence on Metallica, as were Venom, one of the most notorious New Wave of British Heavy Metal bands. Venom was a three-piece band from England whose members went by the names Mantas, Cronos, and Abaddon (a.k.a. Conrad Lant, Jeff Dunn, and Tony Bray). They formed in 1979 and, according to their bios, didn't just play guitar, bass, and drums. Cronos was the "Rabid captor of bestial malevolence," Abaddon the "barbaric guardian to the seven gates of hell," Mantas the "grand master of Hades and Mayhem."

Venom tried to be a combination of Kiss and Motörhead. They wanted their stage show to be bigger than anyone else's and to play the heaviest music imaginable. Venom weren't very talented, but they more than made up for it with aggression and volume. Like Black Sabbath, Venom frightened a generation of fans who thought they were putting their mortal souls in jeopardy by listening to their music. "Venom, as cheeseball as they are, legitimately scared me," says writer Del James. "It was that naïve fear of a band that sang about Satan the way *they* sang about Satan. I said to myself, 'Whoa, this is wrong . . . but I dig it!' "

Like pro wrestlers mocking and challenging their rivals, Venom often trashed other bands, including Metallica. They took pride in the fact that they never opened for anyone, but seeing them play live made it painfully obvious what poor musicians they were. They had a gigantic stage set that could only be described as Studio 54 in hell, and often got into scrapes with fire marshals over their pyro effects. When Venom played in Philadelphia, their effects blew a gigantic hole in the stage.

They dubiously claimed in interviews that the damage bill came to $666.66.

Punk band Black Flag opened for Venom in New Jersey in 1986. "I expected them to go into 'Sex Farm Woman' at any second," wrote Black Flag frontman Henry Rollins in his book *Get in the Van,* referring to the Spinal Tap song. "The guitar player was so bad it was painful. The bass player was hilarious. He would wiggle his tongue and roll his eyes. But he also would fix his hair every fifteen seconds or so. After an hour of 'I can't fucking hear you!' they said, 'Good fucking night New fucking Jersey!' and ran for the dressing room."

Venom are now considered the godfathers of what became "death metal" and "black metal," two genres that took metal to new extremes. Death metal is darker and more morbid-sounding than speed metal, and the vocals are usually very deep, guttural, and unintelligible. Legend has it that the lead singer of the death metal band Obituary often didn't sing actual words—he would just growl and roar like the Cookie Monster on a binge. Many black metal bands grew out of Norway, and their fans believed in the music like they were following a satanic religion. Black metal bands usually wore "corpse paint" or ghoulish makeup. Some tried to prove they were dedicated to the cause by committing evil acts like burning down churches and even murdering musicians in rival bands. (On August 10, 1993, Oystein Aarseth, whose stage name was Euronymous and who was the lead singer of the black metal band Mayhem, was stabbed to death by Count Grishnachkh [real name: Varg Vikernes], lead singer of black metal band Burzum.) It's surprising how heavily black metal bands were influenced by Venom, considering the band themselves didn't take what they were doing that seriously. Any true satanist who went to a Venom or Slayer gig expecting to see ritual sacrifice onstage would have been sorely disappointed.

While Metallica eventually left L.A., disgusted with the hairspray scene, Slayer enjoyed their outcast status of being a speed metal band from

Los Angeles. Forming in 1982, Slayer began playing around the L.A. club scene about the same time Ratt and Mötley Crüe signed with major labels. Along with Metallica, they were one of the only bands in the Southern California area to play extremely heavy and aggressive music. Slayer started out playing Iron Maiden and Judas Priest covers, but guitarist Jeff Hanneman was getting more and more into the punk scene. He would bring punk albums to their practice sessions, and drummer Dave Lombardo started mimicking their rhythms and beats. Like Motörhead, Slayer became a band that both punks and metalheads enjoyed because their music shared intensity and anger.

Lombardo was considered one of the best drummers in the speed metal genre. Few could perform at his level of intensity and speed. He never warmed up before a gig, and easily kept up with Slayer's music, even when it was played twice as fast live. Lombardo had just graduated from high school when Slayer put out their first album in 1983, *Show No Mercy*.

Slayer was notorious for their violent fans, and their concerts were completely out of control. When they played San Diego in 1985, one fan dove from the balcony and went clear through the stage. The road crew dragged him out of the hole and threw him back into the audience. At a 1991 show at the Los Angeles Sports Arena, fans uprooted their chairs and stacked them in a huge pile so they could start a mosh pit. Says Lombardo, "They were controlled by something: 'Get the chairs. Put them in a pile. Do a pit.' They all responded immediately to that call." When a security guard tried to break up the pit, the fans picked him up and threw him out. From the drum riser, Lombardo always had the best seat in the house to watch the pits. "It was the most amazing view that you could ever picture," he remembers. "It was like looking down on a blender. At the end of the show, you saw giant puddles of blood everywhere, and footprints where people stepped in them and continued walking out. That's how intense it was."

Slayer's fans were fanatical about the band and were merciless to opening acts, no matter how heavy they were. Even Metallica in their

Master of Puppets prime probably would have been booed off the stage at a Slayer gig. In 1991, when the band played on the "Clash of the Titans" tour with Megadeth and Anthrax, Slayer's fans chanted the band's name during Megadeth's opening set in Michigan. The fans tore chunks of sod from the lawn area and hurled them at Megadeth's Dave Mustaine, hitting him in the face.

Rick Rubin signed Slayer to his label, Def American Records, in 1986. Def American was first a rap label that featured LL Cool J and the Beastie Boys. Rubin was also a big rock and metal fan and started signing those bands as well. At the time Rubin showed interest in signing Slayer, they were managed by Brian Slagel. Soon after they appeared on one of Slagel's *Metal Massacre* albums, they were signed to Metal Blade. Apparently at first the band didn't have a problem with their manager also running their record label, but they later learned that without their knowledge, Slagel asked Rubin for a ridiculous amount of money to let the band out of their deal with Metal Blade. The band took Slagel to court and were soon free to sign with Def American. Slayer's first album for Rubin, *Reign in Blood,* would be their masterpiece. Rubin had set up a deal with CBS Records to distribute the album, but the label dropped the record a week before it was due in stores because of the song "Angel of Death," about the notorious Nazi concentration-camp doctor Josef Mengele. With the controversy over the PMRC and radio and MTV turning their backs on heavy metal, CBS wanted nothing to do with the album. The label was already dealing with the fallout at this time from a lawsuit against Ozzy Osbourne that claimed that Osbourne's music caused a teenager to kill himself. The label was scared to handle Slayer, knowing they would be a magnet for controversy.

Reign in Blood is considered to be the greatest thrash album of all time, a bludgeoning record that takes the listener through hell and back in twenty-eight minutes. The music was written quickly, shortly before Slayer entered the studio. The band locked themselves into a groove while writing the album and stayed with it all the way through recording. They couldn't go any faster than *Reign in Blood*. They knew they created a standard with the album, and to try to top it would be pointless, which is why the band slowed down on their 1988 follow-up, *South of Heaven*. But soon Slayer sped up again, keeping their sound within the parameters of speed metal. Lombardo wanted Slayer's sound to expand so it wouldn't be so one-dimensional; maybe the band could even have a hit song.

"The band would have had the same longevity, and our popularity wouldn't have gone down that drastically because of a commercial song," says Lombardo. "If it was cleverly done with Rick Rubin at the helm, we could have written a song that was heavy but would have taken us to the next level." Lombardo feels Metallica was smart for distancing themselves from the speed metal tag, which guaranteed they wouldn't get stuck in it. "That's the position I'm in now," he says. "I'm tired of being called the speed metal drummer. There's so much more stuff that I can do."

After briefly quitting the band in 1987, Lombardo returned and would play with Slayer for another five years. Then his wife became pregnant, and he gave the band nine months advance notice. Toward the end of the pregnancy, Slayer asked Lombardo to do some tour dates. Though there weren't many dates on the tour, he didn't want to take any chances and miss the birth of his son. Soon afterward, the band fired Lombardo. At first, he was furious, but he soon realized it was a blessing in disguise. "The best move I made was being there when my son was born," he says. "That was a priority, something I had to do. If I didn't, I was bound to live the rest of my life with regret for choosing [to play a gig] instead of being at something as once-in-a-lifetime as a child being born."

Though Slayer never moved to San Francisco like Metallica, when they played their first gigs there they discovered a whole new world. The San Francisco crowd went nuts for Slayer, and it was in San Francisco that Slayer first saw pits and stage-dives at their shows. Early in the band's career, Slayer wore black eye makeup that gave them a ghoulish look. After their first show in San Francisco, a fan told them, "You guys sounded great, but you know what? It would have sounded a little bit better if you didn't have the makeup." Slayer dropped it the next day. "They took their makeup off and gave it back to Mötley Crüe," jokes Ron Quintana.

The San Francisco metal scene was quite different from L.A., and many of the early speed metal bands gained their first foothold there. When Motörhead developed a following in San Francisco, it started bringing punks and metalheads together. With Quintana starting his underground metal radio show on KUSF, the Old Waldorf Club booking "Metal Mondays" in the early 1980s, and Metallica moving to the city, faster and heavier bands started coming out of the woodwork.

One of the most brutal speed metal bands to come out of San Francisco was Exodus. Like Slayer's *Reign in Blood,* their 1985 debut album, *Bonded by Blood,* is considered a classic of the genre. It took close to a year for *Bonded by Blood* to get released because the band was having problems with the first label they signed with, Torrid Records, and they were trying to get out of their deal. Most die-hard thrash fans had a copy of it on cassette, but they loved the record so much that when it was finally released in the stores, they went out and bought another copy anyway.

Exodus shows were crazed bloodbaths where almost anything could happen. Exodus often played a local club named Ruthie's Inn. The Ruthie's regulars used to pour beer on the dance floor, and moshers would skid up to thirty feet when the pit got really intense. Exodus even had their own security guards called the Slay Team, who beat up potential stage-divers. The band claimed they didn't want anyone falling onstage and damaging their guitar pedals, but according to Ron Quintana, Exodus lead singer Paul Baloff didn't want anyone messing with his hair.

Baloff's stage raps riled up the crowd, and most of the fans knew them by heart. He spoke of killing posers and would even pretend to spot one in the audience, saying, "Bring that poser up here! Let's kill him right now onstage!" Some nights, Baloff would divide the audience down the middle with his hand and challenge each half of the room to see who could thrash the hardest.

Exodus quickly gained momentum in the underground scene, and many in the local scene felt it would be only a matter of time before they were in equal standing with, or even surpassed, Metallica. But Exodus stumbled when they fired Baloff, supposedly over musical differences, before their second album was released in 1987. Baloff was a beloved figure in the S.F. scene, the heart and soul of Exodus, and many of their fans were furious. He was replaced by Steve "Zetro" Sousa, the original singer in Legacy (which later became Testament). The fans were so angry with Baloff's firing that at Sousa's debut gig, the first five rows turned their back on the band for the entire show. Exodus went on to release a number of albums with Sousa, but they never regained their momentum and broke up in the early 1990s.

In the mid-1980s, when Baloff was still in Exodus and Metallica were starting their climb to the top, the San Francisco speed metal scene was thriving. No matter how old you were, you could get involved. Death Angel's drummer was nine years old when the band started, and he played fast and furious behind a miniature drum kit. Alex Skolnick, the talented former guitarist in Testament, was sixteen when he joined the band and had to sneak out of his parents' house to play gigs. Debbie Abono was in her mid-fifties when she began to manage a band named Possessed. Abono started taking her daughters to Motörhead shows, where the members of Possessed first asked her to manage the band. "There's nothing to it," they told her. "All you gotta do is get us shows." Abono agreed and even allowed them to practice at her house.

Everyone went to each other's shows in those days. The members of Metallica, Exodus, and Possessed all went to hear each other play and have fun. Possessed once played with Exodus in Petaluma, California. The members of Metallica came to the show. "The Metallica guys were shooting everyone on stage with water guns," remembers Abono. "But they weren't filled with water." There was a strong spirit of camaraderie in the scene. "I remember everyone was helping everybody else at that time," she says. "I remember Kirk Hammett from Metallica calling me one day, 'Debbie! I just got a magazine, and Possessed is in it!' He was just as excited as we were. It was the best time in the world to be into that music, because everybody supported everybody else." With just a three-song demo tape being traded around, Possessed became immensely popular in Europe while still playing to only a handful of people in San Francisco.

Possessed would record their 1985 debut album, *Seven Churches*, during Easter break because two of the members, guitarist Larry Lalonde and bassist/vocalist Jeff Becerra, were still in high school. The pair graduated because Abono threatened to quit working for the band if they dropped out.

Even though their name was Possessed and their song titles had an evil bent to them ("Burning in Hell," "The Exorcist," etc.), Abono had no idea what the band sang about. When she read the lyric sheet for the *Seven Churches* album, Abono ran for her rosary beads. The band looked over at her, confused, and she said, "I just want the man upstairs to know I didn't know what you were singing about!"

Most of the speed metal bands from the States and abroad were mutual fans and friends of each other. There was never supposed to be a separation between the bands and the fans. Once an opening act was off the stage, they would hang out in the audience and thrashed with everybody else in the pit. In the speed metal scene, rock star was a derogatory term. If a musician in a speed metal band stayed backstage and refused to meet the fans, he was a rock star, a pompous ass who thought he was above everyone else. A speed metal band wouldn't reject success if it came, but success had to come as a result of a band keeping their integrity. No compromises, no selling out.

Unlike most metal bands who dressed up in stage clothes, speed metal bands dressed in their everyday clothes when they played live, and usually their wardrobes consisted of beat-up jeans and sneakers, as well as T-shirts of other bands they liked and were friends with. You wore another band's T-shirt to show your support for them, and for the scene. It would also turn the fans on to new bands they might not have known about otherwise. When the fans saw their favorite musicians wearing another band's shirt, they trusted the band was good. When Metallica were seen wearing T-shirts for the Misfits, a New Jersey punk band, their popularity went through the roof in the metal community. It would also turn their lead singer, Glenn Danzig, into a teenage icon.

Glenn Danzig was a dark, diminutive figure with pasty white skin and an exclusively black wardrobe. He revealed little about himself and liked to maintain an air of mystery. Despite his prince-of-darkness persona, Danzig lived with his parents in New Jersey until he was thirty-two and ran his T-shirt and comic-book business out of their basement.

Danzig originally sang for the punk band the Misfits, which gained prominence once Metallica started wearing their T-shirts and covering their songs. Taking a cue from Danzig, Metallica started dressing all in black and wore black wristbands that covered their forearms. After the Misfits broke up in the mid-1980s, Danzig formed a band called Samhain that later transformed into Danzig in 1987.

When they played the New Music Seminar in New York the following year, Danzig met Rick Rubin. Rubin moved to L.A. in 1987 amid a blizzard of hype. He had started Def Jam Records in his NYU dorm as an undergraduate and made the first LL Cool J record for $400, which sold a reported 120,000 copies. Rubin was a pioneer in making rap mainstream and was responsible for bringing Aerosmith together with Run-DMC for the "Walk This Way" video, the first step of Aerosmith's comeback. However, Rubin had nasty falling-outs with the Beastie Boys and LL Cool J that resulted in lawsuits, but Danzig and Slayer liked working with him. Glenn Danzig and Rubin hit it off because they were both fans of professional wrestling and pornography, but, more important, both had strong opinions on the music industry and where it was headed. Rubin also loved controversy, which Danzig and Slayer certainly knew how to attract.

Rubin wanted to sign Danzig after meeting with Glenn but told the singer that the band needed a better guitar player. Six months later, they were still looking for a guitar player when Glenn met John Christ, who tried out in January 1988 at Top Cat Studios in Manhattan. Christ wanted to make an impression and went wild during his audition. He played so hard he ripped off a fingernail and bled all over the room. After the audition, Rubin told Christ he liked what he played but that the rest of the band was scared of him.

Christ then went back home and practiced like crazy. He couldn't get another audition, however—no one in the band would return his phone calls after his first bloody tryout. So he called Glenn's house and played guitar over the phone until his answering machine ran out of tape. After doing this every day for two or three weeks, Christ was given another audition and got the job. Glenn told him the requirements to play in the band: "You've gotta move up to New Jersey, dye your hair black, shave your mustache, get rid of all your blue jeans, and buy all black jeans and clothes."

Rick Rubin was influential in how Danzig's first album came together. Half the arrangement ideas on the song "Mother," which turned out to be Danzig's biggest hit, were Rubin's. Rubin worshipped AC/DC and recorded his bands the same way: very dry, stripped-down, no reverb. "He was trying to make us sound like AC/DC with different vocals," jokes Christ.

Danzig's fans were usually troubled kids, and Christ points out with a chuckle that teenagers getting arrested on the show *Cops* are often filmed wearing Danzig T-shirts. Some of Glenn Danzig's fans were real-life Beavis and Butt-head characters. Says Christ, "These kids were so nervous, they'd be gigglin' and laughin', 'You guys rock! Heh, heh,

heh. . . . Aw man. . . . dude! Cool!' They never spoke in complete sentences. Some of our fans would be these fourteen-, fifteen-year-old kids about 5'11", 145 pounds, hangin' T-shirt, loose baggy jeans, two different shoes on their feet, workin' out in some cornfield. Sometimes the band would be walkin' down the street, a car would drive by, somebody would raise their fist out the window and go, 'MOTHER!!!' "

When the major labels started signing speed and thrash metal bands in the mid-1980s, Island Records signed Anthrax, the biggest band of their kind to break out of New York. They weren't angry agents of Satan like Slayer, but nice Jewish boys from Queens. Anthrax are now considered pioneers of combining rap and metal when they covered Public Enemy's "Bring the Noise." They also were the first metal band to wear shorts on stage, helping liberate heavy metal fashion from the regimented costumes of leather and Spandex.

Guitarist Scott Ian, along with Metallica's James Hetfield, is one of the best riff-masters in metal. For Ian and Hetfield, the key to making their rhythms ultra-tight was down picking, meaning every note was picked on a downstroke. Hetfield and Ian also used the sides of their thumbs to give their rhythms more tone. Ian would often bleed all over his guitar from scraping off too much skin. He double-tracked his rhythms on record to get them as tight as possible, and down picking was the best way. "If each note is rigidly downstroked perfectly in time, you can match it perfectly," he says. "It was like fascist guitar playing. There is no room for any space or error—each note has to be perfectly down picked. For us, the rhythm was supposed to sound like a machine gun drilling into your head."

Anthrax came together in 1981, the same year as Metallica, and released their first album, *Fistful of Metal,* in 1984 on Megaforce Records. *Among the Living,* one of the band's heaviest and best loved albums, was released in 1987. Two songs on the album, the title cut and "A Skeleton in the Closet," were based on Stephen King stories, *The Stand* and

"Apt Pupil" from the anthology *Different Seasons*. King, in turn, was a big Anthrax fan. Says Ian, "I've read interviews with him where he says when he goes into his room to write, he'll crank Anthrax, because it keeps everybody away when he's trying to have privacy."

But it was in 1985 that a side project Ian started for fun turned the metal community upside down. When the major labels started signing speed metal bands, Anthrax hooked up with Island Records. While recording their first album for the label, 1985's *Spreading the Disease*, Anthrax enlisted a new lead signer, Joey Belladonna. Belladonna had never been in a metal band this fast and intense before, and it took him a while to bond with the members of Anthrax and get used to their style. Ian had already finished recording his guitar tracks and was bored waiting around in the studio. He spent his time drawing cartoons for fun, and invented a crusty-faced ghoul in an army uniform named Sergeant D. Ian then started writing hyperspeed riffs and hardcore songs that were ninety seconds long.

For fun, Ian decided to make a band out of Sgt. D and his stockpile of crazy riffs, calling it Stormtroopers of Death, or S.O.D. for short. He called up Danny Lilker, Anthrax's first bassist, and asked him to join the band, and a behemoth named Billy Milano to sing and personify the Sgt. D character on stage. They rehearsed for a day and recorded an album in two called *Speak English or Die,* which was also released in 1985.

The *Speak English or Die* album was politically incorrect long before the term gained popular currency. The title track and "Fuck the Middle East" were both anti-immigrant songs. "Pre-Menstrual Princess Blues" and "Pussy Whipped" were rants against domineering women. "Douche Crew" was S.O.D.'s diatribe against posers. Some of the songs on the album lasted only several seconds, such as the "extended mix" of the Joan Baez classic "Diamonds and Rust," which was two seconds long.

S.O.D. was heavily criticized for their lyrics. Even though Scott Ian wrote the lyrics, lead singer Billy Milano caught most of the flak for them, being the frontman and the band's focal point. "We were very much aware of what we were doing and how we were satirizing things," says Ian. "People didn't understand political incorrectness back then because we didn't have that [label] then. So of course, the knee-jerk reaction was, 'Oh! "Speak English or die"! That's racist!' Hey, if people don't understand satire, that's not my problem." Whatever outrage the band caused, it certainly wasn't intentional. "We didn't try to do anything with S.O.D. We just did what we did," continues Ian. "There was no responsibility to anything except just doing something that we had fun with."

The *Speak English or Die* album became immensely popular and in spite of the band's satiric origins, many credit *Speak English or Die* with starting the punk and metal "crossover" scene. There were several other hardcore bands that laid the groundwork for this convergence as well. Discharge was a hardcore punk band from England. Their 1982 *Hear Nothing, See Nothing, Say Nothing* album was their crowning achievement, a mercilessly brutal masterpiece. "There was just a level of brutality on that record that, I had never heard before," says Scott Ian. "I could list fifteen bands that, if it wasn't for that record [wouldn't] even be bands, including Anthrax. Without that Discharge record, I don't know what I would have done!"

Listening to Discharge today, it would be easy to mistake them for a speed metal band, because so many speed metal bands borrowed from their sound. As Discharge drummer Terry "Tezz" Roberts recalled, "We made the mistake of waiting for someone to do the crossover sound and make it big with it. It took an American band like Slayer or Metallica to make popular what we were doing years ago."

Like Discharge, D.R.I. (Dirty Rotten Imbeciles) and Corrosion of Conformity helped define the crossover movement. One of the fastest bands around, D.R.I. was able to fit twenty-two songs on a seven-inch EP called *The Dirty Rotten EP.* D.R.I.'s first full-length album, *Dealing With It,* was a classic of the genre. Corrosion of Conformity's sound was ultra-fast and angry, but there were also slow, gloomy parts that sounded like Black Sabbath.

Combining metal and punk created problems. The anger and violence that drove both genres was explosive when the two factions came together. "When metal and punk came together, we were kinda hoping, 'here's a new audience,' and we wouldn't be preaching the message to the converted," said Corrosion of Conformity drummer Reed Mullin. "Instead, they took the superficial shit. They took slamming, doing fanzines, playing fast . . . they missed the fucking point."

Hardcore punk and speed metal shows in Los Angeles were intensely violent. It got to the point where the insurance risks became too great and speed metal and punk bands were exiled to clubs like the Balboa Theatre, located in the heart of South Central L.A., or Fender's Ballroom in nearby Long Beach. Fender's was a notoriously dangerous club that was nicknamed "Fender's Brawlroom." The ceiling was low, and fans sometimes dove off the rafters. Gang violence had infiltrated the scene by the mid-1980s and shows often became bloodbaths between skinheads, longhairs, and members of a local gang called the Suicidals.

Many speed metal bands got tired of seeing their audiences brawling instead of moshing responsibly and enjoying the music. "What people didn't understand about slam dancing is it was actually dancing," says Ian. "People would dance, and they would demonstrate their moshing style. There was a level of respect between the people in the pit, and they knew how to handle themselves responsibly. It was all about expressing yourself physically on the dance floor. When the metal crowd got involved, all that disappeared. It turned into 'who's the biggest jerk-off,' guys pushing and knocking each other down. That's not what it was all about."

Back in New York, the punk/metal crossover didn't come easy either. In February 1985, Scott Ian and James Hetfield went to CBGB's to see Broken Bones, a popular hardcore band founded by Discharge guitarist Tony "Bones" Roberts. A group of skinheads began staring Hetfield down and were ready to beat him up when the massive Billy

Milano of S.O.D. lumbered over and told them, "He's my friend. If you fuck with him, you gotta come to me first." The skinheads fled.

In the wake of S.O.D.'s success, Hetfield and Cliff Burton from Metallica formed their own joke band called Spastic Children, drawing their inspiration from the Mentors. Spastic Children never put out an album, but they played around the Bay Area for fun. Unlike S.O.D., who had great songs, part of the hilarity of Spastic Children was that their music was intentionally awful. The members of Spastic Children would trade off their instruments so each would play as badly as possible (Hetfield was Spastic's drummer, even though he couldn't play drums). "Their shows were so unlistenable, they made the Mentors sound good," recalls Ron Quintana. "They'd play once or twice a year, and the greedy club owners would always mention they were members of Metallica. So half the city would show up expecting Metallica songs, and they had to put up with this incredible torture. They'd start with a riff of a Metallica song, like 'Motorbreath,' then go into a hideous, plodding song like 'I Like Farts.'"

After getting kicked out of Metallica in 1983, Dave Mustaine was driven by an intense hatred toward his former bandmates. He vowed to "kick Metallica's ass" with his new band, and formed Megadeth in 1983 with that promise in mind. Even Lars Ulrich acknowledged that after Dave was fired that he would in all likelihood land on his feet. "I thought Metallica would have gone further with Dave," says Ron Quintana. "Time has proven me wrong. If Metallica only could have contained him...."

When Mustaine was putting Megadeth together, he hired lead guitarist Chris Poland and drummer Gar Samuelson, both jazz musicians. Neither musician had ever heard any of the speed metal bands that were starting to become popular, and Dave hated the jazz music they loved (he often threw their cassettes out the window of the tour bus).

Megadeth's lineup was rounded out by bassist Dave Ellefson, whom everyone called Junior. While the band would change lineups many times, the two Daves remained the core members.

Even with their jazz backgrounds, Poland and Samuelson realized that speed metal was not easy music to play. At the end of every gig, Poland's arm felt stiff as a board from all the fast double picking required of speed metal rhythms. Mustaine's riffs were unorthodox, and Poland initially had a hard time learning his style. But it was Samuelson's drumming that really opened up Megadeth's sound, making the music swing. Megadeth incorporated jazz chops into their music and played in weird time signatures, but never to the point where the listener became lost in a blur of technique. Putting two jazz players in Megadeth is what made their music unique. "It was a wonderful accident, that band," says Poland.

The name Megadeth was taken from a 1982 speech made by Senator Alan Cranston in which he spoke about nuclear disarmament, and it was a fitting name. With enough nuclear weapons to destroy the earth hundreds of times, Cold War paranoia was at its peak in the mid-1980s. The name was misspelled on purpose, probably because spelling it *Megadeath* was thought to be too generic or typical. The whole point of the band, and bands like Metallica, was to go against the clichés that had dominated metal for years.

Megadeth also sported "Choose Deth" stickers on their guitars. In the mid-1980s, when Megadeth were starting to take off, the pop group Wham! was extremely popular, and lead singer George Michael wore shirts that read "Choose Life." In part, it was Megadeth's reaction to Wham!'s upbeat pop. "I said, man, get anybody to choose life except that guy," says Poland. It was also a statement about the band's growing dependence on heroin.

Megadeth was first signed to a small independent label named Combat, which snatched up every speed metal band it could, from Dark Angel to the Crumbsuckers. Megadeth's first album, *Killing Is My Business . . . and Business Is Good!* was released in 1985. The songs were good, but the album's production was terrible. Mustaine would later say that the band spent a lot of the studio budget on heroin. He would also joke that he heard there were ammunition lockers full of dope from the war buried underneath the studio, and his first priority was to find a metal detector. Speed metal fans often didn't mind if an album was recorded poorly, so long as the music was good.

On the road, the members of Megadeth were reckless, frequently getting into fistfights with each other, though they would usually apologize the next day. "We once fought in Japan at the Prince Hotel, and the army came," says Poland. "Our road manager and his interpreter had to go down into the lobby and explain that everything was under control, even though we broke a toilet off the floor and smashed the headboard in half." Sometimes they would wake up amid the ruins of their hotel rooms and think, "Wow, we were really gone last night. We went too far again."

When Megadeth played the Ritz in New York, they were broke and hadn't eaten all day. They were hoping there would be food backstage at the show, but there was none—only alcohol, so they got drunk instead. They were in a bad mood because they were playing with Slayer, whose crowd was murder on opening acts, and Bad Brains, one of the most talented hardcore bands in history.

Poland realized they didn't have a chance on the bill. When they made it to the stage, they were completely inebriated. At the end of the show, Mustaine tried to break his guitar onstage. When a fan started climbing up onstage so he could dive back into the audience, Mustaine swatted him with his guitar like a tennis ball. He swung his guitar around and slashed the video screen behind him. The stage managers brought out a giant hook, as in the days of vaudeville, and yanked Mustaine off the stage.

Soon Megadeth left Combat Records to sign with Capitol Records. In the fall of 1986, they released their second album, *Peace Sells . . . but Who's Buying?* The brilliant studio production sounded great, and the band's musicianship and songwriting had improved by leaps and bounds. The title cut became the band's anthem. Its bass line was featured on the credits of MTV's *Headbanger's Ball* show for years, as were the riffs for "Wake Up Dead," a song about Mustaine's girlfriend threatening to kill him.

But drugs were destroying the band. The band was hooked on junk and constantly sick. During the *Peace Sells* tour in 1986, Mustaine and Ellefson considered firing Samuelson because he was so sick from drug abuse that they were afraid he was going to die on the road. They knew that Poland and Samuelson were old friends, so they pulled Poland aside and told him they were planning to let Samuelson go. Poland put his foot down: They were supposed to be a band and stick together.

Beyond the drugs, there were also artistic differences that constantly caused friction. "It could have been that we were voicing our opinion too much, which Dave doesn't like a lot," says Poland. "Maybe we could have said things more diplomatically. Instead of 'This part sucks,' we could have said, 'You know, Dave, I feel that this section is questionable.' If we weren't on drugs, [the band] wouldn't have been as volatile as it was."

Megadeth was Mustaine's baby, and he fiercely protected his vision. "Dave's ego got in the way a lot, but he knew what he wanted to do and how he wanted to approach it," says Byron Hontas, Megadeth's publicist at Capitol. "With Megadeth, it was all Dave, and he didn't want to hear anybody else's opinion, although when he did, it went in one ear and out the other. I liked Dave, but I think he was a little too tunnel-visioned in his own way."

As if drugs and creative conflicts weren't enough, money was always an issue. One day Poland got into a nasty fight with Mustaine because he needed money. Mustaine told him, "I should just let you guys go." Poland yelled back, "You don't have the balls to let us go. No one else would play with you that's as good as we are." Poland called Mustaine "a pussy" and said he wouldn't fire them. The next day, Mustaine gave him and Samuelson the ax. Not long after losing the Megadeth gig, Poland got sober. "It's hard to get sober when you have money," he says. "There's no reason to. It was easier to get sober when I had nothing."

Soon Mustaine's habit too was unmanageable. Always a workaholic, eventually the drugs became more and more important, getting to the point where he couldn't play anymore. Mustaine was pulled over while driving in 1990, and a drug test revealed he had heroin, cocaine, speed, and alcohol in his blood. Faced with the choice of getting clean or going to jail, Mustaine went into rehab. He relapsed in 1993 and almost died from an overdose of Valium. This scared him enough to get clean, though he recently relapsed and went back into rehab in January 2002. Gar Samuelson died of undisclosed liver complications on July 14, 1999. He was forty-one.

Megadeth went through a number of lineup changes after Poland and Samuelson were fired. Poland feels that as good as Megadeth were when they started, because of the drugs, they were only a mere flicker of what they could have been. Mustaine's rivalry with Metallica continued for many years. After Lars Ulrich said Megadeth was playing it safe with their music, Mustaine retorted by calling Megadeth's 1999 album *Risk*. But he later admitted that the band was in fact playing it safe. As much as *Risk* was supposed to be a step back in the right direction, it was another commercial album that alienated a lot of their die-hard fans. Jeff Wagner, the editor of *Metal Maniacs* magazine, even derisively called it "lite-metal."

Mustaine always wanted Megadeth to be on Metallica's level, or even surpass them, but they never broke through to their level of success. "I wanted to show [Metallica] up," said Mustaine. "As hard as I tried, though, I just couldn't do it. That's where I think we lost a lot of our momentum, because instead of making music for ourselves, we were always competing with other people."

As much as speed metal was about brotherhood and helping each other, Dave Lombardo felt the scene wasn't as tight as it could have been, one reason the genre didn't grow as big as it could have. "It wasn't like today, where bands like Korn and Limp Bizkit were all tight and working together," he says. "Back then, walls were up. Yeah, we had fun, but we didn't use it to our best interests. We knew [the other bands], but we didn't use the relationships like, 'Hey, let's do a tour,' or, 'Hey, let's do a song together.' Now there's that attitude among musicians, and that's great. They need that."

On April 3, 2002, Dave Mustaine announced that he was leaving Megadeth, which in effect broke up the band. A week later, it was announced he was selling his equipment on eBay.

By the early 1990s, many of the classic speed and thrash metal bands had either broken up or moved in more bland, commercial directions. Now there was a whole new generation of younger fans that worshipped a Texas-based band called Pantera, which with each successive release became heavier and more extreme.

Pantera's members are over-the-top characters. They are renowned for their excessive partying, which makes their live performances hit-and-miss. When a writer showed up to interview Pantera guitarist "Dimebag" Darrell Abbott for a cover story in *Guitar* magazine, the journalist had to go out and buy a bottle of Seagrams Seven, two six-packs of Coors Light, and a six-pack of Coke, or there would be no interview. Another subject of endless amusement among Pantera's inner circle is lead singer Phil Anselmo's supposedly fourteen-inch penis. "This is nothing," Anselmo would say. "You should see my dad's."

Metal critic and historian Borivoj Krgin called Pantera's *Far Beyond Driven* album "the most ferocious album to ever be issued through a major label along with Slayer's *Reign in Blood.*" Yet Krgin feels the band's progression to a heavier sound was more forced and contrived than a natural evolution. Pantera originally had big hair and makeup and released four albums independently, which they subsequently tried to bury. The band's first album with heavier music was 1990's *Cowboys From Hell,* their major-label debut. Pantera then tried to convince the world it was their first album ever.

"The band's whole argument is it's a different band musically," says Krgin. "But in my opinion, everybody goes through musical changes throughout the course of their career, and it's natural. It doesn't make it a different band just because you change your style." When Pantera was outed as former Aqua Net abusers, many metal fans questioned the band's integrity. In the '90s, when the anti-hair band sentiment was at its peak, one of the worst things you could be accused of was being one.

Yet for Pantera's fans and friends, there was no question they weren't posing. "One thing about Pantera is they're extremely real," says John Bush, who toured with Pantera when he sang for Anthrax. "There's nothing fake about them at all, and they're great people. That's why they have this following that's stayed true with them."

Pantera's young fans were a new generation of metal enthusiasts who weren't old enough to have listened to the speed metal bands of the 1980s. Many of these fans weren't even aware of pioneers like Exodus or Venom. Exodus performed a big reunion show at the Trocadero theater in San Francisco in 1997. The local metal scene had long since died out, and many of the fans who came to the show hadn't seen each other in years. Exodus put on a brutal show, and it felt like old times again. "One of the things I believe strongly is that those songs deserve to be heard," said Exodus guitarist Gary Holt at the time of their reunion. "They should not be left to the memory banks. Younger kids into Pantera need to learn where the shit started." Paul Baloff died on February 2, 2002, of a stroke. He was forty-one. Anthrax were performing in Tampa when they were told the news, and they held a "moment of noise" in Paul's memory.

On the eve of the release of *Master of Puppets,* Metallica secured a prime slot opening for Ozzy Osbourne. Raised on Black Sabbath, the members of Metallica were in awe of Osbourne, and would suddenly become quiet and whisper, "It's him," whenever he walked into the room. But when Osbourne first heard Metallica playing Black Sabbath songs during soundchecks, he thought they were making fun of him. "Are you trying to give me a hard time?" he asked. He was surprised to find out they were all Black Sabbath fans. After years of getting blasted in the press, it was probably the first time Osbourne really understood his old band's impact.

On tour with Osbourne, Metallica was playing in front of an audience that had never heard them before, and at many of the shows, Osbourne's fans didn't know what to make of them. "At first when we went out with Ozzy, some people booed," said Hetfield. "But some people went, 'Yay!' Most people went, 'Huh?' "

Osbourne's band sported sparkly stage costumes, makeup, and moussepoofed hair. Metallica wore shredded jeans and sneakers held together with duct tape. Onstage, Hetfield and Kirk Hammett would bang their heads at full speed, while Burton's hair took so long to unspill that it looked like he was headbanging in slow motion. They even performed an encore every night, unheard of for an opening act.

Metallica dubbed the jaunt the "Damage Inc. Tour." They were often wild and rambunctious on the road. Hetfield would end up paying huge bills for everything he destroyed on tour, the money deducted from his paychecks. Says former publicist Byron Hontas, "I heard Hetfield got a three-dollar check once on an early leg of a tour, three bucks off ten dates due to damage reports, and that was fine with him." As Hetfield recalled, "We smashed dressing rooms just because you were supposed to. Then you'd get the bill and go, 'Whoa! I didn't know Pete Townshend paid for this lamp!' Come back off the tour, and you haven't made any money. You bought furniture for a bunch of promoters."

Even though they were years away from their peak, Metallica had become the benchmark of success for speed metal and thrash bands. Yet many of the bands that tried to emulate Metallica weren't versatile enough or didn't have the songwriting chops to attract a large audience. "I almost feel like Metallica gave license to a lot of bands to feel like they could get away with murder," says former Elektra A&R exec Michael Alago. "Just like anybody who [thought] they could be in a speed metal or thrash band and never thought the quality of the songs was important."

Alago recalled seeing Metallica as the *Puppets* tour hit Madison Square Garden. While Metallica were onstage, he thought to himself, Next year, we're gonna own this place. The band headed to Europe that summer. By the time they made it to Stockholm, on September 26, Hetfield's arm had healed from a nasty spill on his skateboard, and he could play guitar again. Their next show was in Copenhagen, Denmark.

That night, Burton and Hammett argued over who would sleep in the rear bunk on the right side of the bus. They decided to draw cards to see who would get it. Burton pulled the ace of spades and won. Hetfield usually slept in the bunk next to Burton, but he avoided it that night because it felt drafty, and the cold air would hurt his voice.

At 6:30 on the morning of September 27, everyone was abruptly awoken as the tour bus started to skid along the two-lane highway. As the bus careened off the road, Burton tried to push through the window in his bunk and was halfway out when the bus toppled over into a ditch and landed on top of him. Burton was killed instantly. He was twenty-four. When the bus crashed, Hammett was thrown from his bed and knocked unconscious as the bunks tumbled like dominoes and collapsed into a huge pile. Two members of the road crew were trapped underneath the rubble for three hours before they were rescued.

After the accident, Metallica's tour manager Bobby Schneider said, "Let's get the band together and take them back to the hotel." The band? thought Hetfield. The band is not *the band* right now. It's just three guys. Back at the hotel, Hetfield, Hammett, and Lars Ulrich drank heavily to get through the night. Hetfield smashed out two windows in a drunken rage. Hammett was so rattled by the accident that he refused to sleep with the lights off.

The San Francisco scene was shattered by Burton's death. "Cliff was one of the coolest people I've ever known in my life; he didn't give a shit what anybody thought about him," says photographer Harold Oimen, who was a close friend. "I'd never had a close friend pass away. When Cliff died, it changed my whole outlook on life."

Metallica didn't want their grief to stall the band from moving forward. They had tour dates scheduled in Japan but didn't cancel the shows. They needed to get a new bassist to play those dates, and fast. One of the first bass players they considered was Joey Vera.

Metallica was dreading a cattle-call audition, so they wanted to find someone they already knew and liked. Ulrich called Vera and didn't ask him to join the band or relocate. "Come on up, and let's have some fun [jamming]," he said. Vera stayed up all night thinking about it, and when he called Ulrich the next day, he declined to come up and audition. In the long run, Armored Saint never had the big breakthrough they hoped for, but Vera wasn't willing to abandon his band. "We were more than just a bunch of guys that were in a band together," he says. "It was like family." About a month after the accident, Metallica hired Jason Newsted. Newsted came from a well-off family in Detroit. If you were a Kiss fan and Gene Simmons was your favorite member, you usually ended up playing bass; Simmons was Jason's favorite, and he did. Newsted's family relocated to Phoenix, Arizona, in 1981. He dropped out of high school several months shy of graduating to pursue his dream of becoming a professional musician, which hurt his parents.

Newsted eventually formed Flotsam and Jetsam, inking a deal with Metal Blade Records. In 1986, the band released their debut album, *Doomsday for the Deceiver*. Newsted worked 24/7 to make the band a success, once giving seventeen interviews in a single day, from nine in the morning to ten at night.

Brian Slagel has said he was the one who recommended Newsted to Metallica. According to Jon Sutherland, who worked at Metal Blade at the time, when Flotsam and Jetsam came to L.A. to play at the Country Club, he called Jason into his office, closed the door, and turned the stereo up loud so no one could overhear them. "Jason, Lars called here looking for a bass player," he said. "You can get this gig if you want it. I don't want to break up your band; this is your call. There's no way I can hide this, because it wouldn't be right."

Newsted shot him a strange look. His heart was completely with Flotsam and Jetsam. Somehow, word got back to the rest of the band, and it was like a wake in their dressing room that night. Right as they were gaining momentum and entertaining an offer from Elektra Records, Newsted was going to audition for another band, and his bandmates were not happy. It's hard to say how far Flotsam and Jetsam would have gone if he stayed with them. The band never had a breakthrough, and their singer, Eric AK, quit the band in 2001, frustrated that he was never able to make enough money to live off music.

To prepare for his audition with Metallica, Newsted practiced non-stop for a week. Excitement and adrenaline replaced the need for rest. "That whole week, I didn't sleep," he recalled. "I might have laid down a couple of times. For five days I stayed up and played as long as I could." The audition was terrifying for those who tried out. Some players lasted less than a minute before they were kicked out. One musician came in with a bass that was autographed by a member of Quiet Riot. He was dismissed before he played a note. One fan caught recording the audition had his tape recorder destroyed by Metallica's road crew. One of the musicians who auditioned was Les Claypool, the virtuoso bassist of Primus. He asked Metallica if they wanted to jam on any Isley Brothers songs, and the audition went downhill from there. Jason Newsted made it through his audition with flying colors, and a few nights later he went out drinking with Ulrich and Hetfield at a restaurant called Tommy's Joint, where they told him he had the job. That night, Newsted proved he was able to keep up with Metallica's drinking, another crucial qualification for him to join the band. He flew back to Arizona and told his comrades in Flotsam he was leaving. The band played their last gig with Jason on Halloween night in 1986.

But there was one last test before he was officially a member of Metallica. In November 1986, Metallica were the surprise guests at a Country Club gig with Metal Church and Heretic. The word was out they were going to play, and the club was packed to the gills. Newsted was scared to death. On the second song, "Master of Puppets," everyone's instruments lost power, except his bass and Ulrich's drums. He and Ulrich kept playing the song by themselves, and the entire audience sang in Hetfield's place, chanting the chorus, "MASTER!!!" Newsted was in.

In 1987, the band put together a video tribute to Burton called *Cliff 'Em All*. The video was composed of bootleg footage shot by fans. To get a copy of one video, Ulrich had to call a bootlegger personally to let him know the band really needed a copy and convince him it wasn't a ruse by the FBI. One scene in *Cliff 'Em All*, showed Burton smoking weed with some pals. Some younger, more naïve Metallica fans were upset with this (a guy with hair down to his ass and bell-bottoms a pot smoker?—who would have thought?), but his surviving bandmates wanted to show Cliff in an honest light.

Metallica released their next album, . . . *And Justice for All*, in September 1988. The album title was taken from the film in which Al Pacino plays a lawyer who cracks up after he is blackmailed into defending a man he knows is guilty of rape. After Cliff Burton's death, it's doubtful the title and the cynical tone of the album were coincidental. Coming off his success on Guns N' Roses' *Appetite for Destruction*, Mike Clink was the first producer on *Justice*, but he was soon out the door. Clink wanted the album to have a more organic approach, like *Appetite*, but Hetfield and Ulrich were still a little too rigid in their recording process to loosen up just yet.

. . . *And Justice for All* marked a turning point for the band, with their first video, for the song "One." Up to that point, Metallica had sworn they would never make a video. The song was based on the novel and film *Johnny Got His Gun*, about a soldier who steps on a landmine and becomes a quadriplegic who can't communicate his agony to the outside world because he is left blind, deaf, and unable to speak from the explosion. The video intercut scenes from the film with black-and-white footage of the band. The video, like the song, was grim. Kirk Hammett knew the "One" video was effective when he saw it playing on MTV one night, and afterward the VJ said, "Whoa! Okay, on a lighter note, here's Michael Jackson."

Metallica had hedged their bets with the "One" video. The band had an agreement with Elektra Records that if the video didn't turn out well, it wouldn't be released. If all the hair bands on MTV had this kind of agreement, there would never have been a *Beavis and Butt-head*.

Metallica had been able to get a great deal of control over their music throughout their career. But for Newsted, this freedom didn't extend to him, even after being in the band for over two years. When Metallica were auditioning bassists, they wanted someone who could write, but it increasingly frustrated him that most of his ideas were rejected for the *Justice* album (they did use most of his ideas for the song "Blackened"). The biggest blow for Newsted came when he heard the mixes for the *Justice* album. It was all guitars and drums—and no audible bass. It was as if he never played on the album at all. On the one hand, Newsted had landed his dream gig. Every metal fan fantasizes about joining his favorite band, and with Metallica on their way to becoming one of the world's biggest acts, Newsted's future would be secure. Yet being a natural leader as well as a prolific writer, it was hard for him to accept that Hetfield and Ulrich called the shots and he would have to take a back seat.

Newsted tried to form side projects to get his music heard. When Hetfield found out about it, he went crazy and wouldn't allow Newsted to start another band. Hetfield's reasoning was that he didn't want Newsted's side bands to take away from Metallica, but Hetfield saw nothing hypocritical about appearing on other people's albums himself.

In spite of not having the freedom he wanted, Newsted stuck around.

He would have been a fool not to. Joining Metallica was his dream come true, and for the time being he was willing to make sacrifices. As Cliff Burton had been, Newsted was probably the most down-to-earth member of the band and no matter how popular Metallica became, he always stayed in touch with his roots. "If anything, Jason has become cooler with his success," says Harold Oimen. "Nine times out of ten, if the other guys didn't come out [of their dressing rooms], Jason would spend two, three hours signing autographs a night."

"I had to keep in constant contact with the people every day," said Newsted. "Not for the ego inflation, but for the feeling that I [got] when they talked about what song was their special song, or if it wasn't for us, they would have killed themselves. The thirty seconds that an artist can give to a fan means more than anything. You can't put a price on that bond."

After the turmoil of Cliff Burton's death, Metallica came back stronger than ever and reached a new level of success with *Justice*. The album received rave reviews and was the band's first Top Ten album. When they hit the road for the *Justice* tour, they were finally headlining arenas.

In 1989, Metallica were nominated for the first-ever Grammy award for Best Metal Performance. Metallica were certain the award was theirs. But the Grammys proved how out of touch the recording industry was by giving the award to Jethro Tull. When the award was announced, the audience booed loudly. Metallica finally won their first Grammy for the "Black" album in 1992. In his acceptance speech, Ulrich sarcastically thanked Jethro Tull for not putting out an album that year.

With the success of **Poison,** the prayers of many hard rock and metal fans were finally answered. Sexy girls were now coming to metal concerts. From left to right: Rikki Rocket, Bret Michaels, Bobby Dall, and C. C. DeVille. (Neil Zlozower)

It's So Easy

9

BY ALL ACCOUNTS, it should have been a great night. Two of the biggest bands in the world, the Rolling Stones and Guns N' Roses, were playing together at the Los Angeles Coliseum on October 18, 1989. Guns N' Roses' debut album, *Appetite for Destruction,* had a slow start when it was released on August 1, 1987, but it went to No. 1 on the *Billboard* charts a year later and was now the best-selling debut album in history. Guns N' Roses had risen above the hair bands that dominated the Los Angeles music scene. If any L.A. band had the potential to become the next Rolling Stones, it was G N' R.

Shortly before the Coliseum gigs, Guns N' Roses had been offered the chance to jam onstage with the Rolling Stones for one song in Atlantic City. The band members were big fans, and wanted to play an obscure song called "Salt of the Earth." None of the Rolling Stones could remember how to play it, so shortly before the show, both bands crammed into a trailer to learn the song again. They played the song on a ghetto blaster, and Mick Jagger wrote the lyrics on a sheet of paper so he could memorize them. Guns N' Roses guitarist Izzy Stradlin and Keith Richards played along on acoustic guitars. "This is so cool," Stradlin thought to himself while strumming his guitar. "This is where we could be in ten years."

Guns N' Roses was everything the Rolling Stones used to be: loud, violent, arrogant, and inelegantly wasted. Guitarist Slash once said that

Jagger should have dropped dead after the 1978 *Some Girls* album. With a great show tonight, Guns N' Roses had a good shot of killing him off. Only two shows were booked for the Rolling Stones to play the Coliseum. When Guns N' Roses was added to the bill, demand for tickets was so great that two more shows were scheduled. Guns N' Roses was to be paid over a million dollars for all four Coliseum shows. The Rolling Stones hadn't toured in seven years, and they expected to gross close to $100 million by the tour's end.

But a lot more than money was riding on these shows, more than most people realized. Guns N' Roses had set up these shows to bring the band back together. Drugs were destroying everything the band had worked so hard to build. Just five years earlier, when the band lived in their rehearsal space, singer Axl Rose had drawn up handwritten contracts with the other band members in which using drugs was a serious breach. Unlike many who hid their substance abuse, Rose was unusually candid about the band's drug problems. "Our drug use is not in the past," he said at the time. "We scare the shit out of each other."

Not long before the Rolling Stones concerts, Rose received a birthday present from Stradlin, an expensive Gretsch rockabilly guitar. Trying in his own way to wake up Stradlin about his cocaine problem, Rose smashed the guitar to pieces and sent the shattered remains back to him with a note attached reading: COCAINE SUCKS.

Guns N' Roses did two warm-up shows before the Coliseum gigs. The first was at the Cathouse in Los Angeles, where Guns N' Roses had established their local following; the second was at a downtown club called the Scream, where Jane's Addiction also got their start. That night *RIP Magazine,* one of the country's top metal magazines, was having its third anniversary party. Although it had not been formally announced, everyone knew Guns N' Roses would be the surprise guests.

Few in the audience that night knew that backstage the band members were at each other's throats and threatening to cancel the show. The last billed band ended their set at midnight, and the audience waited until two in the morning when Guns N' Roses finally came onstage—and played a great show. The Cathouse and Scream shows were impressive performances. "The Cathouse show was more than a club show," said the *Los Angeles Times* review. "This was a full-fledged stadium show. This band's ready."

The morning of the first Rolling Stones show, Izzy was on pins and needles. He was facing six months in jail because he had violated his probation from a drug-possession charge by urinating in the trash can of an airplane (the line for the bathroom was too long). The incident earned him the nickname "Wizzy." At 6 A.M., he received a phone call from Axl Rose, completely drunk, telling him that he was quitting the band. Stradlin then called the rest of the band. "It's gonna be a long four days, fellas."

Guns N' Roses went on at 7:30, following the band Living Colour. After their first song, Rose announced to the audience, "I don't like to do this onstage, but unless certain people in this band start getting their act together, this is going to be the last Guns N' Roses show. I'm sick and tired of too many people in this organization dancing with Mr. Brownstone." The 80,000 fans in attendance were stunned.

Slash nearly stormed off the stage. As they tried to continue the show, the other band members stayed in their little boxed areas of the stage. Rose ended the concert by announcing that he was quitting the band. During the Rolling Stones set, Jagger dedicated the song "Mixed Emotions" to Rose.

In the *Los Angeles Times* review of the show, Robert Hilburn wrote that the Rolling Stones "could go on convincingly for another 10 years. Guns N' Roses . . . made you wonder . . . whether they were going to survive the concert." If they were to perform again, it was obvious that Guns N' Roses had a long way to go before dethroning the Rolling Stones.

The next night, Rose threatened not to go on unless Slash first went out onstage and talked to the audience about drugs. At first Slash refused, but, reluctantly, he went on. "There's been a lot written about this band and drugs," he said, standing by himself in the spotlight. "A lot of it is bullshit; a lot of it is true. Last night, you almost saw the last Guns N' Roses gig."

Slash had been coming to the Coliseum since he was a kid to see Van Halen and Aerosmith, hoping he'd be up on that stage one day. "Last night I was up here, and I didn't even know it. Smack isn't what it's all about . . . and we're not going to be one of those weak bands that falls apart over it." With that, the other four members came out onstage, and Guns N' Roses was a band again. The first song they performed was "Patience."

That night no one could predict if Guns N' Roses would ever reach the level of the Rolling Stones or completely self-destruct. As the past two nights had shown, it could go either way. When asked by a reporter what he thought were Guns N' Roses' chances of surviving, Keith Richards said, "Hey, it's not my gig to weigh up others' chances of living or dying, baby. That's what people do to me!"

The most obvious comparison between Guns N' Roses and the Rolling Stones was that Rose and Slash were the band's Jagger and Richards. Like Mick and Keith, Axl and Slash were either making great music together or about to kill each other. As one might expect, the pair's childhoods couldn't have been more different.

Saul Hudson was born in Stoke-on-Trent, England, on July 23, 1965. His father, Anthony, was a graphic designer and met Saul's mother, Ola, a costume designer, in Paris. Anthony Hudson set his sights on the music industry and moved the family to L.A. in the early '70s, where he began designing album covers for David Geffen. Saul grew up among celebrities; frequent visitors to his home included Joni Mitchell and Ron Wood of the Rolling Stones. After his parents divorced, his mother dated David Bowie for a while. One of the celebrities that was often at the house, character actor Seymour Cassel, kept calling Saul Slash, and eventually the name stuck.

Slash grew up around the music business and had seen all the craziness of the lifestyle long before he ever formed a band. "That's the only reason why I've been able to maintain any kind of sanity all the way through my career," he says. "I've been around it so long, nothing really fazes me." Though he grew up in an intensely social environment, Slash was painfully shy, something he carried into adulthood. He started growing his hair out to cover his face because he had a hard time looking people in the eye. Slash's family moved around a lot, and he was primarily on his own by the time he was thirteen. His nomadic childhood made it easier for Slash to be on the road and harder for him to settle down. After Guns N' Roses became successful, he resisted buying a house for years. He felt more comfortable living in apartments because they reminded him of hotel rooms.

Slash met future Guns N' Roses bandmate Steven Adler in the seventh grade. Steven's first instrument was a guitar that he would play along to Kiss records, pushing his tiny stereo to the limit. Inspired to play himself, Slash learned on a one-stringed instrument, unaware he needed another five. As soon as he got a guitar with six strings, he started a band. His grandmother, whom he was very close to, bought him his first good guitar, a B. C. Rich Mockingbird, just like his idol, Joe Perry of Aerosmith, played. "Unfortunately, I hocked it in my drug days. It's one of my few regrets," Slash says. Looking back on his childhood, he says, "My parents were fucking great, and I've always had a lot of freedom. I don't have any horror stories about my upbringing."

Axl Rose was born in Lafayette, Indiana, on February 6, 1962. His natural father left shortly after he was born, and he was raised by his mother and stepfather, Sharon and L. Stephen Bailey. When he was seventeen, Axl found some insurance papers and his mother's diploma and discovered he was born William Rose. He renamed himself W. Rose out of hatred for his stepfather, and legally changed it to W. Axl Rose in 1986, his initials standing for WAR, a fitting coincidence. By outward appearances, Rose looked like an innocent farm boy, with straight red hair, clear blue eyes, and pale freckled skin. Looks were deceiving.

Rose always had a great deal of talent and madness in him. In his high school placement tests, he scored in the top 3 percent of his class, but when he was tested by a psychiatrist, there was also strong evidence of psychosis. Rose was brought up in a strict, religious household. He was an altar boy, sang in the church choir, and taught Sunday school. When he saw people being healed in church, Rose questioned why nothing changed in his life. He often felt he was "cursed" and abandoned by God. "If there's somebody up there," he once said, "I don't know Him."

As a teenager, he continually found himself in violent confrontations with authority figures. He went to jail more than twenty times during his adolescence, once for an entire summer. Always distrustful of the legal system, he sometimes represented himself at his trials.

To Rose, living in Indiana was a dead end. (He called Indiana "Auschwitz" onstage when Guns N' Roses played there in 1991.) While still living in Lafayette, he started singing in bands. Rose knew there was a world beyond Indiana but had no idea how big it was. He had known Jeff Isbell, who later became Guns N' Roses guitarist Izzy Stradlin, since high school. Even before Stradlin knew Rose could sing, he thought to himself, Here's a guy who's completely crazy—he'd be a great singer. Stradlin went to Los Angeles after graduating from high school in 1979. He was the only member of Guns N' Roses to graduate, although bassist Duff McKagan was an honor student at one point and even considered applying to Harvard.

Stradlin was quiet and kept to himself. He never talked about his family and hadn't seen his father for close to ten years before running into him at a Guns N' Roses show in 1988. A year after Stradlin arrived in Los Angeles, Rose decided to join him. He got on a Greyhound bus but ran out of money in St. Louis and had to hitchhike the rest of the way. Not having any idea how big L.A. is, it took Rose a month to find his friend. On a rainy Easter morning, Stradlin heard a knock at his door. There was Rose, standing soaking wet in the doorway.

The five musicians who would eventually make up Guns N' Roses all met as members of various bands around L.A. Slash was working in a music store when he met Stradlin, who was playing with Rose in a band called Hollywood Rose. Slash and Stradlin didn't click musically at the time, but Slash knew he wanted to work with Rose, because "he was the only singer in L.A. who could sing." Live, Rose's performance was ferocious. "Axl didn't have that little snake swag back then," says Vinnie Stiletto, who was friendly with Rose in the 1980s. "He stomped on the stage like a kid throwing a tantrum, just balls out BOMP! BOMP! Attitude from hell." Stiletto wasn't surprised when he found out that Rose had endured a difficult childhood. "I could just picture it, because the tantrum was how he projected himself on stage. All that frustration and anger, he was so revved up."

Stiletto and Rose sometimes spent time hanging out on top of the Bank of America building right above Gazzarri's on the Sunset Strip, talking about their dreams. A lot of musicians would go up to that roof to drink late into the night, as the Strip below them grew empty and quiet. Rose once told Stiletto that his parents refused to let him watch Alice Cooper's appearance on *The Snoop Sisters,* a short-lived '70s television show. "I fucking flipped," said Rose. "I went up to my room and shoved my face in the pillow, screaming!"

At first Slash was uncomfortable playing with other guitarists. He tried to lure Rose away from Stradlin and eventually gave up and joined Hollywood Rose. As they often did, Rose and Slash had a falling-out that led to Slash leaving to join another L.A. band named London. London's greatest distinction was that it was a training ground for musicians who would become successful in other bands. Nikki Sixx left the band to form Mötley Crüe, and both Steven Adler and Izzy Stradlin had been members of London at one time, as was Cinderella drummer Fred Coury. Rose and Stradlin later quit Hollywood Rose to join L.A. Guns. At this point, Slash had been playing with Adler and Duff McKagan. Slash and Rose eventually ran into each other again when they both worked at Tower Video in West Hollywood.

Guns N' Roses officially came together on June 6, 1985. Stradlin and Slash wrote their first song together, "Don't Cry," and after a few days of rehearsal, McKagan booked the band on their first tour. The first date was at the Troubadour in West Hollywood. Before Guns N' Roses played the Troubadour, Stradlin couldn't afford the club's cover charge and had to watch the bands through the front window. When he rode the bus to the Troubadour, he'd often get off a block early so no one knew he didn't have a car.

The day after the Troubadour show, the band and a three-person crew left for Seattle in a beat-up Oldsmobile with a U-Haul trailer behind it. The car gave out somewhere near Fresno. "So we grabbed our guitars and told the crew, 'Get the car fixed and meet us in Seattle,'" remembers Slash. For the next several days, the band hitchhiked their way north. Their first ride was from a truck driver who kept stopping to take speed. Driving for days without sleep, he finally passed out when he stopped at a park. The band tried to wake him up, shaking him and screaming: "Wake up! We gotta get to Seattle!"

The driver eventually dropped them off in Portland, Oregon, and "two of the most adventurous women I've ever met picked us up and put us in the back of a fuckin' Pacer," Slash continues. "It was very generous of them." The band had missed all but one of their scheduled shows by the time they arrived in Seattle. Fewer than twenty people showed up at that show, and the band was never paid. Then they partied for an entire week, and as Slash recalls, "this chick we were all fucking drove us back to L.A. We've been together, more or less, ever since."

By this point, the band members were ready to quit their day jobs and make the band their first priority. The last nine-to-five job Slash ever worked was the first one he was fired from because he spent all his time on the phone taking care of band business.

The entire band moved into their rehearsal space on Gardner Street, off Sunset Boulevard, and "we all sold our souls as a unit at that point," says Slash. Located in a rundown building, their rehearsal space was a dank 12-by-12-foot room with no shower or toilets. The band built a loft from stolen lumber so they had somewhere to sleep. "That's where we all had sex in big groups because there was nowhere else to go."

The band never worried about living in poverty—in fact, they had fun surviving on next to nothing. "It was no rules, no parents, no passing judgment, no 'just say no,' " remembers Del James, a longtime friend of Rose. "We were all very protective of each others' backs. We didn't have much, but what little we had was kill-or-be-killed kind of stuff. People came and went. Some lost faith, some died, some got too strung out to even hang out with us, and that's really something. Then there was this small, loyal circle that was pretty tight."

Like many bands trying to make it in L.A., for Guns N' Roses even eating was a struggle. When they could scrape together three bucks, it was biscuits and grits at Denny's. On Saturdays the local mission served free food to the homeless, and a gay club called Rage served a five A.M. all-you-can-eat buffet. Night Train fortified wine was the drink of choice. At a dollar a bottle, five bucks got the whole band wasted. Even during the recording of *Appetite for Destruction,* the band lived on McDonald's coupons. Slash recalls, "We used to trade coupons with each other: 'I got one for a Coke', 'I got fries', 'Trade you fries for a Coke . . . '

"Every time a label would approach us about signing, they would take us to lunch. Even the labels we didn't want to work with, we had them take us to lunch anyway." After the band signed to Geffen Records in 1986, they often pretended they were still available so they could take advantage of lunch offers.

While Guns N' Roses were establishing themselves, a new band called Poison arrived in town. The four members were, as manager Vicky Hamilton put it, "fresh off the boat from Pennsylvania." Poison singer Bret Michaels used to say he was so determined to make it that when he left for California he tore the rearview mirror off his car so he couldn't look back. When asked why they moved to L.A. instead of New York to make it, the members of Poison would say, "Because L.A.'s a lot farther to come back."

Where many bands wanted their frontman to be the entertainer and the guitarist to take care of the music, vocalist Bret Michaels and guitarist C. C. DeVille *both* took on the entertainer persona. C.C. was the Rodney Dangerfield of rock, with a 200-decibel voice. In another era, he might have wound up a Borscht Belt comedian. Bassist Bobby Dall and drummer Rikki Rockett rounded out the band. Rockett was also a licensed cosmetologist who handled the band's hair and makeup, which they didn't trust to their groupies or girlfriends.

Poison's look was very feminine, and many couldn't tell from photographs if they were male or female. Says photographer Neil Zlozower: "When Poison gave me their first album, I said, 'Wow, who are these girls?' They said, 'Those aren't girls—that's us, you dummy!' " As one *Guitar World* writer put it, "Anyone who dares to claim that his first reaction to the cover of Poison's debut wasn't 'Whoa! These chicks are hot!' is a lying sack of shit."

Poison quickly adapted to the L.A. hustle that many newly arrived bands experienced. With little money to spare, they would move into an apartment, pay the first month's rent, live there for ninety days until they were evicted, then move to another apartment and start all over again. Also, like many local bands at the time, Poison didn't work day jobs and instead found women willing to take care of them. On the wall of their apartment were two lists. One was record-industry contacts; the other was a list of women not allowed to come over unless they bought food or did cleaning.

The women who supported the local musicians in Hollywood held onto the illusion that once a record deal was signed, they'd be repaid for everything they gave. But as soon as bands became successful, they were replaced by models and actresses. It seemed there was never a shortage of women in L.A. to abuse, though, many ending up supporting "suitcase pimps," which was a common term for unemployed musicians who went from girl to girl, on what was called "the couch tour." Many of the women who were attracted to hair bands supported their boyfriends by stripping, which started the joke, "What does a stripper do with her asshole before going to work? Drop him off at rehearsal."

For any struggling band in Los Angeles, self-promotion was key. Taking out an advertisement in the local free magazine *BAM* was expensive, close to a grand for a full page. So most bands would hit Sunset Boulevard on Friday or Saturday night to hand out flyers. Poison made 30,000 flyers per show. C. C. DeVille's mother owned a Kinko's-style copy center named Barbara's Place and was able to print them for free. The telephone poles up and down Sunset Boulevard grew noticeably in thickness with glue and staples, and until the mid-'90s, were still cluttered with staples long after the scene had died out.

When Poison started handing out flyers, the practice wasn't illegal. But eventually their flyer campaign became so excessive that the city of West Hollywood began issuing fines to bands. It was easy to find the musicians—their phone numbers were listed on the flyers for advance ticket sales. Some "posers" and "suitcase pimps" handed out fake flyers for bands that didn't exist, so they had a better shot at getting laid.

Poison's manager at the time, Vicky Hamilton, worked out a deal whereby the Troubadour paid Poison's rent and "fun" bill every month (she also got pizzas on credit from the Rainbow). They drew so well that the band still made money after the shows. The only problem was paying Poison's phone bill, because, as Hamilton remembered, "they were calling Pennsylvania every five minutes."

Even their detractors admired Poison's hard work and tenacity. "Not the music, but their whole stage show impressed me," says Neil Zlozower, a strong supporter of the band in the early days. "For the small amount of money they had to work with then, they used their brains and were very creative. It was fresh; it was fun."

Poison signed with a small independent label, Enigma (who had a distribution deal with Capitol Records), for about $30,000 in 1986. They hooked up with producer Ric Browde, who had worked with Ted

Nugent and Faster Pussycat, and started working on their first album, later titled *Look What the Cat Dragged In*. With $23,000 and eleven days of studio time to make the album, Browde, who had worked under adverse circumstances before, accepted the challenge.

Once they were in the studio, it was clear the band couldn't play very well. Drummer Rikki Rockett couldn't hold a steady beat and accused the tapes of speeding up and down. Browde had to splice so many pieces of tape together that engineer Michael Wagener called it "zebra tape." According to Browde, Bret Michaels had trouble singing on key; C. C. DeVille had to sing the vocal lines first, and Michaels would try to match the notes.

"How we played on the album was how we played," counters DeVille. "That was before ProTools [audio software]; that was before people fixed it up. We went in there and did it in eleven days, so what you hear on the album is [what you get]."

Wagener mixed the album in five days. "I had to pick between a point and getting paid a very small amount. I listened to it and took the very small amount!" Wagener would later call it "one of the big mistakes of my life"—*Look What the Cat Dragged In,* released in August 1986, went on to sell three million copies.

Browde felt the reason why Poison became successful was because Capitol Records had recently fired its entire promotions staff just as Enigma came in with the band. "Capitol had two records that were doing okay [at the time], Crowded House and Poison," he says. "They had no new records in the pipeline for six to nine months, so that's all their promotions staff had to work with. They stayed with *Look What the Cat Dragged In* much longer than any record company would under normal circumstances. That was the real key to Poison's success."

MTV, now playing metal and hard rock again, also gave the album a tremendous boost. With the network playing their videos, Poison went from selling 25,000 records a week to 100,000 a week. "MTV was the single most important thing that broke Poison," says DeVille. "Out of the top ten reasons Poison broke, the first five would be MTV."

The members of Poison and Browde clearly didn't like each other. Notoriously thin-skinned, the band fell out with him over his comments to the press that Poison was "a triumph of image over substance." He told *Creem Magazine,* "There's no musical talent here, with the exception of C. C. DeVille. I told them straight from the beginning, 'Let's do the album from the slant of having a good time and get that across. Luckily it worked.'"

The band badmouthed Browde so much that he thought he'd never work again. Then Poison played live on *The Joan Rivers Show,* and Browde's phone rang off the hook with offers to produce albums. "It was the first time people saw what I had to deal with," he says. "My credibility was restored!"

"The one thing I can say about the '80s is there were a lot of bands making records that couldn't play," says engineer Ross Hogarth. "It says a lot for the talent of certain producers and engineers." When Hogarth engineered the *Wake Me When It's Over* album for Faster Pussycat, it was clear that their drummer at the time couldn't play, mainly because he was hooked on junk. It would sometimes take two days of cutting and splicing to complete a song. Like a jigsaw puzzle, Hogarth and producer John Jansen would chart out what takes were usable. The tapes had so many splices that during playbacks they rhythmically clicked like a metronome when the reels started spinning. It turned out to be worth the effort: The album went platinum.

At first Poison admitted they weren't great musicians, but their motto was: If you can't do something right, do it anyway. Their song "Nothin' but a Good Time" described their M.O. perfectly. As Warrant lead singer Jani Lane put it at the time, "For every band that writes something earth-shatteringly important, there has to be a band that you can go out and drink beer to."

In spite of the criticism Poison received, DeVille says, "I thought the band was good enough to play what we were playing. I joined Poison not because they were the best musicians but because they had something. With Poison, it was obvious there was a spirit that was so huge, you didn't mind taking shit if they said you couldn't play."

DeVille felt stung when his playing came under criticism. "C.C. just got hammered in the press," says Ace Steele, a friend of DeVille's. "The truth of the matter was, C.C. was not a bad guitar player whatsoever. You could have all the money in the world, but all he wanted was that little bit of recognition."

There has always been pressure on rock stars to tell their fans they're not in it for the money, the sex, or the drugs. Success, even when it's well-deserved, often brings cries of "Sellout!" from fans who think the band has lost touch with their roots. If a band hadn't really paid their dues, they might even pretend they struggled through hardship in order to appear more authentic.

Poison openly admitted that they wanted to be stars, they wanted to be rich and famous, and they weren't ashamed of it. Nevertheless, it irritated the band that no one took them seriously. For every album Poison released, the band held meetings at Capitol Records at which they would strategize how to get respect from the critics. Their grievances went around the room: We want the cover of *Rolling Stone*. Why won't *People* do a feature on us? Why did the *Los Angeles Times* fucking destroy us?

"Regardless of their success, everyone thought they were a circus act," says former Capitol publicist Byron Hontas. "No depth, no songs like 'Stairway to Heaven.' They had to satisfy their egos by trying to be something that they weren't. The cover of *Time* wouldn't have been enough." With the label and the promotions staff playing spin doctors between the press and the band, no one told the band members why they weren't taken seriously. "Looking back on it, if I were more honest it probably would have gotten me fired," says Hontas.

Poison came along at a critical time in heavy metal's development. When the band became successful, the effects were evident everywhere. The hardcore metal audience in the '70s and early '80s had been mostly men. When Mr. Big opened for Rush, Rush bassist Geddy Lee thanked them—it was the first time in their twenty-year career they saw women in the audience.

Even for bands that drew a large percentage of women, Poison attracted two to three times more females to their shows. Before Poison, a metal concert wasn't the best place to try to get laid. At a 1988 Metallica show, journalist Jon Sutherland ran into guitarist John Sykes, who played with Thin Lizzy and Whitesnake. Sykes said he was there to pick up girls. "What?" asked Sutherland. "At a Metallica show? It's gonna be 95 precent guys—packed, sweaty, and screaming. If five girls walk through the door, I'll be shocked." Sykes immediately left and went to the Rainbow.

Women did in fact go to heavy metal shows throughout the '70s and '80s, but they usually looked very masculine, making it difficult to tell them apart from the men, and the men who came to the shows outnumbered them by a large margin. Some feel that margin changed in favor of women with the power of MTV. "Once [Metallica] was on MTV, better-looking girls started coming to the shows, just overnight," said former Metallica bassist Jason Newsted. By the mid-'80s, it was believed MTV had a larger female audience than male. Once *Look What the Cat Dragged In* became successful, Poison turned into proverbial kids in the candy store when it came to women. They listed their conquests on a computer by name, city, hair color, and what sex acts they were particularly skilled at performing.

Soon the Sunset Strip became glutted with "glam" bands that copied Poison; eventually, the '80s pop metal bands were lumped under the all-purpose term "hair band." In an era when what you looked like was more important than what you sounded like, many L.A. bands figured they could look good and get signed without having any talent. As producer Beau Hill put it, "Labels expected you could sign any piece-of-shit band, and as long as they had pouty lips, it would go gold."

In the mid-'80s, the Troubadour wouldn't book a band unless they saw a photo of the group first. It didn't matter if the band couldn't play—if they were good-looking guys, more than likely they could bring in enough girls to break even. "There's a lot of bands out there who don't have an image, who don't look very good," said original Warrant guitarist Josh Lewis in 1986. "When it comes down to it, they're not doing well. You can always learn to sound good, but if you're born ugly, there is nothing you can do."

Established artists began to sport big hair and sparkly clothes, though most would regret it a decade later. "Now we look [back] at ourselves—gay wasn't even the word," said Ozzy Osbourne, whose glitzy, glittery costumes in the '80s gave Liberace a run for his money. "Gay people used to come up to us and say, 'What are you fucking *doing,* man?'"

Besides being called a "hair band," Poison was also called a "poser band," implying that they were more concerned about what they looked like than sounded like. "There's a lot of bands out there that are calling us posers," said Rikki Rockett in 1986. "But when you meet them, what they're saying and what they're doing is a totally different thing. We sing about fucking, but then we go ahead and do it."

Bands like Poison ushered metal and hard rock into what could be compared to a bubblegum pop period. Eventually metal magazines began resembling the cover of *Tiger Beat,* with story headlines like, "Write a Poem and Win Warrant's Hearts!"

Arrogant even before stardom, once successful the members of Poison blithely angered many around them. Trying to get the band to agree to do anything was a process. They didn't want to be accessible, and even the people who worked for the band had to jump through a lot of hoops for them. Poison blew off meet-and-greets, interviews, and meeting with radio people. Eventually Poison were barraged by lawsuits. Their former managers, Sanctuary Music, filed a $45.5 million breach-of-contract suit. In 1987, Geffen publicist Bryn Bridenthal sued for assault after Michaels and Dall dumped a bucket of ice water on her head and had her thrown out of a party because Guns N' Roses, a Geffen act, was continually badmouthing them.

Axl Rose had always been close to Bridenthal and considered her a maternal figure. She had to plead with the members of Guns N' Roses not to beat up the members of Poison. Poison claimed the incident was all in fun, but nevertheless Bridenthal won the suit against them. "Make the lawsuit worth our while," said Bobby Dall at the height of the band's legal difficulties. "We don't accept lawsuits under two million dollars."

Another important development in the Los Angeles music scene was the opening of the Cathouse in 1986. The club was founded by Faster Pussycat's Taime Downe and Riki Rachtman, who later went on to host MTV's *Headbanger's Ball*. The first six months the club was open, attendance was low, and it was uncertain whether the club would survive. As Guns N' Roses gained momentum during the same year, so did the Cathouse.

Joseph Brooks was the club DJ from the first night to the last at the Cathouse, and he played the same records that the musicians who frequented the Cathouse listened to at home, everything from the Rolling Stones and Aerosmith to the New York Dolls and Hanoi Rocks. Says Brooks, "When I'd put on 'Whole Lotta Rosie' by AC/DC, Axl would just jump on the dance floor and start dancing all over the place, bumping into people, kicking them out of the way. It was fun to push people's buttons like that."

"The Cathouse was our club; we fuckin' ruled there," recalls Slash. "Some of the most embarrassing things I've ever done in public were done there. That's when I used to wear my top hat all the time, and I'd be passed out naked in a booth with some chick. I fucked so many girls on the floor while people were walking over us."

Sex Pistols guitarist Steve Jones was also a regular at the club. "Steve was in the DJ booth often," says Brooks. "One night he was trying to get this girl to have sex with him in the booth, and she didn't speak any English. So he asked me to play a Sex Pistols song, and he showed her the album cover. Sure enough, he was having full-on sex with her in the booth after I played the song."

Mainstream bands like Bon Jovi and Skid Row started coming to the Cathouse when they came through Los Angeles on tour. The club's reputation grew even larger when Axl Rose wore his Cathouse T-shirt on stage and MTV. Through Rose, Riki Rachtman landed the job hosting *Headbanger's Ball,* which aired on MTV from 1988 to 1994.

"The Cathouse was a comfortable place where a lot of less-than-beautiful people could go to feel beautiful," says Del James. "The club welcomed the unwanted. It was Oz for the addicted." As Rachtman said, "We did for rock and roll what Studio 54 did for cocaine."

In addition to his influential DJ work at the Cathouse, Joseph Brooks also owned Vinyl Fetish, a record store on Melrose Avenue that specialized in rare and hard-to-find albums. Izzy Stradlin made leather bracelets that he sold at the store on consignment. One day Stradlin came in and told Brooks about his new band Guns N' Roses. "Could you please come see us? It would really mean a lot to me." Brooks went to a show and loved the band.

Brooks called several A&R executives, including Tom Zutaut at Geffen, and told them about Guns N' Roses. Brooks invited Zutaut to a show at the Troubadour where the band was opening for Kix, but the executive never showed up. Brooks called him in his office the next day and asked why he didn't come. Zutaut told him he didn't want to pay the drink-ticket minimum, which was five dollars. Brooks again invited Zutaut to the Troubadour, where Guns N' Roses was opening for L.A. Guns. This time, the executive decided to come (Brooks made sure he didn't have to pay the five bucks). Zutaut was blown away by the band and asked Brooks, "Why didn't you tell me about them earlier?"

Zutaut noticed other A&R executives in the audience checking out Guns N' Roses that night. He left after several songs so no one would think he was interested in signing them. At the time, nobody wanted to work with the band because of their reputation for drugs, violence, and unpredictability. But Zutaut saw the band's potential to become huge. It wasn't until Zutaut showed real interest in signing Guns N' Roses that other labels took notice, because he had a strong reputation for signing new artists.

Guns N' Roses signed with Geffen on March 26, 1986. Having developed a shrewd business sense hustling on the street, the band negotiated the Geffen deal themselves. Paul Stanley of Kiss was interested in producing Guns N' Roses; so was Spencer Proffer, who had produced *Metal Health* for Quiet Riot. Clearly, neither was right for Guns N' Roses. When Stanley tried to rewrite several of the band's songs, including "Welcome to the Jungle," he was dismissed. "Anyone tried to 'produce' us, we told them to get the fuck out," says Slash.

Mike Clink eventually landed the job to produce the band's debut album, which they called *Appetite for Destruction*. Clink had begun his career as an engineer in 1975, working in the famous L.A. studio the Record Plant (*Hotel California* was one of the pivotal albums being recorded at the Plant at that time). Clink earned a strong reputation as a top engineer when he worked on Survivor's 1983 No. 1 hit "Eye of the Tiger," from the *Rocky III* soundtrack. Clink was also an engineer on the UFO live album *Strangers in the Night*. In 1986, he moved up to being a full-fledged producer on a Triumph album, *The Sport of Kings,* after the original producer, Ron Nevison, was dismissed.

He ended up working with Guns N' Roses by default. No one wanted to work with the band, but Clink needed to produce a young band to prove himself. "It takes a certain drive and a certain insanity to be a producer," says Ross Hogarth, a friend of Clink. "Guns N' Roses were definitely one of the hardest bands to hang with on a daily basis. I don't know how many other people could have done it."

The band listened to Clink's work and told him what they wanted, and what they didn't want, to sound like. UFO was cool; Survivor wasn't. They agreed to record a demo together to see if they could get along, and they hit it off right away. The band had found a producer who could capture their sound.

Before a note was recorded, Guns N' Roses' reported $75,000 advance was gone. "Me and Izzy had a pretty steady drug habit back then, so I remember how fast we ran out of that," says Slash. "I carried mine around in an envelope with traveler's checks in my back pocket, and was constantly going to check-cashing places, copping all the time. I couldn't put money in the bank, because I had a lien on me from some tax evasion."

At one point, the label figured it would be cheaper to drop the band than make a record, but Tom Zutaut secured enough money from the label to finish the album. According to Clink, the album cost a little over $140,000, which he says was right on budget. Zutaut also asked Alan Niven, who handled another L.A. band, Great White, to manage Guns N' Roses. Niven began managing them in the summer of 1986.

Many of the basic tracks on *Appetite for Destruction* were done in one take. "When you have a band that's as volatile as Guns is, you don't try and milk the band for numerous takes. You just end up losing everybody," said Slash. "Next thing you know, one guy's at a strip bar, another one's around the corner somewhere. You gotta go while the energy flows."

Slash went through countless guitar and amp combinations and had practically given up on generating the right sound from his Jackson and B. C. Rich guitars. Slash then tried a Les Paul with a yellow-and-red "sunburst" finish that blended beautifully with the guitar's quilted wood grain. From that point on, Slash was rarely seen without a Les Paul in his hands. "If it ain't broke, don't fix it," he says. Slash played with almost no effects except for a wah-wah pedal, a device thought to have been left behind in the '70s. Both Slash and Kirk Hammett of Metallica used the effect because they were influenced by Jimi Hendrix. Slash and Bon Jovi guitarist Richie Sambora also used a talk-box, an effect that was last popular when it appeared on the *Frampton Comes Alive* album in 1976.

By 1988, heavy metal music was saturated with fast guitar players who lacked originality and soul. The success of Guns N' Roses helped bring back blues-based guitar. Slash approached his playing by hearing a melody in his head before playing it, instead of just playing fretboard patterns as fast as possible. "It's something that very few guitar players of my generation even paid attention to."

Slash and Stradlin proved to be a unique team. Stradlin's songwriting was vital to the band, and his simple guitar style complimented Slash's playing perfectly. Together they created musical dynamics that most '80s guitarists would have ruined by filling in every space with notes.

The songs on *Appetite for Destruction* were based on actual experiences, and their lyrics would often trigger painful memories for Axl Rose. "We don't hide anything [in our songs]," said Duff McKagan. "It's like, here's your life. Here's the love lost, here's the hurt, here's the good, this is what I've been through."

"Welcome to the Jungle" was about Rose coming to L.A. and learning how to survive on his wits. Many of the kids in the local music scene came to L.A. from small towns hoping to make it, and "Jungle" described what was awaiting them. It was a song for them as much as Rose. "Mr. Brownstone" was a veiled reference to heroin. "A friend of mine thought it was about a building," says Slash. "Out Ta Get Me" was about Rose's conflicts with authority and how he was always finding himself in trouble. "My Michelle" was about Rose's complicated relationship with a former girlfriend, Michelle Young. The song reflected Young's chaotic life. The first line of the song explains that her father worked in the porn industry and her mother died of an overdose. It begins with a dark, mysterious riff that weaves like a spiderweb, "because that's how Axl perceived me," says Young. The tranquility is broken by a heavy riff, "then I explode and exploit myself."

Bored and restless in the San Fernando Valley while recording, the band lived up to their album title. As Slash recalls, "Me and Duff used to take the Guns N' Roses rental van—which there were many—kick the windshield out, drive it through fuckin' walls, and then sneak it back into the rental place late at night." The next day, manager Alan Niven would receive a phone call from the rental company asking, "Do you know what kind of people you're dealing with?"

Guns N' Roses lived at the Oakwood Apartments in Woodland Hills while they recorded the album. One night, they kicked the counters off the bar, broke all the chairs, burned the bed, and smashed the sliding glass doors. The band called the hotel management and told them, "Somebody's broken in!" and demanded a refund. The next morning, the hotel manager and security showed up early in the morning and found the band members passed out on the floor. The manager asked, "So what's the story now?" No one in Guns N' Roses could remember it. They tried making up a story as they went along, but it didn't fly. The band was thrown out immediately.

Appetite for Destruction was released on August 1, 1987, but it was slow to take off. The band figured it would do as well as an average Motörhead album, which was about 100,000 copies. The label was desperate to get their video for "Welcome to the Jungle" on MTV. The album's sales had stalled at around 200,000 copies and without that extra push, the label figured, it was dead. There are two different versions of how Guns N' Roses finally got on MTV. According to Tom Zutaut he went to David Geffen directly, and as a personal favor to Geffen, MTV played the song once at five in the morning on a Sunday. As improbable as it sounds, Zutaut said, "Even in the wee hours of Sunday morning, MTV got so many requests it blew their switchboard."

However, according to Al Coury, who worked independent promotion for Geffen at the time, MTV had to report when a video was added to the network's rotation. MTV didn't want to add the song to their rotation, so Coury asked the program director to just play it once a night for five nights. After several months of Coury's badgering, the program director agreed to play the video for three nights in a row (if a video was played for five nights, the program director was required to report that the song was in "light rotation"). The first night "Jungle" went on at 11:30 P.M. The second night, it was played at 10 P.M.. and again at 3 A.M. MTV called Coury that night to tell him "Welcome to the Jungle" was the most requested video on the network.

Coury then sent out promo singles of the song to radio stations around the country. In big red letters against a black cover it read:

"DON'T REPORT THIS RECORD! . . . Even though it's number one in rotation on MTV. . . . Even though they sell out all their concerts. . . . BUT DON'T REPORT THIS RECORD!"

MTV's decision not to report the song piqued Top Forty radio's interest, and they gave it a listen. "Jungle" became a hit on Top Forty radio first; then the traditional rock radio stations started playing the record, embarrassed to be shown up by the Top Forty stations. The band's popularity snowballed from there. After Geffen had to fight tooth and nail to get Guns N' Roses on MTV, the network started running commercials that bragged, "You heard 'em here first."

In early 1986, the L.A. metal scene finally had its own radio station: KNAC. Formerly a new wave station, KNAC started its "pure rock" format on January 8, 1986, at 6 P.M. The first song they played was AC/DC's "It's a Long Way to the Top."

Metallica's Lars Ulrich felt that KNAC was the best commercial station in the United States. It was one of the only stations in America that played Metallica's epic songs unedited, the longest running over nine minutes. KNAC's programming was like the old days of radio, when the DJ played the more obscure songs from an artist, not just the single. You listened and felt a camaraderie with the DJ: *He likes that song too!* Long songs like Iron Maiden's "Rime of the Ancient Mariner," which clocked in at over thirteen minutes, were great when a DJ wanted to sneak out and smoke a joint.

However, KNAC's signal wasn't very strong. In fact, it was tough to pick up the station in the San Fernando Valley unless one had a cable hookup. Metal fans would drive well out of their way to pick up the station in their cars.

The station management knew that metal fans bought a lot of merchandise, so they created shirts and bumper stickers with the KNAC logo and call numbers, 105.5. Every proud metalhead had a KNAC sticker on his four-wheel-drive vehicle right next to their In-N-Out

Urge (formerly an In-N-Out Burger) sticker. The bumper sticker and T-shirt were simple in design: the KNAC 105.5 logo in white against black. The station didn't have a big budget to work with, and a black-and-white T-shirt was easy and cheap to produce. They also wanted the T-shirt to be like the station's format: bold and in-your-face.

It is estimated that KNAC gave out 200,000 bumper stickers a year, and you could count hundreds in the parking lot of any metal gig in Southern California (even years after KNAC went off the air, you could still spot them on L. A. freeways). KNAC gave away the T-shirts for on-the-air promotions, but they soon became so popular that they went into retail. At some rock shops, they even outsold Guns N' Roses and Metallica T-shirts.

KNAC played Guns N' Roses well before the band became popular, and the band stayed loyal to the station. With Larry Flynt starting his rock magazine *RIP* in 1986, and the Cathouse and KNAC taking off at the same time, the L.A. music scene had a strong support system. Says writer Del James: "There was this momentum and this sense that we were all a part of something bigger than Hollywood or just getting signed to a record contract."

Right after Christmas 1987, Guns N' Roses played several sold-out shows at Perkins Palace, a small theater in Pasadena. Drummer Steven Adler had broken his hand, and Cinderella drummer Fred Coury filled in. Back at the hotel after the show, Rose thanked Coury for helping out. Coury told Rose that Cinderella was going through a difficult time. Lead singer Tom Keifer insisted on having his own limo, away from the rest of the band. "That's fucked up," said Rose. "You guys are supposed to be a band." He then showed Coury the *Appetite* album cover tattooed on his right arm, a crucifix with skulls of the band members at various points of the cross. "See that man?" said Rose pointing to the tattoo. "We're a band here, man. That's Steve right there—he's my bro. He can't be replaced. We're all a band here; we're family."

Guns N' Roses toured extensively throughout 1987 and 1988. They first went on the road opening for the Cult but quickly moved their way up to opening for Mötley Crüe and Alice Cooper. The band members were big fans of Aerosmith and opened for the band on their *Permanent Vacation* tour in July 1988. Guns N' Roses drew a lot of comparisons to Aerosmith; Steven Tyler couldn't help but feel he was looking in a mirror when he met the band.

Aerosmith were now clean and sober. Back in the '70s, when Aerosmith were headlining arenas and stadiums, it seemed more important to keep them on the road and in the studio than to keep them healthy. "It was okay to be drinking away my life," said Tyler. "The manager would come backstage and say, 'Fine. Drink all you want. Just go onstage.' That was great for an alcoholic to hear."

In a band situation, it's extremely difficult to keep one member sober if the rest of the band is still getting high. The key to getting Steven Tyler straight—and to the continuation of Aerosmith—was getting everyone else straight as well. When Aerosmith hit the road, it was the very first time the band had done a sober tour. Only soda and non-alcoholic strawberry daiquiris were served backstage. The band's sobriety and survival were taken seriously, and the rules of conduct were strict; a member of the road crew got fired for having a beer on his day off. With their newfound sobriety, Aerosmith sounded better than ever. After Guns N' Roses played their opening set, Stradlin would watch Aerosmith play, "and they'd sound fucking amazing. I thought, we're gonna have to really pull this shit together to keep up. And with us, even then, it was like the music was already taking a back seat to all the other shit."

On July 23, while Guns N' Roses were still on the Aerosmith tour, "Sweet Child O' Mine" became a No. 1 single. The band wrote the song in just a few minutes, and it was recorded in one take. Most of the band thought it would be filler on *Appetite for Destruction,* a throwaway song—everyone except Axl Rose, who put in the most sincere performance on the song. He dedicated "Sweet Child" to girlfriend Erin Everly.

That summer, young guitarists all over America demanded their teachers show them how to play "Child" 's opening riff. *Musician* magazine voted it "This Year's Mandatory Teenage Guitar Lick" in 1988. Slash came up with the riff as a joke and never liked the song. He considered Guns N' Roses a hard rock band first and foremost. He hated the fact that after touring for a year straight, "Sweet Child O' Mine" turned them into pop stars.

Rose was furious when Tom Zutaut cut "Sweet Child" down so it could be played on the radio and MTV. Their next single, "Paradise City," which clocked in at over six minutes, went to radio and MTV untouched. Bands like Winger and Extreme knew their music had to fit within a certain time frame to get MTV and radio play, and they envied Guns N' Roses for pulling this off.

Appetite for Destruction became the No. 1 album on the *Billboard* charts August 6, 1988, while the band was still on tour with Aerosmith. "Welcome to the Jungle" finally became a Top Ten hit that November. Writer Rob Tannenbaum joined Aerosmith on the road to do a cover story on them for *Rolling Stone* magazine, but Guns N' Roses wound up getting the cover story. "Suddenly the opening act was bigger than we were," recalled former Aerosmith manager Tim Collins.

Appetite for Destruction also put Mike Clink on the map as a hot producer. Many had underestimated Clink when he first championed Guns N' Roses. When the album was released, numerous people came up to him and said the album was "the biggest piece of shit I've ever [heard]. It's just noise—how could you do that record?" A year later, when *Appetite* exploded, those same people came up to him and said, "Oh man, I love that band. I really do."

Appetite for Destruction has gone down in history as one of the best albums of the 1980s. It captured the band's strengths perfectly. The album also became a time capsule, in that Guns N' Roses would never be the same band again. The struggle that the band had gone through made their music all the more honest and authentic. "Rock and roll is not a upper- or middle-class game. It's a lower-class game," says Ric Browde.

"Rich kids rarely make good music and rarely succeed, because there has to be that desperation to it." In their first *Rolling Stone* cover story, Rob Tannenbaum summed up Guns N' Roses' appeal. "Kids may envy or idolize David Lee Roth but they have little in common with him. Axl remains obsessed with the contradictions of adolescence; the unfocused rage, the pervasive doubt, the insecurity and the cockiness, the horniness and the fear. Their songs don't hide the fact that they're confused and screwed up."

"Rock music goes through these surges of really creative, brilliant stuff and then drops into these absolute lows when it almost seems like it's dead," said Slash. "We came along at a time when music was at one of those low points. I guess it was almost like a fluke, really, but we seemed to touch a nerve with everybody."

Guns N' Roses had a hard time adjusting to everyday life following the Aerosmith tour. The band built up an intense level of energy on the road, and to suddenly stop was a recipe for disaster. Slash had always been a workaholic, and he couldn't deal with free time. "As long as I'm playing, I'm okay. Give me a week off doin' nothin', I'm fucked." The band quickly realized they were no longer the same five guys holed up in a tiny rehearsal room but millionaires. For the first time in their lives, they had to be responsible adults, and it overwhelmed them.

With their first album, Guns N' Roses achieved a success few bands would experience, and with that success came new levels of pressure. Axl Rose was becoming aware of what was expected of him, and he was terrified. He constantly threatened to leave the band, once declaring his intention to go pump gas for a living (somehow, it's hard to picture him with an "Axl" patch on his lapel).

Rose would also become unusually thin-skinned to criticism. If anyone didn't understand or agree with him, he flew into rages. He was particularly sensitive to bad reviews of his live performances. Doug Goldstein, the band's manager after Alan Niven was fired, had to hide negative reviews from Rose out of fear he wouldn't show up to the band's next performance if he read them. Rose also tried to make interviewers sign a contract that would give the band and their management complete control over what was being written about them; failure to comply would result in $100,000 damages. It was a move that turned the press against him.

Rose would become megalomanical in his need for control of all things related to the band. Part of his desire to control everything around him had to do with his perfectionism and his insecurity. "Axl was always neurotic about photo shoots or when a show was coming up," says Michelle Young. "He was always afraid he didn't sound perfect. He's very much a perfectionist and very cynical about himself."

Poison hired Tom Werman to produce their second album, *Open Up and Say . . . Aah!* The album would sell five million copies and would feature their biggest single, "Every Rose Has Its Thorn," which went to No. 1 in October 1988.

C. C. DeVille had become close friends with Sam Kinison, the wild ex-preacher whose comedy defined politically incorrect humor. Like John Belushi, Kinison loved the rock and roll life and partied hard. And like Belushi, he secretly wanted to be a rock star and jammed with his famous musician friends. "Sam was the type, you couldn't hold court," says DeVille. "When Sam came over, you had to relinquish the floor because he was so fast and sharp and funny."

Kinison was famous for his screaming, and every time they'd walk into a restaurant together, "everyone just became Sam and would yell, 'Hey, Sam!' The decibel level would be like the Los Angeles airport." One night Sam took DeVille to Spago, the classy L.A. bistro. Laid out in front of DeVille were a number of spoons, forks, and knives. He wasn't sure which utensils to use first and didn't want to look like he didn't know, so he whispered, "Sam, what fork do I use?" Sam told him, "With the prices they charge here, you can use your hands."

DeVille was now living in a big house on Sunset Plaza. According to former Jet Records employee Ace Steele, who was friendly with DeVille, he enjoyed sunbathing nude by the pool. His neighbor, Diana Ross, wasn't happy about it and complained to the city. According to Steele, DeVille got so mad at her that he threatened to hire a bunch of guys to run around his pool naked to piss her off (DeVille doesn't recall this). He would also jam at full volume at six o'clock in the morning and would get numerous letters of complaint shoved under his door from neighbors such as Burt Reynolds and Ice-T.

Poison was finally living their dream of success, but DeVille was free-basing cocaine, a habit that would enslave him for years. He once set his hotel bed on fire when he passed out with the torch still lit. Looking back on those years, he says he's not sure exactly why he turned to drugs. "I ask myself [why] every day," he says. "That's what baffles me. I have a great family, I'm very close to them, I had a great upbringing. Every other thing in my life has a sense of right and wrong except this drug thing. What was it? What was it that made me go? It's one of those things you say to yourself, boy, what a waste."

Guns N' Roses quickly followed up the success of *Appetite for Destruction* with an EP, *G N' R Lies*, which quickly hit the Top Ten, although one track on the recording would cause tremendous controversy. "One in a Million" was similar to "Welcome to the Jungle," in that it described Rose's arrival in Los Angeles and his experience of getting hustled in the Greyhound bus station. The most controversial lines spoke of Rose's problems with "police and niggers" and "immigrants and faggots."

At the time, Rose said he used the word "nigger" because he didn't like boundaries being put on what he could and couldn't say. He also wanted to use the word because it was taboo. He claimed that he hadn't used the word in a racial way but, rather, as "someone who's a pain in your life." He admitted he didn't like homosexuals but denied hating all immigrants, just those that angered him. As far as Rose was concerned, no one had the right to criticize his lyrics if they hadn't experienced what he had when he first arrived in L.A. "There are a large number of black men selling stolen jewelry, crack, heroin, and pot, and most of the drugs are bogus. Rip-off artists [are] trying to misguide every kid that gets off the bus, trying to take the person for whatever they've got. That's how I hit town."

Written into Guns N' Roses' record contract with Geffen was a provision that gave them complete control over their music. But the rest of the band couldn't convince Rose to drop the song. They would have the same problem years later when he insisted on recording a Charles Manson song that Slash refused to play on. "['One in a Million'] was taken exactly how I thought it would be," says Slash. "I had my disagreements with Axl on it. It was just one of those things where I said, 'Fuck it, do whatever you want to do.' But we didn't realize how much influence the band as a whole had, as opposed to it just being blamed on Axl."

The anger over the song was immediate. One critic went so far as to say it was music for "David Duke's America." Gay groups pressured David Geffen to drop Guns N' Roses from his label, and he reportedly received death threats. Izzy Stradlin learned the hard way how much "One in a Million" offended minorities when he spent a day in jail.

The all-black hard rock band Living Colour confronted Rose backstage when both bands opened for the Rolling Stones. Guitarist Vernon Reid spoke for many when he said, "I don't think there was a conscious attempt to hurt people [with the song]. I think there was no thought given to how people would feel."

Slash was also criticized by his family (his mother is African-American) and friends who felt he should have tried to stop Rose from recording "One in a Million." Of course, this was impossible. A member of the band who asked not to be identified told *Details* magazine, "We just let Axl pretty much do what he feels he has to do, 'cause he'll only do it anyways. And if it doesn't work, maybe he might learn something. *Then* maybe we can fix it."

By late 1985, Phil Lynott was considering getting back together with his old friend and Thin Lizzy bandmate Scott Gorham. Gorham was coming off a drug habit and had been clean for a year. When Thin Lizzy were recording their 1979 album *Black Rose* in France, the dealers descended on them, and Gorham and Lynott became addicted to heroin.

Lynott didn't look well. His asthma was acting up, which meant he was using. Guitarist John Sykes, who played with Thin Lizzy on their 1983 *Thunder and Lightning* album, was also concerned about Lynott's health. Sykes told Lynott he was going to take him to the hospital whether he wanted to go or not, but Lynott refused. He was strong-willed and had a temper, which didn't make it easy for Sykes to confront Lynott about his addiction.

Lynott whipped out an acoustic guitar and showed Gorham some things he was working on. Gorham told himself that it wasn't the right time to get back together yet, but he would leave the door open. He knew Lynott had to clean up first because dealing with an addiction on the road was too difficult. Three weeks later, on January 4, 1986, Lynott died of heart failure and pneumonia. He was thirty-five.

In the years after Lynott's passing, Thin Lizzy's cult has grown strong. Metallica had a hit covering their song "Whiskey in the Jar" in 1998, and "The Boys Are Back in Town" has become a staple of classic rock radio. Lynott's fans and former bandmates miss him terribly. "People don't realize that when Phil died, Thin Lizzy didn't just lose a singer or a bass player—we all lost our friend," says Scott Gorham. "I'd rather have him be alive and not be in the band Thin Lizzy than anything else so we can hang out and have a load of laughs like we used to." "I always looked up to Phil and respected him," says John Sykes. "He lived every minute and every second of it. He wasn't fuckin' around, and it wasn't a game. Phil might have had a shortened life on this planet, but I can guarantee that he probably lived more life in his thirty-six years than a fuckin' hundred people lived."

At a point where metal was considered a passing fad, the massive success of **Bon Jovi**'s *Slippery When Wet* album in 1986 brought the music back to radio and MTV. (Neil Zlozower)

Livin' on a Prayer

10

"I'LL NEVER BE SATISFIED. I'M NOT HAPPY THAT WE HAVE THE NO. 1
ALBUM, SINGLE, CD, VIDEO, THAT I SOLD OUT EVERY SHOW AND THAT I
FLY IN MY AIRPLANE AND THAT I CAN BUY A HUGE MANSION IF I WANT
TO. NEXT YEAR, I WANT TO BE BIGGER. I WANT A BIGGER RECORD. I
WANT TO DO MORE SHOWS. I WANT TO BE ABLE TO BUY TWO HOUSES
INSTEAD OF ONE."

—Jon Bon Jovi in 1987

WHILE THEY PACKED ARENAS and boasted heavy rotation on
MTV in the States, many of the L.A. bands had a hard time over in Europe. The hardcore metal fans overseas didn't like hairspray and pop
sensibilities. "The European audience didn't want their metal mixed up
with anything else," says one musician.

Even though they got their start in Europe, Dokken had a difficult
time opening for the German band Accept on a European tour. Accept
was a fierce band that delivered their metal with machine-like precision.
Their anthem "Balls to the Wall" was an apt description of their music.
Dokken lamented that there were no women at the gigs for the entire
two-month tour.

By the mid-1980s, however, a whole new market for metal was
opening up in Japan. The Japanese metal fans were die-hard fanatics
who lived and breathed the music. Robbin Crosby of Ratt once described the letters he would receive from Japanese fans: "In the third
song, second verse, you made a mistake. Was something wrong?" When
the music fell on hard times in the '90s, Japan was one of the last places
a heavy metal band could still headline an arena.

An American band's arrival inspired Beatlemania-style frenzy in Japan.
Lizzy Borden was an L.A. band signed to Metal Blade Records. Back in
the States, they played only clubs, but when they went to Japan, scores
of fans waited for them at the airport. The band was then whisked away

in a limo by security guards in black suits. When they arrived at the hotel, the security changed the codes in the hotel's computers so the fans wouldn't be able to find out where they were staying. In Japan, Lizzy Borden played large theaters and performed on the Japanese equivalents of *American Bandstand* and *The Tonight Show.* "Playing Japan is like a dream," says Lizzy Borden bassist Mike Davis. "It's like flying into another dimension and waking up a rock star."

One of the best ways to break a band in America was to first break them overseas, but few bands were willing to put the effort into touring in Europe and Asia to build that initial following. One manager who understood this philosophy was Doc McGhee. McGhee was already handling Mötley Crüe when he signed on to manage Jon Bon Jovi. McGhee's game plan was to build Bon Jovi in Europe and Japan while his popularity was just starting to grow in the States. As a band, Bon Jovi committed a lot of time and energy to building their following overseas.

"A lot of artists were given that advice, and they just didn't do it," says Jim Lewis, the VP of marketing at PolyGram at the time the label signed Bon Jovi. " 'Oh man, I don't want to go on that fourteen-hour plane ride again to Japan.' Well, Bon Jovi did it." By his second album, Bon Jovi became a superstar in Japan, one of the first of the major '80s hard rock acts to build a substantial following there.

A lot of American bands still don't build their followings overseas, preferring to focus on the United States as their biggest market. Says Joe Elliott of Def Leppard, "Van Halen's best-ever period in Britain was in 1978 when they opened for Black Sabbath. They did a big stadium show opening for Bon Jovi [several years ago]. That was the first time they'd been back there [since]."

Bon Jovi was especially loved in England, and his pictures began filling the pages of *Kerrang!* magazine, then the premier metal magazine in Britain. Bon Jovi opened for Kiss in Europe during their *Animalize* tour in 1985 and as former Kiss guitarist Bruce Kulick recalls, "I remember they were doing New Jersey club material, but it was going over. I giggled about it in a way, because it was like pop Bruce Springsteen, that New Jersey [vibe]. I'm a New Yorker, you can't fool me—I know where that sound comes from!" Bon Jovi's sound was distinctly from the Jersey shore and, like Bruce Springsteen's music, had a working-class-hero feel to it. Bon Jovi was the type of band you'd go to see at a bar after a hard day's work, but they had louder guitars and taller hair.

Jon Bon Jovi was born John Bongiovi on March 2, 1962, in New Jersey. His father was a hairdresser who always cut Jon's locks short. In a bit of poetic justice for Jon, his father later trimmed and colored his son's heap of frosted chestnut hair once he became a superstar. Jon's cousin was Tony Bongiovi, who owned the Power Station recording studio in New York, one of the top studios in the state. Bongiovi had also produced albums for Aerosmith and the Ramones. Jon started working in his cousin's studio after graduating from high school, running errands and sweeping the floors for fifty dollars a week. Tony Bongiovi let young Jon use the studio when no one else was using it, but he still made Jon pay for the time.

When Bon Jovi signed his record deal with PolyGram in 1983, Tony sued him. Tony felt he helped nurture Jon's talent and was owed something in return. His settlement included a producer's credit and fee, royalties from the first album, and a 1 percent royalty on Jon's next two records. The suit alienated Jon from his cousin, and he eventually shortened his last name to Bon Jovi because the label felt his real name was too ethnic. (Bon Jovi's keyboardist David Bryan Rashbaum also changed his name, to David Bryan.)

After he signed his record deal, Bon Jovi came to the label every day and hung out with Jim Lewis and Derek Schulman, the senior vice president at PolyGram. Bon Jovi wanted to learn the business, and he made it his business to learn. "When I first met Jon, he didn't have a dollar in his pocket, and he wanted a real opportunity and a chance to get out there," recalls Lewis.

Despite his desire to make it, it took some time before Jon was acknowledged in the States. For years, the joke went that people thought that Bon Jovi was a spaghetti sauce or a fancy brand of wine (or, like Aldo Nova, he could have been a new model of Italian sports car). Bon Jovi also suffered from the Brad Pitt syndrome: He was frustrated that the press focused on his looks and passed him off as "a heavy metal Shaun Cassidy," as one writer put it.

Jon was upset the critics didn't see any depth in his music, but as he took great pains to point out, Bon Jovi was a hard rock and roll band, pure and simple. There were no deep messages in their music. "We never set out to change the world," he said. "Rock and roll to me was always entertainment; it wasn't a place to be talking about politics or nuclear holocausts. As much as I love U2, it's like, *you* write about that stuff. I ain't concerned."

Like a lot of bands in the '80s, Bon Jovi sported big hair and wore flashy clothes. But by their second album, 1985's *7800° Fahrenheit,* the band tried to move away from that. "If you want to torture me, show me our early videos," Jon said recently. "On our first two albums, we thought that the way to be was to imitate Ratt and Mötley Crüe. You'd sweat, the hairspray would run into your eyes, and your eyes would be burning." He added, "back then, we singlehandedly kept VO5 in business." Jon's hair was so prominently mentioned in the press that when he finally cut it, it was news on CNN.

Jon was fast developing a reputation for being a shrewd businessman. When Bon Jovi opened for Ratt in New Jersey in 1985, both bands were paid equal money. Jon certainly worked harder than most of his contemporaries, but some feel the real genius behind the curtain was manager Doc McGhee. "He's a great star, a great writer, and I think he learned a huge amount from Doc McGhee," says Jim Lewis. "Jon would have been a star no matter who was managing him, but Doc took him further than it naturally would have gone."

"Doc McGhee fought like hell with the promoters to make sure Jon got every cent that was due to him," says Steve Pritchett, who was the director of international marketing at PolyGram. "They were a great combination. Doc is a very shrewd and astute manager, and there was a lot of trust between them."

Bon Jovi brought Cinderella, a band from Philadelphia, to the label in 1985. The band didn't generate a lot of excitement at PolyGram, and only through much cajoling were they offered a record deal. According to Lewis, Bon Jovi told them, "Look, I'm gonna bring this to Columbia tomorrow, and John Kalodner is gonna sign them, unless you sign this band RIGHT NOW!" Reluctantly, the label did sign them, and it would eventually pay off.

When it came to promoting his own band, Bon Jovi was like a politician shaking hands and kissing babies. He did every bit of press and appeared at every radio station he could. He made sure he had a good relationship with everyone at the record company, took them to ballgames, had barbecues, and hung out in bars with them. He even went personally to the *Saturday Night Live* offices offering his band to play on the show (they declined). Short of selling his albums door to door, Bon Jovi did everything possible to get his name out there.

For Bon Jovi's third album, 1986's *Slippery When Wet,* Jon's secret weapon was songwriter Desmond Child. Child first had some success playing in a rock band called Rouge, which released two albums in the '70s. Child wrote his first big hit for Kiss in 1979, "I Was Made for Loving You," a disco song that peaked at No. 11 on the charts. But it was his work with Bon Jovi and the success of *Slippery When Wet* that remade Child's career. Afterward, Kalodner would hire him to work with Aerosmith, and he would go on to write big hits for Cher, Garth Brooks, and Michael Bolton, among others. Jon Bon Jovi was writing for other bands, and he and Child originally wrote Bon Jovi's hit "You Give Love a Bad Name" for Loverboy. Their instincts must have kicked in—they decided to keep the song for themselves.

Radio was on the song from the beginning, and once MTV started playing the video, it delivered the knockout punch. KNAC had played Bon Jovi from the beginning, and he was in turn loyal to the station.

When the *Slippery* tour hit L.A., despite a lot of pressure from PolyGram, Jon would let no radio station promote the concert but KNAC, still an underdog in the ratings to KLOS. "Even when we weren't playing Bon Jovi anymore, because his music had become too mainstream, [in later years] he would still call in and say hi—he never forgot," says Tom Maher, who worked at KNAC until the early 1990s. "I have to give Jon that credit."

Slippery When Wet was selling about 100,000 copies a week out of the gate. Bon Jovi started out its tour opening for Southern rockers .38 Special, but the album took off so fast that .38 Special ended up opening for Bon Jovi. The album hit No. 1 its seventh week of release and was at the top of the charts for eight nonconsecutive weeks. (*Slippery* was competing with Bruce Springsteen's live album and Boston's long-awaited third album, *Third Stage*.) *Slippery When Wet* became the No. 1 album of the year, beating out U2's *The Joshua Tree*. *Slippery* sold over 14 million copies, one of the most successful albums not just of the '80s but of all time.

Bon Jovi would perfectly bridge the gap between pop and metal, and they were in the right place at the right time. "There was a need by the people for a Bon Jovi," said guitarist Richie Sambora. "Just a good-time entertainment band. A bridge between Phil Collins and Whitesnake."

"Bon Jovi really paved the way for metal groups to cross over, in the same way Michael Jackson's *Thriller* opened the floodgates in 1982 for other black R&B artists to cross over," said John Kalodner. He now says the *Slippery When Wet* album was "the pivotal moment in the market changing. That's the record that did it." The public perceptions of heavy metal and hard rock groups were dungeons, black leather, and chains; Bon Jovi were the nice guys, the all-American heroes.

In June 1987, on the heels of *Slippery*'s success, half the *Billboard* Top Ten were hard rock and metal albums, including releases by Bon Jovi, Mötley Crüe, Ozzy Osbourne, Poison, and Whitesnake. The Top 200 featured seventeen other metal acts. *Slippery When Wet* was a record-industry phenomenon that changed the media's perception of metal and hard rock. "There had been numerous predictions that heavy metal was on the way out as a major commercial force," wrote the *Los Angeles Times* at the point of metal and hard rock's resurgence on the charts. Cinderella has actually been credited for first opening up the market again with their debut album, *Night Songs,* which came out in June 1986 and sold three million copies. *Slippery When Wet* hit No. 1 three months later.

As Jon Bon Jovi recalled years later, "We had our first real success on our third album, and fortunately for us, we were given the opportunity to develop a following and hone our songwriting and performance skills in a bigger arena. It would be difficult to think that these days a record company would invest [all that work], and I'm fortunate that in 1983, it was a different time."

Many in the music industry who didn't like metal or hard rock finally saw that the music could make money. Manager Tom Hulett, who handled the Beach Boys and Three Dog Night, had never thought of getting involved with a metal or hard rock band until Bon Jovi's success. He then signed Warrant and told a friend that he made more money with them than with anyone else on his client roster.

A lot of '80s bands that were starting to fade couldn't believe how well Bon Jovi was doing. Kiss tried to follow Bon Jovi to the letter; if they worked with a certain video director or released a live version of a song as the B-side of a single, Simmons and Stanley felt safe following his lead. It almost got to the point where Stanley was scared to make a move without asking, "Did Bon Jovi do it?" first. The biggest rivalry Bon Jovi had was with Mötley Crüe. "Mötley were Doc's first baby," says Charrie Foglio, who worked for Doc McGhee. "They were the first kids, and Bon Jovi were the stepkids. Nikki and Jon were friends in the beginning, but the bigger they got, the more they were competing for Doc's affection, his time, and competing for one being bigger than the other."

In Foglio's view, it seemed to be Mötley Crüe holding the grudge. Jon Bon Jovi tried to be friendly to the band when they ran into each other; Nikki Sixx would usually blow him off. Mötley Crüe took Bon Jovi under their wing when they was first starting out, and when Bon Jovi got bigger, Sixx was envious of his success. "They looked at us as little brothers," said Jon Bon Jovi. "We're nobody's little brothers."

With Bon Jovi riding a tidal wave of success, Jon also helped discover and break another New Jersey band. The members of Skid Row grew up close to the Jersey Shore. Guitarist Dave "the Snake" Sabo lived several blocks away from Jon Bon Jovi in Sayreville, New Jersey, and had played guitar in one of Jon's early bands.

In their early days, Jon Bon Jovi critiqued Skid Row's music and introduced the band to Doc McGhee, who eventually signed them on to McGhee Entertainment (Doc's brother Scott managed the band). Skid Row was in the eye of the hurricane when Bon Jovi took off. They figured they were rubbing elbows with the right people and hoped it would pay off. Jon loved the band but told them they had to get rid of their singer. "We need to find you a superstar," he said.

For a year and a half, Skid Row went without a singer, sticking to a tightly regimented practice schedule five days a week. They even considered playing around as a punk band called This Blows, with bassist Rachel Bolan singing, just so they could get out and play live. Then rock photographer Mark Weiss told the band about someone who sang at his wedding who was a good-looking guy with a great voice, and a total wild man to boot. His name was Sebastian Bach.

Bach was born Sebastian Bierk in the Bahamas. His father owned an art gallery and eventually painted the cover for the band's *Slave to the Grind* album. Bach was on his own and living in Toronto by the time he was fifteen. The members of Skid Row chipped in what little money they could spare to fly him to New Jersey to audition. They all hit it off immediately and spent a week together. Says former Skid Row drummer Rob Affuso, "It was one of the best weeks of my life, because we finally realized we had a full package. Sebastian had balls and everything we needed." He was also all of eighteen years old. Even though he would become a larger-than-life rock star, the kids could relate to Sebastian because he was a kid himself.

One night during their first week together, everyone went out to get White Castle hamburgers wearing their stage clothes, their hair stacked to the sky, at two in the morning. A group of rednecks in the parking lot called them a bunch of faggots, and they began fighting. The Skid Row guys beat the shit out of them. They were now a team. "It was an incredible bonding session," says Affuso. "It really made it official."

Soon Skid Row had label interest, and John Kalodner was close to signing the band. When they entered one club they were going to play, Skid Row noticed a big spread of food and alcohol awaiting them, set up by Atlantic. Then Ahmet Ertegun landed in the parking lot in his helicopter, surrounded by five gorgeous women. He greeted the band and let them know Atlantic would take care of them.

About three months after Bach joined the band, Skid Row opened several shows on Bon Jovi's *Slippery When Wet* tour. They had played only a few club shows. "We were very arrogant; we were very sure of ourselves," says Affuso. "We knew we were great. That came out in the music and the stage show."

The band recorded their debut album in Alpine Valley, Wisconsin, with Michael Wagener producing. Right from the beginning, Wagener knew they had a hit record. All the elements were in place for the band to break. They had good songs, a killer singer, the support of their label, and big tours lined up. "All the lights were on green," says Wagener.

Jon Bon Jovi continued to give the band advice. For their first photo session, Skid Row were completely glammed out, looking like five women. Bon Jovi took one look at the photos and told them, "What the fuck are you guys thinking? This isn't gonna work." He told them they had to work on their image or they would be a flash in the pan. "Don't do this," he said. "You're crazy if you do this."

As with Bon Jovi, Skid Row's success had a lot to do with Doc McGhee. With Bon Jovi, McGhee was managing the biggest band in the world, and with a strong track record, the label figured Skid Row would be the next hit on McGhee's roll. Like Guns N' Roses, Skid Row was the right band at the right time. "We were very much anti-authority," says Affuso. "Do your own thing, stand up for your own rights, do what you believe in—right or wrong, you're going to learn your own way. That kind of a message, it seemed to hit home for a lot of kids."

When Skid Row were recording their self-titled first album, Michael Wagener predicted the band would sell three million records. Skid Row's debut took off at the same time as *Appetite for Destruction*. "When Guns N' Roses hit, we were on the edge of that," says Affuso. "This dirty/pretty band from L.A. all of a sudden became a hit, and we were right on their heels. We were a perfect fit for Atlantic's Guns N' Roses. It was the same image, the same vibe—it was hard, commercially acceptable rock with hard-ass pretty boys." And Skid Row's album did in fact sell three million copies.

Skid Row then hit the road and opened big tours for Bon Jovi, Aerosmith, and Mötley Crüe. It was particularly nerve-wracking for the band playing with Aerosmith because they were Skid Row's idols. But soon problems flared up between Skid Row and Bon Jovi. In exchange for introducing them to Doc McGhee and helping them out, Jon wanted the band's publishing, which became a gold mine once the album became a success. Bon Jovi guitarist Ritchie Sambora also had a share of the money but reportedly gave his back to the band. Years later, Skid Row guitarist Dave Sabo claimed the band never got any money back. The deal was on a declining basis, giving Jon less money with each successive album. "We basically signed a shitty deal, but we all signed it, and contrary to what anyone might say, we all knew what we were doing," Sabo said. "It's just that when success hit, we realized how much we had given up. But we still made a pretty penny ourselves."

Bach complained about this publicly, which angered Jon. Things came to a head on the penultimate night of Skid Row's tour with Bon Jovi. As usual on the last date of a tour, the headliner's road crew was playing pranks on Skid Row, pouring milk on the band from the rafters and chucking eggs at them while they were playing. Announcing their song "Piece of Me," Bach joked, "Jon Bon Jovi should come up here and get a piece of me." Jon wasn't laughing. Backstage, he rushed right past everyone and headed straight for Bach. Both took a shot at each other before security broke them up.

There were other problems that would eventually lead to Skid Row's downfall. The songwriting core of the band had always been Sabo and Bolan. Bach wanted to be a songwriter with the rest of the band, not a passenger along for the ride. Sabo never had a songwriting bond with Bach, and the more the singer tried to force himself into writing with the band, the more uncomfortable it became. Sometimes Bach threatened the band, saying, "It's not a fuckin' song unless I say it's a fucking song."

Skid Row was getting a lot of notice in the media, but the main focus was on Bach. When the band got the cover story in *Rolling Stone* in September 1991, Bach graced the cover alone. "Sebastian was getting a lot of attention, he was Skid Row in the media's eyes, so he started to believe what he was reading," says Affuso. "Granted, he was a great guy, great frontman, an interviewer's dream. But at the same time, we were fighting hard as a band to keep it a unit, not Sebastian and four other members." Bach was also getting attention for the wrong reasons. At the same time Axl Rose was coming under fire for the homophobic lyrics of "One in a Million," Bach took a lot of heat for wearing a T-shirt that was thrown on stage that read: "AIDS Kills Fags Dead." Just as Guns N' Roses caught flak for Rose's actions, so would Skid Row for Bach's. Both Affuso and Sabo would call the T-shirt incident one of the lowest points of the band's career.

"There were many times where I was proud to be in the band with Sebastian," says Affuso. "And there were many times where I felt disgraced, I felt totally humiliated. And that moment was one of them, because he was the spokesperson, so therefore what he said reflected me. Those things really hurt me and basically made me sick. Still to this day I'm judged by that. I wish that didn't happen, it certainly is a very dark moment in my career."

Def Leppard began recording their follow-up album to *Pyromania* in 1984. By New Year's Eve, everyone was enjoying the holidays back in Sheffield when Peter Mensch called Joe Elliott at his parents' home. Mensch asked Elliott if he was sitting down. He expected to hear that someone had died. But when Mensch told him that drummer Rick Allen had been in a car accident and lost his arm, Elliott simply couldn't process the information. He just sat there, stunned. His father quickly put a glass of scotch in his hand.

Elliott took a 180-mile drive to visit Allen in the hospital. When he arrived, Allen was heavily sedated, his eyes opening and closing. Elliott rushed to the bathroom and burst into tears. The doctors had reattached Allen's arm, but after a week they had to remove it because an infection had set in. The band was due back in the studio on January 4, 1985, and they went back to work to keep their minds off their troubles. Says Elliott: "You can't help thinking, 'What's the poor guy gonna do now?' "

Rick Allen spent a lot of time listening to music while he was in the hospital. "That's the thing that upset me the most at first, listening to music," he said. "I'd hear the drums and couldn't help but think, 'Yeah, I used to do that.' " Producer Mutt Lange visited Allen at the hospital and encouraged him to start playing again. Allen went home six weeks after the accident, though he was supposed to be in for at least six months. "They really stuck by Rick Allen when he lost his arm," says Tom Allom. "There was never any talk about getting another drummer. They were so close and so tight as a unit. They'd been a big act when they were kids, and they were gonna stick together."

The recording process for *Hysteria* moved at a glacial pace. Def Leppard had started recording *Hysteria* with MeatLoaf songwriter Jim Steinman producing. After Steinman was let go and close to a year's worth of sessions were scrapped, the band produced the album on their own until late 1985, when Mutt Lange came back to work with them. Elliott lost his voice from overuse, then he caught the mumps. Then Lange broke a kneecap in a car accident.

Surprisingly, as Elliott recalled, "All those delays helped the album. It would have been more in the vein [of] *Pyromania,* more than we wanted it to be. With the added time, we've been able to expand our musical horizons." The Ludwig Drum Company designed a special kit for Allen that he could play with one arm. A little over a year after the kit was built, Allen was up on stage with Def Leppard playing a one-off show at the Monsters of Rock festival in England in 1986.

The band finished recording *Hysteria* in January 1987. Mutt then spent four and a half months mixing the album. "He spent six weeks longer mixing *Hysteria* than he spent recording *High 'n' Dry,*" says Elliott. "He did what we think a producer should do, which is take what you've got and make it better than it is, like Brian Wilson would have done for the Beach Boys, or what George Martin would have done for the Beatles. Listening through a million different versions of a song and doing the edits."

Def Leppard and Mutt Lange looked to the record they were competing with in 1983, Michael Jackson's *Thriller,* which had seven Top Ten singles. Mutt said to the band, "Why can't a rock band have an album with seven singles on it?" *Hysteria* was designed to have numerous singles, à la *Thriller.*

"Mutt knew his way around a ninety-channel [mixing board] like a pilot knew his way around a cockpit," Elliott continues. "He had every single channel doing something. The mix of that record really was a creative work of art. Sometimes he'd run through a song 180 times before he could get into his head how he wanted it to be done. He must have literally almost gone mad doing it." The album took so long to finish that Q-Prime made up T-shirts that said, "Don't Ask," in the style of the Def Leppard logo. The band spent so much money in recording costs that they would have to sell five million albums to break even.

With Def Leppard away as long as they were, it still remained to be seen if they still had an audience. "There was a lot of pressure, obviously," says Jim Lewis. "The label had high expectations, there was a lot of money out on the table, and we had all this internal pressure to try and live up to the last album. The band had high expectations. Cliff and Peter certainly had the highest of expectations. They were out working it hard. There was a lot in place that had to be supported and made sure that it was going to happen."

The album sold well in Britain as soon as it was released in August 1987. It went straight to No. 1 and was, surprisingly, the band's first big hit album in their homeland. "The audience was ready for us in England and got over all the grief of us supposedly selling out to America," says Elliott. There was a new generation of fans just discovering the band that came along after *Pyromania*.

But *Hysteria* was struggling in the States. By Christmas it had sold 2.7 million copies, a respectable sum, but considering how many albums the band sold with *Pyromania*—and how many records they needed to sell to get out of debt—it was a disappointment. "Women," the first of many singles from the album, tanked. The next single, "Animal," cracked the Top Twenty in November 1987. The third single, "Hysteria," actually made it to the Top Ten in February 1988.

The band then toured Europe in May 1988, and "Pour Some Sugar on Me" was released as their next single. It fizzled on rock radio but somehow made it over to Top Forty and became a hit. With the success of the "Sugar" single, the album finally broke. "Summer was coming, and the kids were pulling their surfboards out of the garage and heading to the beach," says Elliott. "It was a very hood-off, drive-down-the-freeway type song. And I think it lit up a generation's summer."

The band originally shot a concept video for "Sugar" but then shot a live video for it instead. "The 'Pour Some Sugar on Me' concept video was the worst video of all time. In fact, MTV wouldn't even play it—that's how bad it was. The concept video had a big, bruising lesbian kind of woman knocking this house down with a big wrecking ball, and we're inside the house as it's collapsing down around us. We put it on our compilation video just so people could see how bad videos can be."

With the success of the "Sugar" single, Def Leppard sold four million copies of *Hysteria* in three months. By August 1988, the album went to No. 1, and the band spent the next twelve weeks fighting Guns N' Roses' *Appetite for Destruction* for the top spot on the charts, along with Van Halen's *OU812* album. "We finally outsold Michael Jackson at last!" says Elliott. (Jackson's follow-up to *Thriller, Bad,* was released the same year as *Hysteria.*).

Hysteria went on to achieve the near-impossible: With eleven million copies sold in the States alone, it actually outperformed *Pyromania.* All the struggle and heartache the band had gone through to record *Hysteria* was worth it. "It was a nightmare to make, but I still enjoy listening to it today," said Elliott. "I'd rather have it that way than have an album that I had a great time making but I can't listen to."

The *Hysteria* tour, which hit the road in October 1987, was performed in the round—the stage was in the middle of the arena, with the audience surrounding the band. In order for the band to get underneath the stage without being detected, the members of Def Leppard hid in laundry bins that roadies would wheel up the aisles to get underneath the stage. Guitarist Phil Collen and bassist Rick Savage shared one bin, and Elliott and guitarist Steve Clark shared another. Clark was claustrophobic and was frightened to be in the bin, and Elliott shared a bin with him to keep him calm. Rick Allen was the only member who didn't ride in a bin. He walked under the stage wearing a wig, sunglasses, and a jacket with a fake arm built in. Eventually, word got out among the fans that the band was being transported in the laundry bins, and as they were being pushed down the aisle, the concertgoers would bang and tap on them, yelling: "We know you're in there!"

Def Leppard had beaten the odds and come back stronger than ever, but the pressure was starting to get to Clark. How would the band follow up the success of *Hysteria* on their next album? On the first night of the *Hysteria* tour, the guitarist smashed his hands against a sink, trying to break them so he wouldn't be able to play. Says Elliott, "Steve was the first and only one of us who was like, 'This is too big for me to deal with,' whereas we were all looking forward to it.

"There were plenty of times when Steve was fine," continues Elliott. "We'd grown up together as a band, and everybody was always there for each other. He always was just a mess when he was left up to his own devices. When everybody else was drinking with him, he was fine. It's just that we all used to stop before him, and that's when he'd be out on his own. But it wasn't an everyday occurrence. Steve was the one who would fall off the wagon more often than not."

Clark's drinking reached a dangerous peak after the *Hysteria* tour. In December 1989, he was found lying in the streets in an alcohol-induced coma. His blood alcohol level was .59. By comparison, John Bonham's blood alcohol level was .41 when he died. In September 1990, the band gave Clark a six-month leave of absence to clean up and get his life together. Before the six months were up, Clark died on January 8, 1991, of an overdose of alcohol and drugs. He was thirty years old.

One of Elliott's fondest memories of Clark was a time when the guitarist was late for rehearsal in 1978. Clark burst into the room and, without saying a word to anyone, plugged in his guitar and said, "Get your ears around this." Clark played them something that he'd written on the bus ride to rehearsal, which became the key riff to their song "Wasted." By coming in with a great riff, it was Clark's apology for being late.

On August 24, 1985, Mötley Crüe headlined the Los Angeles Forum for the first time on their *Theatre of Pain* tour. The band was on their way. It was just like Vince Neil told *Circus* magazine: For four guys who never finished high school, they weren't doing too badly.

Two years later, Mötley Crüe was going from strength to strength and had just released their fourth album, *Girls, Girls, Girls.* "The band was definitely running on solid, full cylinders at that point in time," says

Ross Hogarth, one of the engineers on the album. "Tommy was in love and playing great; the whole band was playing really great."

Tommy was now married to television star Heather Locklear, a true beauty-and-the-beast pairing if there ever was one. Locklear was the good-girl star of *T. J. Hooker* and *Dynasty*. Part of why she married Tommy was out of rebellion. *Dynasty* producer Aaron Spelling just about had a heart attack when he found out she was marrying Tommy Lee. While Lee was dating Locklear, Nikki Sixx was dating singer Vanity; ultimately their relationship would splinter from mutual drug abuse. After she broke up with Sixx, she cleaned up and became a born-again Christian. (Sixx would eventually marry Playmate Brandi Brandt, who was featured in Aerosmith's "Love in an Elevator" video.)

Girls, Girls, Girls was recorded mostly at Rumbo Recorders in the San Fernando Valley, again with Tom Werman producing. During lunch hour, the Candy Cat gentleman's club nearby would empty out, and the studio would be filled with strippers. Mick Mars set up a big-screen TV between the speakers where he watched porno all day while laying down guitar solos. "They were his inspiration," says Hogarth.

The song "Girls, Girls, Girls" became a stripper's anthem. For the *Theatre of Pain* tour, Mötley Crüe had gone on the road with Bon Jovi's security chief, Fred Saunders. Saunders took the band around the country to countless strip bars, many of which wound up mentioned in the lyrics of the song. When the band went to Rick's Cabaret in Houston, Texas, after the release of the *Girls, Girls, Girls* album, they were welcomed like conquering heroes. The strippers were dancing to the album, and the band and the label reps burned through close to $1,000 in forty-five minutes.

Vince Neil frequented so many strip clubs throughout his touring years that he could practically write a Zagat guide to them. One night on a solo tour, he jumped into the audience and pretended to get into a fight; he wanted the show to get canceled so he could get to the Doll House before it closed.

For the *Girls, Girls, Girls* tour, Mötley Crüe took out two of the hottest bands around as their opening acts, Whitesnake and Guns N' Roses. As Rudy Sarzo recalls, the band seemed relatively sober when Whitesnake was opening for them, and the band played well every night. But when Guns N' Roses started opening for them, Mötley Crüe went over the edge with drugs.

On December 22, 1987, Nikki Sixx decided to head to the Cathouse. He was already high on heroin, cocaine, and Valium, and he brought along a bottle of Jack Daniels for the drive. At the Cathouse, he met up with a dealer with the promise of more smack, and they went to a nearby hotel with Guns N' Roses guitarist Slash and drummer Steven Adler. While Slash crashed on the couch, the dealer shot up Sixx, who promptly overdosed and fell to the floor. Adler was unable to drag him to the shower because his arm was in a cast. Instead he kept throwing water on Sixx's face with his good hand and smacking him in the face with his cast until the paramedics arrived on the scene. The attending physician called Cedars-Sinai Medical Center and told them that Sixx would be dead on arrival. The other three members of Mötley Crüe were notified by phone that Sixx had died, which meant the band was dead as well. Mötley Crüe always swore that without the original four members, there would be no band.

In the ambulance, paramedics rammed two needles full of adrenaline into Sixx's chest, and he was revived, à la *Pulp Fiction*. He had been dead for two minutes. He checked himself out of the hospital later that night and hitchhiked home. When he got home, he shot up again. That night, he left a new greeting on his answering machine: "Hi, it's Nikki. I'm not here right now 'cause I'm dead."

Soon after Sixx's near-death experience, all the band members cleaned up and stayed sober, for the time being at least. Comedian Sam Kinison, who partied hard with many heavy metal bands, couldn't believe it. "What are you gonna do now?" he asked the band. "Wreck a salad bar?"

It was still taking Neil time to get the message. He had been in and out of rehab twice the year Sixx OD'd, and his eventual exit from the band several years later was blamed in part on him not staying sober with the rest of the band. Neil was also becoming an embarrassment to the band for getting into bar brawls with guys he thought were hitting on his mud-wrestler wife Sharise. Those close to the band could see it was only a matter of time before things came to a head. Says Charrie Foglio, "The band wanted to be more serious in what they were doing and have it less Vince the playboy, always in trouble. I think when you're around somebody forever, you lose perspective of how much weight they really carry in your outfit."

Girls, Girls, Girls was Mötley Crüe's last album with Werman, and, as the band often did after breaking off a relationship, they blasted their producer in the press even though they had experienced tremendous success with him. Werman was hurt by the split, but he felt the band made the right move by recording their next album, *Dr. Feelgood,* with Bob Rock. "I think we had gone about as far as we were going to go," he says. "Some producer/band combinations can stay together and grow, like George Martin and the Beatles, but others stagnate. I stagnated with Ted Nugent, and I left."

Rock had also engineered Bon Jovi's *Slippery When Wet* and was now making waves as a full-fledged producer himself. With *Dr. Feelgood,* Mötley Crüe would have the biggest album of their career, an unprecedented triumph that went to No. 1 and sold more than five million copies.

Just as the Doors had a strong revival in the early 1980s, Led Zeppelin had a huge resurgence in popularity in 1987 and '88. Since metal and hard rock bands like Guns N' Roses were clearly influenced by classic bands such as the Rolling Stones and Aerosmith, and Aerosmith themselves were coming back stronger than ever, many fans were going back to the roots of metal and hard rock, buying classic albums by the truckload.

But Led Zeppelin's revived popularity was a touchy thing for the surviving members. After John Bonham died, the members of Led Zeppelin decided they couldn't continue without him and then had enough respect for what they'd accomplished not to tarnish it. The three remaining members were reportedly offered $100 million in 1988 to reunite under the name Led Zeppelin—and passed. For years, Robert Plant refused to perform Led Zeppelin songs in his solo concerts, but by 1988 he was finally at peace with the band's legend and singing the songs again. In 1987, as the demand for anything Zeppelin-esque grew, several bands were able to satisfy the public's appetite. One of them was Whitesnake.

Whitesnake lead singer David Coverdale was already a bit of a legend in metal history. He had replaced Ian Gillan in Deep Purple, fronting the band until it collapsed in 1976. Whitesnake struggled along for years, developing a cult following in Europe, but not until 1984 were they able to crack the U.S. market with *Slide It In,* their seventh album. While recording that record, Whitesnake hooked up with guitarist John Sykes, who had also played with Thin Lizzy and Tygers of Pan Tang, a seminal New Wave of British Heavy Metal band.

Whitesnake's *Slide It In* was a minor hit. John Kalodner was Whitesnake's A&R man. Geffen didn't give Kalodner a time limit for when the band had to turn in their follow-up album but told him, "You better make a fucking better record next time." Success for the next Whitesnake album was do-or-die. They had played out the European market, and on the eve of recording their eighth album, they *had* to break the States.

Sykes wanted to bring Whitesnake up to date musically. The band's music was very traditional, blues-based stuff, stuck in the '70s. Sykes loved American guitar players like Eddie Van Halen and Randy Rhoads, and he wanted to give Whitesnake a hot new sound with a metallic edge. For the new album, Whitesnake re-recorded two of their old songs. It was Kalodner's idea to update the 1982 U.K. hit "Here I Go Again," and it became a big hit.

Coverdale rented a villa in France where he and Sykes wrote songs for the follow-up to *Slide It In.* "I had pretty much most of the music in my mind," said Sykes. "It was so easy, quite effortless, really." But the recording of the album was fraught with difficulties. Coverdale reportedly had a sinus infection that prevented him from singing, and both Sykes and Kalodner say that Coverdale was also psychologically blocked. All told, Kalodner worked on the album eighteen months before it was finished, and Coverdale wound up $3 million in debt.

Right before the new album was finished, Coverdale fired everyone in the band. After he was let go, Sykes rushed back into the studio and finished his guitar solos as fast as he could. As far as he was concerned, "[Coverdale] wanted to go it alone 'cause he knew he had a great album under his belt." And indeed, the final product, simply called *Whitesnake,* released in April 1987, was impressive. Sykes contributed a smooth and creamy guitar tone that was heavy without sounding brittle or harsh.

Kalodner put together a new band that included Vivian Campbell and Adrian Vandenberg on guitars, Rudy Sarzo on bass, and Tommy Aldridge on drums. The only musician who had actually played on the album was Vandenberg, who performed the solo on "Here I Go Again." The entire band were dynamite players, but many fans didn't know it was a completely different group of musicians than the one that delivered the music on the album. Sykes wasn't thrilled about this, but he couldn't complain when the royalties started coming in. It was the most money he had ever made as a musician, and both Sykes and Coverdale became millionaires once the album broke.

Marty Callner shot the videos that made Whitesnake famous, "Still of the Night," "Here I Go Again," and "Is This Love?" The first video they shot was "Still of the Night." "They were like Milli Vanilli," recalls Callner. "The guys that were in that video didn't perform on the album. I was directing this nine-minute video and there's no relationship going on [between the members]." In fact, Coverdale had never met most of the musicians until the day of the video shoot.

Callner decided to add another tantalizing element to the video but needed money to shoot it. He had a hard time convincing anyone it was necessary. "The manager told me to fuck off—they weren't going to give me any more money. Same with the record company: They didn't believe in Coverdale. He was broke, living in the Mondrian Hotel, and he was singing commercials for the New York Seltzer Company. That's how he was making a living." Callner's wife convinced Marty to front $30,000 to Coverdale to complete the video.

Callner decided to use Tawny Kitaen as a theme to link all three videos. Kitaen had been involved with Ratt's Robbin Crosby (she appeared on the cover of *Out of the Cellar*), and she was also romantically linked with David Lee Roth and Tommy Lee. Eventually Coverdale and Kitaen fell in love and got married. "He fell head over heels for her," says Geffen's Al Coury. "I think it took three videos, then he married her." Perhaps a *Newsweek* critic put it best when she wrote, "Ten years ago, practically the only woman on [MTV] was Tawny Kitaen. Tawny had stiletto-heeled stilt legs, a centerfold's figure, and about 20 gallons of flowing red hair. She rolled around on the hoods of cars, spread her legs, and helped sell millions of records."

When "Still of the Night" went on to become a "Clip of the Week" on MTV, the *Whitesnake* album sold a million copies in ten days. A big reason for Whitesnake's success was the fact that the album sounded similar to Led Zeppelin, and Coverdale's blond hair and stage moves were reminiscent of Plant's. According to Rudy Sarzo, at least one member of Led Zeppelin enjoyed Whitesnake. He recalled the band receiving a telegram from Jimmy Page when "Still of the Night" became a hit, thanking them for coming up with the best song Led Zeppelin never wrote. Plant, however, was unamused by Whitesnake's success. He publicly ridiculed David Coverdale, dubbing him "David Coverversion." On their next album, Whitesnake recorded another Zeppelin-esque song, "Judgement Day," and Coverdale said he thought of calling it "Up Yours, Robert."

In 1989, Sykes rebounded from the Whitesnake debacle and formed Blue Murder with Carmine Appice of Vanilla Fudge fame, in an attempt to put together a supergroup. After auditioning a number of singers that didn't make the cut, Sykes tried singing and found that he wasn't bad at it.

Blue Murder's self-titled debut had potential to be a hit. Unfortunately, the band had no management to control their finances and spent so much making the album that they had to sell two million copies just to break even. "John was a great guitarist and a great songwriter, but the business sense was not there," says Appice. "The first video for the song 'Valley of the Kings' cost $150,000. We put it on MTV, and MTV didn't want to push it. They said, 'This is not the single. We'll wait for the single.' By the time we released the next song, 'Jelly Roll,' we were all over AOR, but then MTV said, 'Look, we gave you a shot already.' They didn't push the video."

As metal and hard rock headed into the '90s, a lot of acts were getting only one shot to get MTV play. "In the past, records by these bands were able to build on MTV," said Chip Ruggieri, a publicist who worked with a number of '80s bands. "They'd throw a video into overnight rotation, then move it to medium and then heavy rotation. But by the early '90s, all these bands were just being given one shot. MTV would only air [the video for] one single from an album. And if there wasn't a reaction, they just wouldn't play any of the other singles from the album."

The self-titled Whitesnake album, along with Aerosmith's *Permanent Vacation* and Guns N' Roses' *Appetite for Destruction,* pushed Geffen to $175 million in sales by 1989. The *Whitesnake* album alone sold eight million copies. "Whitesnake was our bread and butter for a long time," says Al Coury.

Geffen Records was firing on all cylinders, and heavy metal and hard rock had a lot to do with the label's success. David Geffen was famous for not listening to the bands on his label, but he knew what was successful. One day Jackson Browne came to visit the Geffen offices and was blasted by loud music. "That's my heavy metal band," Geffen told him. "There's a lot of money being made on heavy metal, and I want some."

Granted, it's doubtful that a billionaire living in a Malibu beach house could listen to "Welcome to the Jungle" and relate to where it was coming from, but according to Kalodner, Geffen had "total faith" in his A&R department and in what they wanted to sign. He told them, "I don't know this music anymore; it's up to you [to sign it]."

Re-signing Aerosmith was considered "a career-defining moment" for John Kalodner. Many had written Aerosmith off, but to Kalodner it made perfect sense to bring the band back together. "It was obvious to me; I don't know why other people didn't see it," he says. "You have two superstars, Steven Tyler and Joe Perry, and a band that played incredibly together. I thought to myself, if I can just get their songs back on track, that would be the secret."

Aerosmith's first step back into the spotlight was their re-recording their classic "Walk This Way" with rappers Run-DMC, which peaked at No. 4 on the charts. Just as Eddie Van Halen helped open up Michael Jackson's audience, it took a white band to get rap played on MTV. "It made a big difference in the way people viewed rap music," said hip-hop impresario Russell Simmons. "It was the first significant MTV play that rap had."

After Aerosmith got sober, they released *Permanent Vacation*, which became one of their biggest-selling albums. Marty Callner had seen the Run-DMC video and wanted to work with Aerosmith. His videos for "Dude (Looks Like a Lady)," "Love in an Elevator," and "Cryin' " were also a huge step in reinventing the band. Callner battled MTV's censors over the ultra-sexy content of his videos, but he always found ways to defeat them. For the "Love in an Elevator" video, he put black bars reading "Censored" over supposed nudity in the video.

"It's much more titillating, because you want to know what's under the bar; there's nothing under the bar! You couldn't see anything!

I knew they were going to [change] my stuff, so I'd load it up with more than I wanted in there, so once I made the changes, they'd say 'Look at how cooperative he is.' "

Aerosmith had a love/hate relationship with Callner, just as they did with Kalodner. They loved Callner's videos but weren't happy that they couldn't control his work. One of the biggest complaints Callner received when making videos with Aerosmith (and other metal and hard rock bands) was that some members weren't in the videos enough. (Being that Steven Tyler and Joe Perry were the focus of Aerosmith, the rest of the band was called the "LI3," or the "less interesting three.") To combat this, Callner would pull aside the musicians who felt they weren't getting enough camera time and tell them, "Listen, I'm putting in what's best for that moment. If you're best at the moment, you're going in." This made the band members compete against each other, and Callner got much better onscreen performances.

Also throughout their '80s resurgence, Aerosmith fought with Kalodner over their musical direction. They had a power struggle on the *Pump* album over which songs would go on the album, and Tyler tried to have Kalodner fired during the *Get a Grip* sessions in 1990. But Kalodner stuck to his guns and wouldn't let the band put out an album unless he had hits he could take to radio.

"He would hold the album up, go back in, and bring in new writers," says Al Coury. "He's got his boot camp. That's the basis of John Kalodner's success: He's a good song man. He won't let them out until [they're right]." The band resented the fact that Kalodner and Callner had as much power as they did—but couldn't deny that they helped them achieve their comeback. "Making an Aerosmith record is also about control," said their former manager, Tim Collins. "Who has it, who's losing it, who's on top."

In the summer of 1988, metal went back to the movies with *The Decline of Western Civilization Part II, the Metal Years,* directed by Penelope

Spheeris. The first *Decline* documented the L.A. punk scene from 1979 to 1980, including such bands as X, Fear, and the Germs.

After the success of the first *Decline,* Spheeris carved out a unique niche as a filmmaker. She next made the punk rock urban drama *Suburbia,* which became another cult hit, and *The Boys Next Door,* about two brothers (one played by Charlie Sheen) who go on a killing spree. One critic recently speculated the film could have been the inspiration for *Beavis and Butt-head.*

Spheeris's sequel to *Decline* would be about metal bands, even though the hair bands on the Sunset Strip were a completely separate world from the punk bands she previously chronicled. But Spheeris saw the musicians racing the clock to fame as fascinating material for a film. "They gave it a real human drama," she said. "It's like, 'We're devoted, we're on the verge of being desperate, we have to make it, we're running out of time.' That's heavier drama than you get in a lot of scripted films."

The film features Aerosmith, Stanley and Simmons from Kiss, Lemmy from Motörhead, Poison, and Megadeth. It also showcases a series of local bands that had been struggling for years trying to get a record deal, like London and Odin. Many of the musicians Spheeris interviewed seemed either hopelessly naïve or extremely delusional. Most of them freely admitted they had no backup plans at all. The musicians repeated a mantra over and over throughout the film: "But I *will* make it." With the exception of Janet Gardner, lead singer of Vixen, few of the musicians went anywhere.

A few of the artists interviewed for the film were honest and candid, such as Steven Tyler and Joe Perry of Aerosmith, Lemmy, Ozzy Osbourne, and Alice Cooper. It's clear watching the film that for many of the musicians interviewed the music was secondary, merely a vehicle to get paid and laid. The only thing that was accurate about many of the interviews was it showed how infuriatingly insincere the L.A. scene had become. A number of the male musicians openly bragged that they used the women who supported them. Apparently, many of the musicians related to Spheeris as one of the guys, and freely admitted their disgustingly sexist attitudes.

The strongest moment of *Decline Part II* comes near the end. Spheeris wanted to film W.A.S.P., but according to former guitarist Chris Holmes, when she approached Blackie Lawless, he wanted her to rent out Perkins Palace to film the band lip-synching with a full audience. She didn't have the budget for that and asked Chris if he'd like to be interviewed for the film solo. "Fuck yeah, no problem," he said.

Holmes would be back from a tour that week, and he promised Spheeris he would do it that Sunday. Holmes came home from the road that Wednesday. The limo driver was supposed to just drive Holmes and then go back to the chauffeur company, but Holmes had him stay for several days and bring his friends over to the house where they partied for days.

When Saturday rolled around, Holmes was awake from doing blow and speed all week. That morning at ten o'clock, Spheeris called Holmes. A band she was supposed to film had flaked out on her, and she asked if he could do the interview that day. Not only had Holmes gotten no sleep for three days but, he says, he was still jet-lagged. Yet he agreed to do the interview that day.

As Holmes was leaving the house, his mother Sandy pulled up. She hadn't seen her son in a quite a while, so he told her he was going to do an interview and invited her to come with him. He also brought a shotgun in a guitar case along with him. He figured they could use it for something in the film. Right before they began shooting, Spheeris asked Sandy if she wanted to be in the movie, and she agreed.

For his segment in the film, Holmes floated in a pool in a foam chair while his mother sat on a deck chair. He had a bottle of vodka he continually guzzled from and poured all over himself. Spheeris asked Holmes if the rock and roll lifestyle was dangerous to his health. "Health? What do you mean, health?" he replied, his voice drunken and slurred. "Look at me. What do I look? Forty? Thirty? I'm twenty-nine.

I'm what they call an old fuck." He told Spheeris that within ten years he'd probably be dead.

Holmes looked over at his mother, splashing water at her and trying to make a joke of the interview. "Look at my mom, shit!" he said with a laugh. Spheeris asked Holmes's mother if he drank a lot—as if it weren't already obvious—and Sandy responded, "Just when he's awake." Holmes said, "I'm a full-blown alcoholic. Five pints, five quarts a day, who cares? I'm a happy camper. . . . It's the only thing that makes me free." Throughout the interview, Holmes's mother looked as if she was on the verge of tears.

During the film's premiere, many in the audience openly laughed at Holmes. Years later, the scene is incredibly sad to watch. As one reviewer noted, "I've seen nothing in a movie this year that's more amazing than this dipso millionaire rock star drowning in self-hatred while his mother's face commands the screen. You'll remember that face long after the soundtrack stops echoing in your ears."

Decline, Part II premiered at the Cinerama Dome in Hollywood. One of the poser musicians interviewed for the film rode around in a limo the whole week convinced he was about to become a huge star. Chris Holmes came to the premiere with his mother. His leg was in a cast, and he told reporters he had been shot by the PMRC. London lead singer Nadir D'Priest was interviewed outside the theater by *ABC News*. They had to shoot the right side of his face because he was doing cocaine in the limo on the way to the film and his other nostril was covered in white powder.

Once the film started rolling, many who were in it practically sank in their seats. Odin guitarist Jeff Duncan says he was so embarrassed by the film that he felt like putting a bag over his head before walking out of the theater. Years later, when people recognized him on the street from the movie, he quotes a line from *Animal House:* "Fat, drunk and stupid is no way to go through life, son." Some of the established musicians in the film weren't impressed with it either. "I couldn't believe the amount of horseshit in that film," said Osbourne. "It seemed that all anyone talked about was partying and getting laid. Whatever happened to being in a band and playing music?" (Ironically, Spheeris recently directed a documentary about Osbourne's Ozzfest tour.)

The premiere after-party was at the mansion of Miles Copeland, the founder of I.R.S. Records, where the revelers went through ten kegs in half an hour. The Cathouse's Joseph Brooks DJ'd the festivities. Eventually police helicopters swooped down flashing their lights, and the party dispersed.

London guitarist Lizzie Grey was bitter about the film for years and claimed that Spheeris used his remarks out of context to make him look like an idiot. When asked if any of his remarks were taken out of context, Nadir D'Priest said, "I sure hope so."

Yet there were musicians who appeared in *Decline* who were grateful for the opportunity. "I thought it was pretty cool," says Lizzy Borden guitarist Gene Allen of the band's appearance in the film. "Everybody was portrayed exactly how they are in life. I don't think it hurt. Any exposure is good exposure." Says D'Priest, "Penelope had the right attitude. She wanted the rawness. To me, *Decline* was a giant elevator for all the small bands."

The Decline of Western Civilization Part II opened to good reviews; many critics called it the perfect companion piece to *This is Spinal Tap.* At the time, however, no one could see the film for what it really was: an omen that things would soon be coming to an end.

The Bon Jovi / Mötley Crüe grudge match came to a head in 1989 at the "Make a Difference Foundation" benefit concert in Russia. In 1987, Doc McGhee was arrested for helping a drug ring import 45,000 pounds of marijuana from Colombia to North Carolina (he was to make $10 a pound, $450,000 total). McGhee pleaded guilty to drug importing charges in January 1988 and was sentenced to five years in jail. The sentence was suspended provided he finance an antidrug organization.

McGhee founded the Make a Difference Foundation and set up a benefit concert in Russia that included Bon Jovi, Mötley Crüe, Ozzy Osbourne, and Cinderella, among others. "We called it 'Make a Different Drink Foundation,'" says former Skid Row drummer Rob Affuso. "It was supposed to be this drug- and alcohol-free event, they were making a big deal out of it, we get on the private charter jet, Ozzy's on it, Mötley Crüe, Cinderella, the Scorpions, and everyone's bringing on their own bottles of Jack Daniels and vodka. I do remember that quite clearly! I also do remember that Russian vodka is about eight times as strong as the vodka we have here. We would just go out and order vodka drinks there, and after two drinks I was shitfaced."

When the show finally got under way, Mötley Crüe threw a fit when they found out Bon Jovi would be using pyro effects onstage. Mötley Crüe was without effects and had to share the same stage equipment as Bon Jovi. According to Tommy Lee, there weren't supposed to be any headliners for the Make a Difference show, and every band was supposed to play a stripped-down show with no pyro and no special effects. When Mötley Crüe found out they were "demoted" to opening for the Scorpions and Ozzy Osbourne, they went crazy. The band flew home on their own after performing and fired McGhee when they landed in America. Osbourne himself had issues about opening for Mötley Crüe, and almost left the country without playing. As he was threatening to leave, he ranted to KNAC, who was covering the event live. His interview reputedly went on the air uncensored.

"I don't expect to come to fucking Moscow and have a finger up my ass," said Osbourne. "It's a matter of principle. I don't give a fuck if I open, close, stand outside with a fuckin' banjo. But I don't want to be fucked around by dickheads." Jon Bon Jovi offered his headlining slot to Osbourne to convince him to stay. Struggling to keep the peace, Doc McGhee came up with the solution that Osbourne go on third, and, for pay-per-view TV specials, he would be shown fourth, thus headlining over Mötley Crüe.

At the height of Mötley Crüe's jealousy of Bon Jovi, Jon couldn't help but comment that for a band who put him down for being white-bread, Mötley Crüe no longer had much street credibility. "I can't help wondering how Mötley are gonna carry on being the bad boys of rock with their Rolexes and Ferraris."

In 1988, it was announced that the Monsters of Rock tour would hit the road in America that summer. The tour would feature an impressive lineup of bands: Kingdom Come, Metallica, Dokken, and the Scorpions, with Van Halen headlining. To warm up for the tour, Metallica played a surprise show at the Troubadour, and the place was packed. It was the same club where they had opened for Ratt in 1982.

In spite of the bands' divergent musical styles, once on the road, they all got along well. In between gigs, the bands had a lot of time to hang out and party. There was a lot of personal and chemical camaraderie, and booze and drugs were in abundance. As former Dokken bassist Jeff Pilson recalls, "There were a lot of 3 A.M. phone calls: 'Yeaah, Jeff? Got any?' And usually I did! In that respect, it was a tremendously fun tour."

Even the hard-partying Metallica, who were nicknamed Alcoholica, were surprised at how much chemical intake Van Halen could handle. "They were partyers, no doubt," said James Hetfield. "I couldn't believe how a band could be around that long and party hardcore like that."

The "Monsters" tour didn't live up to expectations. Its stages were twice the size of those for U2 and Bruce Springsteen's recent tours, and its dimensions dwarfed the bands. It also took fifty-one trucks to haul around the 971 tons of equipment. Promoters overestimated the draw of the tour; many shows didn't sell out, and some sold less than half capacity. Some promoters lost money in the six-figure range. "Promoters are praying for breakeven," said one prominent manager. "There was a reasonable, six-truck tour here. Instead they take this fifty-truck tour out, just to gratify their egos, to prove they're larger than life, and then brag about it."

Needless to say, Metallica generated the strongest buzz of the bands featured, and in many ways they carried the tour. When the tour hit Los Angeles, the audience was so hyped up to see Metallica that a riot broke out during the first riff of "Creeping Death" as the band hit the stage at 3:00 P.M. Fifteen thousand people rushed the floor.

"[Metallica] confirmed its reputation as a major new force in the heavy metal world," said one review of the L.A. Monsters of Rock show. "The crowd's response—even apart from the stampede—was remarkable. After that, sets by L.A.'s Dokken and the Scorpions seemed tame and turgid. In the wake of the thunder generated by Metallica's set, these two bands seemed barely there . . . and nothing Van Halen did altered the earlier impression that Metallica is making the metal of the moment—and likely the future." "Dokken was so disheveled as a band at that point, I'd say it added to the defeatism," says Pilson. "Metallica was really, really hot at that point, and the crowd made you know it."

Says former Dokken guitarist George Lynch, "Going on after Metallica was definitely humbling. By Monsters of Rock, we were pretty much demoralized. Don had announced that he was going to split up the band. With this knowledge, going out and trying to play in front of that many people, it was all a dead issue. It was really hard to put your heart and soul into it, especially when you have ill feelings toward somebody else on stage. What was the point? You worked all those years to get there, we were up there, and it was pointless."

Dokken had been falling to pieces long before the Monsters of Rock tour. In April 1988, they were touring with AC/DC in Europe, another hard crowd to win over. Dokken were hoping their fourth album, *Back for the Attack,* would be their big breakthrough, but it didn't live up to expectations. The last date of the AC/DC tour was in Wembley, England. In the limo riding to the gig, Don Dokken told everyone he was leaving Q-Prime Management and suggested everyone else do the same. Then he turned to George Lynch. "And you," he said. "You're an asshole. I don't give a shit what happens to you."

That did it. Lynch lunged at Dokken and began strangling and punching him. Their road manager, Rick Sales, who was riding in the front of the limo, told the driver not to pull over. The band needed to have an all-out fight. When they arrived at the gig, they played the best show of their careers.

The band officially broke up in March 1989. "Don could gain his independence, have the whole juggernaut move in his direction, without having the headaches of having to share the spotlight with anyone else, or the money," says Lynch. "I think that was the main [issue]." He says that when the band was together, they split the money four ways. "A dollar turned into four quarters for everybody," he continues. "That's the way I insisted that it work, so one guy isn't driving a Ferrari and another one's driving a Yugo. It breeds animosity, and we didn't want that. There's enough to go around for everybody if you're successful. We were making half a million a year, each."

The breakup cemented Dokken and Lynch's mutual hatred, and the rest of the band held ill feelings as well. Don later signed a solo deal with Geffen and tried to call it Dokken. Lynch, Pilson, and Mick Brown sued and in effect prevented him from using his own name for his new band, because contractually there was a provision that no one could continue to use the name if the band broke up.

No one could say for certain whether Dokken ever would have had their big break if they had stayed together and continued making albums. There were certainly enough sour feelings among the band members that it could have been difficult to continue making good albums, but Mick Brown, for one, felt regret that Dokken didn't continue and try to realize their full potential. He recently reflected, "We took the brass ring and shoved it down a toilet."

As the 1980s were drawing to a close, **Guns N' Roses** recorded one of the greatest albums of the decade, *Appetite for Destruction,* which to date has sold over sixteen million copies. In the 1990s the original, classic line-up, pictured here, ripped apart, as many bands did during that tumultuous decade for metal and hard rock. From left to right: Steven Adler, Izzy Stradlin, Axl Rose, Duff McKagan, and Slash. (Neil Zlozower)

Slave to the Grind

> **"BACK IN THE '80S, IF YOU TOLD ME TEN YEARS FROM NOW EVERYONE WOULD HAVE SHORT HAIR AND THERE WOULD BE NO GUITAR SOLOS, I WOULD HAVE SAID WHAT PLANET ARE YOU FROM?"**
>
> **—Vinnie Appice**

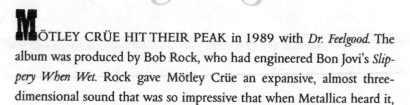

MÖTLEY CRÜE HIT THEIR PEAK in 1989 with *Dr. Feelgood*. The album was produced by Bob Rock, who had engineered Bon Jovi's *Slippery When Wet*. Rock gave Mötley Crüe an expansive, almost three-dimensional sound that was so impressive that when Metallica heard it, they knew they wanted him to produce their next album.

The U.S. tour for *Dr. Feelgood* grossed $25 million (two sold-out shows at the Forum grossed $570,000). Mötley Crüe now had eleven trucks, three buses, and their own plane. The band's overhead was in excess of $300,000 a week. Photographer Neal Preston called the *Dr. Feelgood* show one of the loudest concerts he ever shot. "It was the first time I ever had to use earplugs," he says. "I hate to use earplugs when I'm shooting, because I can't hear my cameras firing."

Yet for all the money Mötley Crüe spent on their shows, Vince Neil still couldn't memorize his stage raps. For years, everything Neil said onstage was written down on large sheets of paper and taped to the stage in front of him, because he was always forgetting his lines. One of those scripts might have looked like this:

"Whew! *Name of city here!!!* Welcome to the world of Mötley Crüe! It's been a long time muthafuckas, but we're back! *Name of city here,* are you with me tonight? I guess the smart people know what rock and roll is on a *Day of week here,* huh? You ain't makin' enough fuckin' noise out there tonight! We ain't startin' over until you make some noise! How many wild muthafuckas are here tonight? I said ... HOW MANY WILD MUTHAFUCKAS ARE HERE TONIGHT?!? Let's make 'em crazy, boys! (Play the next song.)"

When the band used to perform a cover of Elvis's "Jailhouse Rock," Neil didn't know any of the words—he just garbled what sounded like the lyrics into the mike.

At the peak of the band's success, manager Doug Thaler reminded Mötley Crüe how important it was for a band to continue to grow older gracefully, and he mentioned a number of examples: AC/DC, Aerosmith, and Ozzy Osbourne. He hoped Mötley Crüe would follow in their footsteps.

While riding *Dr. Feelgood*'s wave of success, Nikki Sixx sensed that change was in the air. In an MTV interview, he said, "It gets to a point, and I believe we're at that point right now, where you get this kind of dinosaur music mentality going on where everybody looks the same and everybody sounds the same. It's everything punk rebelled against in the '70s. I think it's time for a revolution, a musical revolution. Somebody's gotta do something original here."

Soon the revolution that Sixx had predicted would arrive. What he didn't foresee was Mötley Crüe and many of the bands that thrived in the '80s would soon be in a lot of trouble.

By the late 1980s, hair bands were still getting signed out of L.A. Many of the bands that were successful at the end of the 1980s had even more mainstream pop success with ultra-slick sounds and hit singles than the earlier '80s bands.

Warrant first started storming the Sunset Strip in the mid-'80s, the same time Poison was cutting their teeth in the same clubs. Warrant would make up 20,000 flyers for every show they played. Working in teams, they hit every gig, from clubs to arenas, passing out flyers. With at least three gigs a night in L.A. on average, there was never a shortage of places to advertise.

"It was a great way to meet girls and get into clubs for free, and we started building up a following," recalls Warrant guitarist Erik Turner. "Everybody was fuckin' everybody; it was just a great time. Nobody had any money, but we had a hell of a lot of fun. We took charity wherever we could; we'd go over to our girlfriends' parents and eat as much as possible."

While many local bands only played one gig a month, Warrant played five, sometimes doing mini-tours around San Diego, Fresno, and San Francisco. Their L.A. shows would feature new songs, flyers, and photo shoots. Warrant constantly changed their stage set; one show had a Western saloon design; another featured walls of Marshall amplifiers.

When the first Warrant lineup dissolved, Jani Lane left his band, Plain Jane, on the way back from a gig in San Diego and joined Warrant. At first, Lane drew a lot of comparisons to Poison's Bret Michaels, because they had a similar look, but Lane had his own style of singing and songwriting, and eventually those comparisons fell away.

Warrant was, in fact, friends with Poison in their early club days and learned a lot from them—like how to promote themselves. "They were my favorite live band in L.A.," says Erik Turner. "You'd have all the musicians sitting there with their arms crossed, and then all the chicks are going crazy." Both bands were equally driven to make it, and when Poison got signed, it carved a path for Warrant, but it still took some time for them to get a deal of their own. This was a frustrating period for the band. A number of other bands that had been together for barely ten gigs, like Femme Fatale, were getting major deals because a label needed a hair band on its roster. Warrant stuck it out and eventually signed a deal with Columbia.

Both Warrant's first album, 1988's *Dirty Rotten Filthy Stinking Rich,* and their 1990 sophomore effort, *Cherry Pie,* went double platinum. Many considered the video for "Cherry Pie" the nadir of hair-band sexism, and it was cited in debates about whether sexism in music videos had gone too far. In one scene, a slice of cherry pie falls onto model/actress Bobbie Brown's lap. In another, Brown is literally hosed down by the band, dressed as firemen (the force of the water was so strong that it peeled back her eyelids). According to Jeff Stein, who directed the video, the "Cherry Pie" clip was completely over the top on purpose to spoof the sexism of rock videos. Many didn't get the joke.

Brown has no regrets about being a sex object in a video. "It was a lot of fun, and I got paid very well," she says. "It gave me so much exposure, and regardless of the negative response from it, sex sells—always has, always will. I didn't degrade myself in any way, it was all in fun, and everybody got something out of it. My career went further; Warrant's did too." Lane fell for Brown, and they eventually married and had a child together. *Rolling Stone* named "Cherry Pie" worst video of the year. Stein wore it like a badge of honor.

Another band that fared well at the end of the 1980s was Winger. Beau Hill, who previously worked with Ratt and also produced Warrant's first two albums, would come aboard as Winger's producer. Hill had known singer and bassist Kip Winger since the late 1970s. The two eventually hooked up with guitarist Reb Beach, who had done a lot of session work, and started recording demos. Hill was a friend of Doug Morris, the head of Atlantic Records, and brought Morris Winger's demos; Morris turned them down three times. Recalls Hill, "It had gotten so bad that the third time he turned me down he said, 'Don't you ever bring me that fucking Kip Winger again, ever. I don't even want to hear another note.'"

The band went back to work and whipped up a revamped demo with new songs. Hill called Morris: "Man, I just got this tape in the mail, and I'd love to bring it to Atlantic." Morris agreed to check it out. He liked the band, but Hill wouldn't tell him who it was. They closed a deal to sign the band on a handshake. As Hill was walking out the door, Morris asked—"Well, wait a minute. Aren't you even going to tell me who I signed?" Hill said, "Oh yeah—you signed Kip Winger."

Both Winger's self-titled debut album, released in 1988, and their sophomore effort, 1990's *In the Heart of the Young,* went platinum. Winger's hits included "Headed for a Heartbreak" and their ode to jailbait, "Seventeen." As puerile as some of their music was, Winger was a group of accomplished players. Kip had trained at Juilliard, Reb Beach was a top session musician, and drummer Rod Morgenstein had played with the Dixie Dregs, a jazz/fusion band. Says Hill, "Those guys delivered; they really delivered. They were probably the best live band I've ever heard in my life, because they were the real thing. They could really play." Kip was getting as much attention for his looks as his musicianship. He was hailed as "Metal's New Stud" on the cover of *RIP Magazine* and posed for *Playgirl* (the cover promised: "Kip Winger like you've never seen him before.").

Winger was one '80s band that had a particularly harsh downfall in the '90s. The band blamed the demise of their career on the MTV cartoon *Beavis and Butt-head*. Said Reb Beach, "I remember sitting on the [tour] bus and seeing this new TV show called *Beavis and Butt-head* with a 300-pound, zit-covered kid wearing a Winger T-shirt. Our sales stopped cold."

A lot of the music *Beavis and Butt-head* made fun of was already outdated, so it was hard to really say if these subzero-IQ'd cartoon characters really had any pull on what was "cool" or what "sucked" and wouldn't make it on MTV, but sometimes you had to wonder. John Corabi, who replaced Vince Neil in Mötley Crüe for several years, says one reason MTV pulled Mötley Crüe's "Hooligan's Holiday" video was because the clip moved too fast. Beavis and Butt-head had the same complaint. The show wasn't just a big hit with kids who watched MTV—the cartoon became a nationwide phenomenon. "These guys are the purest form of idiots we've been able to isolate," said David Letterman, a fan of the show. "I think they represent a significant portion of America."

Beau Hill felt Winger became an easy target because of Kip's looks and because in an MTV interview, he had come off as smug and full of himself. He told the interviewer he wanted to "start working on my concerto." Winger also studied ballet and spoke of how he wanted to incorporate it into the band's videos. This was not what the kids wanted to hear. "The kids want [to hear], 'The next record's gonna kick your ass and rock the walls,' " says Hill. "No one wants to watch you ballet-dance around in a tutu, and nobody gives a shit about your next opus. No kid wants to hear that shit. They want to hear, 'I want to go out, find me a blonde, and get laid.' Absolutely, *Beavis and Butt-head* completely ruined Winger's career. But I think if Kip hadn't done all that other stuff, perhaps *Beavis and Butt-head* may have picked on someone else."

Many hair bands sorely lacked a sense of humor, and they couldn't understand that if they hadn't acted pompous and arrogant in the first place, *Beavis and Butt-head* wouldn't have found them such an easy target to bombard. But not every metal musician hated the cartoon. "Tommy was a fan," says Bobbie Brown, who was briefly engaged to Tommy Lee after divorcing with Jani Lane. "They always said cool things about him. They said, 'I hope Tommy Lee jams his drumsticks up Vince Neil's butt.' He laughed and said, 'That's cool.' "

And one band in particular benefited greatly from *Beavis and Butt-head*. White Zombie was a great combination of heavy music and B monster movie kitsch. Michael Alago signed the band to Geffen. He became fast friends with lead singer and chief songwriter Rob Zombie and bassist Sean Yseult, and they spent a lot of time playing Monopoly and Jeopardy board games, and drinking frozen White Russians.

The band's first album for Geffen, *La Sexorcisto: Devil Music Vol. One,* was released in 1992, and sales stalled at around 150,000 copies. One night backstage at a White Zombie gig, *Beavis and Butt-head* creator Mike Judge came backstage to meet Rob Zombie. *Beavis and Butt-head* was the hottest thing on MTV, and everyone rushed up to meet Judge, handing him napkins and handkerchiefs and asking him to draw cartoons for them.

"Mike just took an incredible liking to the music and Rob," says Alago. "Before you knew it, they kept playing the video for 'Thunder Kiss '65.' That helped us get over a stumbling block. Nationally it helped take the record over the top, and eventually it went platinum."

In October 1990, Metallica started recording the follow-up to . . . *And Justice for All.* On *Justice* the band felt insecure as musicians and wanted to prove themselves. Every song was lengthy, with tons of technical riffs. Said Ulrich, "We probably could have made another twelve good songs out of all those riffs on *Justice,* just spread 'em out a little more."

It took Metallica close to a year to record their next album. It was the first time Metallica were working with an actual producer *and* listening to his suggestions. It wasn't easy for Ulrich and James Hetfield to let the rest of the band be involved in the songwriting and have more of a say, but with Bob Rock it happened. The producer told the band, "You guys have never sounded like a band on any of your records," and set out to change that.

Metallica's fifth album was released on August 12, 1991. It was called just *Metallica,* although most people called it "The Black Album," because it had an all-black cover. (Ulrich joked that the band thought of calling the album either *Buy Product* or *Metallica Sucks.*) It went to No. 1 three weeks later and stayed there for a month. The album eventually sold more than ten million copies in the States alone.

"I know we're No. 1 completely on our terms," Ulrich told *Rolling Stone.* "There is an inner satisfaction about that, to give a major 'fuck you' to the business itself and the way you're supposed to play the game and the way we dealt with all that shit up through the mid-1980s. I know there were a lot of bands who went, 'Oh yeah, Metallica, they sell a lot of records, but they can't play or write songs.' " Says Jeff Pilson, "My favorite Lars Ulrich quote of all time is, 'Metallica didn't go to No. 1—No. 1 came to us.' And you know what? The little fucker was right!"

In a *Los Angeles Times* story on the band's newfound mainstream success, one seventeen-year-old fan remarked, "I still like Metallica, but it's getting too popular . . . it's more fun when it's just your band." Ulrich responded, "Obviously, we are not the best kept secret anymore."

For old friends of the band like photographer Harald Oimen, Metallica's success was bittersweet. "In one aspect, I was kinda bummed, because this band was a Bay Area secret, and I didn't want to share them with the rest of the world. But I was happy they were finally getting popular. It was amazing to see them get as big as they did."

Metallica was instantly accessible, and many who weren't fans of the band finally understood what all the fuss was about. They went from "What the fuck is that?" to "That's fucking great." "I had never listened to a Metallica record in my fucking life," says John Kalodner. "I went and bought [. . . *And Justice for All*] and said, 'What the hell is this?' A lot of friends kept telling me Metallica is gonna have great records and things like that. I said, 'Oh okay, fine.' And then the ['Black'] album comes out, and I go and buy it the first day. I put it on, and I said, 'Jesus, what the hell is this record? This is a masterpiece.'"

Ulrich always had a big ego, but it exploded with the success of the "Black" album. He began wearing a white leather jacket like Axl Rose, and the rest of the band started calling him "Starz Ulrich" because of it. Metallica was learning to enjoy the spoils of their success. Gone were the torn blue jeans and sneakers held together with duct tape. Eventually Ulrich would be wearing Gucci, collecting art, and staying in four-star hotels. He bought a three-story mansion with an elevator, indoor racquetball court, screening room, and a grand view of all of San Francisco. Kirk Hammett also bought a three-story house in San Francisco. Being a horror-movie buff, Hammett had his ceilings painted with flashes of lighting and used expensive, vintage monster-movie posters for wallpaper.

When Peter Paterno was running Hollywood Records, he was approached by Queen manager Jim Beach when the band's deal was up at Capitol. "I always thought Queen was still making great records," says Paterno. "They were selling everywhere but America. I don't think they had a record that sold less than three million copies in the rest of the world, even when they couldn't get arrested here." Paterno not only brought Queen to the label but bought their back catalog as well.

Queen hadn't played in America since the early 1980s. Queen were always an arena/stadium band, and they wouldn't come back to the States unless they were on top again. "Freddie, that's all he wanted to do was get big in America again," says Paterno.

But rumors had been circulating for years that singer Freddie Mercury was ill with AIDS. When Lonn Friend reviewed the band's 1989 album, *The Miracle*, for *RIP Magazine*, he addressed those rumors without directly revealing Mercury's illness. Friend pointed out how many of the band's songs seemed to be from the point of view of someone at the end of his life, especially "Was It All Worth It." Friend wrote, "My high-level sources speak of rumors surrounding Freddie's health. If there is any truth to such rumors, it sure puts this record into perspective."

Mercury finally broke the silence on November 22, 1991, acknowledging that he was indeed suffering from AIDS. He died the next day at the age of forty-five. If Freddie had lived, the success of the film *Wayne's World*, featuring their masterpiece "Bohemian Rhapsody," in all likelihood would have brought Queen back to these shores.

Paterno figured it would have taken seven to eight years for Hollywood Records to earn back its investment under normal circumstances, but after Mercury's passing and with the success of *Wayne's World*, Hollywood recouped within three to four months. "Bohemian Rhapsody" was now on heavy rotation on MTV and went to No. 2 on the singles charts on April 4, 1992, almost fifteen years after the song was first a Top Ten hit in the States. "Rhapsody" again went to No. 1 in the United Kingdom. A concert was held at Wembley Stadium in Mercury's honor. Before any bands were announced to perform, 72,000 tickets sold in two hours. The Freddie Mercury Tribute Concert for AIDS Awareness turned out to be an all-star event, featuring a number of artists of all genres performing Queen songs including George Michael, Annie Lennox, Elton John, Metallica, and David Bowie, to name a few. Backstage, there was an argument among the surviving members of Queen. The band couldn't agree whether or not Liza Minnelli was the right choice to sing the last song of the evening, "We Are the Champions." After they gave it some thought, it made sense. One of the most dazzling and glitzy performers in entertainment history closing the show with one of Queen's greatest hits? It's what Mercury would have wanted.

After Mercury's death, the *Los Angeles Times* interviewed a number of musicians and people in the L.A. scene about what, if any, impact AIDS had on rock and roll. "There is definitely a lot of unsafe sex and needles in the Hollywood rock scene," said Riki Rachtman. "And the community is so small . . . if you find a girl who hasn't slept with the singer of at least three bands, keep her. I haven't found her."

"There's always that feeling of, that's never gonna happen to me," says tour manager Alan Reiff. "When Eazy-E died, the rap community was in shock for about seventy-two hours. Now things are back to the same-old. I'm amazed more rockers aren't dead from AIDS now. It's by the grace of God we haven't lost 90 percent of these people."

"For a few years, at the beginning of tours I'd go buy a huge box of condoms and make sure they were in the front lounge, because some bands would say, 'I would've used the rubber—I just didn't have any,' " adds tour manager Larry Morand. "I just did that for the mere sake of [the fact] I'd feel awful if someone I worked with had died of that just because of stupidity."

In 2001, AIDS made news in the hard rock community again. In July of that year, former Ratt guitarist Robbin Crosby announced that he had been in the hospital battling the disease. Crosby was diagnosed in 1994 and believed he contracted the disease from being promiscuous on the road, but it's also possible he contracted AIDS from needles, considering he was a longtime heroin addict. Crosby said that when it was confirmed he had the disease, "It took a while to sink in, like I kind of expected it after all the stuff I had done."

Crosby's drug addiction had cost him his spot in Ratt, his marriage, his home, and on many occasions, nearly his life. "The best thing I can say is, save yourself the grief I've been through, the degradation," he said. "Save yourself from blowing all your money, losing your lover, losing everything you have and not even realizing it's going away because of your love for drugs. Heroin has no payback—it's a no-refund deal. There's nothing like it; there never will be. Because nothing can be that good and you just walk away from it." On June 6, 2002, Crosby passed away after battling AIDS for eight years. He was forty-two years old.

By 1990, Guns N' Roses was back in the studio recording the long-awaited followup to *Appetite for Destruction*. Rose was obsessed with not just following up *Appetite* but surpassing it. Consumed with making the album, he moved into the Record Plant in Hollywood and lived there for a month while recording, smoking pot to relieve his stress.

Rose and model Erin Everly were married in late January 1990 and bought a home in the Hollywood Hills. Before ever moving in, Rose caused over $80,000 in damage to the property, including shoving his $50,000 piano out the window. A year later, the marriage was annulled. Coming from a heavily dysfunctional family, Rose wanted to break the cycle and raise his own family the right way. But the anger that consumed him wouldn't allow it to happen.

If "Sweet Child O' Mine" was dedicated to the love of his life, the song "Estranged," which he wrote for the *Use Your Illusion* albums, was about how devastating it was to lose that love. When Rose introduced the song in concert, he would announce, "As the Stones would say, this song's about a girl who's just a memory."

Eventually it became clear to the members of Guns N' Roses that if Steven Adler wasn't going to get help for his drug addiction, he would have to leave the band. The prospect of having to fire Adler was painful for Slash, since they had been childhood friends. Adler went into drug rehab in 1989, and Don Henley of the Eagles filled in on drums for an

American Music Awards appearance. The only song that features Adler on the *Illusion* albums is "Civil War." Numerous takes of the song had to be edited together to get one cohesive performance. After struggling with the song for two weeks because he was too high to play, he was fired by the band.

The breakup of Rose's marriage and the dismissal of Adler compounded the pressure to top the success of *Appetite*. The *Use Your Illusion* recording sessions were difficult to finish, and if the band couldn't find another drummer soon, they were going to break up. Slash had practically given up when one night he went to see the Cult perform at the Universal Amphitheater in Southern California. Matt Sorum, the Cult's drummer, was hired soon after. Adler was bitter about being fired and later sued the band, complaining that in a band full of junkies, he was fired because the others needed a scapegoat. He received a settlement of $2.5 million.

Adler wasn't a great drummer, but his unique style worked well in the band. When Guns N' Roses played live, Adler would watch Slash tapping his foot for meter. If a song was aggressive and Slash was stomping the stage, Adler's timing would be all over the place. By contrast, Matt Sorum was a better musician, but Slash would later say that Adler's firing "had a big effect on the camaraderie" of the band. "What bound us together was really lacking as soon as we were missing a couple of guys. You just can't reinvent something like that.

"We were the only five guys in L.A. who could have formed Guns N' Roses," he continued. "There's no Guns N' Roses, really, without those particular five guys. The nuances of everyone's individual styles came together with those five people."

The *Use Your Illusion* tour started on May 24, 1991, in East Troy, Wisconsin. The albums still hadn't been released. Axl Rose made it clear that the albums would come out only when he felt they were ready. Some nights, the band members had to fly to the studio after a concert to work on the record. "It was a long process," recalled Mike Clink, who was back with the band producing the *Illusion* albums. "And it's tough to keep up the momentum for that long. When you spend that much time working on a record, some members tend to lose their enthusiasm."

The album took a year and a half to record. All the basic tracks were cut in a month; the rest of the time was spent on overdubs, Rose's vocals as well as writing lyrics, which he hadn't finished when they entered the studio.

The label wanted to release the first part of *Illusion* six months or a year before part two, but the band insisted on putting out both records at once. "There was so much good music between the two record sets we didn't want any of it to get lost with their fan base," says former Geffen executive Al Coury. Guns N' Roses had originally considered making *Appetite for Destruction* a double album but realized it was financially unsound for a debut. One reason the band decided to release so much material at once was because no one was sure if there would ever be another Guns N' Roses album (each CD was the equivalent of a two-record set).

When the *Use Your Illusion* albums were finally released on September 17, 1991, it came out on two separate CDs at the same time. Record stores across the country opened at midnight to sell the albums. Slash didn't want to be in Los Angeles during the hysteria, so he left town for a vacation in Africa the day the albums came out. On the way to the airport, he went to Tower Records on Sunset Boulevard and hid in the back of the store. This was the same Tower Records where he was busted for stealing tapes when he was fourteen years old. Now he was watching the fans, through a one-way mirror, file in to buy the album. The albums went to No. 1 and No. 2 on the charts. Some 1.5 million records were sold the first day, and the albums would sell over seven million in the States alone.

Both *Use Your Illusion* albums were good but many fans who expected an album like *Appetite for Destruction* were disappointed. Slash knew their sound wouldn't be as hardcore as *Appetite* because the band had matured, but change is often tough for metal and hard rock fans to accept.

"Of course, kids hate hearing that, because it reminds them that they're going to get older some day too," he said.

The tour for *Illusion* was planned to run well over two years. The band planned to play arenas the first year and stadium shows the second year. It was hard to believe that with all the success the band had achieved, this would be the first time Guns N' Roses had headlined a full arena tour. Rose had a lot to work through before he was ready to go on the road. To prepare for the tour, it was reported that he was in therapy five hours a day. "I know Axl had a hard childhood," says Michelle Young. "I don't think he realized back then what actually happened until he went into therapy."

In order to survive, Rose had blacked out a lot of his childhood. Little by little, the memories came back to him. He remembered being kidnapped and sexually abused by his father. He recalled his sister had been sexually abused by his stepfather for twenty years. Both children suffered a steady stream of physical violence. According to one friend, Rose was once beaten so badly that there was blood on the walls. He attributed physical problems with his muscles and voice as reactions to his memories.

Rose was also diagnosed as manic depressive, a mental illness that gives those who suffer from it erratic mood swings. While Rose was trying to heal and get ready for the tour, everyone wondered if he would finally conquer his demons.

Skid Row opened the first part of the *Use Your Illusion* tour in 1991. In 1992, the band put out their second album, *Slave to the Grind,* which was much harder in sound than their debut. Skid Row had gotten big during the same period as Warrant and Winger, and didn't want to fall by the wayside like those bands had. The members of Skid Row got together and decided, "We gotta get tougher here," and *Slave to the Grind* was the result.

The band wanted to record a solid *album* without the consideration of hit singles, and indeed, *Slave* had no radio hits, but the album still went to No. 1 on the charts. "That album solidified a base audience for us and allowed us to continue for another four years," says Rob Affuso. Skid Row was convinced they would ride their wave for the next ten years.

For Skid Row, the *Illusion* tour was one big party. "Guns N' Roses brought back the decadence in rock and roll," says Affuso. "You go to a rock show nowadays, it's all about ginseng, bean sprouts, and health drinks. Rock and roll is dangerous, and Guns N' Roses lived that, always." Rose threw parties after every show that cost at least $10,000 a night.

As Rose was trying to get help for his mental and emotional problems, he fell under the influence of psychics and "past-life regressionists," who turned him against many of his friends. Tom Zutaut was one of many frozen out even though he was still the band's A&R representative; Rose refused to speak to him. "One time we had a meeting with Axl, and he left to go to the dentist," recalls Al Coury. "His psychics told him he had to change the fillings in his teeth because his current ones were giving him bad vibes."

Skid Row often had to play extended opening sets on the *Illusion* tour because no one could find Rose. On some nights, they had to play every song they knew, including covers, until Rose felt like showing up. His psychic friends had told him he performed better late at night, and often the audience had to wait up to two hours after Skid Row's set was finished before Guns N' Roses would hit the stage. The tickets for the concerts on that tour didn't have a starting time on them—only question marks. "Axl would be like, 'I can't go on until 11:17 and thirty seconds because that's when my healer told me the stars are aligned right," jokes Affuso. The fans grew tired of having to wait so long, but Rose didn't care. "If you were getting laid, you wouldn't be so worried about what time it was," he countered.

Throughout the *Illusion* tour, Rose complained onstage about everything and anything that bothered him, and his tirades took up a lot of time during their concerts. If a concert exceeded the local curfew, the band was fined. Guns N' Roses ended up paying hundreds of thousands of dollars in fines. This was a major sore point for the rest of the band because the money came out of their pockets as well, even though it was clearly Rose's fault they were going on late. Slash regretted having to go on late so often during the tour. "When you want to go and you're ready to go, that's when you're ready to go," he says. "After you drink half a gallon of vodka and four cups of coffee and you're still waiting to go on, that can be a hindrance."

As the frontman, Rose often abused his power. Before the *Illusion* tour started, he demanded the rights to the name Guns N' Roses or he wouldn't tour. Not wanting to face millions of dollars in losses, his bandmates agreed to give him the rights. They would soon deeply regret their decision.

The tour pulled into the Riverport Performing Arts Center in St. Louis, Missouri, on July 2, 1991. During the song "Rocket Queen," Rose noticed a biker in the crowd taking pictures and asked security to take the camera from him. When they didn't, Rose jumped into the audience and tried to take it away himself. Back onstage and pissed off beyond belief, he told the crowd he was leaving, threw down his microphone, and stormed off. Ten minutes later, the houselights came up, and the crowd began to riot. The band tried to get back onstage to finish the show, but the riot was already under way. The audience rushed the stage and tore down the drums and amps. Fans tore through the amp grills to steal the speakers. One fan was caught running away with guitars. The lighting rig and monitor boards were taken. Damage was estimated at $200,000.

Rose blamed the promoters and security staff later as well as the crowd for starting the riot. As far as he was concerned, the band fulfilled their contractual obligations by playing for ninety minutes, and the audience's behavior, Rose felt, didn't merit anything more.

The riot received extensive coverage on CNN. Some fans believed the band's version of events, while many felt there was no excuse for Rose to storm off stage. Guns N' Roses had experienced riots at their shows before, but the crowds had never frightened them until the St. Louis show. It was the first time they realized how much power they had over an audience. A decade after the fact, Slash didn't blame anyone for the riot, only saying that the St. Louis show "was one of those gigs that was just fucked."

The St. Louis riot rattled Izzy Stradlin so much that he left the band shortly afterward. "What's to stop us from having some more people trampled because the singer doesn't like something?" he said. The final straw for Stradlin came when Rose tried to make him sign a contract that would demote his position in the band and cut down his royalties. "I've been [here] from day one—why should I do that?" said Stradlin. "Fuck you—I'll go play the Whisky." Guitarist Gilby Clarke, a longtime friend of Slash's, was Stradlin's replacement.

Several weeks after the St. Louis riot, Guns N' Roses played four sold-out shows at the Los Angeles Forum. The final performance lasted three and a half hours. It was one of those nights the band could have played forever, but they had to stop because they ran out of songs, a completely opposite experience from the St. Louis show.

In the February 1992 issue of *RIP*, Skid Row was on the cover. So was a Seattle trio called Nirvana, in a small-boxed picture. In her feature story on the band, Katherine Turman wrote, "Nirvana has struck a chord. It may be out of tune, but it's universal."

The same year, *RIP* held its fifth-anniversary party at the Hollywood Palladium. The bill included Temple of the Dog, Alice in Chains, Pearl Jam, and Soundgarden (the night before, Pearl Jam played to seven people at the Mason Jar in Arizona). Guns N' Roses bassist Duff McKagan jammed with Alice in Chains on "Man in the Box," and Pearl Jam frontman Eddie Vedder crowd-surfed during Soundgarden's set. Spinal Tap headlined the show. Between sets, a song played over the P.A. system called "Smells Like Teen Spirit," caused a great deal of buzzing in the audience. As music journalist Kim Neely recalled, the fans waiting for Spinal Tap came "to pay tribute to a band that was a walking parody of every arena rock cliché in the book. But at that moment, singing along with Kurt Cobain, what they were really doing was bidding those rituals farewell."

At first, expectations at Geffen weren't huge for Nirvana's *Nevermind* album. The label was hoping to sell 50,000 copies, and if they were able to sell half that, they would be happy. Geffen executive John Rosenfelder slipped a copy of *Nevermind* to David Geffen's limo driver on the sly. Rosenfelder was hoping that Geffen would like what he was hearing while he was being chauffeured around, and in turn get the label behind the band.

Nevermind was released on September 24, 1991. It broke the Top Forty in its fourth week on the *Billboard* charts. The label printed fewer than 50,000 copies and were caught off guard that the album took off so fast. *Nevermind* was completely sold out for several weeks. By January 11, 1992, *Nevermind* was No. 1. The video for "Smells Like Teen Spirit" was all over MTV. While many metal bands were making videos that cost in the six-figure range, "Spirit" cost just $25,000 to shoot. "Poison would not be heard from again until VH-1's *Behind the Music*," wrote one critic years after the Seattle explosion. "When I saw Nirvana, I said, 'Oh God, this is gonna be trouble,'" says C. C. DeVille. "Poison got so far away from our first record. When you start to rely on lasers and bombs and the show and here comes Kurt Cobain singing these songs with so much rage and intensity, that doesn't need any lasers and bombs. It wasn't any musical sins we did. When the pendulum swings, you get enough of something, it goes the other way."

In 1992, Mötley Crüe fans were shocked when Vince Neil was ousted from the band. Neil said he was fired; the rest of the band maintained that he quit. The cry of outrage from the fans was immediate. One fan wrote to *RIP Magazine,* "I watched you during the MTV Rockumentary (I have it on video, if you would like to see it), and I heard Vince say, 'Mötley Crüe has always been Nikki, Tommy, Mick, and me. I couldn't even imagine playing with anybody else. I would rather call it quits.' Please don't tell me you've been lying all this time. I really couldn't stand that." Many of the letters that fans sent to *RIP* pointed out that the other band members had also told MTV that the band would break up if any of the members left and that they were the best of friends.

As for why the split happened, former manager Doug Thaler says, "My take on it is that the whole thing was just a side effect of addictive behavior disorder. I think that if they'd gone the Aerosmith route and stayed with it like in the *Dr. Feelgood* days, the Vince split would have never happened. I don't know where that would leave the band now, but I have to believe it would leave them in pretty much the same place that Aerosmith is currently enjoying."

In an interview in *Spin* magazine not long before the breakup, Nikki Sixx said he really enjoyed an L.A. band called the Scream that was founded by singer John Corabi. Corabi read the article and called Doug Thaler's office to leave Sixx a message thanking him. When he called in, Thaler was talking to Sixx on the other line. Sixx said he wanted Corabi to try out for the band. "Well, I'm not gonna call the label and go, 'Hey, we wanna steal their singer,' " said Thaler. "I have no way of getting in touch with him." Thaler's secretary then put the message from Corabi on his desk. Five minutes later, Corabi got a call from Sixx and Tommy Lee, and he was in the band by February 1992.

Speculation abounded about whether Mötley Crüe could go without Neil and whether the massive $25 million contract the band had just signed with Elektra would pay off. Corabi paid no attention to any of the speculation. Joining Mötley Crüe was the opportunity of a lifetime. He was a good songwriter, and he told the band he wouldn't cruise on their nostalgia. He wanted to write and contribute to the music, and the rest of the band wanted that as well. They started writing songs together right away.

The band waited a while before recording, because they wanted to make sure they got along with Corabi; they didn't want to have to trade singers again. They spent a year hanging out, jamming, and writing together. Nikki Sixx had started a family with Brandi Brandt and wanted to spend time with his newborn son, Gunnar. Mick Mars had just gotten married as well, and Tommy Lee was still married to Heather Locklear and wanted to spend time with her as well. When they finally got down to recording with Bob Rock, the album took over a year to make and cost $2 million.

Not long before Vince Neil was fired, Mötley Crüe had renewed their deal with Elektra Records for $25 million. When the band signed the deal, many in the industry were shocked. Aerosmith had signed a huge deal with Sony in 1991 for a reported $30 million and a 25 percent royalty rate. At the time, Aerosmith still owed Geffen two more albums, and Steven Tyler would be pushing fifty before delivering their first album to Sony. The band and their manager, Tim Collins, were confident they'd deliver. Yet bassist Tom Hamilton admitted, "The Sony deal became this big thing hanging over us. It was exciting but also threatening."

The last album Aerosmith recorded for Geffen was *Get a Grip*. As usual, recording the album was a difficult process fraught with tension. When John Kalodner didn't like the songs the band were writing, he brought in outside writers again, and the band resented the control Kalodner wielded. But Kalodner would maintain his job wasn't to be their friend, it was to get the best possible record he could out of the band.

The second single released off *Get a Grip*, "Eat the Rich," almost caused the album to tank, but once again Marty Callner's videos saved the day, reinventing Aerosmith for the MTV generation. With the video for "Cryin'," Callner brought them up to date, making a female the hero of "Cryin'." "The times reflected a change in that it was no longer acceptable to have girls in garter belts," says Callner.

This did not sit well with Steven Tyler. According to Callner, Tyler called him after seeing the "Cryin' " video and told him he didn't think Alicia Silverstone was sexy. Callner assured him, "Steven, this is the sexiest video you've ever done, even if she's only wearing jeans and a flannel shirt." After Callner's videos, *Get a Grip* exploded. "Aerosmith made a hell of a lot of money off that video," said Silverstone. "Their sales tripled. They would have been crazy not to ask me back."

Along with re-signing Mötley Crüe in 1992, Elektra had also signed Anthrax for a deal reportedly in the $10 million range. Although executive Bob Krasnow didn't like the music, Mötley Crüe, Metallica, and Anthrax have all said they had good working relationships with him. "We had a great experience with him," says Anthrax guitarist Scott Ian. "Krasnow didn't like the music, he never claimed to understand heavy metal, but he knew it was successful, and he knew it sold records. He let people [at the label] do their jobs." After Krasnow left Elektra, Ian felt the new regime at Elektra hurt the metal bands on the roster. According to Ian, at a meeting at the label, new CEO Sylvia Rhone put Anthrax's contract on the table and said, "I never made this deal; I never would have signed this band."

"The WEA group [Warner Bros., Elektra, and Atlantic] in the period of a year had three different CEOs," says Corabi. "Krasnow got Mötley that huge deal, Anita Baker a big deal, Natalie Cole a big deal, and he gave Anthrax $10 million. All these records came out prior to ours, and they were just commercial disasters. So Time Warner, who owns that whole fuckin' umbrella, is sitting up there going, 'What the fuck is going on here?' And they told Krasnow, 'If the Mötley record doesn't explode, you're done.' And this is all shit I heard in meetings; we were carrying the weight of the whole label."

Mötley Crüe's album with Corabi, released in April 1994 and simply titled *Mötley Crüe,* entered the *Billboard* charts at No. 7, and the first video, "Hooligan's Holiday," debuted in heavy rotation on MTV. Three weeks after the album came out, Elektra stopped promoting the album because Krasnow had left the company. According to Corabi, MTV stopped supporting the video because it was clear the label wasn't enthusiastic about supporting the band. Three months after its release, the album disappeared off the Top 200 altogether and stalled at around 300,000 copies sold.

Despite its poor sales, *Mötley Crüe* was a strong record and will probably become the band's "lost classic" album, like Kiss's *Creatures of the Night.* Says current Metal Blade president Mike Faley, "Had somebody heard that record, sight unseen, without being told it was a Mötley record, people probably would have liked it. It's a very heavy, powerful record. But once you say it's a new Mötley Crüe record, people already have a preconceived notion of what they're going to get."

The following tour did poorly as well. On previous tours, Mötley Crüe could easily sell out several nights at the Forum. On August 28, 1994, the band had a different homecoming at the Hollywood Palladium, which holds a little over 3,000 people (2,700 tickets were sold). Most of the band's tours had lasted over a year, covering the entire United States and Europe. This tour was scheduled for three months but lasted only ten weeks. One show was reportedly canceled when an estimated 900 tickets were sold in advance.

The new Mötley Crüe put on a loud, good-time rock and roll show at the Palladium, but as hard as John Corabi tried, he clearly wasn't welcomed by the old-guard fans. When Corabi went up to the mike for his stage raps, he didn't read from a script. "Thanks for sticking around," he said to the audience. "There's a lot of fucked-up shit going on in the industry right now. The music industry doesn't give a shit about you or music. If we stick together, they can't stop us." Toward the end of the show, Nikki Sixx dedicated a song called "Hammered" "to our record company, which sucks dick."

In a 1994 cover story for *Kerrang!* magazine, Mötley Crüe clearly couldn't get a grip on what was happening to them. Sixx claimed the band "deflated" its career on purpose because "Dude, it was so big it was scary. All those limos ... me and Tommy *hate* limos! Dude, we rode in the luggage van nearly every day because we were dying to get real. ..."

This was the usual party line for many bands that struggled in the '90s. Some musicians were more candid in unguarded moments: "Whenever you hear that 'getting back to the audience thing,' take it from me, it's because the bands can't sell out the big places anymore," said former Billy Idol guitarist Steve Stevens when he was playing in Vince Neil's solo band. "It's the poor excuse for when your record isn't selling: 'We wanna get back in touch with our fans.' Bullshit!"

All of the problems that plagued Mötley Crüe were finally adding up. There were seismic executive shifts at their label when the album was released, it was six years since they last released an album, and they had a brand new singer. "I mean, every possible thing that could have been against you was against the band," says Corabi. "And in hindsight, even Nikki will admit it, they never should have called the band Mötley Crüe. After Vince left, it should have been 'That's it, but here's Mick, Tommy, Nikki, and this new guy.' Everyone I've talked to says that's what we should have done. We should have changed the name of the band, because nothing was the same. And I think it kind of rubbed the fans the wrong way."

As with many bands, Mötley Crüe had beggars and hangers-on who took advantage of them. "People took advantage of Nikki," says Corabi. "People took advantage of Tommy; I saw it happen. One night we went out, and we all ended up at a hotel. There was a whole hotel room of people around, and I don't even know half of them. 'Hey, Nikki, go get me some blow.' 'Hey, Nikki, go get some Ecstasy.' They were just working him, and poor Nikki was obliterated, because he had his bouts with falling off the wagon. He'd give the person money, and they'd go run off and get some blow or Ecstasy or booze. And he'd wake up the next day and go, 'Fuck, man, I had like a grand in my pocket.' "

Mötley Crüe tried to reconvene and record another album. Says Corabi, "Unfortunately, I think what happened is instead of taking responsibility for everything we did to ourselves, the band went around, pointed fingers at everybody else, and cleaned house." Thaler was fired, and practically everyone who had worked for the band followed out the door.

The band then signed with Left Bank Management, which had helped resuscitate Meat Loaf and Duran Duran. The band tried for a year to record a new album, but Sixx was making Corabi's life miserable. He constantly told him that he couldn't sing and couldn't play; it seemed the band was trying to drive him crazy so that he'd quit. Corabi was so unhappy that he was relieved when they finally fired him. Though his tenure in Mötley Crüe ended badly, Corabi has a lot of respect for Sixx. "He's fucking brilliant," he says. "He's amazingly smart. Nikki was incredibly generous."

Even if Mötley Crüe faced a backlash after Vince Neil's firing, the singer wasn't faring much better on his own. He signed an $18 million solo deal with Warner Bros., but his solo career never got off the ground. Neil was often a comedy of errors on the road. After a gig, he had to have a hot pizza and bottled Coors Light waiting for him. One night, he got locked out of his bus, and no one could hear him yelling to let him back in. Tour manager Larry Morand showed up with a fresh pizza while Neil was throwing a tantrum outside. Once on the bus, the singer got so mad at Morand that he threw the pizza at him. He missed and hit a groupie, and Morand burst out laughing at the sight of her covered in hot, dripping cheese and sauce. Furious, Neil grabbed a slice that was stuck to her and hurled it again toward Morand. He missed again and hit their bus driver. Morand couldn't stop laughing for ten minutes.

At the end of Neil's 1996 solo tour, he said onstage that the next time you'd see him, he'd be back in Mötley Crüe, and he was right. One rumor published in *BAM* magazine said the label wouldn't support any album the band did without Neil, and that's why he was back in the band. According to Corabi, Allen Kovac, president of Left Bank Management, even told him, "It doesn't matter who's singing for this band—the label is just not gonna promote it, the kids are just not gonna buy it, so we gotta let you go." Sixx denied that the label forced them into bringing Neil back. "It was a band decision." Mötley Crüe made their reunion with Neil official at the 1997 American Music Awards. Expectations were high for a comeback. The band hoped to sell two and a half million copies of their new album, get back into the arenas, and pretend the Seattle explosion never happened.

Right after Mötley Crüe performed, Alice Cooper and Pat Boone came out to announce the nominees for Best Heavy Metal/Hard Rock award. Boone lived next door to Ozzy Osbourne, which seemed to have an effect on him—he'd just released his first heavy metal album. He came on stage wearing rub-on tattoos and leather head to toe. Cooper uttered the understatement of the year: "Well, Pat, does this mean heavy metal is dead?"

Mötley Crüe's next album with Neil in tow, *Generation Swine,* stalled at about 250,000 copies (the album they did with Corabi had sold more). Venues were about 63 percent full on the tour. As one critic speculated, "Perhaps the fundamental problem facing Mötley Crüe in the '90s is that more people have seen their drummer's substantial penis than heard a single song they have recorded in the last seven years," referring to the infamous Tommy Lee and Pamela Anderson home porno tape.

During the *Generation Swine* tour, Nikki called a bouncer who roughed up a female fan "a nigger" on stage. After the incident, Lee commented, "I'm not a fucking racist, but only a dumb fucking nigger would hit a girl." The band was now trying to get out of their Elektra deal. Sixx would publicly call the label's CEO, Sylvia Rhone, "a cunt," and at one show encouraged the audience to chant "Fuck Elektra." An article in *Spin* chronicled the *Swine* tour, including the "nigger" incident and Sixx's comment about Rhone. "I stopped listening to Mötley Crüe when I grew up," wrote one *Spin* reader. "I think that's why America stopped listening too." Another wrote, "In response to your most unnecessary article on Mötley Crüe, I would like to say thank you to Kurt Cobain, Eddie Vedder, Perry Farrell, Sonic Youth and the Breeders. In the early '90s, these [bands] not only ridded radio and MTV of embarrassing bands like the Crüe, they also put them to shame. Wake up boys—the big-shot, big money, bimbo, racist, misogynist days of rock are over."

Tommy's marriage to Pamela Anderson was falling apart as well. In February 1998, during an argument, Lee kicked Anderson, and she flew across the room as she held onto their son. "I had to call 911," she later said. "He could have done anything at that point. What really frightened me was that he had no regard for his children. The babies were crying and hyperventilating. I was shaking and screaming and holding the babies when he kicked me in the back. I thought, 'There's nothing I can do if he's not even listening to his children.'" He pleaded no contest to felony spousal abuse in April 1998 and spent four months in jail. He refused to let his kids visit him; he didn't want them to see their father that way.

After getting out of jail, Lee went public on a maudlin self-pity trip, seemingly having no clue why he had been sent to jail. He denied he was abusive toward women, though he clearly had a history of it and told stories confirming it in several interviews. In *Spin,* he recalled a story of punching a woman off her bicycle in Stockholm for calling him a "stupid American." In Mötley Crüe's authorized biography, *The Dirt,* Lee recalled punching a onetime girlfriend's teeth out onto the pavement of the Sunset Strip for calling his mother "a cunt."

While he was in jail, Lee decided he would leave Mötley Crüe, promising to finish off by doing a greatest-hits tour. At an airport in Las Vegas, Neil sucker-punched Lee in the face and challenged him to a fight, knowing that if Lee hit him back, he'd go back to jail for violating probation. Neil got in his face and screamed, "Fuck you! What are you going to do about it? You gonna hit me?" Lee threw Neil to the ground, and the band's security chief separated the two into different corners like children. "Police!" Neil screamed. "Police! I've been assaulted!" Lee then demanded his own bus and dressing room or he wouldn't finish the tour. When the tour hit San Francisco, Sixx got so fed up with Neil that he punched him at the airport. After Lee left the band, he stopped speaking to Sixx. The two had been as close as brothers, practically joined at the hip. Now, said Sixx, "He cut off seventeen years of friendship cold."

The members of Mötley Crüe endured a number of tragedies in the '90s. Vince Neil lost daughter Skylar to cancer at the age of four. He filed for bankruptcy, and his marriage to Playmate Heidi Mark ended in divorce after fifteen months. Nikki Sixx fell off the wagon hard, going back into heroin, and saw his marriage to Playmate Donna D'Errico collapse from his infidelities (they've since gotten back together). Tommy Lee was hit with a tragedy when a young child drowned in his swimming pool during a birthday party for his son Brandon.

Mötley Crüe's downfall was an embarrassing one for a once-mighty band. Thaler's advice of growing old gracefully went unheeded. "I hate to say it, but I really believe that for the most part, people don't really know what to make of Mötley anymore," says John Corabi. "I don't think *Mötley* knows what to make of Mötley anymore. You could ask Gene Simmons why did Kiss reunite, and he's gonna say for the money. And love him or hate him, Gene's fans know he's gonna be honest.

"You have guys in Mötley Crüe giving interviews that if any member of Mötley leaves, they're just gonna break up. Then they fire Vince, and I come in. They didn't break up. Now they say *this* is the guy; Vince was a buffoon. It got 'em in trouble with a lot of fans. Then after I got fired, I was the guy that couldn't sing, can't perform, who's the buffoon. They take Vince back, but when they do it, they say it's not for the money, and maybe it isn't. But the bottom line is, now you've got your fans saying wait a minute, this ain't real. From the fans I talked to, they just don't believe it anymore. And if the fans ain't buyin' it, nobody else is going to either."

For the second part of the *Use Your Illusion* tour, Metallica and Guns N' Roses joined together for a stadium tour. The members of both bands were friends and mutual fans. Lars Ulrich had often flown down to L.A. to catch Guns N' Roses shows before the band had a record deal.

On tour, both Metallica and Guns N' Roses played full sets (two hours-plus each), and instead of sharing, each band had its own stage, which took a long time to set up and break down. Because of the long sets and set-up times, some shows went on almost until morning.

The band Faith No More, also longtime friends of Metallica, opened half of the joint tour and couldn't help but notice how bloated Guns N' Roses had become. "I'm getting more and more confused about who's who in Guns N' Roses," said keyboardist Roddy Bottum. "On stage now there's a horn section, two chick backup singers, two keyboard players, an airline pilot, a basketball coach, a coupla car mechanics." Bottum told *Spin*, "Their scene was about excess, excess, excess. There were more strippers than road crew." It was a strong lesson to Metallica, showing them what they would never want to become. James Hetfield said that Guns N' Roses were no longer a band but "a guy and some other guys."

The tour ended Metallica's friendship with Guns N' Roses. By this point, Axl Rose was not just an overbearing taskmaster with his band. He wouldn't grant Metallica what they wanted as co-headliners, thinking they didn't deserve it. But what Rose didn't realize was that Metallica sold six million copies of the "Black" album during the tour alone while Guns N' Roses' audience was dwindling rapidly.

It was clear that being in Guns N' Roses wasn't fun anymore. Slash loathed having to play ballads, and now they were taking up much of the show. The band members began going through the motions and weren't speaking to each other onstage anymore. Many nights on tour,

Duff McKagan woke up in the middle of the night, having no idea where he was. He'd run to the window, look outside, and try to figure it out. Some nights he would sit alone in his hotel room in tears, pleading, "Please, let there be a show soon."

On August 8, 1992, the tour reached Montreal. Metallica's concerts were now featuring full pyroeffects with twelve-foot high, 3,200-degree flames. During the introduction to their song "Fade to Black," Hetfield was confused where he was supposed to stand onstage and walked into an area of the stage where he was engulfed in fire. Holding his doubleneck guitar in front of him helped minimize the burns. If he had inhaled, the flames would have gone down his throat and scorched his internal organs, killing him instantly. Hetfield was rushed to the hospital with second- and third-degree burns. The rest of the band had no idea whether he would survive. That night while he was recuperating in the hospital, someone gave him a radio so he could listen to music and take his mind off his injuries. Flipping around the stations, he heard something about a riot.

After the accident, Guns N' Roses were asked if they could go on early to calm the agitated audience. Metallica were hoping that they would play a great three-hour show and turn around the evening's bad fortunes.

Instead, Axl Rose stormed offstage after 55 minutes because he was angry about the monitor systems and having to strain his voice. Reports vary as to what Rose said onstage that night before leaving. One had him saying, "If anybody here is interested, this will be our last show for a long time." (Another claimed he said, "Sorry, hope you get your money back.") The result was another full-scale riot. Both bands weren't allowed to leave the venue until 4:30 in the morning, when everything was finally under control.

As the riot was under way, Kirk Hammett was ready to have a nervous breakdown. Rose seemed less concerned. "The kids outside are turning over cop cars," he said. "Cool!" Hammett thought, Man, this guy really doesn't get it. While the other three members of Metallica waited backstage, having no idea if Hetfield was okay or not, Rose sipped champagne, acting as though nothing had happened. It reminded Hammett of the emperor Nero fiddling while Rome burned.

Hetfield was released from the hospital the next day and began physical therapy. It took several weeks for him to even make a fist, but he was determined to play guitar again. Seventeen days later, Metallica was back on tour with former roadie and Metal Church guitarist John Marshall taking over on guitar while James sang.

As they had done throughout their career, the members of Metallica put their misfortunes behind them and even cracked jokes about the Montreal show. After Hetfield was out of danger, the band called him "Flames Hetfield." The "Black" tour ended safely on July 4, 1993, in Belgium. It was a long, hard tour, and Metallica swore they would never be out on the road that long again. By that point, there was little the band had to prove anymore.

"You feel that sting, huh, big boy? That's *pride fuckin'* with ya!"

—Bruce Willis in *Pulp Fiction*

THE FIRST TIME Jani Lane ever walked into the Columbia Records building, he saw a gigantic poster of Warrant's *Dirty Rotten Filthy Stinking Rich* cover on the wall above the president's secretary's desk. When he walked into the Columbia offices before the release of the band's third album, 1992's *Dog Eat Dog,* a huge Alice in Chains poster had replaced it.

Lane searched his memory. Alice in Chains, he thought. Didn't they just open for us? In fact, when Warrant played Seattle, the label had asked if they could add Alice in Chains to the bill, because they wanted to see them live before they signed them. Staring now at the gigantic poster, the writing was literally on the wall. Hello, Seattle, he thought. Goodbye, Warrant.

Warrant was gearing up for a big tour and had bought a huge stage from Whitesnake shaped like a giant W. Warrant took to the road for the *Dog Eat Dog* album, but thirty shows in, Lane quit the band, in part because he was going through a painful divorce from Bobbie Brown. The thirty shows had bombed. Adding to the band's misfortune, manager Tom Hulett had died.

Warrant's merchandise company then sued the band to try

and recoup lost merchandise money from the canceled tour. "Everybody just came after us like we were Bank of America, sitting on millions of dollars," says bassist Jerry Dixon. According to Dixon and guitarist Erik Turner, Warrant's next manager then ripped off the band while they were fighting for survival, and from then on they decided to conduct all the band business themselves.

Turner and Dixon admit that when they were riding high on the wave of success, they didn't care that much about making money and put a lot of what they earned back into the band. Says Turner: "I think a lot of it had to do with, one, we'd never had money, two, we never thought it was going to end, and three, all the people that we worked with we trusted, which was a big fuckin' mistake, 'cause we found out a lot of them ripped us off. As soon as we fell on hard times, not only did they not help us out, some of them went out of their way to fuckin' come after us."

It was a hard transition for the band to go from being top dogs to not even getting their phone calls returned. The band would call Columbia repeatedly to discuss what they should do next. Says Jerry Dixon, "We used to leave messages like, 'We want to continue on—do we have a deal? We need five seconds: a yes, a no, kiss my ass, suck my dick . . .' Nothing." Six months later, the band received a letter informing them they had been dropped. Says Erik Turner, "We thought, we'd been at the label for five years, we sold seven million albums for them—it's not that much, but it's still not bad. We thought that we could get a phone call."

Eventually Warrant re-formed with Jani Lane, and it was apparent that even throughout their turmoil, they managed to keep a sense of humor. During one ride on their tour bus, Dixon was talking to the current road crew about the band's glory days. At Warrant's peak, they were spending $225,000 a week on tour, and all their roadies were on salary year-round. They even helped one tour manager buy a house. Finally Lane walked in and told the roadies, "Basically, what he's telling you guys is you all fucked up! You should have worked with us before!"

As with many '80s bands, the touring juggernaut for Poison had to keep rolling, and it would cost them dearly. Some tours went from seventeen to nineteen months in length, with little rest time built in. "Toward the end of the third album, I remember feeling tired," says guitarist C. C. DeVille. "I remember feeling like I was a little bit drained. I was getting high, Bobby and I were both getting high a lot, and we really needed to stop. We really needed to take a break. If we had taken a break right after that album, it might have been a real good thing. But that's not the way it goes."

Since albums had become so textured and layered in the 1980s, performers needed help to re-create their music live. Poison had their background vocals sampled through a keyboard. One night DeVille and vocalist Bret Michaels were arguing, and DeVille said, "Just go on stage and shake your ass. No one listens to your voice anyway—that's what we've got a keyboard player for."

While DeVille's drug problem was clearly out of hand, what led to his departure from Poison was, of all things, when he showed up to the 1991 MTV Video Music Awards with his hair dyed shocking pink. He wanted to make an outrageous appearance like Cher or Madonna. The other members of Poison, at this point taking themselves too seriously, were not amused. "I knew they were going to get upset with me," DeVille recalled. "I figured if they were going to get upset with me over something like this, then it's time to leave." Michaels groused afterward, "[DeVille] wanted to be taken seriously as a guitar player and then he would come out onstage looking like Bozo the fucking Clown!"

DeVille was replaced by Richie Kotzen, a whiz-kid shred guitarist, whom Poison obviously picked up to try and blow DeVille away, just like David Lee Roth had recruited Steve Vai to try and blow away Eddie Van Halen. "He has tons of credibility," said Michaels. "The critics take him seriously!" Kotzen eventually got kicked out of Poison for having an affair with drummer Rikki Rockett's girlfriend.

When Nirvana hit, several bands that thrived in the '80s, like Poison and Mötley Crüe, lost key members. If DeVille had stayed with Poison, would they have been able to co-exist with Seattle? "With the music Poison was playing by then? No," he says. "We were done. I was done, and that meant musically, the band was done. I needed some fresh people to play with, and I wanted to do some fresh things."

After years of being out of the limelight and not being able to get his career back on track, DeVille got sober in 1995. "Normally when you stop, it's because you get arrested or you go broke," he said. "I could have kept going, because my resources were not about to run out. But I felt myself going insane. I would hear voices." Soon after DeVille got sober, he ran into Rainbow owner Mario Maglieri, and Mario gave him a huge bear hug and kissed him. "I'm so glad you're off that shit," said Maglieri. "Stay that way!"

Bands from the '80s often play the blame game as to why their careers went downhill but rarely accept much of the blame themselves. DeVille said, with a surprising degree of honesty, "You look back, and you realize we were a bunch of spoiled fucking brats. How dare we complain? Being a drug addict, or anytime you're famous and things like that happen, you lose touch with reality because [it] doesn't feel like it applies to you. You forget that you have to grow up. I had everything, and I just didn't see it. It's embarrassing that we could be so childish. We were clearing a hundred grand a night doing what we loved, and we argued constantly about pissy stuff. They should hand everyone who enters Hollywood an owner's manual for real life. We certainly could have used it."

When Gene Simmons and Paul Stanley appeared on *Headbanger's Ball* in 1993, host Riki Rachtman posed the inevitable question: "Is it possible, picture like four stadium dates, only four, [doing] the old show. Ever gonna happen?" The pair swore it would never happen. "That's too easy," said Simmons. "And then what's the difference between us and a Vegas show?"

Kiss would head into the 1990s without drummer Eric Carr, who died of cancer in 1990 at the age of forty-one. Carr had played in the band longer than Peter Criss and was the best drummer in the band's history. Carr was friendly, down-to-earth, and always available to Kiss fans. "He really cared about the fans," says Carrie Stevens, Carr's girlfriend. "He always stopped to talk to them, he always wrote back to them, he really appreciated that they were fans. Eric did a lot more than just be the drummer of Kiss."

Kiss wasn't packing 'em in as they had in the makeup days, but the band spent money like it was still the 1970s. In 1989, Paul Stanley went on a solo tour and stayed in a top hotel when the tour hit Manhattan, even though he had an apartment in town. The band had socked away money in tax shelters. By the '80s, there were new people working in the IRS but who were reevaluating these tax shelters. By the end of the decade Kiss owed millions in taxes, plus interest (a settlement was reached in 1989).

In 1988, the band fired and sued their business managers, Glickman/Marks (the suit was dismissed). The band then hired Jesse Hilsen, Stanley's psychotherapist, to handle their business affairs. He allegedly took off with the profits from one of their tours and hasn't been seen since.

With new drummer Eric Singer in tow, Kiss hailed their 1992 release *Revenge* as their big comeback album. Bob Ezrin was back on board as producer to try and recapture the magic of the old days. "I always felt Kiss did better when they worked with an outside producer who has power and clout and can help form the sound," says Bruce Kulick. "A guy like Ezrin is your classic producer, which is so valuable. He can write, help engineer, and psychologically get everybody to do the right thing; that's a big job. I kind of regret that we didn't have more people like Ezrin or more of that kind of an effort on other albums we did."

Revenge was supposed to be a step back in the right direction for Kiss, yet its sales and the subsequent tour floundered. "If *Revenge* had come out five years earlier, it would have done better," says Kulick. "To get a gold record in 1992 was damn hard for the kind of music we were doing."

Yet no matter what, Simmons and Stanley were still determined not to go back to working with Ace Frehley and Peter Criss. "I kept asking Gene for years to put the band back together, and he never wanted to do it," says Bill Aucoin. "He felt he and Paul did all the work, and Ace and Peter didn't really work hard at it. And I told him, appealing to the main side of Gene, 'The only way you're ever gonna make money again is if you put the band back together.' No promoter would give them a date anymore. The reason why they did the Kiss Conventions on their own was they couldn't tour anymore. No promoter would put the money up to do a Kiss show."

Simmons and Stanley finally reunited with Frehley and Criss for an MTV *Unplugged* special in October 1995. By January 1996, Kulick and Eric Singer were informed that Frehley and Criss were coming back, and so was the greasepaint. Both Kulick and Singer were put on hold and were paid for the year. In August 1996, they were officially let go.

Kulick had played guitar in Kiss for twelve years, longer than Frehley. "I had enough business sense to know they were going to put the makeup on again at some point," he says. "When it happened, it was the kind of shock where you knew it was going to happen all along, but it's still weird when it happens."

While the anti-'80s sentiment was stronger than ever, Kulick was stung when many wrote off the years he worked with Kiss entirely. "What hurt the most was all the press that acted like Kiss didn't mean anything from 1983 to 1996," he continues. "That was a slap in the face that I won't forget." Simmons was certainly one musician who led the charge against the decade, telling one reporter, "I would say most of the '80s was a complete waste of time." Simmons claimed that he was a "pop moron" throughout much of the decade. "I sold out; I became a corporate whore. I was seduced into not being myself. People held big checks in front of my face and said, 'Let's have a hit single.'"

As most predicted, the Kiss reunion tour was a huge success. Here was a whole new generation of fans who hadn't even been born when Kiss were at their peak in the '70s, flocking to see a Kiss show in record numbers. Simmons never got his wish of being on the cover of *Rolling Stone,* but the band did make the cover of *Forbes,* which one would think would be a bigger honor for Simmons. The magazine reported that their 1996 tour made $700,000 in ticket sales a night. The promoters received as little as 4 percent; 3 percent went to their booking agents, CAA; and their current manager, Doc McGhee, got only 5 percent of the net. Frehley and Criss, once equal partners in Kiss, were now paid employees earning a salary, plus a small percentage of the net.

In addition to the income that *Forbes* reported, Simmons also charged bands $2,500 a night to open for them. (Lizzy Borden was going to open a Kiss Tour in the late 1980s, but had to bow out because it would have been too expensive for them to do it.)

One published rumor claimed that Simmons and Stanley took in over $20 million apiece from the reunion tour's profits; Frehley and Criss were allegedly offered less than $2 million each. As Simmons liked to put it, four guys are in a car, but two have to sit in the back seat.

As the Kiss reunion stretched well past the time that Simmons had said the band would officially come to an end, they became a good example why bands shouldn't keep going past a certain point. Peter Criss was fired from the band in 2001, and now Eric Singer is playing in the band wearing Criss's makeup. Tommy Thayer, former guitarist of Black 'N Blue and Gene Simmons's personal assistant, has also currently been playing gigs in Ace Frehley's makeup and costume.

Reunions are normally shotgun marriages of convenience; the Eagles didn't call their tour "Hell Freezes Over" for nothing. Yet the Kiss reunion gave a lot of '80s bands renewed hope that they could reunite and be successful. The reunion also proved that no matter how much the other members of a band hated each other, they could get along long enough to potentially make a nice fortune. Or could they?

One of the most unlikely reunions of all the 1980s bands was Dokken. After Jeff Pilson's band War & Peace broke up in 1992, Don Dokken's solo career stalled as well. The two soon started writing songs again, drummer Mick Brown rejoined them, and they began playing again.

At first, all involved thought the new project would be a Don Dokken solo album, because Pilson didn't think it was a good idea to reform Dokken without George Lynch. After the three had recorded an entire album, Lynch reluctantly came back on board, and in December 1994, there was a full-fledged Dokken reunion. They fittingly titled their first album back together *Dysfunctional*. Lynch admitted, "money talks."

Dokken hoped that with John Kalodner signing them to Sony, they could have an Aerosmith-style comeback as well. According to Pilson, Sony was behind the band, and Kalodner got radio behind them too. The problem was, "The band self-destructed at that point," he says. "Was the anti-'80s sentiment still in place? Yes, it was still there. So I think we would have met resistance at certain levels anyway, but we definitely did self-destruct."

Sure enough, old wounds between Dokken and Lynch opened up. Dokken did a radio show that was broadcast to two hundred stations via satellite. The band was to play live, then do an interview. Before they were scheduled to go on, Lynch was fiddling with his guitar sound, and the engineers worried that his adjustments would mess up the mix. Don told Lynch not to change his sound and Lynch said, through clenched teeth, "Don't tell me what to do." He then threw down his guitar and walked out. The red light came on, and there was no Lynch. The band had recorded their soundcheck on digital audio tape, which was played on the air, fooling the listeners into thinking they were actually playing live. During the interview, Pilson pretended he was George. "I would answer for me and I would answer for George," he says. "Considering how shaken up I was, I think I did pretty damn good! Let's put it this way—nobody on the other end knew."

Eventually Lynch was fired from the band, and sued the other three members over money he said he was owed for rejoining the band and for playing on their summer tour. Dokken continued on, replacing Lynch with former Winger guitarist Reb Beach.

"Personally, my expectations aren't overly high for the band, but I'm gonna shoot for the moon," said Pilson. "If I only make it halfway, that's fine. We're not gonna give up. We're still gonna come up with quality work. You never know when the market's gonna change. If you can survive the tide, you can swim to shore." Not long after saying this, he had a falling-out with Don Dokken and left the band again. Pilson recently reconciled with George Lynch after they're not speaking to each other for four years, and formed a new band together. Dokken is currently touring and recording with only two original members, Don and drummer Mick Brown.

The *Use Your Illusion* tour ended on July 17, 1993, with Guns N' Roses having played close to two hundred shows. Axl Rose went into hiding at his Malibu compound. In one of his last interviews, conducted over the phone, he said, "I think there's a great fear of the unknown, and my new thing is, 'I am the unknown.'"

The same year, the band released an album of covers called *The Spaghetti Incident.* It featured a song by Charles Manson called "Look at Your Game, Girl." The band had complete control of their music written into their contracts and as with "One in a Million," no one could convince Rose that releasing the song was a bad idea. David Geffen didn't know about the Manson song until he saw a report about it on CNN while he was on vacation in Barbados, and, predictably, he went crazy.

A year later, just as the O. J. Simpson trial was getting under way, Rose's ex-wife Erin Everly and former fiancée supermodel Stephanie Seymour filed domestic-violence suits against Rose, who claimed he was the one who was attacked by Everly and Seymour and that his actions were in self-defense. Both suits were settled, Seymour's reportedly for

$400,000. A number of other lawsuits from embittered people in Rose's life kept him drowning in litigation for years.

Relations between Rose and the rest of the band were also growing increasingly strained. Stradlin's replacement, guitarist Gilby Clarke, left the band in 1994. Clarke and Slash were close friends, and his departure caused a huge falling-out between Slash and Rose. Slash wrote material for a new Guns N' Roses album, all of which Rose rejected. Slash didn't want the material to go to waste and started another band to keep himself busy while waiting for Guns N' Roses to get started again. Axl went crazy over this and threatened to sue. Slash's new band, Slash's Snakepit, featured Gilby Clarke, drummer Matt Sorum, and bassist Mike Inez from Alice in Chains (Chains lead singer Layne Staley's heroin addiction had kept that band inactive for years). They jokingly nicknamed themselves The Wayward Musicians Suffering From LSD, LSD being an acronym for "Lead Singer's Disease."

After returning from a tour with Slash's Snakepit in 1995, Slash tried to stay in Guns N' Roses. But he eventually ran out of reasons to stick around, and officially left the band in October 1996. When Rose sent a fax to MTV confirming Slash's departure, he patronized his remaining bandmates, warning them that if *they* didn't get their act together, there would be "no more Guns N' Roses." A *Rolling Stone* report on Slash's departure stated that a new Guns N' Roses album should be expected in 1997. "I'd be dead by now if I stayed," said Slash. "I can't handle that much inactivity or that much negative energy to the point where doing what I love is completely turned the opposite way and I hate it."

Soon enough, what was left of the lineup completely collapsed. Matt Sorum was fired in April 1997, and Duff McKagan left at the end of the year. The revolving door was spinning at top speed. Rose had so many musicians and producers going in and out of the studio that one needed a scorecard just to keep up. Even Quiet Riot's Kevin DuBrow called Rose's replacing the classic lineup with hired guns "a perfect example of career self-destruction. I should know!"

Recording the next Guns N' Roses album was a long, belabored process. At last report, over $8 million has been spent in the studio, with no music yet released. "Axl is a guy that in my opinion is really afraid to get back out in the marketplace," speculates producer Beau Hill. "Because as long as he doesn't release that record, he can't fail."

Guns N' Roses did release a lackluster live album in 2000. During the mixing process, Rose refused to communicate with Slash or McKagan directly, and they never saw one another. The tracks were selected and approved with their managers acting as the go-betweens. Even for an album with classic songs, the album struggled to go gold.

Since Rose now owned the name Guns N' Roses, he was free to put together any lineup he wanted. Former manager Alan Niven believed that Rose had taken control of the name so he could do a solo album and receive the big advance money a Guns N' Roses album would command, reportedly in the neighborhood of $10 million.

Many hope that one day Guns N' Roses will reunite the original members, yet it's doubtful that Rose will ever allow it to happen. Slash has remained friendly with the ex-members of the band, and they perform on each other's solo albums and continue to support one another. None of them has spoken to Rose in years. Oddly enough, Slash and Stradlin haven't ruled out participating in a Guns N' Roses reunion if one were to take place. Stradlin recently said that he could go into the studio with Slash and McKagan and make a Guns N' Roses album in a week . . . but God knows how long the vocals would take.

In one of the few interviews he's deigned to grant after the breakup, Rose said the band's breakup was Slash's fault, not his. "There was an effort to bring me down," he said, melodramatically. "It was a king-of-the-mountain thing."

After years of inactivity, speculation and canceled returns, it was announced that Guns N' Roses would play the Rock in Rio festival in January 2001 and, before that, a New Year's Eve show at House of Blues in Las Vegas. The show was scheduled to go on at one in the morning, meaning the gig would start on the first day of the first month of 2001 at one in the morning. (01/01/01 at 1 A.M.)

Of course, Guns N' Roses didn't hit the stage anywhere near one in the morning. Rose's new band performed their first song, "Welcome to the Jungle," at 3:30 A.M. "Good morning," Rose told the audience. "I've just woke up. I've been taking a nap for about eight years."

At both shows, the new Guns N' Roses played mostly old songs. Both the Vegas and Rio shows received rave reviews, and it seemed that for the moment, the press perception of Rose had turned around. Now hopes were high that their new album, *Chinese Democracy,* would actually get released, and the band could perhaps have a big return to glory. But a scheduled summer 2001 tour was canceled at the last minute. According to one report, the tour was canceled because Rose was suffering from a botched hair transplant which left "big scarred patches on the back of his head" that were "incredibly painful." The dates were rescheduled for winter, then canceled again.

Guns N' Roses would play two more shows in Vegas, at the end of 2001 at the Hard Rock Hotel. At the first show, on December 29, Slash wanted to see the band but was barred from entering the venue. Rose threatened to walk offstage if any ex-member of the band was in attendance. During the show, Rose also insulted his former bandmates during one of his stage rants, and the audience booed.

Meanwhile, Guns N' Roses' first and best album, *Appetite for Destruction,* has sold over 16 million copies to date and sells 200,000 copies a year. *Appetite* is also a sad reminder of what could have been.

Even though Slash had seen practically everything growing up around the music industry, he was bewildered by the collapse of the band. "I heard so many disillusioning stories about some of my favorite rock bands," he says. "And I thought, 'Okay, I learned from other people's mistakes,' which I have. But I never thought [we] would go that route."

When the Seattle bands came in, Eddie Van Halen, like many musicians, was terrified. Van Halen hadn't put out a new album since 1991, and

Eddie was wondering if the band still had an audience. He was backstage at the last show Nirvana ever played in Los Angeles in late 1993. Drunk and feeling sorry for himself, he told the band, "I'm washed up. You guys are what's happening now."

Yet Van Halen's next album, *Balance,* released in 1995, was another No. 1 hit and was one of the band's best albums in years. Van Halen sold out two nights at the Forum during the tour. "The eternal dudes rock on," hailed the *Los Angeles Times* when Van Halen triumphantly came back to town. "Here's a band that has stayed on top for nearly two decades by being true to itself, transcending every trend and weathering every whim of pop fashion."

After the *Balance* tour, Sammy Hagar felt that they all needed to take some time off. Eddie and Alex Van Halen were having health problems that had to be dealt with. Eddie needed a hip replacement, and Alex played with a full neck brace because of problems with his vertebrae. Hagar's new wife was expecting a child.

Hagar put out a greatest-hits solo album, stirring bad blood between him and the rest of the band. Hagar had once said that bands put out greatest-hits albums only when they needed the money, and after a costly divorce, Hagar needed the money. The album was released so he could generate money to pay off the lump sum he owed his wife. This did not sit well with Eddie and Alex. They told Sammy, just as David Lee Roth had ordered Eddie years earlier, that they didn't want him to do solo albums.

While the band was supposed to be taking a break, manager Ray Daniels proposed they write some songs for the film *Twister,* which promised to be a big hit in the summer of 1996. Hagar didn't like Daniels, but Alex Van Halen was Ray's brother-in-law. Hagar felt he'd be outvoted on key decisions. According to Hagar, Daniels told Van Halen that the money generated from the film's soundtrack could carry them through the rest of the year. While recording the songs for the *Twister* soundtrack, Hagar and Eddie constantly bickered in the studio.

For all the grief Eddie and Alex gave Hagar for releasing a solo album, Hagar got angry at them for wanting to do a greatest-hits album themselves, which would feature material with Roth. Hagar didn't want the classic-era Van Halen on the same CD as his songs, Eddie claimed, because he didn't want his music compared to Roth's. According to Hagar, he swallowed his pride and proposed that the band release two greatest-hits albums, one with his material and one with Roth's, and let the fans pick which they liked best. (Eddie denied this, and told *Guitar* magazine, "He was afraid Roth's would outsell his, so we made it one CD, half and half.")

Hagar left to be with his wife, who had just given birth, and Eddie told him he had to come back to the studio and work on lyrics by six o'clock the next day, or he shouldn't bother coming back at all. Hagar stayed with his wife. A showdown happened on Father's Day over the phone. According to Hagar, Eddie told him, "You're always thinking of yourself; you never do anything I ask of you. You've always been a solo artist; you might as well go back to being a solo artist." Then Eddie dropped the bomb: He was working with David Lee Roth again. "You, behind my back, are working with Roth?" yelled Hagar. "You fucking piece of shit! If what you two are doing is better than anything you and I can do, I'll blow you both!" Eddie allegedly responded: "Well, I wouldn't say that, man—this stuff is pretty good."

Eddie claimed that Sammy Hagar wanted to go back to his solo career. He would also later say, "I practically begged Sammy to stay in the band, but he wanted out," and claimed that Hagar pledged to keep relations friendly but then went to the press, slamming the band.

"Everything that Eddie has said about me is the total opposite of what really happened," countered Hagar. "Eddie says I wanted to be a solo artist. No, Eddie wanted to be a solo artist." Years after the split, Hagar said, "I've always been a solo artist. In Van Halen, I was a solo artist, and they used it against me. Looking back, it was time to break up. The way it happened was wrong."

Roth contacted Eddie when Van Halen was preparing their greatest-hits album. Eddie asked Roth to work on some songs with the band to add "spice" to the album. Eddie has always claimed he never asked Roth to rejoin the band. "The idea was not for him to be in the band again but to try and get him out of the Vegas trip he was in. Let him establish himself as a rock and roll singer again so he could put together a new band and do his own thing."

Van Halen recorded two songs for *The Best Of: Volume One* with Roth, "Me Wise Magic," and "Can't Get This Stuff Anymore." Roth was forced to record his vocals in a separate room away from the band. Alex Van Halen said that Roth tried hard, but where it would take the band several takes to nail a song, it took Roth two weeks to cut his vocals. The singer wasn't happy with how the greatest-hits album came out anyway. "Half the album is some other singer," he said.

When the band appeared on the MTV Video Music Awards on September 4, 1996, everything fell apart. As they appeared on stage, Roth was greeted with overwhelming applause. This was the most attention he'd received from an audience in years, and he basked in it. As his ego filled up the room, it became difficult to breathe. The rest of the band was clearly embarrassed to be on the same stage with him.

After a disastrous press conference, Roth and Eddie blew up at each other privately. According to Eddie, Roth told him he "fucking better not" talk about his hip surgery to the press. Roth considered it "selfish" and "bad manners." Even though Roth's solo career had completely stalled and he needed a Van Halen reunion to resuscitate it, he apparently still thought he was in a position where he could play hardball with Eddie. He told the guitarist, "Tonight's about *me,* not your fucking hip," and threatened Eddie he "better not" bring it up again. Eddie then blew a gasket, screaming, "Nobody ever talks to me like that! You ever talk to me like that [again], I'm going to kick you in your fucking balls! You fucking hear me?" Roth was soon out of the picture. "I don't need that kind of negative energy around me," said Eddie. "I don't know how to explain it, but Dave kinda sucks the life out of me."

Eddie thought a reunion that rode on their past and trying to relive the glory days would be ripping off the band's fans. "You don't know how much money was thrown at us to do a reunion tour with Roth," he said. "Probably more than the gross national product of East and West Germany put together. Some things are just better left to memory. I mean, if anyone saw him in Las Vegas—I'm sorry, but the thrill is gone."

It was a very messy, and contradictory, three-way feud between Hagar, Roth, and Eddie Van Halen. Whoever was truly at fault, the fans were furious with Eddie. Those who had never seen Roth with the band and were salivating for his return were disappointed that the dream reunion would never happen.

On October 2, 1996, Roth sent out an open letter addressed "To Whom This May Interest." The letter opened: "You've probably heard rumors that Van Halen and I will not be consummating our highly publicized reunion. And since neither Edward, Alex, nor Michael have corroborated or denied the gossip, I would like to go on the record with the following: Eddie did it."

However, in his letter, Roth did write: "A 'couple of songs' was all I knew for sure when Edward and I got together. . . . At that time, the band tiptoed around me sprinkling sentiments like, 'this isn't a sure thing, Dave; this doesn't mean anything long term, Dave; we're still auditioning other singers, Dave." Roth concluded, melodramatically, "If I am guilty of anything, I'm guilty of denial. I wanted to believe it just as much as anyone else."

Once the news broke that the reunion would never happen, fans posted furious messages on the Internet. One fan called Eddie "a communist." Another resigned as a fan-club president. Another wrote, "We made Van Halen and we can break them!" When David Lee Roth arrived at the premiere of Howard Stern's film *Private Parts* at Madison Square Garden, the fans in attendance began to chant, "Eddie Sucks!"

Hagar's replacement in Van Halen was Gary Cherone. Cherone was the lead singer of Extreme, a band from Boston whose song "More Than Words" had been a No. 1 hit. According to Hagar, "I know they had already thought of Gary Cherone as a spare part, in case something unexpected happened." Eddie denied that Cherone was hired three months before Roth was fired. According to one report, other singers were being auditioned in August, and Eddie did confirm having a phone conversation with him that month, but said he didn't meet him until after the MTV ceremony.

Before it was announced Cherone was the new singer, Eddie said, "If Gary's in, he's in for life—that's it. And if anything ever does happen, then I'll score movies or whatever, but that would be the end of Van Halen. I'll take up tuba."

Hagar said that if the band had been successful with Cherone, he would have been upset about it. "I probably wouldn't have been too easy-going about it if [the album] had sold four or five million, or the shows had sold out like they did with me," he said. "It would have been like, 'Damn, they don't need Sammy!'" It turned out Hagar had nothing to worry about. Van Halen's album with Cherone, *Van Halen III*, was the worst-selling album of their career when it was released in 1998, and the tour went poorly as well.

Soon Cherone was out of Van Halen as well. According to a report in *Rolling Stone*, he "left" halfway through recording their new album. But according to a source who was friendly with Cherone, he was given his walking papers right before the album was completed.

One often-repeated story is that Van Halen was given an ultimatum to get either Roth or Hagar back in the band or they would be dropped, which was denied.

Van Halen laid low after Cherone left the band, and it became public knowledge that Eddie was battling cancer. While he was receiving treatment, behind the scenes he and Roth were trying to patch things up. One published report claimed the two were having late-night meetings at Crazy Girls, one of Roth's favorite strip clubs on Sunset, trying to work out reunion plans, and that the supposed reunion would go under the moniker Van Halen With David Lee Roth, which was probably a demand of Roth's.

The latest reunion attempt was never announced officially because it was always on the verge of falling apart, and sure enough, it did. Roth tried to get his deal to return to Van Halen in writing this time. Trying to draw up an agreement for Roth to rejoin the band and having to deal with Roth's lawyers "made the cancer seem like a tiny zit on my ass," said Eddie. Another reunion attempt had failed. The band reportedly recorded three songs with him that will probably never see the light of day.

In December 2001, Van Halen lost their record deal with Warner Bros., a relationship that had lasted twenty-five years. The Van Halen saga would then take a turn into the twilight zone when it was announced in April 2002 that David Lee Roth and Sammy Hagar would be touring together, a venture the press jokingly dubbed "Sans Halen."

It remains to be seen if Van Halen will ever be able to pull itself out of limbo. Whatever musical trends that came along that threatened hard rock's existence—disco, punk, grunge—Van Halen survived, which makes the band's collapse even more bewildering to comprehend.

Who knows what the real deal is with Eddie. Considering the fact that Michael Anthony is playing guest spots with Hagar and Roth on their tour (something the Van Halen brothers reportedly forbid him from doing), and that the band has no singer, no management, and no record deal, it's safe to say the Van Halen camp is still in turmoil.

After the 1991 release of Skid Row's *Slave to the Grind*, the band didn't release another album until 1995. One reason given why Skid Row took so long between albums was their manager advised them to "wait for all this Seattle shit to die down." But according to drummer Rob Affuso, there was a long gap because the band was barely getting along.

Cinderella, whom Bon Jovi also championed, had also been inactive for much of the '90s. It took them four years to follow up their last hit album, *Heartbreak Station*. A year was spent for lead singer Tom Keifer's recovery when he developed cysts on his vocal cords as a result of his raspy, screechy singing style. By the time their next album, *Still Climbing,* was finished and released in 1994, the musical climate had changed. The record company told the band to strongly consider changing their name and cutting their hair.

Affuso didn't totally blame Seattle for Skid Row falling apart. If the band was stronger, he felt, they could have laid low, written some good songs, and come back with another hit album. But the band was falling apart from within. Then, when Doug Morris got fired from Atlantic, his entire staff went with him. No one was left at the label who was behind the band anymore. There was no support from radio, and no support on the road. Headlining a sold-out arena had been par for the course for the band, and now they couldn't sell out a large club.

"I can now see why so many ex-rock stars are drug addicts," says Affuso. "You go through this incredible high, you've obtained your dream, you're living it, and then it's over. You're still trying to find that high, and so many people look for it in drugs. I did it for a short time; luckily, I didn't get too serious and realized it wasn't working. But I can see how it can downfall so many people."

The follow up to *Slave to the Grind* was 1995's *Subhuman Race.* The album fared poorly, and guitarist Sabo would call the tour for the album one of the worst experiences of his life. Sabo was proud of the record, but he feels that no matter how good it was, it would have flopped regardless. "We could have released *Back in Black,* and it wouldn't have mattered," he said. "It just wasn't our time anymore."

Sabo and Bach eventually had a bad falling-out and Sabo swore he'd never play with the singer again. The band splintered in late 1996. The other members minus Bach formed a group called Ozone Monday. Affuso would eventually leave, and when the band changed their name back to Skid Row with another singer, he was furious. He always felt that without the original members, it wasn't Skid Row.

Affuso made peace with his bandmates backstage when they opened for Kiss in 2000. (Rumor has it they called themselves Skid Row again and opened for Kiss because they owed Doc McGhee a lot of money, a charge guitarist Scotty Hill has denied.) Affuso is still upset that they're touring under the Skid Row name, but he accepts it and is back on friendly terms with the band. He'd like to see the original five get back together, but, like Aerosmith, he feels they would need to get together in a program where everyone talks out their differences with a counselor or a moderator. Affuso doesn't think the other guys could get into the same room with Sebastian Bach without everyone beating the shit out of each other, but he feels that maybe they should do it anyway, to get it out of their systems.

Meanwhile, Jon Bon Jovi had managed to keep his band together during some tough periods, during which he started an acting career and even modeled for Versace. In 2000, the band had a Top Ten album with *Crush*. Max Martin, the producer for numerous teen pop groups, including Britney Spears and the Backstreet Boys, worked on the single "It's My Life," which sounded similar to the Backstreet Boys' "Larger Than Life." Jon didn't appreciate a reporter questioning whether he was going for mainstream acceptance by working with Martin. "You're wasting your time going there," he warned angrily. "If this is what you're going to write your article about, you're jerking yourself off."

After the mega-successes of *Pyromania* and *Hysteria* in the 1980s, Def Leppard lost a bit of footing over the next decade. After the death of Steve Clark in 1990, the band was ready to quit. Phil Collen told Joe Elliott, "This is not fun for me anymore. I'd rather do something else. Fuck, I think I'd rather be a plumber."

Yet late in the decade, aided by a brutally honest *Behind the Music* special, Def Leppard was doing better than they had in years. In 1999, the band earned a gold record for their *Euphoria* album and had a radio hit with the song "Promises." Granted, a gold record may not seem like much compared to the mega-millions they sold with *Pyromania* and *Hysteria*, but in '90s terms it was a success.

Like Metallica, in the face of tragedy Def Leppard grew stronger and were able to stay together, while numerous '80s bands splintered over the most trivial reasons. "I'll tell you right now, I honestly do believe if we have one more traumatic experience, it probably would signal the end of the band," says Elliott. "I think just out of a dignity factor we'd say, 'You know what? It's just not worth it anymore.'

"When a challenge had been put in front of us, we've risen to it for twenty years. But how much longer do we have to prove to this higher power or to ourselves that we can get over this? There comes a time where you have to say no. It hasn't happened yet, and I hope in the next thirty years it doesn't happen. We've done a lot of growing up into adulthood, and we did it as a team. That's a fantastic achievement."

After the tremendous success of the "Black" album, Metallica wanted to renegotiate their deal with Elektra (they had kept the same deal they signed back in 1983). Elektra chairman Bob Krasnow and Metallica had an agreement to renegotiate the band's deal, but when Robert Morgado became chairman and CEO of Warner Music Group, he would not give the band what they wanted.

Metallica sued Elektra Records on September 27, 1994, to get out of their deal, citing California Labor Code 2855, a law that prohibits personal-service contracts holding anyone longer than seven years. Elektra countersued for $100 million. The lawsuit came during a turbulent year at WEA.

"There were a lot of issues wrapped around that one issue," says Peter Paterno, the band's attorney, who represented them on the case. "There was the issue of whether or not the contract was enforceable, but it wasn't, and what damages were available for breaking it. In Metallica's case, it was a really bad case for the record company if they had lost, because Metallica was operating on the first agreement they ever signed, and it was never renegotiated."

Though Metallica had officially recorded only four albums under their seven-album deal, they could have argued that releases such as the *Garage Days Revisited* EP and the *Binge and Purge* box set could have fulfilled the deal. The other ace they had up their sleeve was the seven-years clause. Says Paterno, "We knew the seven-year deal existed, [and] we'd wait until the deal was up."

The suit was settled three months after it was filed. According to one report, Metallica now owned their master tapes, split recording and video expenses with Elektra 50/50, and received a similar share of the profits as well. No one in the music business ever wanted to test a suit like this, because if a band won, countless artists would be able to get out of their existing deals.

Metallica's next album, *Load,* came out in 1996. It was a radical departure from the "Black" album, and the fans weren't happy. Angry letters poured into the guitar magazines. "The band that set the path for many heavy metal bands and was the whole reason I like heavy metal has shit on everyone and followed the alternative bandwagon," wrote one. Another read, "After reading your Metallica article, I couldn't resist writing in to point out what a total fraud they've become. Instead of recording something that was contemporary but true to their roots, they decided to be a softer, more commercial version of Soundgarden. They deny it, but they totally sold out in the hopes that they would sell more albums than the last time out. Isn't this the same band that threw darts at Kip Winger's picture?" While on tour with White Zombie in 1996, Pantera lead singer Phil Anselmo took a shot at Metallica every chance he could. "Admit it," he said onstage at the Forum. "It's good to have us around now that Metallica let us all down."

But from the band's point of view, making the "Black" album twice would really be selling out. Says Steffan Chirazi, a veteran metal journalist and longtime friend of the band, "If you can step back from the fact that they didn't make *Master of Puppets, Part Ten* like everyone wanted them to, they've really been more independently minded in what they've done since the 'Black' album than any other band who's sold that many records. Who would have done what they did with *Load*? If you want to talk in pure commercial terms, what might very well be the quickest way to lose your fans is to do [an album] like that. Of course, it didn't matter to them, because they didn't give a shit. I'm sure their label wasn't impressed they didn't try and repeat the 'Black' album. And look who was vindicated in the end. They were."

Load sold well—not the monster sales of the "Black" album, but Lars Ulrich had expected that. He felt that one of the biggest mistakes a band can make is thinking they'll stay at that peak of success forever. "I believe that you don't have more than one gargantuan record in your career," he said. "I don't think it's possible. You have a record like *Back in Black*. You have a record like *Synchronicity*. You have a record like *Nevermind*. Or you have a record like the 'Black' album. But you don't have more than one like that."

Metallica has managed to survive and sell millions of records when many bands had fallen apart. "Most of those hair bands are followers, and they will follow any trend if the trend is against them," says Ron Quintana. "Metallica didn't give a shit, and they did it their way. You can see who all the followers and leaders were in the past ten to fifteen years."

Metallica had endured a lot of bad press over their war with the music-download website Napster, and they endured further bad P.R. when they were interviewed for the April 2001 issue of *Playboy*. Rob Tannenbaum spoke to the band for *Playboy* and reported, "I've never seen a band so quarrelsome and fractious," and considering that Tannenbaum did the first *Rolling Stone* cover story on Guns N' Roses, that's saying something. At the time Tannenbaum spoke to the band, the members of Metallica weren't speaking to each other, and there was tremendous friction between Jason Newsted and James Hetfield over the former's desire to record a solo album.

Judging by the mail the article received, the readers of *Playboy* grew sour reading Metallica's complaining.

On January 17, 2001, a statement was released to the press that after fourteen years, Jason Newsted was leaving Metallica. "Due to private and personal reasons, and the physical damage that I have done to myself over the years while playing the music that I love, I must step away from the band," the statement read. Just as leaving the band he built from the ground up, Flotsam and Jetsam, had been a hard move to make, Newsted said that choosing to leave Metallica was "the most difficult" decision of his life. He sent "love, thanks, and best wishes" to the band, and the three remaining members.

Newsted ultimately left the band over issues of respect. He made Metallica his top priority and put everything in his life on hold for the band's needs. "Whatever I had to do with Metallica [came] before anything else," said Newsted not long after he left. "But then to not get the respect that I felt I needed when I held [the band] in such high regard, that combination wasn't good after a lot of years."

Again in the face of loss, Metallica kept going forward. After the departure of Newsted, they returned to the studio to record a new album. But sessions were soon put on hold when Hetfield entered rehab. In spite of the turmoil that Metallica's gone through lately, there's little doubt they will soldier on and continue. They've overcome much tougher obstacles before.

Once it looked as though alternative music was finally on the wane, a number of hard rock and heavy metal bands tried to reunite for an Aerosmith-style comeback. Ratt was one band that for years tried to reunite. The band's *Detonator* album, released in 1990, was slick and polished. "The last record that we made wasn't a record that I wanted to make," says bassist Juan Croucier. "I wanted to have something that was really in-your-face and hardcore Ratt. Strip it down, lose that '80s production." It didn't happen. When Croucier saw the success of the Metallica song "Enter Sandman," and that they could succeed in commercial terms with a heavy sound, he said to himself, "Fuckin' A, we blew it."

When Ratt broke up in 1992, no one in the band was getting along, and they decided it would be a cold day in hell before they would play together again. Yet in a strange way, guitarist Warren DeMartini felt it was a blessing in disguise that the band broke up before the entire heavy metal/hard rock market collapsed.

For years, drummer Bobby Blotzer pushed hard to make a reunion happen. DeMartini, the most talented member of the group, was one of the last holdouts.

When Ratt finally got back together, they had a powerful ally in their corner. Just as he brought Aerosmith back from oblivion, John Kalodner now had his own label imprint at Sony, Portrait Records, and hoped to do the same with a handful of '80s artists as he'd done with Aerosmith. He signed Ratt, Cinderella, Great White, C. C. DeVille's new band Samantha Seven, Pat Benatar, and Iron Maiden. Unlike many executives in the music business, Kalodner was a big fan of hard rock and heavy metal, and he did everything he could to support the music.

The bands that ruled the '80s now found themselves in a strange position. The alternative bands that put out their music on independent labels throughout the '80s were now on major labels, while the metal and hard rock groups that glutted the majors now could only get deals with struggling indie labels. With Kalodner's interest, this was the first time many of these bands had the chance of being on a major label again. Kalodner was also able to get Ratt and Great White radio play, which hadn't happened in quite some time either.

Kalodner felt a big mistake the majors made was not scaling down the record deals of many '80s artists when their careers cooled down. On the eve of Great White and Ratt releasing their albums for Portrait, Kalodner said, "I think these bands can have gold records. I'm not sure they can sell four million units; in fact, I doubt that. But if you have a proper perspective and keep the budgets in line with sales expectations, then I think these groups can be moderately successful and continue to have [careers]."

Yet the same poison that destroyed Ratt the first time around bubbled to the surface again. Ratt's album for Portrait didn't perform well, and

Pearcy left the group six days before the band was scheduled to hit the road on a tour. The promoters were furious and wanted their money back. Pearcy cryptically told the press he didn't quit and he wasn't fired (he evaporated?). The band then did a showcase gig for John Kalodner at the Viper Room with a new singer. Kalodner wasn't impressed and dropped the band from the label, though he offered to keep them on if they changed their name, which the band refused to do. "I'm not gonna start from scratch," said Blotzer, even though at this point, that's exactly what the band had to do. Other acts on the label spiraled downward rapidly as well (three members of Great White quit within a year).

Even in the most reduced circumstances, certain bands behaved as though they were still headlining the Forum. Another '80s reunion that no one was waiting for was W.A.S.P., who toured with Motörhead in 1997. Motörhead chose not to headline the tour, even though they were the bigger act of the two. Blackie Lawless often delayed Motörhead's soundchecks until right before the doors of the venue opened, leaving the band with no time to prepare. When both bands had to share a dressing room, Lawless threw all of Motörhead's clothes and belongings into the hallway while they were onstage. Lemmy got so fed up with his bullshit that he ended up decking Lawless, and Motörhead left the tour.

Considering the market for metal in the '90s resembled the Sahara Desert, one would think a band would be grateful to have a major label interested in signing them. Many of the '80s artists never understood that success was a privilege, not a right. Most bands were lucky enough to get one break at success; many of the '80s artists did get second chances and blew them.

Even Kalodner got frustrated with the prima-donna antics of certain musicians he had fought hard to champion. "All those bands from the '80s were difficult because they all hate each other and they still think it's the '80s," he says. "It's almost not worth my time to do those records. I mean, I really wanted to try it, and then it's probably not worth my effort to do so."

Right before Portrait released the new albums from Ratt and Great White in 1999, they advertised them with full-page ads. The ads had a clever tagline that the '80s bands should have taken as a warning: "Never forget your past. It'll come back to kick your ass."

And yet, not every band reunion was a disaster. Along with Kiss, Black Sabbath had the most successful reunion of any metal or hard rock band. In 1992, Black Sabbath had reunited with Ronnie James Dio and Vinnie Appice and was slated to open for Ozzy Osbourne on his "retirement" tour when it came to the Pacific Amphitheater in Costa Mesa, California. The original Black Sabbath lineup would then reconvene and play several songs for an encore at the end of the night. But Dio refused to open for Osbourne and left Black Sabbath, this time for good. Former Judas Priest vocal god Rob Halford came on board to fill in for the show. He hadn't learned all the lyrics and taped them to the monitors for reference. Halford spent a good deal of the set crouched down on one knee in a hardcore pose while singing; because he wasn't a young man anymore, he had to crouch down and squint his eyes to see the lyrics.

Black Sabbath planned a full-fledged reunion tour with Osbourne in 1992, but he backed out at the last minute. They tried again in 1998. Rehearsing for the tour, Bill Ward suffered a heart attack, and Vinnie Appice was ready to go in case he had to fill in. Ward rose to the occasion just in time and wasn't replaced for the tour.

The reunion tour was a huge success, selling out arenas around the country, and finally Black Sabbath gained some (begrudging) respect from the critics. One critic made fun of the fact that all the members put together were nearly two hundred years old in age, but there was no denying that when they got back together again, the music held up very well. "Tony is still one of the heaviest motherfuckers in the world," said Osbourne.

Before the tour started, the band set up camp at a farm in Wales. "We rehearsed in some house near where Shakespeare used to live or something," says Appice. "It was in the middle of nowhere. Everything's in the middle of nowhere in England!" Appice loved to sit at dinner with the four members of Sabbath, who would reminisce about the old days when their van used to break down and they had to push it to gigs. "And it was nice to see them not around managers," says Appice. "No outside people. Just the boys shootin' the shit."

When Nirvana hit in 1992, the entire traditional metal and hard rock market collapsed, practically overnight. It's hard to remember anything like it happening in the history of the music business. One by one, the support systems that kept heavy metal alive began to crumble.

The beloved Cathouse, the club that defined the Guns N' Roses generation, closed after five years nonstop in 1992. Says DJ Joseph Brooks, "The scene changed; it wasn't vital anymore." Those who were now coming to the Cathouse didn't request Queen and Guns N' Roses but Nirvana and Nine Inch Nails. When Brooks would sneak in some Hanoi Rocks, nobody would dance to it. The Cathouse staff decided to end things on a positive note. Says Brooks: "Five years is a long time, and in the club world it's a *really* long time!"

In late 1994, KNAC was sold to a Spanish station. KNAC's last day on the air was February 15, 1995. To show their gratitude for all the station's support, Metallica's Lars Ulrich and James Hetfield were guest DJs for the final day. Metallica's "Fade to Black" was the last song the station ever played. At 1:59 P.M., they signed off and went to the Spanish format without a moment of silence.

In a memorial letter printed in the *Los Angeles Times,* Michael Wolffe spoke for metalheads all over Southern California when he wrote that KNAC was "the call letters of my youth and the soundtrack to my innocence." Countless bands and fans felt the loss immediately.

It was tough for metal fans in the L.A. area to let go of the music they loved. In the late '90s, a number of tribute bands began playing the L.A.

clubs that were still open. Most of these tribute bands were made up of musicians who played the Strip in the '80s but never made it. The most popular was the Atomic Punks, which only played Roth-era Van Halen. Bands that paid tribute to everyone from Cheap Trick to Ratt began springing up all over Los Angeles. It was nostalgia for the fans who wished they could go back in time and see the bands they loved.

Many of the L.A. bands that were headlining arenas in the 1980s are now playing the same clubs they started in. According to Jimmy D, an L.A. promoter who books a lot of '80s bands, Quiet Riot and L.A. Guns usually make anywhere between $3,500 and $6,000 a show. He says a tribute band can make anywhere from $100 to $3,000 a show. Atomic Punks make around $2,000 a show and are actually able to tour.

"There's been talk of the '80s bands coming back," says Jimmy D. "Radio's not gonna go that way at all. But there's always gonna be people who want to see Ratt or L.A. Guns. They never seem to have a lack of people who want to come and see them. There's talk of Tuff [an '80s L.A. club band] coming back, and none of those guys have hair anymore. It wouldn't be the same."

It wasn't just the American metal market that dwindled; the Japanese market changed by the end of the decade as well. Where Japan was once a safe haven for bands where they could headline arenas and be hailed as kings, now Japanese fans were discovering bands from their own country and listening to alternative, techno and hardcore instead of metal.

MTV was clearly one of the most crucial support systems that metal had in the '80s. Once the channel stopped playing traditional metal in the '90s, many of the '80s musicians did an about-face in terms of their attitude toward the channel, calling MTV an evil entity. Sebastian Bach, hardly a Rhodes scholar, blamed MTV for illiteracy. "I think MTV is a cancerous poison," said Steve Vai. "It glorifies violence, loveless sex, drugs, and stupidity. Thanks to MTV, there are no more real musicians."

The most common complaint was that the only reason the Seattle bands became popular (which were followed by teen performers like Britney Spears and N'Sync) was because MTV "spoon-fed" them to mindless kids. But hadn't MTV made metal and hard rock a Top Ten phenomenon in the '80s? Says Marty Callner, "I think the pros far out-weighed the cons with MTV. When Aerosmith sold out Warsaw, Poland, in thirty minutes without ever playing there, I knew the only way these people were exposed to them were by videos."

Throughout the '80s, guitar players practiced endlessly to achieve ef-fortless technique and staggering musical abilities. Now with the advent of Seattle, technique-heavy guitar solos, and the era of the guitar hero, was dead. At its peak, the Guitar Institute of Technology, a music school located in the heart of Hollywood that taught musicians how to "shred" on their instruments, had seven hundred students in enrollment, at $5,000 each. In 1997 it was down to fewer than three hundred.

"Rock stars were heroes, and the music had great solos, lots of hooks, cool arrangements, and made you feel good," said former Winger gui-tarist Reb Beach. "Now there's poor music, no guitar, bad writing, and crappy arrangements—no wonder it makes you feel so bummed out."

The great guitar companies of the 1980s such as Jackson, B. C. Rich, and Kramer suffered as well. Grover Jackson left the company he founded, Jackson Guitars, in 1990, and the quality of the instruments went downhill without his guidance. Kramer went bankrupt and out of business. B. C. Rich went back to making the same quality instruments they constructed in the '70s and '80s when their founder, Bernie Rico, came back to the company (Rico passed away in 1999). The classic gui-tar companies that were almost put out of business in the 1980s, such as Fender and Gibson, came back strong in the '90s and were popularized by the likes of Kurt Cobain and Pearl Jam's Mike McCready.

Yet after countless bands faded away into memory, one of the strong-est entities on the L.A. scene, the Rainbow Bar and Grill, stood strong. Many people from the '80s still come back without fear of a dress code or a karaoke night. "I can go in there tonight and see the same people I've seen there for twenty years, wondering if they're ever gonna get a job," says former Rainbow doorman John McBurnie.

When the Rainbow celebrated its twenty-fifth anniversary, hundreds of rockers came out to celebrate, hoping the music they loved in the '80s would one day return. At the bar, Jon Sutherland ran into Lemmy, who laid down $20 for drinks. Sutherland reminded him that it was an open bar that night and drinks were on the house. Lemmy turned to Motör-head's guitarist and said, "Lemme buy ya a drink."

It may no longer be the 1980s, but the spirit of the Rainbow is always willing. "I gotta tell ya somethin' about sex stories right now," says owner Mario Maglieri. "This happened recently. I was talkin' to this girl out front, gorgeous girl. A guy comes over, starts kissin' her, and before you know it, she's givin' him head! I'm goin', 'What the fuck are you doin'?!? Stop that!' It was at 2 A.M., there were so many people trying to get out [of the restaurant], I'm stuck in the middle. It stopped traffic, I had to break that up, I almost had a riot out there. That's twice in two weeks, two Saturdays in a row." Maglieri could only shrug and say, "That's the Rainbow."

For many '80s musicians, losing their careers wasn't nearly as bad as the one thing they've always dreaded: losing their hair. For many musicians, going bald was a sign of having to face mortality. A whole industry of wigs and extensions grew up in L.A. just for rockers.

"A lot of the guys [I worked with] had wigs," says one photographer. "I'm doin' a Kiss session. The band shows up, we're kinda waiting around, then the studio door rings. I open it up, there's a guy standing there with a briefcase. He says, 'I'm here for Gene Simmons.' The guy opens up this briefcase, and it's Gene's wig! It was no Hollywood Boulevard Halloween wig, it was like a Ted Danson/Burt Reynolds wig." Says Alan Reiff, who worked with Kiss for years, "On Friday, Gene's hair was down to his shoulders. On Saturday, it's down to his chest. A member of the band said to me, 'That Minoxidil's a mother-fucker.'"

Some speculate that a lot of musicians lost their hair because of the extra-strength hairspray to keep their hair up. "Let's put it this way, the guys with the biggest egos lost their hair first," says former Poison manager Vicky Hamilton.

Vanity has always been integral to being a rock star. For years, many metal bands wore tight spandex with no underwear to show off their girth in photos and on stage. Just as a wig could cover what you were missing on your head, bands like Iron Maiden had secret pouches in the front of their spandex that they stuffed to make the bulges bigger. Many bands used socks; some used dildoes, because they looked more realistic. According to photographer John Harrell, who shot numerous bands throughout the '80s and '90s, there's an art to rolling up the socks just right to make the bulge look realistic. "You have to use one sock instead of two," he says, having watched many musicians do this before a shoot. "One pair of socks can work, but you have to twirl them a certain way. They get longer, and it takes away some of the thickness. You can't just roll 'em up."

What these bands went through almost became a formula in itself. Years of struggle + overnight success − humility − maturity + tremendous arrogance + millions of dollars + a lot of drugs − millions of dollars − success = VH-1 *Behind the Music* special.

Blame went in every other direction for why the scene went down. "It was all the bands they signed *after* us," said Jon Bon Jovi. "Oh God, it made you embarrassed, what it became." When it became extremely unpopular to be a former metal or hard rock band, many musicians did everything they could to distance themselves from the past. "It wasn't real sincere on my part, what I went through in the '80s," said George Lynch. "I wasn't really happy in the '80s," said Warren DeMartini before reuniting with Ratt. "The gigs were great, but the whole process wasn't very healthy."

"I was known as the metal guy, which I wasn't," said Riki Rachtman, practically attacking a reporter who asked him about his days hosting *Headbanger's Ball*. "I never picked one video the whole time I was at MTV! I never said I was metal." Then again, considering what a mediocre interviewer and shameless backslapper he was on *Headbanger's Ball,* perhaps Rachtman was smart to distance himself from his past.

In the 1990s, metal became an embarrassment to be called or compared to. When Soundgarden won a Grammy for best metal performer, they made it clear during their acceptance speech that they resented being classified as metal. Singer Chris Cornell had the chutzpah to say that Soundgarden hadn't been influenced, "not even slightly," by '70s heavy metal. This makes you wonder how the cover of Black Sabbath's "Into the Void" wound up on a special edition of their *Badmotor-finger* CD. "Eddie Vedder dressed up like Kiss like everyone else," said former Pearl Jam drummer Dave Abbruzzese. "But all of the sudden it wasn't politically correct to admit it. It just wasn't part of the marketing plan."

Many metal and hard rock musicians privately held the alternative scene in contempt. The geeks that bullies like Sebastian Bach used to beat up in school were now making millions and sleeping with his groupies while he was back struggling in the clubs. No wonder he called the alternative explosion "Revenge of the Nerds."

When '80s bands began distancing themselves from their pasts, it angered the fans they still had left. These were the fans who bought their albums in good times and bad, and spent most of their disposable income on albums, concert tickets, and T-shirts. To hear a band say they weren't sincere about what they were doing was a real slap in the face to the fans. It was as if many of the '80s bands said, "Yeah, we put out a lot of shitty albums, but we got your money anyway!"

Some bands felt it was only a matter of time before the pendulum would swing back their way again. "A lot of bands from the '80s thought they were going to ride out Seattle like AC/DC rode out punk and new wave," says music journalist Jon Sutherland. "I'm surprised these bands crashed so heavy, so fast. I'm surprised that the fans gave up on them so quick. When you grew up on Kiss, you didn't give up on them because they had one bad record. You'd wait until the next one, and you did that for years."

It wasn't just the bands that were out of work. Record executives and producers associated with the era had to find other lines of work as well. "I kind of thought everything would remain the same forever," says Tom Werman. "I thought as long as adolescent males are out there, there will always be hard rock and I will always make it. I had no idea that the nature of the music would change. I never factored change into my life or anyone else's."

After their careers went south, a lot of the musicians had spent so much of their lives playing in bands that they had a very difficult time readjusting to regular life, or finding normal employment. After L.A. band Rough Cutt got dropped from Warner Bros., lead singer Paul Shortino applied for a job at the Wherehouse, a Southern California record store chain. He hadn't worked a day job in close to ten years, and on his application he wrote, "You probably sold some of my records [here]."

Many '80s musicians blame the record labels, MTV, the Seattle bands, and *Beavis and Butt-head* for bringing their careers to an end. And many '80s musicians remain bitter that their glory days are behind them. But it's naïve to blame the downfall of the '80s bands solely on one factor, whether it's Poison, Warrant, *Beavis and Butt-head,* or Nirvana. It was only a matter of time before the music had to change. Ultimately, listeners grew tired of how smug, arrogant, and phony the hair bands came off, and couldn't stomach it anymore.

But in the late 1990s, a new generation of artists would create a unique style of music that combined elements of heavy metal with grunge, funk, hip hop and other genres. The music industry would dub this new style of music "nu metal" and it would become incredibly popular with fans who were more familiar with Kurt Cobain than Randy Rhoads. For many bands that took on the "nu metal" label, such as Limp Bizkit and Korn, the metal sound is only one ingredient of their music. The instrument of choice for nu metal guitarists is the Ibanez seven string guitar (an instrument invented by Steve Vai), which gives their riffs even more depth and texture.

The distance that many '80s bands demanded to keep themselves away from the fans would eventually cost them, and by the time they tried to reconnect with their fan base in the '90s, it was already too late. The fans who bought their records were either alienated by their arrogance or had grown up and out of the music by the '90s. "It's unfortunate that a lot of the bands who were popular in the '80s really couldn't go out and talk to the kids, so they could see for themselves that there's no conspiracy against them," said Kalodner. "Something just changed."

For the bands that are still left, trying to maintain their careers has been an uphill struggle. "It's so much harder than it was ten years ago," says Scott Ian. "Metal never had a lot of radio, but ten years ago you had KNAC, you had ZROCK [a metal station in Texas]. Now in some cities you don't even have rock stations anymore—you have alternative and classic rock. A lot of the avenues and roads we used to have to market ourselves outside of MTV and radio don't exist anymore. Labels don't even have rock departments anymore.

"The little spark needs to happen somewhere to light the fire again. What that is, I couldn't tell you. I don't know what's going to stop this kind of music from getting smaller and smaller."

SOURCE NOTES

AI= Author's Interview.

INTRODUCTION

p. ix: "I've been there and back": Kurt Loder, *Bat Chain Puller,* St. Martin's Press, 1987.

p. xi: Origin of the term heavy metal: Stephen Davis, *Hammer of the Gods,* William Morrow, 1985; Jim DeRogatis, *Let It Blurt,* Broadway Books, 2000; Art Fein, "L.A. Musical History Tour," *2.13.61,* 1998.

CHAPTER 1: IN THE BEGINNING

p. 3: AI, Greg D'Angelo.

Ozzy thought, and following: *Don't Blame Me,* directed by Jeb Brien, Sony Music, 1991.

"We got sick and tired": Steven Rosen, *Wheels of Confusion,* Castle Communications, 1996.

p. 4: The members of Black Sabbath grew up within a mile of each other: AI, Bill Ward.

Ward's memories of Aston and "There was a lot of pride": *Wheels of Confusion.*

p. 5: "It used to tear me apart" and "I had to": Mick Wall, *Diary of a Madman,* Zomba Publishing, 1986.

Details of Osbourne's arrest and jail stay: Nick Ravo, "Ozzy Osbourne: The Icon Profile," *Icon,* June 1997; *Diary of a Madman.*

Shopping center where he'd cop dope: *Diary of a Madman.*

How Ozzy and Tony met, and Tony beat up Ozzy in high school: Robert V. Conte and C. J. Henderson, *Black Sabbath: The Ozzy Osbourne Years,* Studio Chikara, 2000; *The Black Sabbath Story, Volume One: 1970–1978,* directed by Martin Baker, Castle Communications, 1991.

pp. 5–6: Iommi losing his fingertips: Jas Obrecht, editor, *Masters of Heavy Metal,* Quill, 1984; *The Last Supper,* directed by Jeb Brien and Monica Hardiman, Sony Music, 1999.

Iommi was inspired by Django Reinhardt: *Masters of Metal.*

Iommi forming the "power chord," and couldn't feel the strings when he played: Lisa Sharken, "The Masters of Reality Return," *Vintage Guitar,* January 1999.

"The guy had a lot of:" John Stix, "Ozzy Osbourne: Metal's Heavy Is the Patron Saint of Rock Guitar," *Guitar for the Practicing Musician,* October 1984.

Both Led Zeppelin and the Jeff Beck Group covered the Willie Dixon blues classic "You Shook Me": AI, Neal Preston.

"Nobody would know what was going to happen": AI, Ward.

p. 7: "I didn't hear Black Sabbath's music coming from": AI, Richard Cole.

"Let's face it": Mike Stark, *Black Sabbath: An Oral History,* Avon, 1998.

"It just seemed like the right thing to do": AI, Ward.

Sabbath used to go to clubs where Jeff Beck was booked to perform: Steve Tarshis, *Original Black Sabbath,* Amsco Publications, 1985.

p. 8: A band had to be good enough to play London: Martin Melhuish and Mark Hall, *Wired for Sound,* Quarry Music Books, 1999.

Marquee club information and "If this is hell": Jay Jay French, "Rock Climbing: The Marquee," *Guitar for the Practicing Musician,* September 1988.

[Marquee] wouldn't let them come back until they bathed: Chris Welch, *Black Sabbath,* Bobcat Books, 1982.

"They were the dirtiest": AI, Tom Allom.

Fourteen labels rejected the band: Welch, *Black Sabbath*; Ravo, "Icon Profile."

Isn't it strange: Stark, *An Oral History.*

p. 9: What the album cost: AI, Tom Allom.

Sabbath playing at nuclear volume in the studio, "You can't turn it up," and "We don't turn down, man": AI, Allom; *The Last Supper.*

"Louder Than Zeppelin": Lester Bangs, "Bring Your Mother to the Gas Chamber," *Creem,* June–July 1972.

Didn't think the band would last long: Ravo.

"sounds like the gates of hell opening": Ibid.

"We were four guys": AI, Ward.

p. 10: Penicillin shot into his rear story: *Diary of a Madman.*

Roadies would wheel them up to their rooms and "emergency booze": AI, Ward.

"I was always afraid": AI, Ward.

"Honestly": *Diary of a Madman.*

How "Paranoid" was written: AI, Allom. *Wheels of Confusion* confirmed that the song was added to the album at the last minute.

p. 11: Geezer didn't know what "paranoid" meant: *The Black Sabbath Story, Volume One.*

The band saw used needles all over the arena floor: Bangs, "Bring Your Mother to the Gas Chamber."

"Wow. My mom won't even" and "Sabbath was forbidden": Robert Hilburn, "Metallica's Voyage to the Mainstream," *Los Angeles Times,* October 27, 1991.

Played the Fillmore East with Rod Stewart: *Wheels of Confusion.*

[Master of Reality] was written and recorded in three weeks: AI, Allom.

p. 12: "Psssffftt! Psssffftt! Psssffftt!": *The Black Sabbath Story, Volume One.*

Iommi played with Jethro Tull and saw Ian was clearly in control: *Wheels of Confusion.*

Ozzy sang off to the side of the stage: Conte and Henderson, *Black Sabbath: The Ozzy Osbourne Years.*

"was like one big Roman orgy": Jeff Kitts, "Miracle Man," *Guitar School,* December 1995.

drug references in *Snowblind*: AI, Ward.

Warner Brothers didn't see the band until they opened for Van Halen: Bob Nalbandian, "Geezer Butler," *Shockwaves* No. 1, August/September 1996.

"Nobody likes us except": Welch, *Black Sabbath.*

"I don't give one fuck": Lonn Friend, "John Kalodner: A&R Guru," *Album Network Magazine,* n.d. Clipping provided by Jon Sutherland.

p. 13: "Ultimately, it's the kids": Roy Trakin, "Another Number One Smash for Bon Jovi," *Circus,* January 31, 1989.

"Despite the blitzkreig": Bangs, "Bring Your Mother to the Gas Chamber."

Black Sabbath going from one star to three in the *Rolling Stone Album Guide*: Dave Marsh and John Swenson, editors, *The Rolling Stone Record Guide,* Random House, 1979; Anthony De Curtis and James Henke, editors, with Holly George-Warren, *The Rolling Stone Album Guide,* Random House, 1992.

pp. 13–14: Sabbath's lawsuits: Welch; Conte and Henderson.

"I liked the first four albums": Tim Jones, "The Ozzman Returneth," *Record Collector,* August 1999.

The songs on *Sabotage* dealing with their internal troubles: Ravo; Conte and Henderson.

"You've got to be really careful": Alicia Morgan, "Black Sabbath: An Interview with Tony Iommi," *Metal Maniacs,* August 1994.

Jimmy Page and John Paul Jones's studio musician background: Stephen Davis, *Hammer of the Gods,* William Morrow, 1985; Richard Cole, *Stairway to Heaven: Led Zeppelin Uncensored,* HarperCollins, 1992; *Guitar Player Presents the Best of Led Zeppelin,* 1994.

p. 15: Blind Faith information: Craig Rosen, *The Billboard Book of Number One Albums,* Billboard Books, 1996.

John Entwistle and Keith Moon were thinking of leaving the Who and "lead balloon" comment: Chris Jisi, "The Return of Thunderfingers," *Guitar Player,* August 1989.

Jimmy meeting with Terry Reid and Plant meeting Page for the first time: Cole, *Stairway to Heaven*.

"He had this bricklayer's ability": Davis, *Hammer of the Gods*.

"The P.A. systems at concerts": AI, Carmine Appice.

The relationship between Bonham and Sabbath and Bonham was the best man at Tony Iommi's wedding: Alan Paul and Brad Tolinski, "Heavyweight Champs," *Guitar World*, August 1992;*Wheels of Confusion*.

Bonham thrown out of a club because the soundcheck was too loud, and the countless bands he was kicked out of: *Wheels of Confusion*.

Drums covered with blood by the end of the show: Rosen, *Billboard Book of Number One Albums*.

p. 16: Bonham leaves Tim Rose: Cole, *Stairway to Heaven*.

"the room just *exploded*": Davis, *Hammer of the Gods*.

Details of the recording of the first album: Ibid.

"distance is depth: Ibid.

"the guitar army": *Guitar Player Presents the Best of Led Zeppelin*.

Peter Grant background: Davis, *Hammer of the Gods*.

p. 17: Details of Atlantic deal: Ibid.

Zeppelin II and *II* info: Ibid.

Overdubs on *Presence* done in one night: *Guitar Player Presents the Best of Led Zeppelin*.

"If you can't get it": AI, Eddie Kramer.

Airplanes, ringing telephones and coughing in the background: Rosen, *Billboard Book of Number One Albums*; John Stix, "The Music of Jimmy Page and Led Zeppelin," *Guitar,* March 1994; Chuck Eddy, "The Making of Led Zeppelin's (Untitled Fourth LP)," *Rolling Stone,* May 15, 1997.

"If it was an accident": AI, Kramer.

p. 18: Information on *Zeppelin IV*: Davis, *Hammer*.

"We decided that": Ibid.

The band insisted "Stairway" never be released as a single: The Editors of Rolling Stone, *The Rolling Stone Interviews 1967–1980,* St. Martin's Press, 1981.

" 'Stairway' crystallized the essence": Ibid.

Zeppelin IV sold over 22 million copies: Jenny Eliscu, "The Eagles: 26 Million Served," *Rolling Stone,* January 20, 2000.

"Stairway to Heaven" reportedly the most requested song in the history of commercial radio: Alan Di Perna, "The History of Hard Rock: The Seventies," *Guitar World,* March 2001.

"accidentally fallen open" and "accidentally perfect": Cameron Crowe, "Led Zeppelin," *Rolling Stone,* October 15, 1992.

p. 19: Bonham didn't use a drum riser: AI, Cole.

Zeppelin also had a very small road crew: AI, Cole.

Details of the Starship and limos: AI, Neal Preston and Michael Bruce; Billy James, *No More Mr. Nice Guy,* SAF Publishing, 1996; Davis, *Hammer of the Gods.*

p. 20: "you just tucked away those photographs": AI, Preston.

Neil Zlozower taking pictures of the band at the Hyatt House, and Peter Grant demanding the photos and negatives: AI, Neil Zlozower; Gary Graff, "In the Light," *Guitar World,* March 1996.

"The pictures that appealed to me," and following: AI, Preston.

p. 21: "The bottle stayed up in the air": AI, Preston.

When Zlozower started shooting bands, and information on rock and roll photography in the 1970s: AIs, Zlozower and John Harrell.

Some have said this rule started with Rod Stewart: AI, Rick Gould.

Metallica prefers photographers to shoot the *last* three songs: AIs, Rick Gould and Alex Solca.

"Robert was basically a hippie," and following: AI, Preston.

Page was well versed in the works of Aleister Crowley: Davis, *Hammer of the Gods.*

Page bought and lived in Crowley's manor: Editors of Rolling Stone, *The Rolling Stone Interviews.*

p. 22: "A lot of people can't be on their own": Ibid.

"He'd get on the Starship": AI, Preston.

Bonham was also jealous: AI, Preston. Also confirmed in Davis, *Hammer of the Gods.*

"We had a great time": AI, Carmine Appice.

the shark incident: Davis, *Hammer of the Gods*; Cole, *Stairway to Heaven.*

Could rent fishing poles in the lobby of the Edgewater Inn: Ed Grant, "The Alice Cooper Band," *Psychotronic* 31.

Appice ran into Frank Zappa: AI, Appice.

p. 23: "During the second Madison Square Garden show": Cole, *Stairway to Heaven.*

"the black sheep of English hard rock": Crowe, "Led Zeppelin," *Rolling Stone,* October 15, 1992.

Karen Carpenter beating Bonham in the *Playboy* music poll: Davis, *Hammer of the Gods.*

"Zeppelin really had": AI, Preston.

Grant almost never allowed the band to be filmed or videotaped: AI, Cole.

"If MTV had existed": S. L. Duff, "White Zombie: Welcome to the Warp Asylum," *RIP,* April 1995.

p. 24: Zeppelin's 90/10 tour split: Davis, *Hammer of the Gods.*

The Rolling Stones only got 60/40: Stephen Davis, *Old Gods, Almost Dead,* Broadway Books, 2001.

"[Grant] had the": AI, Preston.

"when Peter Grant": AI, Appice.

p. 25: "We were a flower-power": Robin Platts, "Purple Reign," *Discoveries,* November 1999.

How Deep Purple got the "Loudest Band in the World" tag: Ibid.

Blackmore's customized Marshall amps and "I'd rather play a little": *Masters of Heavy Metal.*

"cut any guitarist alive": Cameron Crowe, *Fast Times at Ridgemont High,* Simon and Schuster, 1981. A character in the book cited a quote Blackmore made in *Guitar Player* magazine.

Mötley Crüe had Hammond organ hidden in the power chords: AI, Tom Werman.

p. 26: Some bands had such disdain for keyboard players: AI, Claude Schnell.

Details of the recording of the *Machine Head* album: Joe Lalaina, "On the Record: Deep Purple's Machine Head," *Guitar World,* August 2000; Cameron Crowe, "Deep Purple: Self Evaluation Time Again," *Rolling Stone,* n.d. Clipping provided by Allison Grachowski.

pp. 26–27: Details for the Montreux incident that inspired the song "Smoke on the Water": Ian Gillen with David Cohen, *Child in Time,* MBS Publishing, 1993.

The title "Smoke on the Water" came to Roger Glover in his sleep and following: Platts, *Discoveries.*

Gillen sneaked a groupie underneath Lord's Hammond organ and following: Gillen and Cohen, *Child in Time.*

CHAPTER 2: HALLOWED BE MY NAME

p. 29: "Everyone needs a gimmick": Danny Fields and Randi Reisfield, *16 Magazine: Who's Your Fave Rave?,* Boulevard Books, 1997.

"year of the follicle": Alice Cooper with Steven Gaines, *Me, Alice,* Putnam, 1976.

Furnier felt rock and roll had more heroes, and following: *Prime Cuts,* directed by Neal Preston, PolyGram Video, 1991.

"I fear mediocrity": *Me, Alice.*

pp. 29–30: Details of Cooper's family and upbringing: Ibid.

Cooper's near death from typhoid, "the cursed Furnier nose," and following: Ibid.

Details of the high schools days of the Alice Cooper band and the Earwigs: *Prime Cuts.*

The late night jams in the desert: Ed Grant, "The Alice Cooper Band," *Psychotronic* 31.

p. 31: Alice Cooper's name: *Me, Alice* and *Prime Cuts*.

The "Don't Blow Your Mind" single: Alice Cooper collector Steve Darrow mentioned in AI that the single is very rare and worth a lot of money, reputedly thousands of dollars.

The band decided Vincent would become the character of Cooper: Michael Bruce with Billy James, *No More Mr. Nice Guy*, SAF Publishing, 1996.

Cooper equated being a villain with being an outsider: *Me, Alice*.

"Most people": Lonn Friend, "Alice Cooper: Prince of Darkness/Lord of Light" knac.com, October 5, 2000.

Alice's [Furnier's] parents were shocked by the Beatles and the Rolling Stones: *Prime Cuts*.

Glen Buxton put on makeup first: *Me, Alice*.

pp. 31–32: See-through pants story: *No More Mr. Nice Guy*.

The band moved to a house in Topanga and Cooper's encounters with Jim Morrison: *Me, Alice*.

The band cleared out a room of 6,000 people in three songs: Joe Smith, *Off the Record*, Warner Books, 1988.

Fans would buy tickets and not go to the gigs: *No More Mr. Nice Guy*.

Shep Gordon meeting the band details: *No More Mr. Nice Guy*; *Me, Alice*; Grant, "The Alice Cooper Band."

p. 33: "that Vince guy": *No More Mr. Nice Guy*.

Cooper meeting Frank Zappa: *Prime Cuts* and *Me, Alice*.

Signed to Straight for $6,000 and All our struggles are over: *Me, Alice*.

The Toronto Rock and Roll Festival and chicken incident details: *Prime Cuts*; Grant, "The Alice Cooper Band."

p. 34: "That was the original": S. L. Duff, "Alice Cooper: The Trashman Cometh," *RIP*, October 1989.

"the Blue Army": Stephen Davis, *Walk This Way*, Avon, 1997.

"Our band is the epitome": Bob Greene, *Billion Dollar Baby*, Signet, 1974.

For $50,000, Warner got James Taylor, Ronstadt, and Cooper: *No More Mr. Nice Guy*; Grant.

p. 35: Ezrin information, working at Nimbus Nine and seeing the band at Max's Kansas City: AI, Bob Ezrin.

"You have no right to stop this show!": *Me, Alice*.

"What the fuck was that?," and following: AI, Ezrin.

p. 36: Warner would not finance another Alice Cooper album: *Me, Alice*.

Rehearsed ten to twelve hours a day: Ibid.

If the prisoners in the yard liked the music: Russell Hall, "The Alice Cooper," *Goldmine*, May 19, 2000.

"We kept a lot of the madness": AI, Ezrin.

"Pretend you're desperate": *Me, Alice.*

"I argued with him": Tom Forsythe, "The Recurring Nightmare," *Guitar for the Practicing Musician,* 1989.

p. 37: Ezrin thought Cooper was singing, "I'm edgy": AI, Ezrin.

Gordon reportedly paid people: *No More Mr. Nice Guy.*

The band even made hundreds of calls themselves: *No More Mr. Nice Guy* and *Me, Alice.*

"That was the boner": *Me, Alice.*

Details of the mansion where the band lived: *No More Mr. Nice Guy.*

" 'Eighteen' Changed Alice Cooper": *Village Voice* review reprinted in *No More Mr. Nice Guy.*

" 'Eighteen' became our license to kill": Joe Smith, *Off the Record.*

p. 38: Warner Brothers considered Alice Cooper's success a fluke: Russell Hall, "The Alice Cooper Band," *Goldmine,* May 19, 2000.

"We started to incorporate": Christopher Scapelliti, "Well Hung," *Guitar World,* July 1999.

"God Bless America" was played at the end of every show: Greene, *Billion Dollar Baby.*

Alice was terrified of snakes at first: *No More*; Alice also confirmed this in *Off the Record.*

Kachina laying in Alice's lap for a famous poster: Poster is shown in *Prime Cuts.*

A substitute snake was brought in: AI, Steve Hunter, former guitarist in the Alice Cooper band, 1975–1979.

pp. 38–39: Sword through the leg story: AI, Brian "Renfield" Nelson, Cooper's personal assistant.

The evolution of the props, "low budget radical," and "He loved his electric chair": AI, Ezrin.

Cooper looked at their shows as a rock and roll morality play: Scapelliti, *Well Hung.*

"Shakespeare would have been": *Me, Alice.*

The gallows were built by the Warner Bros. prop department: Grant and *No More Mr. Nice Guy.*

The guillotine was built by the Amazing Randi, and the band wanted the audience to believe every show could be Alice's last: Greene.

The band hired a Broadway producer who had worked with Liza Minelli and the band's lighting director got an equal cut: Grant and *No More.*

Cooper said bandmates didn't want to do the wild stage show: *Prime Cuts.*

"dancing musical": Grant.

"The whole band": Hall.

p. 40: "I think we liberated": Scapelliti. In Michael Bruce's autobiography, *No More Mr. Nice Guy,* he also recalled that Elton John came to see Alice perform at the Hollywood Bowl on the *School's Out* tour and after the show said, "Alice, you really showed me what show business is all about." Bruce also recalled it wasn't long after that show that Elton began wearing his crazy stage costumes on stage. The song "All the Young Girls Love Alice" on Elton John's *Goodbye Yellow Brick Road* album is his tribute to Cooper.

"the happiest, most exhilarating moment": David Wild, "The Making of 'School's Out,'" *Rolling Stone,* June 9–July 23, 1998.

Panties raining from the skies: Grant, Bruce.

The recording of the song "School's Out," "one of the best moments," and following: AI, Ezrin.

p. 41: The harmonies for *Billion Dollar Babies* were structured like "Row, row, row your Boat": *No More Mr. Nice Guy.*

Details of *Billion Dollar Babies* tour: *Me, Alice* and *No More Mr. Nice Guy.*

"If Alice Cooper was destroying anyone": *Me, Alice.*

fourteen-year-old Canadian boy was found hung: AI, Ezrin. Confirmed in *Me, Alice* and *No More Mr. Nice Guy.*

"I thought if we had": AI, Ezrin.

p. 42: Starship details: AI, Preston; *No More Mr. Nice Guy*; *Hammer of the Gods.*

Watching *Deep Throat* on the Starship: *Billion Dollar Baby.*

The tensions on the tour, "I write No. 1 songs," and following: Ibid.

p. 43: The tour's grosses and expenses: *No More Mr. Nice Guy.*

Alice used to say that whenever someone asked him where he lived: *Prime Cuts.*

pp. 43–44: *Muscle of Love* details: *No More Mr. Nice Guy.*

Glen Buxton's downfall: *No More Mr. Nice Guy* and Hall.

Breakup of the original band: *No More Mr. Nice Guy* and Hall.

"Alice is a good guy": Hall.

p. 45: Downfall of Bruce's solo act and "It was only": *No More Mr. Nice Guy.*

Details for the Nightmare tour: Hall.

pp. 45–46: Details of Vincent Price guesting on the *Nightmare* album and Ezrin quotes: AI, Ezrin.

"Alice must have": Craig Rosen, "Bladerunner," *BAM,* July 13, 1990.

Ike and Tina Turner covered "Only Women Bleed": Ike and Tina's version of the song is on Ike and Tina Turner, *Greatest Hits, No. 2,* WEA/Atlantic, 1988.

Gloria Steinem rumored to have sent Alice a telegram: AI, Hunter.

"When Alice": Slash interviewed by John Harrell, quoted with permission.

"Joe! There's a course down there!", and Alice kept his clubs in the equipment truck: AI, Hunter.

Cooper watching the Marx Brothers with Groucho: AI, Hunter.

p. 47: Cooper helping to save the Hollywood sign: AI, Nelson.

"Do you know": *Billion Dollar Baby*.

Alice Cooper's appearance on the *Midnight Special*: B. R. Hunter, *The Midnight Special 1972–1981: Late Night's Original Rock 'n' Roll Show*, VH-1 Books, 1997.

Cooper observed Keith Moon killing himself being "Keith Moon" 24 hours a day: Tony Fletcher, *Moon*, Avon, 1999.

"I think [Cooper] drank more": *No More Mr. Nice Guy*.

p. 48: Simmons was lost without the makeup: Bob Nalbandian, Vinnie Vincent, Aardshok, Fall 1986. Also confirmed by Gene himself in Jaan Uhelszki, "Confessions of a Kissette," *BAM*, September 10, 1993.

"If you're not careful": AI, Hunter.

Kiss formed an Alice Cooper tribute band and "They got four guys with makeup": *No More Mr. Nice Guy*.

Kiss wanted to be like the Dolls: Barney Hoyskyns, *Glam!*, Pocket Books, 1998.

pp. 48–49: Details of the recording of the first New York Dolls album, "In the end," and glam/glitter was laid to rest on October 11, 1974: Ibid.

"they figured": Ibid.

"Anybody who held me back": Ken Sharp, "Last Kiss," *Goldmine*, June 2, 2000.

"In Israel": David Rensin, "Twenty Questions: Gene Simmons," *Playboy*, December 1988.

p. 50: "I wanted to kill": Chris Lendt, *Kiss and Sell*, Billboard Books, 1997.

Gene and Paul's first meeting: As told to Jeff Kitts and Ken Sharp, *Kisstory*, Kisstory Ltd., 1994.

Details of Wicked Lester, Coronel's dismissal, and "There was no reason": Ibid.

"anything to make it": "Kiss Live 1973-1993," magazine special.

"flash and balls": Ibid.

Ace's first meeting with Gene and Paul details and details of Ace Frehley's clothes: Jeff Kitts, "Kiss and Tell," *Guitar World*, August 1993; AI, Rik Fox, who was friends with Peter Criss and knew the band in the early days.

p. 51: They wanted to call the band a four-letter word: Rensin.

Paul came up with the name: *Kisstory*.

At first, some thought they were a soft rock group: AI, Zlozower.

Details of Criss's erratic behavior: Lendt, *Kiss and Sell*; AI, Fritz Postelwaite; Margaret Moser and Bill Crawford, *Rock Stars Do the Dumbest Things*, Renaissance Books, 1998.

pp. 51–52: Rehearsals at the loft: AI, Rik Fox.

The development of the band's makeup: Jeff Kitts, "Kiss N' Makeup," *Guitar World*, September 1996.

Details of the Hotel Diplomat meeting and "Let's get together": AI, Bill Aucoin.

"Neil wanted to work": AI, Aucoin.

Three of Bogart's biggest acts, Kiss, the Village People, and Parliament: AI, Cecil Holmes Jr. Cecil Jr. worked at Casablanca as a teenager and his father, Cecil Sr., was an executive at the label.

"I think this kind of garish stuff": Smith, *Off the Record.*

p. 53: "Warner Brothers never really," and following: AI, Aucoin.

Soon a secret memo: AI, Aucoin. That a memo was circulated and Neil went crazy over it was also generally confirmed in Fredric Dannen, *Hit Men,* Random House, 1990.

"How could you do this," and following: AI, Aucoin

p. 54: "They could have been laughed": AI, Fritz Postelwaite.

Early on in the band's career and following: AI, Aucoin.

Magazines would get photos of the band without makeup and the fans voted they didn't want to see them: Kiss interview for the late night cable show *Night Flight,* 1983.

"To tell you the truth": Kitts, "Kiss and Tell."

Brands of makeup the band wore: Kitts, "Kiss N' Makeup."

pp. 54–55: Peter would sweat and smush his makeup: AI, Fox.

Kiss dyed their hair darker: Ed Przydzical, Ace Frehley, *Guitar for the Practicing Musician,* January 1985.

No facial hair allowed: Bruce Pollack, Paul Stanley, *Guitar for the Practicing Musician,* January 1985.

Ozzy Osbourne wouldn't consider hiring bassist Greg Chaisson: John Stix, "Edging Forward," *Guitar for the Practicing Musician,* June 1989.

Kiss played New York only once a month: *Kisstory.*

They lost a little on each show, but made up for it with volume: AI, Postelwaite.

"the opening chords," and following: AI, Postelwaite.

Aucoin financed Kiss's first tour and following: AI, Aucoin.

p. 56: The black community thought Kiss were a black group in whiteface: AI, Aucoin.

The label made sure the next album was already in the stores: AI, Aucoin.

Kiss touring with Blue Öyster Cult and Queen details: Mike Henry, "The Ten Best Concerts That I Can Hardly Remember," *Shockwaves,* Spring 1997.

"Rock and Roll All Night" written in Eugene, Oregon: Przydzical, *Guitar for the Practicing Musician.*

p. 57: "They were what the record company": Platts, *Discoveries.*

If they were able to capture that live energy and excitement: Cherrie Foglio and Paul Stanley, "Smashes, Thrashes, and Other Shit," *RIP,* September 1989.

One local high school, AI, Aucoin.

Bogart didn't have Kiss's advance money: AI, Aucoin; *Kisstory.*

Aucoin got a huge check delivered: AI, Aucoin.

Frampton Comes Alive! sales and weeks on the charts: Hunter, *The Midnight Special*; Fred Goodman, *The Mansion on the Hill,* Random House, 1997.

p. 58: "I do remember" and "It's anything but flawless": Ken Sharp, "The Roar of the Greasepaint, the Smell of the Crowd," *Goldmine,* October 15, 1993.

"Only the drums": AI, Kramer.

"As far as the live show": AI, Postelwaite.

Limos and room service ran twenty-four hours a day: AI, Postelwaite.

Frehley always had at least $5,000 in his pockets: Kitts, "Kiss and Tell."

Kiss grossed $119 million: Robert La Franco, "Retread Rock," *Forbes,* September 23, 1996.

$52 million was made through merchandising: AI, Aucoin.

"Why don't you guys put out belt buckles": Peter S. Greenberg, "Stocks, Bonds, Rock n' Roll," *Playboy,* January 1981.

p. 59: "The merchandising was": AI, Chris Lendt.

The merchandising profit was split 50/50 and following: Lendt, *Kiss and Sell.*

"All this is taken": AI, Lendt.

"I think it was the mentality of": AI, Preston.

p. 60: "It all felt very fleeting": Cameron Crowe interview by Vera Anderson, quoted with permission.

Outside the window of Bogart's office: Lendt, *Kiss and Sell.*

Some artists had provisions put in to their contracts about billboards: Fein, *Musical History Tour.*

The movie studios had no room to advertise their films: AI, Aucoin.

"You walked into Casablanca": Nancy Griffin and Kim Masters, *Hit and Run,* Simon and Schuster, 1996.

p. 61: Some went to record labels to score: AI, Barry Levine.

Bogart's appearance and the Casablanca parking lot: Griffin and Masters; Lendt; Dannen.

"When it came to": Kitts, "Kiss and Tell."

"As far as what took place": AI, Postelwaite.

"That's Gene's oxygen": AI, Bruce Kulick.

"Gene is pretty much": Barry Levine, *The Kiss Years,* Studio Chikara, 1997.

p. 62: "I fuck everything": Uncredited, "The Girls of Kiss," *Playboy,* March 1999.

"That's really the biggest kick": Paul Elliot, "Kings of the Night Time World," *Kerrang!,* March 27, 1999.

Thirteen women lined up outside Gene's bathroom, and "It was almost like": AI, Levine; Levine, *The Kiss Years.*

"He really looked like": Gretchen Edgren, *Inside the Playboy Mansion*, General Publishing Group, 1999.

"To be fair," and following: AI, Postelwaite.

p. 63: "Gene would demand," and roadie covered in spit story: AI, Aucoin.

pp. 63–64: Peter and Fritz pulling the prank on Gene story: AI, Postelwaite.

CHAPTER 3: ON FIRE

p. 66: "I forgot the words all of a sudden": *Frank, Dean and Sammy: An Evening With the Rat Pack*, 1965 television special.

"I FORGOT THE FUCKIN' WORDS!!!": Taken from a video copy of Van Halen's performance at the US Festival, May 29, 1983.

pp. 66–67: Anaheim Stadium recollections: AI, Steve Mercer, a local fan who went to many shows throughout the 1970s.

pp. 67–68: Peter Grant could be seen walking down the hotel hallway: AI, Preston.

Not only did Led Zeppelin headline and following: Davis, *Hammer of the Gods*.

The entire Forum turned into one big bong hit: AI, Mercer.

Keith Moon jammed on "Whole Lotta Love": Cole, *Stairway to Heaven;* Henry, "The Ten Best Concerts I Barely Remember."

p. 69: Dr. Larry Information and "Henry" and "Charlie": AI, Preston; Davis, *Hammer of the Gods.*

"Dr. Larry used to pull": AI, Preston.

Dr. Larry's quaaludes for girls barter: Davis, *Old Gods, Almost Dead.*

Oakland incident: Bill Graham and Robert Greenfield, *Bill Graham Presents,* Delta, 1992.

Graham wouldn't book the band again, which meant they would never play the Bay Area again: Davis, *Hammer of the Gods*; K. J. Doughton, *Metallica Unbound,* Warner Books, 1993, Metallica lead singer James Hetfield recalled Bill Graham getting pissed off at Metallica for several incidents, including trashing a trailer backstage, and until Hetfield apologized to Graham, he swore he would never book them again. Hetfield recalled that he had to apologize, because without Graham's support, they wouldn't be able to play San Francisco, their home base, again.

p. 70: "I had a couple of": Smith, *Off the Record.*

Details of the beginning of Queen: David Thomas, "Their Britannic Majesties Request," *Mojo,* August 1999.

"We all had": Jas Obrecht, "Brian May: Queen's Flash Guitarist," *Guitar Player,* January 1983.

Details of Brian May's "Red Special" guitar: "Lisa Sharken, King of Queen," *Guitar School,* April 1996.

"Can do things I could only": Jacques Lowe, editor, *Queen's Greatest Pix*, Quartet Books, 1981.

"Freddie started out": Alan Di Perna, "A Kind of Magic," *Guitar World*, October 1998.

The band didn't know Freddie Mercury was gay until 1974: Ibid.

p. 71: "It was like saying": AI, Neal Preston.

The band was broke and in need of another hit: Thomas, *Mojo*.

"Bum, bum, bum": Sharken, *King of Queen*.

"I've added a few" and following: Ibid.

p. 72: Whenever you stomp and clap that thunderous beat: Uncle Joe Benson, a famous DJ for the L.A. radio station KLOS, mentioned this anecdote when he played Queen's *News of the World* LP on his Sunday night program, *The Seventh Day*. Anecdote reconfirmed: AI, Joe Benson.

"That seems to be my": AI, Ezrin.

At first, many fans didn't like the *Destroyer* album: Sharp, *The Roar of the Greasepaint*; *Kisstory*.

Ezrin wrote the famous Spanish interlude to "Detroit Rock City": AI, Ezrin.

Details of the song "Beth" and Ezrin quotes: AI, Ezrin.

p. 73: Disc jockeys flipped the single and played "Beth" instead: *Kisstory*.

Some didn't know it was Kiss on first listen: Paul Gilbert Entry, "Kudos to Kiss," *Guitar for the Practicing Musician*, June 1994.

"If I never play another gig": Chris Ingham, *Get in the Van*, Metal Hammer, 55.

"We could have played": AI, D'Angelo.

"They were an excellent," and following: AI, Postelwaite.

p. 74: Ted Nugent made music for his Bronco: AI, Ric Browde.

"Rush Limbaugh with a guitar": AI, Browde.

Nugent almost didn't make it to Cal Jam: Michael B. Smith, "The Super-Energized Ted Nugent: It's the Nature of the Beast," *Goldmine*, February 25, 2000.

pp. 74–75: Details of Kulick playing on *Alive II*: AI, Bob Kulick.

Gene and Paul bobbing the head of the doll: *Kisstory*.

"Best you ever played": AI, Bob Kulick.

The "Dream On" single saved Aerosmith from being dropped: Martin Huxley, *Aerosmith*, St. Martin's Press, 1995.

p. 76: Hidden deep in the lyrics of "Walk This Way": Davis, *Walk This Way*.

"Joe, it's way too fuckin' loud!": Ibid.

"Steven sure looked like": Huxley.

Joey Kramer came up with the name and drew it on his textbooks: David Wild, "The Band That Wouldn't Die," *Rolling Stone*, April 5, 1990.

p. 77: Details of Boston's formation, background information on Scholz, and the band's struggle to get a record deal: "The Encyclopedia of Record Producers, Hit Men"; Craig Anderson, "Star Tech," *Guitar World,* February 1990; AI, Werman.

"the band Boston existed on my basement tape recorder": Larry Lange, EE-Times.com, 4/17/98. Article provided by Paul Duran.

"pure fantasy": Ibid.

Scholz was considered the "genius": AI, Doreen Courtwright. Courtwright was a publicist at Epic, Boston's label, for thirteen years.

p. 78: Most of the guitars on *Hysteria* recorded with a Rockman: Alan DiPerna, "Of Life and Def," *Guitar World,* July 1999.

The details of the long delay in between *Don't Look Back,* and *Third Stage:* Dannen, *Hit Men.*

Cost of first Boston album: "Encyclopedia of Record Producers."

ushered in "the long, cold winter": *Rolling Stone Album Guide,* 1992 edition.

"where you could be," and following: AI, Kalodner.

pp. 78–79: Details of the birth and childhood of Phil Lynott: Philomena Lynott, *My Boy,* Hot Press Books, 1995.

How Thin Lizzy's guitar harmonies developed: AI, Scott Gorham.

p. 79: Lynott's lyrical inspiration for "Black Rose," "The Boys Are Back in Town," and "Cowboy Song": AI, Gorham. All subsequent Gorham quotes, AI, Gorham.

p. 80: "Leave the stage covered in blood": Mark Putterford, "Phil Lynott: The Rocker," *Omnibus,* 1998.

The Miami Showband was gunned down, "You came to a Thin Lizzy gig," "They'd look at a picture," and "As far as flat out racism": AI, Gorham.

p. 81: Jon Sutherland felt Sound Barrier was considered one of the most talented L.A. bands on the scene: AI, Jon Sutherland.

"They used to send out": AI, Jon Sutherland.

The label had reservations about putting Sound Barrier's photo on the cover: Sharon Liveten, "Sound Barrier: Breaking New Ground," *Hit Parader,* March 1985.

"I've heard people say": AI, Sutherland.

"This [tour] is something": Lonn Friend, *Anthrax*; "Living Colour: The Integration of Metal, U.K. Style," *RIP,* August 1989.

"A lot of my black friends": Joe Gore, "The Groove According to Fishbone," *Guitar Player,* August 1989.

pp. 81–82: Mike Kelley's encounter with Eddie Van Halen: AI, Mike Kelley.

Background on Eddie's family: David Wild, "Balancing Act," *Rolling Stone,* April 6, 1995.

One of the most important lessons Eddie learned and following: Steven Rosen, "The Life and Times of Edward Van Halen," *Guitar World*, July 1985.

"I can't play a scale": Steven Rosen, "Jimmy Page: The Interview," *Guitar World*, July 1986.

Eddie learned to play guitar: Eddie Van Halen, "Reflections on Eric Clapton," *Guitar Player*, July 1985.

p. 83: "Dave's ability to be normal": confidential source.

"The thing you gotta understand": AI, Neil Zlozower.

"forced zaniness" and "one bitter dude": Mark Coleman, "New Rock Bios Dish the Dirt on Aerosmith, Van Halen, and David Bowie," *Rolling Stone*, October 16, 1997.

"Primarily motivated by fear and revenge": Charles M. Young, "The Oddest Couple: Can It Last?", *Musician*, June 1984.

Which Axl Rose later took to heart: Rob Tannenbaum, "The Hard Truth About Guns N' Roses," *Rolling Stone*, November 17, 1988.

Background Information on Eddie and David's early bands: Rosen and Wild.

Eddie claimed the reason they brought Roth on: Wild, "Balancing Act."

Roth claimed it was his idea to call the band Van Halen: David Lee Roth, *Crazy from the Heat*, Hyperion, 1997.

Alex Van Halen joked: Jodi Summers, "Metal Mind Tease," *RIP*, November 1988.

p. 84: Details of the David Lee Roth house and rehearsal room: AIs, Gary Osby and Debbie Rodriquez. Both were caretakers on the Roth estate before the band broke.

The band had to hide their beer when Roth's father came downstairs and "I have surgery": Tom Broderick, Jeff Hausman, "The Club Days," *The Inside* 8.

Roth's father wanted his son to go back to college, and following: AI, Osby.

Eddie would put plastic covers over his amps: Rosen, "Life and Times of Eddie Van Halen"; Joseph Bosso, "Monster of Rock," *Guitar World*, February 1990.

The band played disco covers: Michael Anthony, "The Last of the Pre-Van Halen Band," *Guitar for the Practicing Musician*, December 1987.

p. 85: "Back in the club days": Chuck Cristafulli, "Ain't Talkin' 'Bout Love," *Los Angeles Times*, October 20, 1996.

Van Halen playing the Southern California party circuit, and cramming high school lockers with flyers: *Best of Guitar Player: Van Halen Unpublished Interviews*, 1994.

Van Halen brought with them a new influx of girls: AI, Hernando Courtwright.

They eventually moved all the way up to playing the Pasadena Civic: *Van Halen Unpublished Interviews* and AI, Marshall Berle.

For their stage shows, and following: *Crazy from the Heat* and AI, Kevin Martin.

Like a director, and following: AI, Osby.

"I really give": AI, Kevin Martin.

p. 86: "I'd rather bomb": Vic Garbarini, "Tracks of His Tears," *Guitar World,* April 1998.

"You have to watch": Mötley Crüe and Neil Strauss, *The Dirt,* Regan Books, 2001.

Eddie lived with his parents until hooking up with Valerie Bertinelli: Wild, "Balancing Act."

p. 87: "The Rock Star," and "The Musician": Debby Miller, "Van Halen's Split Personality," *Rolling Stone,* June 21, 1984.

"Let me show you," and following: AI, Steve Mercer.

Interior of the Starwood: AIs, Brian O' Brien, Jon Sutherland, Mark Danielson, Steve Mercer, and John Arnold.

The Starwood's unlimited guest list: AIs, O'Brien and Arnold.

"Even if": AI, O'Brien.

p. 88: The bathroom graffiti and "David Lee Roth Stuffs": AI, O'Brien.

Details of Camp Quaalude: AI, Kevin Martin.

"For distribution at the box office," and the Starwood was raided twenty-five times a month: Mike Sager, "The Devil and John Holmes," *Rolling Stone,* June 15, 1989.

"I think the statute of limitations": AI, Slash.

Celebrities that came to the Starwood: AI, O'Brien.

Kiss being spotted in the balcony: AI, Juan Croucier.

pp. 88–89: "Back then," and following: AI, O'Brien.

One night John Belushi jammed with Aerosmith and following: AI, Danny Johnson.

Gene Simmons came to see the Boyz at the Starwood: George Lynch, "Kudos to Kiss," *Guitar for the Practicing Musician,* June 1994.

"Great band, but": Steven Blush, "Runnin' with the Devil," *Seconds Magazine* 26.

Aucoin's response to Van Halen: AI, Aucoin.

"Van Halen started," and following: AI, Kelley.

"He aped a lot of": AI, O'Brien.

Roth wasn't confident with his stage raps and told corny jokes: This is evident on several Van Halen live show soundboard tapes that were provided to the author by several sources. The shows were taped circa 1976.

Ted Templeman wanted them to replace Roth with Hagar: AI's Aucoin. This story was also told to me by Greg Leon, a local guitar rival of Eddie's from the 1970s several years before Aucoin told me the story. Aucoin says he heard it directly from Templeman on a number of occasions. In the book *Guitar World Presents Eddie Van Halen,* a compilation of Eddie's *Guitar World* interviews, he was asked about this by interviewer Steve Rosen, and Eddie said: "I remember hearing something like that."

p. 90: Van Halen's royalties were split four ways: Young, *The Oddest Couple.*

"Van Halen was so cocky": AI, Martin.

"They took a piece of our ass," and "A La Fart": AI, O'Brien.

"They smoked all of us": AI, Kevin DuBrow.

pp. 90–91: Stormer information and "Van Halen had the tunes": AI, Gary Holland.

Marshall Berle was handling the reopening of the Whisky and following: AI, Marshall Berle.

The band didn't know how to shop the demo: *Guitar Player Presents Unpublished Interviews.*

Harper's Bizarre information: *Encyclopedia of Record Producers.*

Berle set up a show at the Starwood and following: AI, Berle.

p. 92: "Within a week": *Masters of Heavy Metal.*

"I thought after": AI, George Lynch.

"When Van Halen got a deal": AI, Chris Holmes.

"I remember how jealous": AI, Kevin Martin.

The first Van Halen album took less than a month, and following: AI, Berle.

"I think that's the mark": *Encyclopedia of Record Producers.*

Templeman mostly helped them structure their songs: Ted Templeman and Gene Santoro, "Edward's Producer on the Brown Sound," *Guitar World,* July 1985.

p. 93: At Templeman's suggestion, and following: *Guitar World Presents Eddie Van Halen.*

Frank Zappa even thanked Eddie: Roth, *Crazy from the Heat.* In the photo section of the book, an article Nancy Griffin wrote on Van Halen for *Life* is reprinted, and in the text the article says that Frank Zappa thanked Eddie for reinventing the instrument.

Details of Eddie's homemade guitars: Richard Hogan, "Eddie Van Halen Probes His Past and Present," *Circus,* October 31, 1986; AI, Karl Sandoval, who did guitar-building work for Eddie as well.

The guitar grew bigger and bigger every gig from the paint layers: AI, Gary Holland.

Roth drove his old, beat-up clunker and following: AI, Berle.

p. 94: The TV set falling to its death, and the fire extinguisher fights in the hallway: AI, Berle; Joe Bosso, *Guitar World,* February 1990.

Van Halen banned from the Holiday Inn chain: AI, Scotty Ross.

"Hugh Jazz": C. J. Chilvers, *The Van Halen Encyclopedia,* Malpractice Publishing, 1999.

Billy Sheehan opened forty shows for Van Halen in 1980 and following: AI, Billy Sheehan.

The M&M clause: The Editors of *Esquire, Bad News: The Best of Esquire Magazine's Dubious Achievements 1961–1984,* Avon, 1984.

Roth explained the reason the clause was in the contract: Steven Blush, "Runnin' with the Devil," *Seconds* 26.

pp. 94–95: Eddie bought several rare Les Paul guitars: AI, Norman Harris, owner of Norm's Rare Guitars.

Eddie and Alex retired their father from working: AI, Steven Rosen. Rosen was a close friend of Eddie's who wrote about him extensively for *Guitar World.*

Jan Van Halen would burst into tears of happiness: Wild, "Balancing Act."

"Well, you know": AI, Mark Dansziesen.

"Don't blame me for the errors": Blush, *Runnin' with the Devil.*

"It's kind of like incest": Bosso, *Monster of Rock.*

"It really bummed me out when everyone ripped off": Andy Widders-Ellis, "Slash: The Hands Behind the Hype," *Guitar Player,* December 1991.

"The more people that hate you": *Guitar Player Presents Van Halen Unpublished Interviews.*

"I was petrified when I heard": AI, Bruce Kulick.

p. 96: "God, he was disgustingly brilliant": Jennifer Schwartz, "Smear Tactics," *BAM,* April 5, 1996.

"I don't know what's going to happen": *Masters of Heavy Metal.*

CHAPTER 4: ON YOUR FEET OR ON YOUR KNEES

p. 98: "Randy was at about": Joe Lalaina, "Randy to the Max," *Guitar World,* June 1987.

"There was more heart": Mike Gitter, "Birthed Too Late," *Metal Maniacs,* August 1993.

"It might have been a little": Matt Resnicoff, "The Clown Prince of Rock Guitar," *Guitar World,* January 1988.

p. 99: "You get on the road": Huxley, *Aerosmith.*

Tyler was so used to living in hotels: Smith, *Off the Record.*

"We started to see how": Ibid.

"It got to the point": Wild, *The Band That Wouldn't Die.*

pp. 99–100: Details of the *Draw the Line* recording sessions and "the coke lines," and following: Davis, *Walk This Way.*

pp. 100–101: All a record label needed was one huge hit: Anthony Haden Guest, *The Last Party,* William Morrow, 1997.

PolyGram's sales topped $1.2 billion and following: Dannen, *Hit Men.*

Shipping an album gold and getting it shipped back platinum: Ibid.

Bill Aucoin liked to say: AI, Aucoin.

Neil Bogart was against the idea until: AI, Aucoin.

Distributors ordered a million units of the solo albums: Lendt, *Kiss and Sell.*

"Each band member": AI, Kramer.

The solo albums sold approximately 600–700,000 copies per member and "[Bogart] pressed so many": Dannen, *Hit Men.*

p. 102: Details of the Dynasty tour: AIs, Postelwaite and Lendt; Lendt, *Kiss and Sell.*

pp. 102–103: Details of *Unmasked* album, Eric Carr joining the band, and Kiss only doing one show in the states: Lendt, *Kiss and Sell.*

Carr's disastrous debut as "The Hawk": Lendt, *Kiss and Sell.*

PolyGram bought out the other 50 percent of PolyGram: Griffin; Masters, *Hit and Run.*

Details of Australian tour: AI, Aucoin.

"We actually did [*The Elder*]": Ken Sharp, "The Roar of the Greasepaint, the Smell of the Crowd," *Goldmine,* October 15, 1993.

The Elder was designed as one of the first multimedia concepts: AI, Lendt.

pp. 103–104: "dead right" and following: AI, Ezrin.

Ace recorded the solos in his home studio: AI, Ezrin.

"Ace's Bomb Shelter": Przydzical, *Guitar for the Practicing Musician,* January 1985.

Frehley said Eric was a hired gun, could be outvoted on decisions: Sharp, "Roar of the Greasepaint."

Frehley smashed his cassette copy, wanted the album shelved and was outvoted: Sharp; Kitts, "Kiss and Tell."

Ace Frehley totaling his car and losing his driver's license: Jeff Kitts, "Rock Soldiers," *Guitar World,* August 1993.

p. 105: "You know something?": AI, Ezrin.

Details of the beginnings of AC/DC: Martin Huxley, *AC/DC: The World's Heaviest Rock,* Boxtree Books, 1996.

Scott often wore vests two sizes too small: Clinton Walker, *Highway to Hell,* Sidgwick and Jackson, 1994.

"Bon didn't have a mean bone in his body": Ibid.

p. 106: Angus would go through several SGs a year: Steven Rosen, "Angus!", *Guitar World,* March 1984.

"It's as if the music is hanging on": AI, Tony Platt. All following Platt quotes from author's interview.

"[Chris Williams] plays very little": Billy Sheehan, "Bass Secrets Column," *Guitar for the Practicing Musician,* March 1986.

"The truth is": AI, Beau Hill.

p. 107: "The main thing with AC/DC": AI, Platt.

The goal was to record an album: AI, Platt.

Details of Kramer producing *Highway to Hell,* Lange coming aboard, Lange background information, and the hours the band spent in the studio: Walker.

"We learned a lot": Ibid.

"If Mutt and I": AI, Platt.

Van Halen, Sammy Hagar, and Foreigner wouldn't take them as an opening act: Huxley, *AC/DC: The World's Heaviest Rock.*

p. 108: "When you're sleeping with the singer's sock": Ibid.

Scott was writing lyrics and following: Walker.

"You know, the thing about Bon": AI, Platt.

Malcolm later admitted *Back In Black:* David Glessner, "Let There Be Talk," knac.com, August 30, 2000.

p. 109: Platt playing the album for Atlantic Records and "Yeah, that's what I was thinking": AI, Platt.

The Clash and Billy Idol taunting Zeppelin: Davis, *Hammer of the Gods.*

Page took a backseat on the band's next album: Rosen, *Billboard Book of Number One Albums.*

pp. 109–110: It took Plant half the first show to get over his stage fright: Davis, *Hammer of the Gods.*

Bonham's death: Ibid.

Page didn't pick up a guitar for three years: Winston Cummings, "The Firm: A Matter of Pride," *Hit Parader,* August 1985.

"the most boring guitarist": *Diary of a Madman.*

p. 111: "They just stomped Black Sabbath to death": AI, Grover Jackson.

"Why are you yelling at us?": Rick Evans, "On the Set With Ozzy Osbourne," *Hit Parader,* November 1985.

After Black Sabbath finished the tour, and following: Rosen, *Wheels of Confusion.*

"It was the end of Black Sabbath": Stark, *Black Sabbath: An Oral History.*

Iommi was ready to leave the band and following: Ibid.

p. 112: One night Dio had laryngitis: AI, Claude Schnell.

The roadies sometimes put an orange crate in front of the microphone stand: AI, Larry Morand.

"Say hello to Ronnie": Ozzy Osbourne MTV concert special shot at Irvine Meadows (now the Verizon Wireless Amphitheatre), 1982.

Dio would spend up to five hours signing autographs: AIs, Schnell and Vinnie Appice.

The managers and former managers were still fighting each other, and Sabbath toured Europe first: Stark.

p. 113: Ward missed four gigs and following: Ibid.

Ward later got sober in the mid-1980s after winding up on the streets: AI, Ward, and Stark.

Appice's first gig in Hawaii, and dry ice explosion in England: AI, Appice.

Dio and Iommi accused each other of turning up their own mixes: Stark.

Everyone in the band agrees that it didn't happen: Ibid; AI, Appice.

p. 114: The band wound up in separate limos: AI, Appice.

"It surprised me": AI, Schnell.

Dio went from opening act to headlining theaters in two months: AI, Schnell.

The bus would be rockin' till three in the morning: AI, Appice.

Ozzy signed away all rights, and following: Wall, *Diary of a Madman*; Stark; Rob Tannenbaum, "Dear Superstar," *Blender,* November 2001.

p. 115: "we counted on it": AI, Kevin DuBrow.

Thirty-two labels passed on the band: Billy Cioffi, "All-American Hero," *Guitar World,* June 1987.

One local fan ran to his car, grabbed his acoustic: "Letters to the Editor," *Guitar for the Practicing Musician,* April 1994. Michael Vangerov wrote this in a letter to the magazine, recalling his memories of Randy Rhoads.

The record executives would tell them to write a song just like a current hit on the charts: AI, Rudy Sarzo.

p. 116: "Who's Ozzy Osbourne?", and following: AI, Robert Olshever. Olshever ran a local L.A. magazine called *Raw Power,* and promoted local shows in the 1970s. Slaughter bassist Dana Strum has said he got Randy into Ozzy's band. Olshever says it was on his recommendation that Dana called Randy and told him about the Ozzy gig.

Randy's mother convinced him to audition: *Masters of Heavy Metal.*

Ozzy was stoned out of his mind during the audition: Brad Tolinski, "The Good, the Bad, the Ozzy!", *Guitar World,* June 1990.

"I don't know what I got": *Masters of Heavy Metal.*

Ozzy told a friend he had a dream and following: Tolinski.

"I put all my eggs": AI, DuBrow.

Ozzy's new solo band reminded him and following: Stark. *Diary of a Madman* also confirms the lineup for the first two albums.

p. 117: In Black Sabbath, Osbourne could never: Tolinski.

Ozzy viewed Randy not just as a collaborator, but an equal: AI, Sarzo.

Sharon paid for much of the tour out of her own pocket and had to mortgage her home: AI, Sarzo.

The band often had to play for free: Sharon Osbourne, "The Truth About the Tragedy," *Guitar World,* June 1987.

"I can honestly tell you": AI, Sarzo.

Once when Arden suspected a promoter was cheating her: Steve Hochman, "Batty About Each Other," *Los Angeles Times,* June 18, 2000.

pp. 117–118: They sold out a show at the Academy of Music and following: AI, Sarzo.

Ozzy biting the head of the dove, Ozzy was banned from entering the CBS building, and label wouldn't promote the album if he pulled a stunt like that again: Jon Wiederhorn, "Ozzy Osbourne Q&A," *Rolling Stone,* June 16, 1997; *Diary of a Madman.*

Ozzy's stage space and the Bat Incident: AI, Sarzo; Evans, *Hit Parader,* November 1985.

p. 119: "I love you": Evans.

"Hey, man": AI, Sarzo.

pp. 119–120: Ozzy shaving his head, the carafe story, and Ozzy stealing the shoes story: AI, Sarzo.

Ozzy relieved himself out an open window: *Don't Blame Me.*

With his first royalty payments, Randy bought an expensive classical guitar: *Masters of Heavy Metal.*

Rhoads looked up teachers in the phone book, ended up teaching them instead: Ibid.

Rhoads took his mother to Mazatlan and "Randy loved his mother": AI, Ace Steele.

pp. 120–121: Jackson Guitars information: AI, Grover Jackson.

"Grover was always very good": AI, C. C. DeVille.

Randy Rhoads walked into Jackson's shop, and following: AI, Jackson.

Randy wasn't going to stay in the band much longer, and wanted to get a classical degree: Steve Baltin, "Remembering Randy Rhoads," *Guitar One,* March 2001; Alan di Perna, "Crazy Train," *Guitar World,* March 2002.

pp. 121–122: Details of the crash: AI, Sarzo, Diary.

"I suppose when he died": *Don't Blame Me.*

"I feel somewhat": Tim Jones, "The Ozzman Returneth," *Record Collector,* August 1999.

pp. 122–123: Grover's unfinished guitar and "People ask me": AI, Jackson. The author was shown the unfinished guitar when he interviewed Jackson.

Chet Thompson information and quotes: Chet Thompson, "Randy Rhoads' Private Lessons," *Guitar for the Practicing Musician,* August 1990.

Kevin DuBrow got a call: AI, DuBrow.

Ozzy said if it wasn't for his wife forcing him to continue the tour: *Diary of a Madman.*

Randy's dream had been to play Madison Square Garden: Sharon Osbourne, "The Truth About the Tragedy."

"The saddest moment," and following: AI, Sarzo.

p. 124: Details of the *Speak of the Devil* album and "The record company had me by the balls": Stix.

Ozzy's lyrics notebook and desk lamp on the chair: AI, Sarzo.

Wylde wine cork story: AI, Mark Leialoha. Leialoha is a photographer who shot many metal bands and was eating with Ozzy and Zakk when the latter did this.

p. 125: "We have full blown": Daina Darzin, "After Two Decades of Rock, Is Ozzy Happy at Last?", *Circus,* January 31, 1989.

"The truth is": Kitts, *Miracle Man.*

CHAPTER 5: LIVING AFTER MIDNIGHT

p. 127: "Gary and Billy sat": David St. Clair, *Say You Love Satan,* St. Martin's Press, 1987.

"Bee Gees Free Weekends": *Keppel Road: The Life and Music of the Bee Gees,* directed by Tony Cash, PolyGram Video, 1997.

Stephen Dahl and the "Disco Sucks" movement: Haden-Guest, *The Last Party.*

pp. 127–128: The Knack went Gold: AI, Hernando Courtwright. Confirmed in Brendan Mullen and Marc Spitz, *We Got the Neutron Bomb,* Three Rivers Press, 2001.

"Knuke the Knack": *Rolling Stone Album Guide,* 1992 edition.

"Rock music was becoming," and following: AI, Joe Elliott.

"You listen to those": AI, Scott Ian.

p. 129: Details of Derek Riggs's artwork and Eddie, Iron Maiden's mascot: Mick Wall, *Run to the Hills,* Sanctuary, 1998.

p. 178: "Sometimes you fell in love": AI, Aucoin.

"The established bands": AI, Jon Sutherland.

pp. 129–130: Quintana fanzine information: AI, Ron Quintana.

"The punk attitudes": Albert Bouchard and Deborah Frost, "Lars Ulrich: Master of Metal," *Modern Drummer,* June 1987.

"Every day was like": AI, Quintana.

Fans in Italy were so fanatical: AI, Alex Solca.

"You find out about a cool record": AI, Del James.

p. 131: Joe Elliott used to draw rock and roll posters, and following: AI, Joe Elliott.

p. 132: Geoff Barton creating the term "The New Wave of British Heavy Metal": Steve Beebee, *MTV Headbanger's Ball: Chaos A.D. Rock in the Nineties,* Simon and Schuster U.K./MTV Books, 1997.

The EP landed on the desk of Cliff Burnstein, and following: AI, Elliott.

Burnstein worked A&R for Mercury and signed Rush: Jory Farr, *Moguls and Madmen,* Simon and Schuster, 1994.

Def Leppard went to see Led Zeppelin, and following: AI, Elliott.

Mensch hooked Def Leppard up with AC/DC on their *Highway to Hell* tour and soon became their manager: AI, Elliott.

pp. 132–133: Details of the recording of *On Through the Night*: AI, Tom Allom.

High and Dry going Gold with the help of MTV and "There's this new thing": AI, Elliott.

Music videos first being played on *Top of the Pops* and following: Tom Mc-Grath, *MTV: The Making of a Revolution,* Running Press, 1996.

p. 134: Details of *The Midnight Special* and *Don Kirshner's Rock Concert*: Tim Brooks and Earle Marsh, *The Complete Directory to Prime Time Network TV Shows,* Ballantine Books, 1981.

"Don Kirshner's shows": Uncredited, "In the Classic Way, *Guitar for the Practicing Musician,* September 1988.

p. 134–135: The creation of MTV and following: McGrath.

Marty Callner information and quotes: AI, Marty Callner.

Rickie Lee Jones said she wrote the songs and their videos at the same time: McGrath.

"Because of the unbelievable promotional": David Coverdale and John Stix, "The David Coverdale Story: His Lordship Right Here," *Guitar for the Practicing Musician,* February 1990.

pp. 135–136: "Once everyone knew that MTV": AI, Beau Hill.

"the Last of the Mohicans": Elizabeth Gilber, "Unleash the Ripper," *GQ,* September 1998.

Priest took their name from a Bob Dylan song: Karl French and Chip Rowe, *This Is Spinal Tap: The Official Companion,* Bloomsbury, 2000.

"Where we lived": *Judas Priest: Metal Works '73–93,* directed by Jerry Duller, Sony Music Entertainment, 1993.

Priest helped lay the groundwork for the speed-metal bands: *Metal Works.* This was also pointed out to me by research assistant Skylaire Alfvegren.

The struggles of Priest's early years: Steve Gett, *Heavy Duty,* Cherry Lane Publishing, 1984; AI, Tom Allom.

K. K. Downing's troubled adolescence and "I suppose it was my": Bill Milkowski, "Judas Priest's Scorching Twin Leads," *Guitar World,* July 1984.

p. 137: Halford knew he was gay at 13 and following: Judy Wieder, Rob Halford, "Stuck Between a Rock and a Hard Place," *The Advocate,* May 12, 1998.

It was never a problem among them until the 1990s: Gilbert, *Unleash the Ripper.*

Rob began shopping for leather and studs: Wieder, "Stuck Between a Rock and a Hard Place."

"Rob was very instrumental": Gett, *Heavy Duty.*

Performing "Take on the World" on *Top of the Pops* with Donnie and Marie: Ibid.

p. 138: The Harley-Davidson deal: *Metal Works.*

"By definition": Skylaire Alfvegren, "Breaking the Law," *L.A. Weekly,* April 10–16, 1998. Clipping provided by Skylaire Alfvegren.

To me, heavy metal": AI, Allom.

"a mama's boy": AI, Sutherland.

p. 139: Slagel had always wanted to start his own record label and following: AI, John Kornarens.

"Oh wow!": AI, Sutherland.

"To this day": Chris Croker, *Frayed Ends of Metal,* St. Martin's Press, 1993.

"a bunch of people drinking and roaring": Jodi Summers, "Lars Ulrich: Big Bang Theory," *RIP Magazine Presents Metallica,* 1988.

"If you look like you have": Jodi Summers, "Metallica: Waking Up With a Headache," *RIP,* January 1988.

pp. 139–140: Ulrich, Slagel, and Kornarens hanging out together and buying records: AI, Kornarens.

No one believed Ulrich would ever put it together: Crocker; K. J. Doughton, *Metallica: Unbound,* Warner Books, 1993.

Hetfield and Ulrich seemed destined to meet: Michael Corcoran, "Speed Thrills," *Creem,* vol. 2, 1, 1991.

Ulrich's audition: Crocker.

Lloyd Grant providing the lead for "Hit the Lights": Doughton.

pp. 140–141: Ulrich making it to the studio at three o'clock and following: AI, Kornarens.

The first *Metal Massacre* cost $2,400 and following: AIs, Kornarens and Sutherland.

Quintana asked Lars which name would be cooler: Summers, *Big Bang Theory.*

"I think the idea to form": AI, Kornarens.

Hetfield's father owned a trucking company: David Fricke, "Pretty Hate Machine," *Rolling Stone,* June 27, 1996.

p. 142: "My mom needed to be": Rob Tannenbaum, "Playboy Interview: Metallica," *Playboy,* April 2001.

"Seek and Destroy" influenced by Diamond Head and "One" influenced by Venom: Doughton and Jeff Kitts, "Prime Cuts: Metal Reflectors," *Guitar World,* October 1991.

"We just put the two heads together": David Fricke, *Garage Inc.* liner notes, Elektra Records, 1998.

Metallica did covers of their favorite bands live, didn't tell anyone they weren't originals: Ibid.

"it interferes with my drinking": Joe Gore, "Metallica Rules!", *Guitar Player,* April 1989.

pp. 142–143: The story of the *No Life Til Leather* demo and "Mild bootlegging does not detract": Doughton.

The rock clubs wouldn't book them because they thought they were a punk band: Gore, "Metallica Rules!"

They played too fast, too loud: Joe Gore, "Metal Age Crisis," *Guitar Player,* September 1991; "Metallica Rules!"

The hair bands condescended to them: Ibid.

Metallica's first gig in San Francisco with Hans Naughty: Doughton; Metallica's *Behind the Music* special.

Burton got the band to relocate to S. F.: Doughton.

p. 144: Jonny Z. released from a halfway house started Metal Heaven with $180: Farr, *Moguls and Madmen.*

"We would make our pilgrimages," and following: Al, Ian.

Jonny Z and his wife Marsha, and "That's why my kids": Farr.

p. 145: There was no hot water: S. L. Duff, "Lightning Strikes Thrice," *Music Connection,* May 26–June 8, 1986.

The band sometimes ate raw hotdogs: Adrianne Stone, "The Moshin' Chronicles," *RIP,* January 1989.

Mustaine partly fired because of his drinking: Doughton.

Mustaine's account of fight with Hetfield: Joel McIver, "Deth, Where Is Thy Sting?", *Record Collector,* October 1999.

McGovney's account of fight with Hetfield: Pat O' Connor, "Metallica," *Shockwaves,* Spring 1997.

Hammett's bandmates told him they wouldn't take him back: Corcoran, *Speed Thrills.*

pp. 145–146: Mustaine was woken up and told he was fired: *Behind the Music* special; Doughton.

"We were there rehearsing": Al, D'Angelo.

"kick Metallica's ass": Doughton.

If Hammett didn't work out and following: *Behind the Music.*

Hammett and Hetfield bonded: Tannenbaum, "Playboy Interview."

"None of us were": Bruce Pollock, "In the Tradition," *Guitar for the Practicing Musician,* November 1989.

Kill 'Em All is what they wanted to do: "Cliff 'Em All" home video, 1988.

Easter's Canceled: Corcoran, *Speed Thrills.*

"At first, a lot of people": Al, Harald Oimen.

p. 147: Michael Alago seeing Metallica in New York and following: AI, Michael Alago and Crocker, *Frayed Ends of Metal.*

"Is there gonna be lots of beer?": Crocker.

Kill 'Em All tour rider: John Kornarens had a copy of this rider, which he showed me and allowed me to take notes from when I interviewed him.

To help the press understand Metallica: AI, Byron Hantas.

pp. 147–148: Cliff Burnstein and Peter Mensch information: Farr, *Moguls and Madmen.*

Burnstein and Mensch were looking to sign an indie metal band and following: Duff, *Lightning Strikes Thrice.*

"the CNN years": David Fricke, "Metallica," *Rolling Stone,* November 14, 1991.

"It was my favorite amp, man!": David Fricke, "Don't Tread on Me," *Rolling Stone,* April 15, 1993.

The band got countless letters from fans telling them "Fade to Black" saved their lives: Ibid.

pp. 148–149: "It was having absolute": AI, Alago.

"Metallica knew where they wanted": AI, Hantas.

"Metallica takes care of their fans": AI, Hantas.

Hetfield remembered how it felt: David Fricke, "Heavy Metal Justice," *Rolling Stone,* January 12, 1989.

Metallica resented having to go to a record signing in a limo: Sue Cummings, "Road Warriors," *Spin,* August 1986.

"In the beginning": AI, Hantas.

p. 150: "If you had told me": *A Year and a Half in the Life of Metallica,* directed by Adam Dubin, Elektra Video, 1992.

"If one of them gets a haircut": Cummings, "Road Warriors."

Def Leppard entered the studio, and following: AI, Elliott.

p. 151: The label figured that by the third album and following: AI, Jim Lewis.

Details of the *Pyromania* tour: AI, Elliott.

"It was only Michael Jackson": AI, Elliott.

"Because of Quiet Riot": AI, Pilson.

CHAPTER 6: BREAKING THE SILENCE

p. 153: "I had never heard anybody called dude": Charrie Foglio, "Mötley's Motlier Days," *RIP,* January 1989.

The downfall of the Starwood and Ed Nash: Sager, *The Devil and John Holmes.*

"I'm really glad that I got": AI, Mercer.

"It was good to be part": AI, John Arnold.

pp. 153–154: Suite 19 information: AI, Greg Leon. Leon was their guitar player.

Lee's father supported his son's music, went to the shows, and soundproofed the house: AI, Will Boyett, Lee's former friend.

p. 155: Leon helped introduce Lee to Nikki: AI, Leon. In Tommy Lee's interviews featured in *The Dirt* he confirms this.

"Nikki had auditioned for Suite 19": AI, Leon.

"I don't have a son," and following: Mötley Crüe and Strauss, *The Dirt*.

"I'm gonna get three slugs": Confidential source.

Mars attended the same high school as Dan Quayle: Charrie Foglio and Mick Mars, *The Silent Shredder, RIP Magazine Presents Mötley Crüe*, 1989.

Lee, Sixx, and Mars found Neil at the Starwood and "I don't care if he can sing": Steve Gett, "The Mötley Crüe Story," *Guitar for the Practicing Musician*, September 1985.

pp. 155–156: "All Vince cares about": Michael Kaplan, "The Swingin' Sounds of the Dust Brothers," *Los Angeles*, February 1997.

Neil wanted to be like Jerry Buss or Hugh Hefner when he got old: Handleman, "Money for Nothing"; Neil Strauss, "Checking In with Hugh Hefner," *Rolling Stone*, April 1, 1999.

Lee once broke Neil's nose in a fight: Evelyn McDonnell and Ann Powers, editors, *Rock She Wrote*, Delta Books, 1992. This book is a compilation of music stories written by women; a story by Deborah Frost, "White Noise: How Heavy Metal Rules," which ran in *The Village Voice* in June 18, 1985, is reprinted in the book.

"I didn't want to go completely": Steve Gett, "Dressing for Success," *Guitar for the Practicing Musician*, August 1984.

Sweet show at Santa Monica Civic: AI, Joe Burman, who was there.

Mötley became a band on January 17, 1981: Gett, "The Mötley Crüe Story."

The Pookie's Gig: AIs, Boyett and Gett.

pp. 156–157: Sixx sprayed his hair upside down: AI, Boyett.

Coverdale said the reason why bands had big hair: "Random Notes," *Rolling Stone*, October 22, 1987.

"arena," "stadium," and "lobby" hair levels: AI, Sarzo.

Nikki singed off his leg hair: AI, Vicky Hamilton. Hamilton was one of the first managers for Poison and Guns N' Roses, and she helped out Mötley Crüe in their early days as well.

The band constructed their stage costumes out of: AI, Mark Pietrosky, a memorabilia collector who has a large Crüe collection.

By 1985, they were spending: Susan Paterno, "Theatre of Justice," *BAM*, November 29, 1985.

The Whisky followed them around the corner to their apartment: AI, Boyett.
Roth and the Scorpions were regulars: AIs, Dan Starr and Danzsiesen.
Drugs were usually easy to score: AI, Danzsiesen.
"Some of the [punks]": AI, Cletus Nelson.
   pp. 157–158: Doug Weston was facing financial ruin and had to take on a partner: Robert Hilburn, "A Man Who Had a Passion For the Art of the Troubador," *Los Angeles Times,* February 16, 2000.
Incident at Oki Dog: AI, Nelson.
Coffman information: AI, Hernando Courtwright.
Levine set up two showcase gigs for the band at the Santa Monica Civic: AI, Barry Levine.
Hernando Courtwright tried to get the band signed and following: AI, Hernando Courtwright.
   p. 159: Doug Thaler background information: AI, Doug Thaler.
"You should check this out": AI, Courtwright.
Doreen tried to get Mötley Crüe signed to Epic and following: AI, Doreen Courtwright.
"I didn't realize what they could be": AI, Tom Werman.
Werman soon left his job: *Encyclopedia of Record Producers.*
"You don't need ears to be a talent scout": *The Dirt.*
   p. 160: Meeting with Krasnow: AI, Werman. Krasnow's dislike of metal was also confirmed in *The Dirt.* See also Dee Snider, "The Four F Syndrome," *RIP,* January 1995.
"The record companies don't know": Phillip Bashe, *Heavy Metal Thunder,* Dolphin/Doubleday, 1985.
Werman in the studio with Mötley Crüe: AI, Werman.
Sixx had to play "Red Hot" with his arm in a cast, Werman joked: Tom Beaujour, "Smashed Hits," *Guitar World,* September 1999; AI, Werman.
For a nice Jewish boy from Boston, it was like hanging out with the mob. AI, Werman.
   p. 161: McGhee promised the band whatever the label wouldn't pay for, he'd take care of: *The Dirt.*
Elektra didn't want to pay for a gatefold: AI, Courtwright.
Shout at the Devil recording budget and Werman was called at Pebble Beach a month after its release: AI, Werman.
When Sixx saw kids dressed up as Mötley on Halloween: Charrie Foglio, "Nikki Sixx: The King of Sleaze!", *RIP Presents Mötley Crüe,* 1989.
"Is Mötley Crüe's Bad Image For Real?" and following: Dennis Hunt, "Is Mötley Crüe's Bad Image For Real?", *Los Angeles Times,* November 13, 1983.
"cute, naïve, nice guys": Paterno, "Theatre of Justice."

pp. 161–162: "I don't like to look back": Hunt, "Is Mötley Crüe's Bad Image for Real?"

Bill Holdship on the road with Dokken incident: Adrianne Stone, "Rock Journalism: Tales from the Trenches," *RIP,* April 1995.

"There was a lot of pressure": AI, George Lynch.

He would often binge for days and Sixx had to be carried onto the plane: Beaujour, *Smashed Hits.*

When Zlozower's girlfriend picked him up at the airport: AI, Neil Zlozower.

pp. 162–163: Sixx found out at the airport and following: AI, Zlozower.

Details of the crash: *Mötley Crüe: Behind the Music* special; Michael Goldberg and Neil Sentenced, *Rolling Stone* 460.

The accident happened before Hanoi were scheduled to play the Roxy: AI, Jon Sutherland.

"I believe that": AI, John Kalodner.

Zutaut offered the members of Hanoi a lot of money to re-form: This was first told to me in an AI with Sutherland, and he recalled its being Kalodner who made the offer. Kalodner says it was Zutaut who was interested in getting the band to reunite.

Nikki Sixx had the chutzpah to ask Monroe if he wanted to start another band: Charrie Foglio and Mike Monroe, "The Life and Death of Hanoi Rocks," *RIP,* January 1992. Monroe also told this to Sutherland in an interview as well.

Details of sentence: Goldberg.

Neil had already been found guilty of another drunk driving charge: This detail is on the Chronological Crüe website (ozemail.com.au/~Crüekiss/ exclusive) in the site's history of the band.

"Ira Reiner had a complete": AI, Charrie Foglio.

p. 164: "My biggest regret as a manager": *The Dirt.*

MTV's most requested video for four months: Chronological Crüe.

Sixx bringing two shopping bags of candy bars to the studio: AI, Werman.

pp. 164–165: Quiet Riot's show at the Troubadour details: AI, Dan Starr, a fan and observer from the period who was there.

"We took advantage of the term": John Stix, "Quiet Riot: Metal of the Road," *Guitar for the Practicing Musician,* June 1984.

"I'm getting vertigo": AI, Starr.

Details of "Cum On Feel the Noize," and the recording of *Metal Health:* AI, Kevin DuBrow.

p. 166: Tour details: AI, DuBrow and Carlos Cavazo, "The More You Know, the More You Can Play," *Guitar Player,* June 1984.

"One of the scariest audiences": Jeff Gilbert, "The Father, the Son, and the Holy Grunge," *Guitar World,* February 1995.

The US Festival cost Wozniac $18 million: Kathryn Harris, " 'Woz' Spends a Chunk of His Roll on Rock," *Los Angeles Times,* May 27, 1983.

"One of the richest guys in America": AI, Jeff Black. Black worked for concert promoters Wolf and Rissmiller, and worked at the US Festival.

Details of Van Halen's US Festival deal: Geoff Belland and Jeff Hausman, "Big Fat $$$$: The US Festival Revisited," *The Inside Magazine,* Spring 1996, No. 5.

Quiet Riot ran into Van Halen in the lobby: AIs, Kevin DuBrow and Rudy Sarzo.

"There were so many people," and following: AI, DuBrow.

"A local club band": Stu Simone, "US '83: Day Two," *BAM,* June 17, 1983.

pp. 166–167: Loverboy tour details and quotes: AI, DuBrow.

MTV started playing the video for "Cum On Feel the Noize," and following: Cavazo, "The More You Know, the More You Can Play."

"I've been approached by lots": Ibid.

"In the past": Rob Andrews, "Lights, Camera, Action!", *Hit Parader,* March 1985.

The night Quiet Riot found out *Metal Health* went to No. 1: AI, DuBrow.

p. 168: *Metal Health* sold three million copies by November 1983: Cavazo, "The More You Know, the More You Can Play."

Piazza's love of Saint and "gave me a mental edge": John Bush and Bob Nalbandian, "Anthrax Vocalist John Bush Goes Up to Bat With Baseball Superstar Mike Piazza," *Shockwaves,* August/September 1996, No. 1.

Saint came up with their name after seeing *Excalibur:* Jodi Summers, "Metal Mind Tease," *RIP,* November 1988.

pp. 168–169: Details of Armored Saint's costumes: AI, Joey Vera.

The auto accident with Lee and Vera: AI, Vera.

pp. 169–170: Bush turned down singing for Metallica, and "It just wasn't": AI, John Bush.

Chrysalis didn't know how to market the band and following: AIs, Vera and Sutherland.

Saint on tour with Metallica and "Hey, don't take this the wrong way": AI, Vera.

Holmes's mother bought the buzzsaw blades: AI, Chris Holmes.

Costumes were inspired by *The Road Warrior* and splinters in Holmes's rear end: AI, Holmes.

The flames making the spiders on the ceiling flee: AIs, Betsy, David Carruth, and Robbie Settles of the band Bitch, who were a top draw at the Troubadour along with W.A.S.P.

p. 171: Holmes knocked out by flying rump roast: David Hiltbrand, "Live in the Raw" video review, *People,* August 22, 1988.

Arthur Kane had to be carried offstage by a roadie: Seen at the last Killer

Kane show by Starwood regular Joe Burman. In the article "Classic Rocks" by Alan Di Perna in *Guitar World* (July 1997), Joe Perry mentioned how Kane had to be carried around when he was drunk. As Perry recalled in the article, "Arthur Kane's the first guy I ever saw where I said, 'Hey, he's an alcoholic.' "

Rik Fox came up with the name W.A.S.P.: AI, Rik Fox. Confirmed by former W.A.S.P. guitarist Randy Piper.

Holmes peeing off the ledge of the building: AI, Charrie Foglio, who was at the party and saw it happen.

p. 172: Lawless's shelves lined with books how to intimidate people: AI, Gary Holland, who played drums with Blackie briefly.

"Yep, that's about the size of it": AI, Piper.

Smallwood threatened to pull Iron Maiden off the label: AI, Holmes.

Lawless assured Browde: AI, Browde. Dan Starr also used to know Lawless back in the '70s and '80s, and in an AI with Starr, he recalled Lawless's talking about gambling away his money in Vegas and having to walk miles to the airport because he couldn't afford a cab.

Metallica were ordered out of the dressing room and had to change in a garden shed: AI, Holmes.

"Blackie would go out of his way": AI, Vera.

When the tour hit Canada: Doughton, *Metallica: Unbound*.

p. 173: Dokken made their first album with the money they were advanced and following: AI, Lynch.

The band rehearsed in a wine cellar and the mold forming in the drums and amps: AI, Michael Wagener, who produced the *Breaking the Chains* album.

Dokken were going to sign to Elektra but the deal wouldn't close and following: AIs, Lynch and Pilson.

p. 174: "The plan all along": AI, Pilson.

"[We're] like a husband and wife": Sylvie Simmons, "A Little Piece of the Rock," *Kerrang!*, n.d. Clipping provided by Dan Starr.

Lynch's studio time was scheduled during the day, Don's at night: *Encyclopedia of Record Producers*.

Some tracks were recorded in separate states: Adrianne Stone, "Ear Candy," *RIP*, February 1988.

"We had so many mishaps": AI, Lynch.

Dokken denied wearing a wig: "Twenty Questions With Don Dokken," *Metal-Sludge*, March 14, 2000.

Lynch's pants split and "I lost a little hair there": AI, Lynch.

Volcano erupting during the "Just Got Lucky" shoot: AI, Lynch.

pp. 174–175: "There was a great model": AI, Lynch.

"We were very hungry and very focused": AI, Pilson.

"one of the best guitar players": AI, Werman.

The struggle to get "Alone Again" on the album: AIs, Pilson and Wagener.

p. 176: "You know that collection of power ballads": AI, Werman.

"Other bands were wearin' bandanas": *It Came From the Eighties: Metal Goes Pop!*, MTV special, 1996.

The costumes cost $3,000: AI, Lynch.

"clown outfits": John Stix, "Conversation Piece," *Guitar for the Practicing Musician*, February 1989.

A decade later Don admitted he was embarrassed by the costumes as well: *It Came From the Eighties.*

Lynch also wanted the music to progress to where: Billy Cioffi, "Dokken at the Crossroads," *Creem Metal Special*, n.d.

p. 177: Mötley Crüe's stage set inspired by *Escape from New York*: AI, Barry Levine.

Photographers couldn't shoot Bon Jovi unshaven: Adrianne Stone, "Bon Jovi Does Jersey," *RIP*, July 1989.

"We can't be [photographed] when I'm in": Paterno, "Theatre of Justice."

"That's where we spent": AI, Ian.

p. 178: Dio underwrote the tour with T-shirt money: confidential source.

"It became just as important": Roth, *Crazy from the Heat.*

"A kid puts on": *Rock She Wrote.*

"As much flak": AI, Pilson.

pp. 178–179: Even someone's mother could like a Ratt song: Steve Gett, "The Year of the Ratt," *Guitar for the Practicing Musician*, December 1984.

Ratt were pleased they played with Huey Lewis and the Cars: Jeff Tamarkin, "Ratt: Best New Artist," *Circus*, February 26, 1985.

The early days of the band details: Frank Meyer, "Ratt and Roll," knac.com, December 23, 1999.

The three P's, and Ratt Mansion West: Meyer, "Ratt and Roll."

The Gladiators names: AI, Robbin Crosby.

pp. 179–180: Berle backing the first E.P.: AI, Berle.

KLOS and KMET both played the single: Melinda Lewis, "Ratt: Racing to the Top of the Heap," *Music Connection*, August 30–September 12, 1984.

Ratt industry showcase at the Beverly Theatre: Ibid.

Ratt wanted Tom Allom and following: AI, Beau Hill.

pp. 180–181: Details of the writing and recording of *Out of the Cellar*: AI, Hill.

"the melody in their rhythm": John Stix, "Beating the Sophomore Blues," *Guitar for the Practicing Musician*, December 1985.

The label was having trouble getting radio play for "Round and Round" and MTV saved the day: AI, Berle.

Out of the Cellar would chart for over a year and sell more than three million copies: Steven Dougherty, "Loud, Brash, and Subtle as a Chainsaw, Ratt Cuts Itself a Piece of the Hard Rock Pie," *People,* n.d. Clipping provided by Dan Starr.

"MTV can take": AI, Berle.

Ratt lined their bus with bras and panties: Dougherty.

"Show Your Tits": Ibid.

pp. 181–182: The first big arena show opening for ZZ Top and following: AI, Croucier.

Slated to open for Alcatrazz, flipped a coin: AI, John Harrell, who was there that night shooting the bands.

Also opened for Fastway and Mama's Boys: AI, Blotzer.

Squire's managers tried to tell Ratt what to do and following: AI, Berle.

"Hey man, haven't you heard?", and following: AI, Croucier.

p. 183: "We don't have that offensive": Jeff Tamarkin, "Ratt: Best New Artist," *Circus,* February 16, 1985.

The only bands that could compete with Ratt: Pearcy said this in a 1985 MTV interview, which was replayed on *It Came From the Eighties: Metal Goes Pop.*

Pearcy fought with Croucier over his stage act: AIs with Dan Starr (who saw Pearcy taping the lines Croucier was not supposed to cross on stage), Mike Kelley (who was close friends with Bobby and Juan), and Croucier.

Pearcy stuffing his pants legend and posing for *Playgirl:* Pearcy addressed the stories of stuffing socks down his pants and confirmed that he didn't show all in *Playgirl* in Adrianne Stone, "Killer Kwotes," *RIP,* March 1988.

A $50,000 deposit was put on the studio and the band was under pressure to write: AI, Blotzer; also confirmed by Hill.

"You know something?": AI, Hill.

"All the bands I've ever worked with": AI, Berle.

p. 184: "The first effort of an artist": AI, Claude Schnell.

p. 185: "Ratt's biggest problem": Paul Gallotta, "Longplayers," *Circus,* January 31, 1989.

Quiet Riot signed away their publishing to Proffer: *Quiet Riot: Behind the Music* special.

The band did have legal council: AI, DuBrow. Proffer confirmed on *Behind the Music.*

The band figured they'd become successful by their third album: AI, DuBrow.

"I'm certainly not set financially": Alan Paul, "The Down Boys," *Guitar World,* April 1997.

p. 186: DuBrow's interview for *Hit Parader* and "If hair was gold": AI, DuBrow. All following DuBrow quotes, unless noted otherwise, are from AI, DuBrow.

Details of *Condition Critical* album and tour: AI, DuBrow.

The stage elevators breaking down on tour: AI, Sarzo.

"platinum failure": Jodi Summers, "Quiet Riot," *Aardshok*, Fall 1986.

When Rudy Sarzo opened up *Hit Parader* and saw a dartboard of DuBrow: AI, Sarzo.

p. 187: "You can't walk on": *Quiet Riot: Behind the Music.*

The stage set up backwards story in Pittsburgh: AI, Keel guitarist Mar Ferrari.

Quiet Riot played their last show on December 7, 1986: Katherine Turman, "Quiet Riot: The Band That Wouldn't Die!," *RIP*, March 1988.

The band changed their airline flights and slipped a ticket under DuBrow's door: AI, DuBrow.

pp. 187–188: DuBrow failed to pay a settlement and following: "Whammy Bar: News and Notes," *Guitar World*, April 1999.

"I think that if I had": AI, DuBrow

CHAPTER 7: PUSH COMES TO SHOVE

p. 190: "Every night": David Fricke, "Can This Be Love*?*," *Rolling Stone*, July 3, 1986.

Eddie trying to record the solo to "Push Comes to Shove": *Guitar World Presents Van Halen.*

Eddie began writing music for a solo album: Jeff Hausman, "VHTimeline 2," *The Inside*, Summer 1995, No. 2.

According to Alex Van Halen: Fricke, "Can This Be Love?"

Warner Bros. didn't release any singles from the album: Hausman, "VHTimeline 2."

Fair Warning was one of Billy Corgan's favorites: Billy Corgan, "Best of Both Worlds," *Guitar World*, April 1996.

p. 191: Roth kept Eddie away from Simmons: Roth, *Crazy from the Heat.*

Details of Eddie playing on "Beat It": Bosso, *Monster of Rock.*

Roth claimed if he had known: *Crazy from the Heat.*

"What did Edward do": Debby Miller, "Van Halen's Split Personality."

"You're a guitar hero": Steven Rosen, "On the Road," *Guitar World*, September 1986.

p. 192: Eddie claimed the only song he could come up with was "Jump": Richard Hogan, "Eddie Van Halen Probes His Past and Present," *Circus*, October 31, 1986.

Blondes were ordered off the tour bus: AI, Steven Rosen, who was on the bus with Van Halen once when this happened. Also confirmed in Steve Dougherty and Todd Gold, "High Jumping Hagar Helps Van Halen Forget Roth," *People,* June 23, 1986.

Dee Snider considered dying his hair: Chilvers, *The Van Halen Encyclopedia.*

Roth didn't want wives on the road: Dougherty and Gold.

Roth insisted Bertinelli not come on tour: Fricke, "Can This Be Love?"

Roth compared her to David St. Hubbins's wife: Blush, "Runnin' with the Devil."

Roth hit on Valerie first but was rebuffed: *Guitar World Presents Van Halen.*

Eddie thought Roth was jealous: Wild, "Balancing Act."

Bertinelli felt he wanted to keep Eddie miserable: Debby Bull, Valerie Bertinelli interview, January 1987.

p. 193: "He either didn't anticipate," and following: AI, Schnell.

Atlantic had previously rejected their demo five times: Snider, "The Four F Syndrome."

"Illegetimus non Carborundum est": Uncredited, Dee Snider, *People Special Issue: Rock n' Roll Then and Now!,* June 17, 1996.

pp. 193–194: Snider beat up anyone who heckled the band: Smith, *Off the Record.*

The Reading Festival incident: Bryan Reeseman, "You Can't Stop Rock n' Roll," *Goldmine,* January 28, 2000.

Snider singled people out in the audience: Uncredited, "Rip Rap Column," *RIP,* May 1988. In this installment of "Rip Rap," White Lion guitarist Vito Bratta recalled seeing Twisted Sister live and being one of the people who got singled out and cursed.

Snider cursing out the balcony: *Rock City News,* September 17–October 1, 1994.

Snider telling Mendoza to meet the fans or he was fired: AI, Alan Reiff. Reiff is a road manager who also worked at a number of clubs back East, including L'Amours. Twisted Sister and Zebra were both huge club bands at the time, and Reiff saw this incident happen at a club show.

Marty Callner met with Ahmet Ertegun: AI, Callner.

p. 195: "My father was not": AI, Dee Snider.

The "We're Not Gonna Take It" video cited by the PMRC and the video being influenced by Warner Bros. cartoons: AI, Callner.

"If ever there was a video band": AI, Callner.

It took Twisted Sister six years of playing clubs: AI, Snider.

"I'm always tickled": AI, Snider.

Snider presented a Grammy in 1985: Reeseman, *You Can't Stop Rock and Roll.*

"I was viewed as selling out": Ibid.

pp. 195–196: MTV usually rejected bands for not being attractive: Steven Levy, "Ad Nauseam," *Rolling Stone,* December 8, 1983.

"pioneered ugly way before": AI, Snider.

"All those bands": AI, Snider.

Come Out and Play cost $300,000: Linda Maleski, "Fun Vids Broaden Twisted Sister's Appeal," *Billboard,* n.d. Clipping Provided by Dan Starr.

The tour was canceled after eighteen shows: Charrie Foglio, "The Demise of Dokken," *RIP,* May 1989.

"I went from being scary": AI, Snider.

p. 197: "All of the sudden": Snider, "The Four F Syndrome."

James Hetfield once joked: Tom Beaujour, "Born Again," *Guitar World,* July 1996.

Snider was deeply in debt: *People,* June 17, 1996.

"As crazy as things got on the high side," and following: AI, Snider.

Band members now speaking again: Reeseman.

The downfall of Snider's Desperado: AI; Snider, "The Four F Syndrome."

"I don't want to bury it": AI, Snider.

p. 198: Green Day played "We're Not Gonna Take It": AI, Snider.

p. 198: "I'm sure there's a picture or two of me," and "Look mommy": AI, Snider.

Kramer went from $1 million to $15 million and "instant credibility": AI, Henry Vaccaro.

p. 199: "guitar whores" and "You played the guitar": Kevin Kelly, "The World According to Dean," *Guitar Shop,* December 1995.

Yngwie Malmsteem's childhood: Jas Obrecht, "Yngwie Malmsteem," *Guitar Player,* May 1985; Joe Lalaina, "Yngwie Malmsteen: Like Him or Not, He Demands Your Attention," *Guitar World,* January 1986.

"What this guy does with a violin": Obrecht.

pp. 199–200: "broken chords," and Yngwie's licks made sense fast or slow observation: Lalaina.

Yngwie came across like a classical musician stuck in a time warp: AI, Rik Fox, who played bass in Steeler, made this observation.

"Yngwie is God": Obrecht.

p. 201: "The pole's gotta go": AI, Jon Sutherland, who was there at the Mason Jar when Yngwie demanded this.

Yngwie threw Faster Pussycat out of their dressing room: "Rip Rap Column," *RIP,* March 1988.

"Malmsteen and I broke up over": Bryan Reeseman, "Shamelessly '80s! Volume 5: Graham Bonnet and Joe Lynn Turner," knac.com, November 16, 2001.

"The God with the Chip": This story appeared in *Guitar World* in July 1984.

Rosen punching Yngwie incident: AI, Rosen.

Malmsteem's car accident, arrest, bankruptcy filing: Joe Lalaina, "Damn the Torpedoes," *Guitar World,* August 1994.

"Unfortunately, as bad of a reputation," and following: AI, Sheehan.

p. 202: Sheehan drove a Pinto with the emergency spare tire: Billy Sheehan/ Yngwie Malmsteen cover story, John Stix, *Guitar for the Practicing Musician,* March 1986.

Sheehan's call to Van Halen: AI, Sheehan.

p. 203: "The audience loves to see pain up there": Smith, *Off the Record.*

"People ask": Blush, *Runnin' with the Devil.*

Sheehan arrived in Los Angeles, and following: AI, Sheehan.

p. 204: Steve Stevens was considered: AI, Mike Fahley.

Steve Vai attended Berkley: John Stix, "Steve Vai," *Guitar for the Practicing Musician,* March 1986.

"Steve will say": Tom Mulhern, "Billy Sheehan," *Guitar Player,* December 1986.

"I'm bummed for Van Halen": Hank Bordowitz, "Billy Sheehan: The First Bassman," *The Best of Metal Mania.*

"No, there's no chance we'll ever get back together": "Backpages" column, Lou O' Neil Jr. *Circus,* December 31, 1986.

p. 205: Ted Nugent telling Eddie to get a new singer and move on at the NAMM show: AI, Sammy Sanchez. Sanchez is a former roadie for Nugent who was there when this happened.

Details of Eddie searching for a new singer, and finding Hagar: Fricke, "Can This Be Love?"

David Geffen did not want Hagar to leave: Tom King, *The Operator,* Random House, 2000.

A bitter feud resulted between Geffen and Ostin: Ibid.

They almost changed their name to *Sammy Hagar* and following: Fricke, "Can This Be Love?"

p. 206: Roth said he found the phrase on a watermelon sticker: Roth, *Crazy from the Heat.*

"When I listen to those tracks now": AI, Steve Vai.

Twisted Sister considered making a movie: Barbara Nellis, "Fast Tracks" column, *Playboy,* July 1985.

Details of the proposed *Crazy from the Heat* movie: Roth, *Crazy from the Heat.*

p. 207: "I wasn't trying to": AI, Steve Vai.

Set list for Van Halen *5150* tour in Fricke article. Set list for Roth tour confirmed in AI, Vai.

"It shows me": Rosen, *On the Road.*

Hagar burning the pro-Dave banner: Jon Dworkow, "Why Is Edward Always Smiling?", *Guitar World,* July 1987.

"Hagar the horrible": Howard Stern, *Private Parts,* Simon and Schuster, 1993.

p. 208: On the first night of the *Eat 'Em and Smile* tour and following: AI, Vai.

Roth brought out an empty video camera to hype up the crowd: AI, Sheehan.

"You couldn't see a better": AI, Mike Fahley.

pp. 208–209: "It was a fantastic time": AI, Vai.

Sheehan hated the *Skyscraper* album: "Twenty Questions with Billy Sheehan," *Metal Sludge,* 8/10/99.

Working for Roth, there were three things you never mentioned: Confirmed by several confidential sources.

"Bad Career Move" list, and "With the inevitable split": *People Weekly 25 Years! Special Anniversary Issue,* March 15–22, 1999.

Sheehan believes and Vai feels: AIs, Sheehan and Vai.

p. 210: Some in the audience booed Roth: David J. Criblez, Geoff Bell, "DLR Live!", *The Inside,* Winter 1996, 4.

"I think David Lee Roth": AI, John McBurnie.

"You walked in the place": AI, Jon Sutherland.

Mario Maglieri's pre-Rainbow jobs: Tom Maguire, Mario Maglieri, *Shockwaves,* Spring 1997; AI, Mario Maglieri.

Supposedly the first restaurant to open on Sunset: AI, McBurnie.

DiMaggio and Monroe met at Villa Nova: Richard Ben Cramer, *Joe DiMaggio: The Hero's Life,* Simon and Schuster, 2001.

When Led Zeppelin came to L.A. and following: AI, Richard Cole.

p. 211: Slash sneaking into the Rainbow in drag incident: AI, Slash.

"Sweet Child O' Mine" signaled last call: AI, Patty Johnson, former Rainbow waitress.

What tables were popular with bands: AI, McBurnie.

pp. 211–212: "Around 11 o'clock": AI, Hantas.

Lonn Friend received his introduction: AI, Lonn Friend.

"No one cared," and "Now that's the Rainbow": Lonn Friend, "Rock's Outer Limits," *Hustler,* April 1985.

The watch drawer: AI, Hantas.

"I just gave a watch": AI, Maglieri.

The restaurant started using shorter tablecloths: AI, Sheehan.

The phone booth had to be moved outside: AIs, Sheehan and McBurnie.

"I was in there": AI, McBurnie.

"We let 'em": AI, Maglieri.

p. 213: Chris Holmes contracting syphilis: AI, Holmes.

Mötley Crüe's "PSP" passes: *Rock She Wrote.*

"Let's go upstairs," and "Why fool around?": Roth, *Crazy from the Heat.*

"This looks like a 1989": AI, Jerry Dixon.

"Marry a rock star," and following: AI, Julia Nine.

p. 214: Hidden cameras on the tour bus: AI, Hantas.

"May those tapes": Tom Beaujour, "Metal Memories with George Lynch," *Guitar World,* September 1999.

"I thought marriage": AI, Slash.

"tried to be married" and "I'd explain, 'Oh, I gotta go for one second' ": Blair R. Fischer, "Top Ten Jobs We Could Think Of: Rock Star," Playboy.com.

p. 215: It took Reiner four and a half years to sell the film, and following: David Rosenthal, "Rob Reiner: Playboy Interview," *Playboy,* July 1985.

Tufnel seen reading a racing magazine and Beck is an auto enthusiast: You can see this in the film, but Jeff Beck also pointed this out when he was interviewed in the January 1990 *Guitar World* by Brad Tolinski in the article "Jeff Beck, Strat Cat." Beck recalled with a laugh: "Do you know that one scene in the airport? Did you notice that Nigel is reading a hot rod magazine—the bloody bastard!"

The film was shot in five weeks on a $2.2 million budget and following: Uncredited, "Reiner's *This Is Spinal Tap* Set For Cult Status in U.S., Now Opening in U.K.," *Screen International,* September 8, 1984. The outline for *Spinal Tap* was also reprinted in French and Row, *This Is Spinal Tap: The Official Companion.* That much of the film was improvised is confirmed in a report by Jimmy Summers, *Boxoffice,* May 1984.

Embassy issued press kits featuring fake bios, lyric sheets, and a million albums returned: Mark Leviton, "Spinal Tap's Metal Memories," *BAM,* March 23, 1984.

Spinal Tap previewed in a Dallas shopping mall: Aljean Harmetz, "Reiner Has the Last Laugh with His Rock Spoof," *New York Times,* April 25, 1984.

"Jesus, what is this?": Michael London, "Film Clips," *Los Angeles Times,* March 21, 1984.

pp. 215–216: "The funniest rock and roll movie": Merill Schindler, "*This Is Spinal Tap:* Rock 'n' Droll," *Los Angeles Times,* March 1984.

"it almost becomes the thing": David Denby, *This Is Spinal Tap* review, *New York,* March 19, 1984.

The first time Eddie Van Halen saw the film, and "Everything in that movie": Bosso, *Monster of Rock.*

"That's us!": AI, Lynch.

Steven Tyler almost couldn't, and "That movie was way too close": Wild, *The Band That Wouldn't Die.*

"The closer we got to the real thing": Clark Collis, "Stairway to Eleven," *Mojo,* November 2000.

Black Sabbath's Stonehenge set, and the fog obscuring the lyric sheets: Gillen and Cohen, *Child In Time.*

p. 217: Vinnie Appice trapped in the pyramid and the roadies trying to pry him loose: AIs, Vinnie Appice and Scotty Ross.

Venues where metal bands played in the '80s were vaudeville venues, had to open all the doors before you found the stage: AI, Sarzo.

When Great White opened for Whitesnake: AI, Gary Holland.

During one Danzig show: AI, John Christ.

As George Lynch put it: AI, Lynch.

pp. 217–218: David St. Hubbins called the film "a hatchet job," and following: Collis, "Stairway to Eleven."

"I've seen rock bands": Richard Cromelin, "Held By a Monster Magnet," *Los Angeles Times,* March 11, 1999.

pp. 218–221: Information on the PMRC, the PMRC hearings, and Frank Zappa's involvement in the fight against them: Linda Martin and Kerry Segrave, *Anti-Rock: The Opposition to Rock 'n' Roll,* Da Capo Press, 1993; Frank Zappa and Peter Occhiogrosso, *The Real Frank Zappa Book,* Poseidon Press, 1989.

p. 220: Zappa reconciled with Gore: AI, Gail Zappa.

"It's a shame": Geoff Boucher, "Tipper's Refrain," *Los Angeles Times,* August 17, 2000.

The Mentors record sales doubled: Jeff Silberman, Metal Blade Records: The Cutting Edge for Headbangers. *BAM,* April 11, 1986.

p. 221: In January 1985, and following: Patrick Goldstein, "KMET Joins the Ranks of Metal Defectors," *Los Angeles Times,* March 17, 1985.

Record labels were nervous about selling a record without the support of MTV: Greg Ptacek, "Video Rebuff Rattles Rosters," *Billboard,* April 27, 1985.

The "Just Got Lucky" single falling flat when MTV pulled the plug on metal: Foglio, "The Demise of Dokken."

Armored Saint didn't make a video for *Delirious Nomad* album because they knew MTV wouldn't play it: AI, Vera.

p. 222: "MTV had a profound": AI, Lynch.

"Without MTV": AI, Sarzo.

CHAPTER 8: BONDED BY BLOOD

p. 224: "I know our music": Kenny Kerner, "Slayer: Speed Thrills," *Music Connection,* May 26–June 8, 1986.

"MTV wasn't our concern": AI, Alago.

pp. 224–225: Bruce Dickenson felt the band had done, and following: Wall, *Run to the Hills.*

"stagnate and just drift": Ibid.

"Neither Steve nor I": Ibid.

"I felt the time": Ibid.

p. 226: "Lemme a fiver": Joel McIver, "Mil-Lemmy-Um," *Record Collector,* January 2000.

Story behind "Ace of Spades": Liner notes for Motörhead's *No Remorse* album, written by Lemmy, 1984 Bronze/Island Records.

"They're the bravest, dumbest": AI, Sutherland.

When Lemmy went to the Rainbow: AI, John McBurnie.

Motörhead never had a gold or platinum album: Jon Sutherland pointed this out to me in an AI, and RIAA has no listing of Motörhead being awarded a gold or platinum album.

p. 227: Lemmy's suitcase full of books: AI, Sarzo.

Venom's real names: Jason Ankeny, Venom bio, cd.now.com.

"Rabid captor of bestial malevolence," and following: All the members of Venom are credited this way on the back cover of their *Black Metal* album.

Venom tried to be a combination of Motörhead and Kiss: Ankeny.

"Venom, as cheeseball as they are": AI, Del James.

Venom talked trash about other bands: AI, Borivoj Krgin.

The band got into scrapes with fire marshalls: Lloyd Lea, "Venom," *It's All Over* fanzine, Summer 1986.

pp. 227–228: When Venom played the Capital Theatre in Philadelphia, and $666.66: AI, Krign.

"I expected them to go into," and following: Henry Rollins, "Get In the Van," *2.13.61,* 1994.

Details of Euronymous's murder: Michael Moynihan and Didrik Soderlind, *Lords of Chaos,* Feral House Press, 1998.

p. 229: Hanneman would bring punk albums to their practice sessions and following: AI, Dave Lombardo.

Fan balcony diving into the stage in San Diego: Uncredited, "Brief Encounter: Jim Dulin, Slayer's Road Manager," *It's All Over* fanzine.

"They were controlled by something": AI, Lombardo. All subsequent quotes, unless noted, are from AI, Dave Lombardo.

p. 230: Mustaine being hit in the face with sod: AI, Lombardo.

Details of Slayer falling out with Slagel and signing with Rubin: Kerner, "Speed Thrills." Jon Sutherland, who worked at Metal Blade at the time, also said in an AI that Slayer sued Metal Blade to get out of their deal and won.

Details of CBS's dropping Def Jam and Slayer: Patrick Goldstein, "CBS: A Case of Heavy Metal Poisoning?", *Los Angeles Times,* October 12, 1986.

The music was written very quickly before they entered the studio: AI, Lombardo.

p. 231: Lombardo wanted Slayer's sound to expand, and following: AI, Lombardo.

Details of Lombardo getting fired from Slayer: AI, Lombardo; also confirmed in Borivoj Krgin, "Life After Slayer," *Metal Maniacs,* August 1993.

p. 232: "You guys sounded great": AI, Lombardo.

"They took their makeup off": AI, Quintana.

When Motörhead developed a following, and following: AI, Quintana.

It took close to a year for *Bonded by Blood* to get released: Ron Quintana, "Exodus," *Aardshok,* Fall 1986.

Fans bought the album even though they had it on tape: AI, Don Kaye.

Ruthies crowd pouring beer on the dance floor: AI, Quintana.

The band claimed: Uncredited, "A Triple Shot of Speed: Exodus, Possessed, Death Angel," *It's All Over.*

Baloff didn't want anyone messing with his hair: AI, Quintana.

p. 233: "Bring that poser up here!": AI, Quintana.

Baloff would divide the audience down the middle: "Exodus," *Aardshok.*

The fans turning their back on Exodus: AI, Eric Peterson, Testament guitarist.

Death Angel's drummer played behind a miniature drum set: AI, Peterson.

Alex Skolnick had to sneak out of his parents' house to play gigs: AI, Peterson.

"There's nothing to it": AI, Debbie Abono. All subsequent Abono quotes are from AI, Abono.

p. 234: Possessed broke in Europe first while still playing clubs in S.F.: AI, Quintana.

Details of Possessed, Abono managing them, and the recording of *Seven Churches:* AI, Abono.

p. 235: Danzig lived with his parents: AI, John Christ.

When Danzig met Rick: Legs McNeil, "Danzig," *Spin,* January 1991.

Details of Rubin starting Def Jam in his dorm: Farr, *Moguls and Madmen.*

Rubin had fallouts with the Beastie Boys and LL Cool J: Ibid.

p. 236: Glenn and Rick hit it off because: AI, Christ.

Christ's bloody audition: AI, Christ.

Christ leaving his licks on Glenn's answering machine: AI, Christ.

"You gotta move up to New Jersey": AI, Christ. All subsequent Danzig information from AI, Christ.

p. 237: Ian would scrape his fingers downpicking: Joe Gore, "Viva Anthrax!", *Guitar Player,* February 1991.

"If each note": AI, Ian. All subsequent Ian quotes from AI.

pp. 238–239: The creation of S.O.D. and all subsequent S.O.D. information: AI, Ian.

"We made the mistake": Mike Gitter, "Broken Bones: Maximum Mandible Damage," *Creem Close Up: Thrash Metal,* November 1988.

p. 240: "When metal and punk came together": Chris Bade, video interview with Corrosion of Conformity, *Creepy Crawl Video Magazine,* 1992.

Insurance risks to book bands became too great: Bernard Doe, "Terror Rising," *Metal Forces* 24, 1987.

Fender's and the violence of the L.A. scene: The author went to a number of speed metal and punk shows in the late 1980s and early 1990s and observed a lot of the violence and craziness that went on in those days. In D.R.I.'s home video, "Live at the Ritz," some of the footage was shot at Fenders, where you can clearly see people hanging and diving from the roof; it's usually what punks and speed metal fans remember about the club, along with the excessive violence that went on.

pp. 240–241: Metallica and Anthrax going to see Broken Bones at CBGB: AI, Ian.

Spastic Children information: AI, Ron Quintana; Doughton, *Metallica Unbound.*

"Their shows": AI, Quintana.

"kick Metallica's ass": Doughton, *Metallica Unbound.*

"I thought Metallica": AI, Quintana.

Poland and Gar hadn't heard speed metal before joining 'Deth and Dave threw their tapes out the window of the tour bus: AI, Chris Poland.

p. 242: At the end of every gig, and following: AI, Poland.

"It was a wonderful": AI, Poland. All following Poland quotes are from AI.

Megadeth name taken from political speech: Jon Wiederhorn, "Bending Metal," *Penthouse,* May 2000.

Reasoning behind the "Choose Deth" stickers: AI, Poland.

Megadeth spent most of the production money on dope: Frank Meyer, "Megadeth's Dave Mustaine Makes a Killing," knac.com, November 26, 2001.

Dave joked about the ammunition lockers: Jeff Wagner, "Megadeth: Cryptically Speaking," *Metal Maniacs,* October 1997.

p. 243: Megadeth got into fistfights, the army coming to the hotel in Japan, and the Slayer gig at the Ritz: AI, Poland.

p. 244: The details of Megadeth's first lineup break-up: AI, Poland.

"Wake Up Dead" about Dave's psycho girlfriend: AI, Poland.

"Dave's ego got in the way a lot": AI, Hantas.

p. 245: Mustaine getting to the point where he couldn't play anymore and getting pulled over in 1990: Mikal Gilmore, "Heavy Metal Thunder," *Rolling Stone,* July 11–25, 1991.

"lite-metal": Wiederhorn, "Bending Metal."

"I wanted to show": Phil Alexander, "The Countdown to Extinction," *Raw*, July 8–21, 1992.

"It wasn't like today": AI, Lombardo.

pp. 245–246: Megadeth's break-up, Mustaine going back into rehab, and Mustaine selling his equipment on Ebay: Sefany Jones, "Dave Mustaine Leaves Megadeth!", knac.com, April 3, 2002; Jon Wiederhorn, "Megadeth Pack It In After Nearly 20 Years," Mtv.com, April 3, 1002; Tokemaster General, "Dave Mustaine Puts Equipment Up For Sale," knac.com, April 15, 2002.

No Seagrams and Coke, no interview: Jon Wiederhorn, "Drunk, Disorderly, and Devastating," *Guitar*, May 1999.

The legend of Phil's dick and "This is nothing": Lynn Snowden, *Nine Lives*, W.W. Norton, 1994.

"the most ferocious album": Borivoj Krgin, Aural Assaults record reviews section, review of *Far Beyond Driven*, *Metal Maniacs*, August 1994.

Yet Krgin feels: AI, Krgin.

p. 247: "The band's whole argument is": AI, Krgin.

Pantera formerly a hair band: Early photos of Pantera in glam garb have appeared in *Metal Maniacs* magazine and in Lynn Snowden's article, "Hair Today, Gone Tomorrow," which appeared in the February 1996 issue of *Spin*. Hair band pictures of Pantera and Alice in Chains (when the members of AIC were in earlier bands like Diamond Lie and Sleaze), have also appeared on the website metal-sludge.com. Alice in Chains and STP's being former hair bands also confirmed in Snowden article.

"One thing about Pantera": AI, John Bush.

Exodus reunion show brought out fans who hadn't seen each other in ten years: AI, Quintana.

"One of the things I believe": Jeff Wagner, "Exodus Re-Bonded," *Metal Maniacs*, October 1997.

Baloff's death and Anthrax held a "moment of noise" for him: Frank Meyer, "Exodus's Paul Baloff Passes Away After Suffering a Stroke," knac.com, February 1, 2002; Frank Meyer, "Exodus Carry On . . . But for How Long," knac.com, February 5, 2002.

"It's him": Corcoran, "Speed Thrills," *Creem*.

p. 248: "Are you trying to," and Ozzy was surprised to find out: Pollock, "In the Tradition," *Guitar for the Practicing Musician*.

"At first": Paul Gallotta, "Metallica Do It Their Way," *Circus*, n.d.

James and Kirk banging their heads at full speed, Cliff looked like slow motion: I have to thank Harald Oimen for pointing this out to me in AI; thanks, Harald!

"I heard Hetfield": AI, Hantas.

"We smashed dressing rooms": Tannenbaum, "Playboy Interview."

p. 249: "I almost feel like": AI, Alago.

Alago thought, Next year: AI, Alago.

Details of the bus accident and Cliff Burton's death: Doughton, "Crocker: Behind the Music."

p. 250: "Cliff was one": AI, Oimen.

Joey Vera being contacted for the bassist slot, and "We were more": AI, Vera.

Jason Newsted's early years: Doughton.

Jason doing seventeen interviews in a day: AI, Sutherland.

pp. 250–251: Sutherland telling Newsted about the Metallica gig and following: AI, Sutherland.

Erik AK quitting the band: Frank Meyer, "Flotsam and Jetsam Vocalist Retires!," knac.com, August 24, 2001.

pp. 251–252: Newsted's audition: Doughton, "Playboy Interview"; *Behind the Music.*

"that whole week": "Playboy Interview."

The last test gig at the Country Club: Doughton and the author also listened to an audiotape of the show, which included the power failure during "Master of Puppets."

To get a copy of the video: AI, Oimen.

Some fans were upset with Cliff smoking pot: In *RIP* magazine, June 1988, one letter of the month to the magazine dealt with a fan's disappointment with the video showing Cliff smoking pot. *Kerrang!* magazine also did a story on Metallica in 1988 while they were recording . . . *And Justice For All,* which dealt with some fans being surprised by Cliff smoking pot in the video.

Reason why Clink left: AI, Mike Clink.

p. 253: "Whoa! Okay, on a lighter note": Beebee, *Headbanger's Ball.*

The band could can the "One" video if it didn't turn out right: Jeff Kitts, "Is Metallica in Search of White Bread Status?", *Metal Mania,* September 1989.

No audible bass on the album: Confirmed in numerous articles on Metallica including "Playboy Interview"; Beebee, *Headbanger's Ball*; "Metal Age Crisis," *Guitar Player.*

Hetfield went crazy when Jason tried a solo band, didn't see anything hypocritical about doing it himself: Fricke, "Pretty Hate Machine"; "Playboy Interview."

p. 254: "If anything": AI, Oimen.

"I had to keep": Jason Newsted interview by John Harrell; quoted with permission.

Metallica were certain the Grammy was theirs, and the audience booed loudly: Kitts, "Is Metallica Searching For White Bread Status?"

Lars thanked Jethro Tull: *A Year and a Half in the Life of Metallica.*

CHAPTER 9: IT'S SO EASY

p. 256: "Guns N' Roses is the most": This widely reported quote was reprinted in Danny Sugerman, *Destruction,* St. Martin's Press, 1991.

Guns N' Roses jamming with the Stones, relearning "Salt of the Earth," and "This is so cool, this is where we could be": Nick Kent, "Losing Their Illusions," *Details,* December 1991.

pp. 256–257: Jagger should have dropped dead after *Some Girls:* Sugerman, *Destruction.*

The Stones hadn't toured in seven years and expected to make $100 million: Robert Hilburn, "Still the Greatest," *Los Angeles Times,* October 20, 1989.

The band had to sign anti-drug contracts: Sugerman.

"Our drug use is not in the past": Del James, "Axl Rose: The Rolling Stone Interview," *Rolling Stone,* August 10, 1989.

Axl smashing the guitar and COCAINE SUCKS: AI, Vinni Stiletto, a friend of the band from the 1980s. Generally confirmed by Slash in AI.

Details and reviews of the Cathouse and Scream gigs: Jonathan Gold, "Guns N' Roses Lets 'er Rip in Stone Warmup," *Los Angeles Times,* October 13, 1989; AI, Marty Temme, a photographer who shot the show.

p. 258: Izzy peeing on the airplane, Axl calling at six in the morning, and "It's gonna be a long four days": Sugerman.

"I don't like to do this onstage": Ibid.

Slash nearly stormed off the stage, everyone stayed in their boxed areas of the stage, Axl announced he was quitting: Jeffrey Ressner and Lonn Friend, "Slash: The Rolling Stone Interview," *Rolling Stone,* January 24, 1991.

Jagger dedicated "Mixed Emotions" to Axl: Mark Putterford, "Over the Top," *Omnibus* 1993.

"could go on convincingly": Robert Hilburn, "The Winner and Still Champ, The Rolling Stones," *Los Angeles Times,* October 20, 1989.

Axl wouldn't perform unless Slash talked about drugs before the show: AIs, Ressner and Friend.

pp. 258–259: "There's been a lot written": Sugerman.

Slash had been coming to the Coliseum since he was a kid: AI, Slash.

"Last night I was up here," and the first song they performed was "Patience": Sugerman.

"Hey, it's not my gig": Kent, *Losing Their Illusions.*

pp. 259–260: Details of Slash's childhood: AI, Slash and Friend; Ressner.

"That's the only reason why": AI, Slash.

Slash grew his hair out to cover his eyes: Kim Neely, "Guns N' Roses," *Rolling Stone,* September 5, 1991.

Apartments reminded Slash of hotel rooms: Mark Rowland: "Appetite for Reconstruction," *Musician,* December 1990.

Steven played along to Kiss records, Slash first learned on a one string guitar, grandmother bought him a B. C. Rich, "Unfortunately, I hocked it," and "My parents": AI, Slash.

pp. 260–261: Details of Axl's childhood, finding out who his real father was, changing his name to W. Axl Rose: Rob Tannenbaum, "The Hard Truth About Guns N' Roses," November 17, 1988; Kim Neely, "Axl Rose: The Rolling Stone Interview," *Rolling Stone*, April 2, 1992; Sugerman.

He scored in the top 3 percent: Del James, "Axl Rose: The Rolling Stone Interview," *Rolling Stone*, August 10, 1989.

evidence of psychosis: Tannebaum, "The Hard Truth About Guns N' Roses."

"cursed," and "If there's someone up there": Sugerman.

Axl called Indiana "Auschwitz": Kim Neely, "Guns N' Roses," *Rolling Stone*, September 5, 1991.

Izzy thought, Here's a guy who's: Mick Wall, "In Too Deep," *Classic Rock*, June 2001.

Stradlin was the only one with a diploma, Duff McKagan was an honor student: Neely, "Guns N' Roses"; Tannenbaum, "The Hard Truth."

Stradlin hadn't seen his father in close to ten years, ran into him backstage: Mark Rowland, "Guns N' Roses," *Musician Heavy Metal Special Issue*, 1989.

Axl got on a Greyhound, ran out of money, hitchhiked the rest of the way: "Guns N' Roses Fact Sheet," *Rock of the '80's II Magazine Special*, November 1988. Rose Rolling Stone interview by James also confirmed he hitchhiked his way to Los Angeles.

p. 262: Axl showed up at his door: Rowland.

How the members of GNR met each other and "he was the only singer in L.A.": Sugerman; Rowland; Uncredited; "In the Tradition," *Guitar for the Practicing Musician*; and AI, Slash.

"Axl didn't have that," and "I could just picture it": AI, Vinni Stiletto.

Stiletto and Axl hanging out on top of Bank of America and "I fucking flipped": AI, Stiletto.

p. 263: Guns N' Roses officially started on June 6, 1985, and following: Sugerman.

Izzy couldn't afford the club's cover charge and had to watch bands through the window: AI, Stiletto.

When he rode the bus to the Troubadour: AI, Stiletto.

Details and Slash quotes on the band's trip to Seattle: AI, Slash.

Less than twenty people showed up and the band never got paid: Sugerman.

"this chick we were all fucking": AI, Slash.

The last nine-to-five job Slash had: Sugerman.

pp. 263–264: "we all sold our souls": AI, Slash.

Details of the Gardner rehearsal room, and the band built a loft out of stolen lumber: Tannenbaum, "The Hard Truth About Guns N' Roses."

"That's where we all had sex": AI, Slash.

It was fun surviving: AI, Slash.

"It was no rules": AI, Del James.

The band would eat at Rage: Debbie Metal, "Guns & Roses: Live Like a Lunatic," *RIP,* May 1987.

"Every time a label would approach us" and following: AI, Slash.

"fresh off the boat": Pleasant Gehman, "To Be Smart, Young, and Female During the Strip's Metal Heydaze," *BAM,* June 16, 1995.

pp. 264–265: Bret Michaels said he tore the rear-view mirror off: AI, Vicky Hamilton.

"Because L.A.'s a lot farther to come back": AI, Scotty Ross. Ross was their tour manager before going to work for Van Halen.

Rocket was a licensed cosmetologist: Chris Marlowe, "12 on 4," *Raw,* October 4–17, 1989.

Poison didn't trust their girlfriends to do their hair: AI, John Harrell.

"When Poison gave me their first album": AI, Zlozower.

"Anyone who dares claim": Tom Beaujour, "Comb Runs," *Guitar World,* September 1999.

Poison would move into an apartment, pay the first months rent: Bobby Dall and Charrie Foglio, "The Days of Wine and Ramen," *RIP,* n.d. Clipping provided by Jon Sutherland.

On the wall of their apartment were two lists: Gehman. The members of Poison also confirmed that women bought them food and took care of their apartments in the film *Decline and Fall of the Western Civilization Part II: The Metal Years,* directed by Penelope Spheeris, New Line Cinema, 1988.

p. 266: Poison made 30,000 flyers per show, and his mother owned Barbara's Place: Dall, "Days of Wine and Ramen"; AI, Hamilton.

The city of West Hollywood began issuing fines: The author recalled this happening when he was friends with a number of small bands, who complained about its becoming harder and harder to "flyer" the strip.

p. 361: "Posers" and "suitcase pimps" handing out fake flyers: AI, Ace Steele.

Hamilton worked out a deal, and following: AI, Hamilton.

"Not the music": AI, Zlozower.

pp. 266–267: Ric Browde's account of working with Poison in the studio: AI, Ric Browde.

"How we played": AI, C. C. DeVille.

Wagener mixed the album in five days, "I had to pick," and "one of the big mistakes": AI, Wagener.

"Capitol had two records": AI, Browde.

Poison went from selling 25,000 a week to 100,000: Mark Rowland, "Heavy Metal Is Sinking to the Top," *Los Angeles Times,* June 19, 1987.

"MTV was the single most": AI, DeVille.

p. 268: "a triumph of image": AI, Browde.

"There's no musical talent": Teri Saccone, "Posin' or Poison?", *Creem Metal Special,* 1988.

"It was the first time": AI, Browde.

"The one thing I can say about the '80s," and splicing the drum tracks together for Faster Pussycat: AI, Ross Hogarth, who engineered the album.

"For every band that writes": Judy Wieder, "Warrant Update," *Creem Metal Special Issue: Poison, Warrant and Other Hard-Rockin' Bands,* 1991.

"I thought the band": AI, DeVille.

p. 269: Poison held meetings at Capitol Records, and "Regardless of their success": AI, Byron Hantas. Poison being thin-skinned to criticism, and bewildered why the critics don't like them, was also brought up by the band themselves in Steve Appleford, "Gone Today, Hair Tomorrow," *New Times,* October 24–30, 1996.

pp. 269–270: When Mr. Big opened for Rush: AI, Billy Sheehan.

Sutherland running into Sykes and Appice at the Metallica Troubadour show: AI, Sutherland.

"Once [Metallica] was on MTV": Tannebaum, "Metallica: Playboy Interview."

It was believed MTV had a larger female audience: Mark Rowland, "Heavy Metal Is Sinking to the Top," *Los Angeles Times,* June 19, 1987.

Poison listed their conquests on a computer: Daina Darzin, "Poison Trivia," *Poison, Warrant, and Other Hard Rockin' Bands.*

"Labels expected you could sign": *Encyclopedia of Record Producers.*

The Troubador wouldn't book a band unless they saw a picture first: Billy Cioffi and Tom Kidd, "Beauty of the Beast: The Metal Mentality," *Music Connection,* May 26–June 8, 1986.

p. 271: "There's a lot of bands": Karen Burch, "Stairway to Heavy," *Music Connection,* May 26–June 8, 1986.

"Now we look [back]": Chris Sumner, "The Wisdom of Oz," *High Times,* March 1999.

"There's a lot of bands out there": Lloyd Lea, Lisa Fleming, "A Poison Sampler," *It's All Over* fanzine, summer 1986.

"Write a Poem and Win": *Poison, Warrant, and Other Hard Rockin' Bands.*

Poison didn't want to be accessible, and following: AI, Hantas. One published example of Bret Michaels blowing people off is in a story Beth Nussbaum wrote on the band for *Rock Scene* magazine. At the beginning of the story, she says "I flew all the way to Atlanta and chased Bret halfway across the state of Georgia for two days, trying to get this interview." She reports she had to pull him out of "another cheap soiree" to do the interview. There was also a photo session planned for the story, which Michaels blew off completely. Reprinted in Beth Nussbaum, "Poison's Bret Michaels: The Story About What Happens When Nice Guys Become Famous," *Rock of the '80's II Magazine Special,* 1988.

Sanctuary's suit against Poison: Jon Sutherland, "Toxic Shock: Poison Swallow the Antidote to Success," *BAM,* June 3, 1988.

Bryn Bridenthal getting thrown out of party, sued band and won: Adrianne Stone, "Inside Axl Rose's Turbulent World," *Circus,* January 31, 1989.

Axl considered Bridenthal a maternal figure: The Editors of Rolling Stone, *Takin' Care of Business: Rolling Stone 30th Anniversary Issue: Women of Rock,* November 13, 1997.

pp. 271–272: She had to plead with the members of GNR not to beat up members of Poison: Stone, "Inside Axl Rose's Turbulent World."

"Make the lawsuit worth our while": Sutherland, "Toxic Shock."

The beginnings of the Cathouse: AI, Joseph Brooks.

What bands the Cathouse played and "When I'd put on": AI, Brooks.

"The Cathouse was our club": AI, Slash.

"Steve was in the DJ booth often": AI, Brooks.

p. 273: Bon Jovi and Skid Row started coming to the Cathouse: AI, Brooks.

Rikki Ratchman got the *Headbanger's Ball* gig through Axl: Marc Spitz, "Just a Little Patience," *Spin,* July 1999.

"The Cathouse was": AI, Del James.

"We did for rock and roll": "Twenty Questions with Rikki Rachtman," *Metal Sludge,* 9/14/99.

Joseph Brooks owned Vinyl Fetish and Izzy came in to tell him about his new band: AI, Brooks.

Details of Brooks trying to get Zutaut to come see the band: AI, Brooks.

He left after several songs so no one would think he was interested in signing them: Farr, *Moguls and Madmen.*

pp. 273–274: It wasn't until Zutaut wanted to sign them that other labels took notice: AI, Slash.

Proffer and Stanley were interested in producing the band: Sugerman, *Appetite for Destruction.*

When Stanley tried to rewrite several of the band's songs: Chris Gill, "Young Guns," *Guitar World,* January 2000.

"Anyone tried to 'produce' us": AI, Slash.

Clink began his career, and following: AI, Mike Clink.

Clink needed to produce a young band to prove himself, and "It takes a certain drive": AI, Ross Hogarth.

UFO was cool; Survivor was not: AI, Clink.

They recorded a demo to see if they could get along, and following: AI, Clink.

pp. 274–275: "Me and Izzy had a pretty steady": AI, Slash.

The label figured it would be cheaper to drop the band: Sugerman, *Appetite for Destruction.*

The album's cost: AI, Clink.

Zutaut asked Alan Niven to manage the band: Sugerman.

"When you have a band": J. D. Considine, "Off the Record: Guns N' Roses Appetite for Destruction," *Guitar World,* December 1996.

"If it ain't broke": AI, Slash.

p. 276: "It's something that": Andy Widders-Ellis, "Slash: The Hands Behind the Hype," *Guitar Player,* December 1991.

"We don't hide anything": Jeanne Marie Laskas, "On the road with Guns N' Roses," *Life,* December 1, 1992.

"A friend of mine thought it was about": AI, Slash.

"because that's how Axl perceived me": AI, Michelle Young.

"Me and Duff used to take," and following: AI, Slash.

p. 277: The band getting kicked out of the Oakwoods: AI, Slash.

Tom Zutaut's version of how Guns broke on MTV: Marc Spitz, "Just a Little Patience," *Spin,* July 1999.

Coury's version of how Guns got on MTV: AI, Coury. Jon Sutherland also mentioned to me that he had one of the singles with the "Don't Report This Record" sleeve.

p. 278: How getting Guns N' Roses on MTV broke them on Top 40, then AOR: AI, Coury.

"You heard 'em here first": Sugerman. "You heard 'em here first" was something MTV would say on commercials telling viewers what bands they could expect to see on the network, and they would usually use that catch-phrase on bands after they'd broken through.

The first song KNAC played on January 8, 1986: Bob Nalbandian, interview with program director Jimmy Christopher, *Aardshok,* Fall 1986.

Lars Ulrich felt KNAC was the best commercial station in the United States: Cummings, "Road Warriors."

DJ's liked to play "Rime of the Ancient Mariner" when they wanted to smoke a joint: AI, KNAC DJ Moshin' John.

Metal fans would drive well out of their way, and following information about KNAC and its merchandise: AI, Tom Maher, who worked at KNAC for a number of years before going to work for Guns N' Roses manager Doug Goldstein.

p. 279: "There was this momentum": AI, Del James.

Back at the hotel after the show, "That's fucked up": AI, Vinni Stiletto, who was at the hotel after the show.

p. 280: Steven Tyler felt he was looking in a mirror: Davis, "Walk This Way."

"It was okay to be drinking away": Smith, *Off the Record.*

Only soda and nonalcoholic daiquiris were served backstage, and a roadie was fired for having a beer: AI, John Harrell, who's worked for Aerosmith for many years.

"and they'd sound fucking amazing": Mick Wall, "In Too Deep," *Classic Rock,* June 2001.

The band wrote the song in a few minutes, most of the band thought it would be filler: Sugerman.

The song was recorded in one take: Spitz, "Just a Little Patience"; also confirmed in AI, Clink.

p. 281: "This Year's Mandatory": *Musician: The Year in Music* special issue, 1988.

Slash came up with the riff as a joke and never liked the song: AI, Slash.

He hated the fact that after touring for a year: Neely, "Guns N' Roses," *Rolling Stone,* September 5, 1991.

Bands like Winger and Extreme knew their music had to fit a time frame and envied GNR for pulling it off: Alan DiPerna, "Power Trio," *Guitar World,* May 1990.

Rolling Stone were going to put Aerosmith on the cover, then went with GNR, and "suddenly the opening act": Davis, "Walk This Way."

"the biggest piece of shit," and "Oh man, I love that band": AI, Clink.

"Rock 'n' roll is not": AI, Browde.

p. 282: "Kids may envy or idolize": Rob Tannenbaum, "The Hard Truth About Guns N' Roses," *Rolling Stone,* November 17, 1988.

"Rock music goes through": Beebee, *Headbanger's Ball.*

"As long as I'm playing": AI, Slash.

Axl threatened to jump ship and pump gas: Tannenbaum.

Goldstein had to hide negative reviews: Marc Spitz, "Just a Little Patience," *Spin,* July 1999.

p. 283: "Axl was always neurotic": AI, Young.

"Sam was the type": AI, DeVille.

"everyone just became," and Spago story: Laurel Fishman, "Sam Kinison: The Last Laugh," *RIP,* October 1992.

p. 284: C.C. sunbathing naked and threatening to hire people to run around naked, and DeVille doesn't recall: AIs, Ace Steele and DeVille.

He would jam at six in the morning, and letters of complaints shoved under his door: AI, DeVille.

DeVille's bed caught on fire: Uncredited, "Who's the Man?", *Stuff,* October 2000.

"I ask myself": AI, DeVille.

Axl's explanation of the "One In a Million" lyrics and "There are a large number": Del James, "Axl Rose: The Rolling Stone Interview," *Rolling Stone,* August 10, 1989.

p. 285: GNR had complete control over their music: David Sheff, "Playboy Interview: David Geffen," *Playboy,* September 1994.

"['One in a Million'] was taken exactly": AI, Slash.

Gay groups pressured David Geffen to drop the band, and he reportedly received death threats: Fred Goodman, *Mansion on the Hill,* Random House, 1997.

Izzy Stradlin learned the hard way: Nick Kent, "Losing Their Illusions," *Details,* December 1991.

"I don't think there was": Harold Steinblatt, "Vivid Imagination," *Guitar World,* June 1990.

Slash was also criticized by his family: Rowland, "Appetite for Reconstruction."

"We just let": Kent, "Losing Their Illusions."

p. 286: Drug addiction in Thin Lizzy and the details of Gorham's last meetings with Lynott: AI, Scott Gorham.

Sykes told Lynott he was going to take him to the hospital, and following: AI, Sykes.

"People don't realize": AI, Gorham.

"I always looked up to Phil": AI, John Sykes.

CHAPTER 10: LIVIN' ON A PRAYER

p. 288: "I'll never be satisfied": Susan Orlean, "The Kids Are Alright," *Rolling Stone,* May 21, 1987.

"the third song, second verse": Laurel Fishman, "Hail! Hail! The Gang's All Here (Almost)," *RIP,* May 1989.

pp. 288–289: Lizzy Borden playing in Japan and Mike Davis quotes: AI, Mike Davis.

"A lot of artists": AI, Jim Lewis.

"Van Halen's best-ever period": AI, Joe Elliott.

pp. 289–290: "I remember they were doing": AI, Bruce Kulick.

Jon Bon Jovi's early years, his relationship with cousin Tony Bongiovi, and

Jon and David changing their names: Orlean; Rob Tannenbaum, "Bon Voyage," *Rolling Stone,* February 9, 1989.

Jon came to the label every day, and "When I first met Jon": AI, Lewis. All subsequent Lewis quotes from AI.

p. 291: "a heavy metal Shaun Cassidy": Deirdre Donahue, "Bon Jovi's Pretty Metal," *USA Today,* September 19, 1988.

"We never set out": Ian Cronna, editor, *The Rock Yearbook 1988,* St. Martin's Press, 1988. Bon Jovi entry written by David Keeps.

"If you want to torture me": Christine Muhlke, "Man of Style: Bon Jovi," *In Style,* May 2000.

"back then, we singlehandedly": Evgina Peretz, "Bon Jovi Does Hollywood," *Vanity Fair,* May 2000.

When he finally cut his hair: Ibid.

"He's a great star": AI, Lewis.

"Doc McGhee fought": AI, Steve Pritchett.

p. 292: Cinderella didn't generate a lot of excitement at PolyGram and following: AI, Lewis.

Jon did every bit of press, and following: AI, Lewis.

Offered Bon Jovi to play *Saturday Night Live:* Orlean.

Child and Jon originally wrote the song for Loverboy: Craig Rosen, *Billboard Book of Number One Albums.*

p. 293: Jon would let no other radio station promote the concert, and "Even when we weren't": AI, Tom Maher.

Bon Jovi opened for .38 Special, then .38 opened for them: AI, Pritchett.

"There was a need by the people for a Bon Jovi": Tannenbaum, "Bon Voyage."

"Bon Jovi really paved the way": Susan Spillman, "Heavy Metal Bangs Into the Mainstream," *USA Today,* September 17, 1987.

"the pivotal moment": AI, Kalodner.

In June 1987: Steve Pond, "Full-Metal Racket," *Rolling Stone,* August 13, 1987.

p. 294: Cinderella broke first: Ibid.; King, *The Operator.*

"We had our first real": Allison Stewart, "Bon Jovi: Video Interview," cdnow.com.

Tom Hulett signed Warrant and told a friend: AI, Pritchett, who was the friend Hulett told this to.

Kiss tried to follow Bon Jovi to the letter, and "Did Bon Jovi do it?": Lendt, *Kiss and Sell.*

"Mötley were Doc's": AI, Foglio.

In Foglio's view, and following: AI, Foglio.

p. 295: "They looked at us as": Malcolm Dome, "Long Gone Jon," *Raw,* September 5–18, 1990.

pp. 295–296: Sabo and Bach background information: David Wild, "Pretty Bad Boys," *Rolling Stone,* September 19, 1991.

pp. 295–296: "We need to find you," and following details on the formation of Skid Row, the White Castle parking lot brawl, and signing to Atlantic: AI, Rob Affuso. All subsequent Affuso quotes: AI, Affuso.

Kalodner came close to signing Skid Row: AI, Affuso. Confirmed by AI, Kalodner.

Wagener knew they had a hit record, and "all the lights were on green": AI, Wagener.

"What the fuck are you guys thinking?": AI, Affuso. Bon Jovi had also spoken about changing his own band's image in Muhlke, "Bon Jovi: Man of Style": "On our first two albums, we thought that the way to be was to imitate Ratt and Mötley Crüe. It wasn't until our third album that we realized, The hell with this. Go home, be who you are. And fortunately for us, that has helped the longevity of the band." He also said he wanted the cover of the *Slippery When Wet* album to just have the band's logo and the album title because as one report put it, he was tired of photos that 'make us look like chicks.' ": David Handelman, "Bon Jovi Makes Good with 'A Bad Name,' " *Rolling Stone,* November 20, 1986.

p. 297: Wagener predicted the album would sell three million: AIs, Affuso and Wagener.

Bon Jovi had Skid Row's publishing: Confirmed in "Wild, Pretty Bad Boys" and "Twenty Questions With Dave 'The Snake' Sabo," *Metal Sludge,* 4/18/00.

Sambora reportedly gave his share back, Sabo claimed the band didn't get any money back: "Wild, Pretty Bad Boys" and "Twenty Questions."

"We basically signed": "Twenty Questions."

pp. 297–298: Incident backstage with Jon and Sebastian: "Twenty Questions"; also confirmed in AI, Affuso.

The songwriting core of Skid Row, and Bach trying to write made them uncomfortable: AI, Affuso.

"It's not a fuckin' song": AI, Affuso.

AIDS Kills Fags Dead T-shirt one of their lowest points: "Twenty Questions" and AI, Affuso. In response to the incident, Bach would say in Wild's story: "People hand me shirts all the time. I didn't realize then that anybody gave a shit about what it says on my chest. Now I know. I'm sorry."

p. 299: The news of Allen losing his arm on New Year's reaching Joe Elliott, and following details: Beebee, *Headbanger's Ball.*

Joe took a 180-mile drive, and following: AI, Joe Elliott.

Allen's arm was sewn back on, then removed when infection set in: *Def Leppard: Behind the Music Special.*

"You can't help thinking": AI, Elliott.

"That's the thing that upset": David Fricke, "To Hell and Back," *Rolling Stone*, April 30, 1992.

Lange visited Allen and encouraged him, Allen went home six weeks, was supposed to be in for six months: AI, Elliott.

"They really stuck by": AI, Tom Allom.

pp. 299–300: The further problems that plagued the *Hysteria* album: Dennis Hunt, "From Hot to Cold to *Hysteria*," *Los Angeles Times*, November 22, 1987.

"All those delays": Ibid.

"He spent," and following: AI, Elliott.

"Why can't a rock band have an album": AI, Elliott.

"Don't Ask": Lars Ulrich was photographed wearing one of these shirts on the cover of *Music Connection* magazine, May 26–June 8, 1986.

The band had to sell five million to break even: *Behind the Music Special*.

pp. 300–301: "There was a lot of pressure": AI, Lewis.

"The audience was ready": AI, Elliott.

Hysteria's progress on the American charts: AI, Elliott. Confirmed in *Billboard Book of Top 40 Albums and Singles*.

The success story of the "Pour Some Sugar on Me" single, the story behind the first video, why it became a live video, and Elliott quotes: AI, Elliott.

p. 302: "We finally": AI, Elliott.

"It was a nightmare": Rosen, *Billboard Book of Number One Albums*.

The band getting sneaked in under the stage in the laundry bins, Rick Allen walking down the aisle in disguise, and "We know you're in there!": AI, Elliott.

Clark trying to break his hands: *Behind the Music*.

pp. 302–303: "Steve was the first": AI, Elliott.

Clark's blood alcohol level: Fricke, "To Hell and Back."

Clark writing the riff for "Wasted" on the bus story: AI, Elliott.

For four guys who never finished high school: Ben Liemer, "Mötley Crüe: Smokin' in the Studio," *Circus*, October 31, 1986.

"The band was definitely running on": AI, Ross Hogarth.

p. 304: Locklear partly married Lee out of rebellion: Rob Tannenbaum, "Venus de Melrose," *Details*, October 1994.

Aaron Spelling just about had a heart attack: Jodie Gould, *Heather!*, Citadel Press, 1995.

Sixx relationship with Vanity fell apart from mutual drug use: *The Dirt*.

Vanity later became a born-again Christian: Sarah Cristobal and Michael Martin, "Where Are They Now?", *Gear*, November 2000.

Mötley emptying out the Candy Cat, Mick's porno setup, and "They were his inspiration": AI, Hogarth.

Saunders: AI, Hogarth.

Mötley's visit to Rick's Cabaret and blowing through $1,000 in 45 minutes: AI, Byron Hantas.

Neil starting a fight so he could get to the Doll House: AI, Larry Morand.

p. 305: Mötley was relatively sober on tour with Whitesnake: AI, Sarzo.

Details of Nikki Sixx's o.d. and near-death experience: Charrie Foglio, "The New Age of Mötley Crüe," *RIP*, August 1989; Sylvie Simmons, "Good Times, Bad Times," *Raw*, October 4–17, 1989; Marc Spitz, "Just a Little Patience," *Spin*, July 1999; *Behind the Music Special*.

"What are you gonna do now?": Margaret Moser and Bill Crawford, *Rock Stars Do the Dumbest Things*, Renaissance Books, 1998.

pp. 305–306: Part of Vince getting fired was not staying sober: AI, Foglio.

Neil getting into bar brawls thinking people were hitting on Sharise: In an interview with Gerry Gittleson in *Rock City News*, August 18–September 1, 1990, Maglieri said Vince had to get kicked out of the Rainbow because he'd fight with people he thought was "goosing his old lady." Neil bar brawl incidents are also recalled in *The Dirt*.

"The band wanted to be more serious": AI, Foglio.

Mötley blasted Tom Werman in the press: Simmons, "Good Times, Bad Times." Sixx also insulted Werman in the band's book, *The Dirt*, although it's hard to imagine why Mötley did three albums with him in a row if they didn't think he was a good producer or didn't think he knew what he was doing.

"I think we had gone": AI, Werman.

p. 307: Led Zeppelin offered $100 million to reunite: Robert LaFranco, "Retread Rock," *Forbes*, September 23, 1996.

Plant wouldn't perform Zeppelin songs for years: Davis, *Hammer of the Gods*.

"You better": AI, Kalodner.

Whitesnake had played out the European market: Uncredited, "Through the Years With David Coverdale," *Rock Beat*, June 1988.

Sykes wanted to give Whitesnake a hot new sound: AI, John Sykes.

It was Kalodner's idea to update "Here I Go Again": AIs, John Sykes and John Kalodner.

p. 308: "I had pretty much most of the music": Katherine Turman, "Investigating Blue Murder," *RIP*, August 1989.

Coverdale had a sinus infection: *Rock Beat*, June 1988.

Sykes and Kalodner say Kalodner was psychologically blocked: AIs, Kalodner and Sykes.

Album took eighteen months, Coverdale $3 million in debt: Coverdale and Stix, "Lordship Right Here."

Sykes rushed back into the studio to cut his solos: Uncredited Sykes bio on www.johnsykes.com.

"[Coverdale] wanted to go at it alone": Turman, "Investigating Blue Murder." Sykes wasn't thrilled about this, and following: AI, Sykes.

"They were like Milli Vanilli": AI, Callner.

Coverdale had never met most of the musicians until the day of the video shoot: AI, Kalodner.

Callner decided to add another element to the video: AIs, Callner and Sarzo.

p. 309: "The manager told me": AI, Callner.

Other rock stars who were in relationships with Tawny Kitaen: Michael Roche, "Tawny Kitaen: The Kitten Roars," *Chatter,* October 1995.

"He fell head over heels": AI, Al Coury.

"Ten years ago": Karen Schoemer, "Skanks But No Skanks," *Newsweek,* January 13, 1997.

When "Still of the Night" became a "Clip of the Week": AI, Callner.

Sarzo recalled the band receiving a telegram from Jimmy Page: AI, Sarzo.

"David Coverversion": Davis, *Hammer of the Gods,* Boulevard Books, 1997 (paperback).

"Up Yours, Robert": Dante Bonutto, "It's a Man's World in Whitesnake," *Raw,* November 29–December 12, 1989.

Formed Blue Murder to try and put a new supergroup together: AI, Carmine Appice.

p. 310: Sykes tried singing: Turman, "Investigating Blue Murder."

The band didn't have management to control finances, had to sell two million to break even, and "John was a great guitarist": AI, Carmine Appice.

"In the past": Alan DiPerna, "Who Killed the Hair Bands," *Musician,* May 1995.

Geffen's sales that year: Dannen, *Hit Men.*

"Whitesnake was our": AI, Coury.

pp. 310–311: Jackson Browne visit and "That's my heavy metal band": John Seabrook, "The Many Lives of David Geffen," *The New Yorker,* February 23–March 2, 1998.

"total faith" and "I don't know this": AI, Kalodner.

"a career-defining moment": Christopher Scapelliti, "Hair Raiser," *Guitar World,* September 1999.

"It was obvious to me": AI, Kalodner.

"It made a big difference": Russell Simmons, "Into the Mainstream," *Newsweek,* June 28, 1999.

Callner had seen the Run-DMC video and wanted to work with Aerosmith: AI, Callner.

p. 312: The "Censored" black bars and "it's much more titillating": AI, Callner.

Aerosmith had a love/hate relationship, and following: AI, Callner.

"less interesting three": Johnny Angel, "Kickin' Back with Jack Douglas," knac.com, February 28, 2000.

"He would hold the album up": AI, Coury.

pp. 312–313: "Making an Aerosmith record": Davis, *Walk This Way*.

The Boys Next Door could have been the influence for *Beavis and Butt-head*: Michael Weldon, "Reviews," *Psychotronic* 31, 1999.

"They gave it a real human drama": J. D. McCulley, "Love Among the Ruins," *BAM*, June 3, 1988.

p. 314: Details of how Chris Holmes got into *Decline and Fall II*: AI, Holmes. Holmes dialog in *Decline and Fall II* is taken directly from the film.

p. 315: "I've seen nothing": *California Magazine*, June 1988.

One of the poser musicians rode around in a limo: AI, Browde.

Chris Holmes came to the premiere and following: *L.A. Weekly*, June 10, 1988.

They had to shoot the right side of Nadir's face: AI, Nadir D'Priest.

pp. 315–316: Jeff Duncan says, and "Fat, drunk and stupid": AI, Jeff Duncan. Jon Sutherland, who was at the premiere, recalled the crowd reaction being akin to something like a "collective groan."

"I couldn't believe": Tolinski, "The Good, the Bad, The Ozzy!"

The after-party at Miles Copland's mansion: AIs, Jon Sutherland and Byron Hantas; *L.A. Weekly*, June 10, 1988.

Lizzy Grey was bitter and following: AI, Grey.

"I sure hope so": AI, D'Priest.

"I thought it was": AI, Gene Allen.

"Penelope had the right": AI, D'Priest.

Many critics called it: Reviews of the film that said this include a review by Stephen Fried for *GQ* quoted in the newspaper ads ("It's hard to watch *Decline and Fall Part II* without being reminded of Rob Reiner's hilarious *This Is Spinal Tap*"), Janet Maslin's review of the film in the *New York Times*, which appeared June 17, 1988 and said it would make the perfect companion piece to *Tap*, and Michael Weldon's review of the film in *The Psychotronic Video Guide* (St. Martin's Press, 1996), which said it would make a "perfect double bill" with *Tap*.

pp. 316–317: Details of Doc McGhee bust: Farr, "Moguls and Madmen"; Tannebaum, "Bon Voyage".

"We called it": AI, Affuso.

According to Tommy Lee, and following: *The Dirt*; Charrie Foglio, *Rockin' in Russia Collector's Issue*, Tempo Publishing, 1989; AI, Foglio, who was at the event.

"I don't expect to come to": Cassette copy of Ozzy Osbourne interview with KNAC deejay Tawn Mastery, provided to the author by Bob Nalbandian.

p. 318: "I can't help wondering": Dome, "Long Gone Jon."

It was the same club where they opened for Ratt in 1982: Crocker.

The bands got along on a personal level, and following: AI, Pilson.

Chemical camaraderie, and "Got any?": AI, Pilson.

"They were partyers": Doughton, *Metallica Unbound.*

pp. 318–319: Details and logistics of the Monsters tour, what some promoters lost, and "Promoters are praying": Keith Moerer and Dave Zimmer, "The Belly of the Beast," *BAM,* July 1, 1988.

A riot broke out during "Creeping Death": Steve Hochman, "From Monsters to a Quiet Charmer," *Los Angeles Times,* July 26, 1988. The author was also at the L.A. Monsters of Rock gig and saw the riot happen first hand.

"[Metallica] confirmed its reputation": Hochman, "From Monsters to a Quiet Charmer."

"Dokken was so disheveled": AI, Pilson.

"Going on after Metallica": AI, Lynch.

p. 320: The fight in the limo: Foglio, "The Demise of Dokken."

"Don could gain his," and following: AI, Lynch.

The band sued Don from using the name Dokken: AI, Pilson.

"We took the brass ring": "Twenty Questions with Mick Brown," *Metal Sludge,* 2/5/02.

CHAPTER 11: SLAVE TO THE GRIND

p. 322: "Back in the '80s": AI, Vinnie Appice.

The U.S. tour for *Dr. Feelgood* gross: Steffan Chirazi, "All SCrüed Up?!", *Kerrang!* 505.

Neal Preston called the "Dr. Feelgood" show, and following: AI, Preston.

Mötley now had eleven trucks, and overhead figure: AI, Doug Thaler.

The stage rap scripts: Handleman, "Money for Nothing and the Chicks For Free."

"Whew!": This is what Neil said, word for word, in between a song on the Dr. Feelgood tour. Dialogue taken from a video shoot of a Dr. Feelgood tour show in New Jersey.

p. 323: Vince didn't know any of the words to "Jailhouse Rock": Bill Kinison and Steve Delsohn, *Brother Sam,* William Morrow, 1994.

Doug Thaler reminded them: AI, Thaler.

"It gets to a point": *It Came From the Eighties: Metal Goes Pop!*

pp. 323–324: Warrant's beginnings and Erik Turner and Jerry Dixon quotes: AIs, Erik Turner and Jerry Dixon.

Femme Fatale were barely together for ten gigs: AIs Turner and Dixon, "Twenty Questions with Lorraine Lewis," *Metal Sludge,* 4/23/02.

According to Jeff Stein: AI, Jeff Stein.

p. 325: "It was a lot of fun": AI, Bobbie Brown.

Rolling Stone awarded it Worst Video, and Stein wore it like a badge of honor: AI, Stein.

Hill bringing Winger's demos to Doug Morris and how they eventually got signed: AI, Beau Hill.

p. 326: "Those guys delivered": AI, Hill.

"Metal's New Stud": This was on the cover of the July 1989 issue of *RIP*.

"Kip Winger like you've never seen him before": The cover of *Playgirl* where Kip appeared was reprinted in "Twenty Questions with Kip Winger," *Metal Sludge*, 11/27/01.

"I remember sitting": Paul, "The Down Boys."

Beavis and Butt-Head had the same complaint: AI, John Corabi.

"I think they represent": Tom Shales, "David Letterman: Playboy Interview," *Playboy*, January 1994.

p. 327: "The kids want [to hear]": AI, Hill.

"Tommy was a fan": AI, Brown.

Beavis and Butt-head helped White Zombie break, Alago's experiences with White Zombie, and "Mike just took": AI, Alago.

p. 328: "We probably": Fricke, "Metallica."

"You guys have never": Ibid.

Buy Product, Metallica Sucks: Mark Putterford, *Guns N' Roses: Over the Top,* Omnibus, 1993.

"I know we're Number 1": Fricke, "Metallica."

"My favorite": AI, Pilson.

pp. 328–329: "I still like Metallica," and "Obviously, we are not": Robert Hilburn, "Metallica's Voyage to the Mainstream," *Los Angeles Times,* October 27, 1991.

"In one aspect": AI, Oimen.

"I had never listened to a Metallica record": AI, Kalodner.

Lars started wearing a white leather jacket, and "Starz Ulrich": Uncredited, "Viva Rock Stars," *Spin,* April 1999.

Ulrich and Hammett's spoils of success: AI, Kornarens, David Fricke, "Married to Metal," *Rolling Stone,* May 18, 1995; Steffan Chirazi, "Captain Kirk," *Guitar,* August 1999.

pp. 329–330: Hollywood Records buying the Queen catalog and Peter Paterno quotes: AI, Peter Paterno.

"My high-level sources": Lonn Friend, "Ear Candy," *RIP,* September 1989.

Before any bands were announced to perform, 72,000 tickets sold in two hours: AI, Paterno.

p. 331: Queen arguing whether Liza Minnelli was right to sign "We Are the Champions," and following: AI, Neal Preston, who was the official photographer for the show.

"There is definitely a lot": Chuck Phillips and Steve Hochman, "Sex, Drugs, Rock . . . and AIDS," *Los Angeles Times,* November 26, 1991.

"There's always that feeling of": AI, Reiff.

"For a few years": AI, Morand.

Robbin Crosby announced he had AIDS: Frank Meyer, "Robbin Crosby Fighting AIDS," knac.com, July 13, 2001.

p. 332: Crosby's drug addiction would cost him, and "The best thing I can say is": AI, Robbin Crosby.

Axl moved into the Record Plant and smoked pot to relieve his stress: Jeanne Marie Laskas, "On the Road with Guns N' Roses," *Life,* December 1, 1992; Del James, "I, Axl," *RIP,* September 1993.

Axl damaged the house: Spitz, "Just a Little Patience"; Sugerman.

Axl wanted to break the cycle: Spitz; Wilkinson, "The Lost Years."

"As the Stones would say": Del James, "Here Today, Gone to Hell (And Lovin' It)," *RIP,* September 1991.

Don Henley filled in on drums: Sugerman.

p. 333: Numerous takes had to be edited together: Lonn Friend, "Guns N' Roses from the Inside," *RIP,* March 1992.

After two weeks, he was fired: Sugerman.

Slash finding Matt Sorum at the Universal Amphitheater: Friend and Ressner.

Adler complained in a band full of junkies: Sugerman.

Adler won a settlement of $2.5 million: Nick Kent, "Who's Afraid of Axl Rose?," *Icon,* October 1997.

Adler would watch Slash tapping his foot: Rowland, "Appetite for Reconstruction."

"had a big effect on the camaraderie," and "what held us together": Robert Cherry, "Rock of Ages," *Guitar One,* June 2002.

"We were the only five guys": AI, Slash.

"It was a long process": *Encyclopedia of Record Producers.*

p. 334: The album took a year and a half to record, and following: AI, Clink.

"There was so much good music": AI, Coury.

Originally *Appetite* was going to be a double album: Adrianne Stone, "Inside Axl Rose's Turbulent World," *Circus,* January 31, 1989.

The band released a double album because no one was sure if there would be another album: Rowland, "Appetite for Reconstruction."

Slash watching the fans file in to buy the album at Tower where he was busted as a kid: AI, Slash.

First day sales of the *Use Your Illusions* albums: Steve Hochman, "Marketing Triumph for Guns N' Roses," *Los Angeles Times,* September 18, 1991; Sugerman.

p. 335: "Of course, kids hate hearing that": Rowland, "Appetite for Reconstruction."

"I know Axl had a hard childhood": AI, Young.

Axl's recollections of childhood abuse: Kim Neely, "Axl Rose: The Rolling Stone Interview," *Rolling Stone,* April 2, 1992.

According to one friend, Rose was once beaten so badly: AI, Stiletto.

"We gotta get tougher here": AI, Affuso. All following Affuso quotes are from AI, Affuso.

p. 336: Details about Skid Row on the *Use Your Illusions* tour: AI, Affuso.

Axl fell under the influence of psychics: Farr, *Moguls and Madmen;* Peter Wilkinson, "Axl Rose: The Lost Years," *Rolling Stone,* May 11, 2000.

Tom Zutaut was one of many frozen out: Farr, *Moguls and Madmen.*

"One time we had a meeting": AI, Coury.

Skid Row often had to play extended sets, and following: AI, Affuso; Spitz, "Just a Little Patience."

The tickets didn't have a starting time, only question marks: AI, Affuso.

"If you were getting laid": Kim Neely, "Axl Rose: The Rolling Stone Interview."

p. 337: "When you want to go and you're ready to go": AI, Slash.

Axl demanding the rights to the name or he wouldn't tour: Spitz, "Just a Little Patience." Zutaut's account was also confirmed in Duff McKagan's interview of John Harrell for *Burrn!* magazine, cited with permission. This was also generally confirmed in Wilkinson, "Axl Rose: The Lost Years."

Details of the St. Louis riot: Widders-Ellis, "The Hands Behind the Hype."

As far as he was concerned, the band fulfilled their obligations, and the way the audience behaved: Neely, "Axl Rose: The Rolling Stone Interview."

p. 338: The crowds had never frightened them, and following: Widders-Ellis.

"What's to stop us": Mick Wall, "In Too Deep," *Classic Rock,* June 2001.

"I've been [here] from day one": Ibid. Rose also confirmed he wanted Izzy to accept less money because he didn't feel Izzy was working hard enough in the band in Neely, "Axl Rose: The Rolling Stone Interview."

Details of Forum show: *RIP,* December 1991. The magazine nominated this show as the gig of the year.

"Nirvana has struck a chord": Katherine Turman, "Smells Like Nirvana," *RIP,* February 1992.

Details of the 1992 *RIP* Party: Kim Neely, *Five Against One,* Penguin, 1998; Adrianne Stone, "Gig of the Month: *RIP*'s Fifth Anniversary Blowout," *RIP,* February 1992.

p. 339: "to pay tribute to a band": Neely, *Five Against One.*

Geffen executive John Rosenfelder slipped a copy of *Nevermind*: Charles Cross, *Heavier Than Heaven,* Hyperion, 2001.

Details of the explosion of the *Nevermind* album, and cost of "Teen Spirit" video: Cross, *Heavier Than Heaven*; Mark Binelli, "Anarchy in the U.S.," *Rolling Stone,* September 13, 2001.

"Poison would not be heard from again": Rob Tannenbaum, "The 100 Greatest Music Videos Ever Made," *TV Guide,* December 4, 1999.

"When I saw Nirvana": AI, C. C. DeVille.

Neil said he was fired, the rest of the band said he quit: *Behind the Music Special.*

p. 340: "I watched you during the MTV Rockumentary," and following: "We the Crüeheads: Letters From RIP Readers," *RIP,* June 1992.

"My take on it is": AI, Thaler.

Details of how Corabi joined the band: AI, John Corabi.

p. 341: By one estimate, the album took over a year and cost $2 million: AI, Thaler.

Terms of Aerosmith deal: Huxley, *Aerosmith.*

But as Kalodner maintained, his job wasn't to be their pal: AI, Kalodner.

"The times reflected a change": AI, Callner.

p. 342: Tyler called him after seeing the "Cryin' " video: AI, Callner.

"Aerosmith made a hell of a lot": Rich Cohen, "Ballad of a Teenage Queen," *Rolling Stone,* September 7, 1995.

"We had a great experience with him," and "I never made this deal": AI, Ian.

"The WEA Group," and details of the Mötley Crüe album fairing poorly: AI, Corabi.

p. 343: "Had somebody heard that record": AI, Fahley.

Attendance of Hollywood Palladium show: AI, Thaler.

One show was reportedly canceled: Chirazi, "All Screwed Up?!"

The band's show at the Palladium, "Thanks for sticking around," and "to our record company": The author was present at the Palladium show.

pp. 343–344: "deflated," and "Dude, it was so big": Chirazi, "All Screwed Up?!"

"Whenever you hear that": Uncredited, "Vince Neil: Everyone's Invited to Check Out Exposed," *Kiss Live 1973–1993 Magazine Special.*

"I mean, every possible thing": AI, Corabi. All following Corabi quotes are from AI, Corabi.

p. 345: Neil signed an $18 million dollar solo deal: Alan DiPerna, "Who Killed the Hair Bands?"

The pizza incident: AI, Larry Morand.

Neil said the next time you'd see him: Gerri Miller, "Mötley Crüe: Reunited and Rocking on Generation Swine," *Metal Edge,* July 1997.

Rumored label wouldn't release an album without Vince: "Hearsay Column," *BAM* May 19, 1996.

p. 346: "It doesn't matter who's singing for this band": AI, Corabi.

"It was a band decision": Miller, "Reunited and Rocking on Generation Swine."

The band hoped to sell two and a half million: Neil Strauss, "Shout at the Bouncer," *Spin*, March 1998.

"Well, Pat, does this mean heavy metal is dead": Review of American Music Awards, *Los Angeles Times*, January 29, 1997.

Sales of *Swine*, venues 63 percent full, "Perhaps the fundamental": Strauss, "Shout at the Bouncer."

"I'm not a fucking racist," "a cunt," and "fuck Elektra": Ibid.

pp. 346–347: "Letters to *Spin* Magazine": "Going Postal," *Spin*, June 1998.

"I had to call 911": Suzan Colon, "I'm a Real Drama Mama!", *Jane*, Summer 1998.

He refused to let his kids visit him in jail: Tommy Lee interview with Catherine Crier, *Fox Files* TV show.

Lee recalled punching a woman off her bicycle for calling him a "stupid American," and punching his then girlfriend for calling his mother "a cunt": Dean Kuipers, "Beyond the Valley of the Ultra Glam Boys," *Spin*, January 1990. Anecdote reprinted in *Spin Special Anniversary Issue 1985–2000, April 2000*, and *The Dirt*.

p. 347–348: Neil and Lee fighting in a Vegas airport: AI, John Harrell and Anthony Bozza; "Tommy Lee Q&A," *Rolling Stone*, January 20, 2000.

"He cut off seventeen years": Kate Sullivan, "Exit the Theatre of Pain," *Spin*, January 2000.

The tragedies that struck Mötley Crüe: Vince would lose his daughter: Todd Gold and Vince Neil, "Losing Skylar," *People*, October 16, 1995.

Vince Neil's marriage ended after fifteen months: Knac.com Pure Rock Newswire, 9.2.01.

Vince Neil filed for bankruptcy: Uncredited, "Vince Neil Sues His Lawyers," Rock 'n' Roll World: The Fan's Rock Super Site.

Nikki fell back into heroin and cheated on Donna on the road, drowning accident at Tommy's house: Philip Wilding, "Sixx Appeal," *Classic Rock*, October 2001.

"I hate to say it," and following: AI, John Corabi.

p. 349: Lars Ulrich often flew down: AI, Sutherland.

Both bands had their own stages, and some shows went almost until morning: Jeff Kitts, "Metallica, Guns N' Roses, Faith No More: Why It Didn't Work," *Metal Maniacs*, February 1993.

"I'm getting more and more": Putterford, *Over the Top*.

"Their scene was about": Spitz, "Just a Little Patience."

It was a strong lesson to Metallica: *Behind the Music Special.*

"A guy and some other guys": Fricke, "Don't Tread on Me."

Metallica sold six million copies of the "Black" album during the tour: Farr, *Moguls and Madmen.*

Slash hated playing the power ballads: Slash's hatred of power ballads has been well documented (hence his dislike of "Sweet Child O' Mine"), and when asked in an interview why the first *Snakepit* album didn't have many ballads, he said, "One ballad for me is always enough." Chris Gill, "Snake and Bake," *Guitar Player,* May 1995.

It wasn't fun anymore, and the members of the band stopped speaking to each other on stage: Mike G, Duff McKagan: "A Serious Case of That Beautiful Mind Disease," *Metal Edge,* June 1999.

p. 350: Duff would wake up in the middle of the night, and "Please, let there be": Jeanne Marie Laskas, "On the Road With Guns N' Roses," *Life,* December 1, 1992.

Details of Hetfield's accident during "Fade to Black": Uncredited, "Testing Metallica's Mettle," *People,* November 9, 1992.

Flipping around the stations, he heard about a riot: Fricke, "Don't Tread on Me."

"If anybody here is interested": Putterford, *Over the Top.*

"Sorry, hope you get": Kitts, "Metallica, Guns N' Roses, Faith No More: Why It Didn't Work."

"The kids outside are turning over cop cars": Beebee, *Headbanger's Ball.*

p. 351: It reminded Hammett of Nero fiddling while Rome burned: *Behind the Music Special.*

Hetfield's recovery and return to the tour: "Testing Metallica's Mettle."

"Flames Hetfield": AI, Oimen.

CHAPTER 12: DON'T KNOW WHAT YA GOT 'TIL IT'S GONE

p. 352: From the film *Pulp Fiction,* written and directed by Quentin Tarantino, Miramax, 1994.

Lane seeing the *Alice In Chains* poster and his thoughts: Lorraine Ali, "Devil's Haircut," *Rolling Stone,* August 21, 1997; Di Perna, "Who Killed the Hair Bands?"

Alice In Chains opened for Warrant so the label could see them: AIs, Jerry Dixon and Erik Turner.

Warrant bought a stage in the shape of a giant W: AI, Larry Morand.

Thirty shows in, Lane quit the band: AIs, Jerry Dixon and Erik Turner. All following Warrant information and quotes: AIs, Dixon and Turner.

p. 353: During one ride on their tour bus, and "Basically, what he's telling you guys": AI, Larry Morand.

p. 354: Some tours went seventeen to nineteen months in length: AI, Scotty Ross.

"Toward the end": AI, DeVille.

"Just go on stage": Tom Farrell, "C. C. DeVille: Goodbye Poison, Hello World," *RIP,* July 1991.

The band getting upset with C.C. for dyeing his hair red, and "I knew they were going": Ibid.

"[C.C.] wanted to be taken seriously": Judy Wieder, "Poison: Back on the Attack," *RIP,* October 1992.

p. 355: "With the music Poison": AI, DeVille.

"Normally when you stop": Andrew Dansby, "Poison's C. C. DeVille Returns with Samantha Seven," rollingstone.com., June 10, 2000. Clipping provided by Karen Sundell.

"I'm so glad you're": AI, Maglieri.

"You look back," and "I had everything": Paul, "The Down Boys."

Gene and Paul interview on *Headbanger's Ball:* Taken directly from a copy of *Headbanger's Ball* episode from 1993, where Gene and Paul were promoting the *Alive III* album.

p. 356: "He really cared": AI, Carrie Stevens.

Stanley stayed at a top hotel even though his apartment was in town: AI, Alan Reiff.

Kiss getting in trouble because of tax shelters: Lendt, *Kiss and Sell.*

Jesse Hilsen allegedly took off with the profits and hasn't been seen since: Lendt; Robert LaFranco, "Retread Rock," *Forbes,* September 23, 1996.

"I always felt": AI, Bruce Kulick.

"If *Revenge* had come out": AI, Bruce Kulick.

pp. 357: "I kept asking Gene": AI, Bill Aucoin.

Details of Ace and Peter rejoining Kiss, and "I had enough": AI, Bruce Kulick.

"What hurt the most": AI, Bruce Kulick.

"I would say": Mark Blackwell, "Gene, Gene, the Drivin' Machine," *Bikini,* March 1996.

"pop moron," and "I sold out": Uhelszki, "Confessions of a Kissette."

p. 358: Simmons never got his wish of being on the cover of *Rolling Stone.* Charrie Foglio, who was back working with Doc McGhee when he was managing Kiss, told me that Gene and Paul would have loved to have been on the cover of *Rolling Stone,* and even offered to make her their publicist if she could nail the cover story.

Details of the financial take of the 1996 Kiss reunion tour: LaFranco, "Retread Rock."

Gene charged bands to open for Kiss: Rhoda Penmark, "My Black Pages" column, *The New Times*, October 17–23, 1996; AI, Jon Sutherland, who worked at Metal Blade (Lizzy's label when they were offered the tour); also confirmed in AI, Gene Allen, former Lizzy Borden guitarist.

Published rumor Gene and Paul got $20 million, Ace and Peter got less than $2 million: Edna Gundersen, "Kiss: Ready to Lay One on the U.S.A.," *USA Today*, June 13, 1996; "Hearsay" column, *BAM*, May 3, 1996.

Four guys in a car, two have to sit in the back: R. J. Smith, "It's Alive," *Spin*, August 1996.

Tommy Thayer now in Ace's makeup, Eric Singer now in Peter's: Knac.com Pure Rock Newswire, March 15, 2002; Singer's bio on pearldrums.com, which confirms he's back in Kiss for their endless "farewell" tour; pictures of Eric in Peter's makeup and costumes on kissonline.com

p. 359: "money talks": Geri Miller, "George Lynch: Return of the Mob," *Metal Edge*, May 1999.

"The band self-destructed": AI, Pilson.

Lynch leaving the radio show and Jeff imitating his voice: AI, Pilson.

p. 360: Lynch was fired, then sued the band: Miller, "Return of the Mob."

"Personally": AI, Pilson.

Pilson left Dokken, then reunited with Lynch: Frank Meyer, "Rockin' Without Dokken: Jeff Pilson & George Lynch Unite In New Band," knac.com, November 2, 2001.

"I think there's a": Del James, "I, Axl," *RIP*, September 1993.

Geffen didn't know about the Manson song: Sheff, "Playboy Interview."

p. 360–361: Details of the Erin Everly and Stephanie Seymour lawsuits and settlements: Uncredited, "Bye, Bye Love," *People*, July 18, 1994; Nick Kent, "Who's Afraid of Axl Rose?", *Icon*, October 1997; Wilkinson, "The Lost Years."

Axl threatened to sue Slash: AI, Slash.

"The Wayward Musicians Suffering from LSD": Mike Mettler, "Slash's Snakepit," *Guitar for the Practicing Musician*, April 1995.

Slash leaving the band, and "no more Guns N' Roses": Matt Hendrickson, "Slash Leaves Guns N' Roses," *Rolling Stone*, December 12, 1996.

"I'd be dead by now": Dale Turner, "A Serpent's Tale," *Guitar One*, April 2000.

"a perfect example": "Twenty Questions With Kevin DuBrow," *Metal Sludge*, 7/19/01.

p. 362: At last report, $8 million has been spent: Phil Sutcliffe, "Didn't You Used to Be Axl Rose?", *Q*, July 2001.

"Axl is a guy": AI, Hill.

The tracks were selected and approved with their people as go-betweens: Wilkinson, "The Lost Years."

Former Guns manager Alan Niven believed: Kent, "Who's Afraid of Axl Rose?"

Slash and Stradlin haven't ruled out a reunion, and writing a new album could come in a week: Wall, "In Too Deep."

Rose blamed the breakup on Slash: Kurt Loder, MTV interview with Axl Rose, November 8, 1999.

"There was an effort": David Wild, "Axl Speaks," *Rolling Stone,* February 3, 2000.

pp. 362–363: Details of the Guns N' Roses Vegas gig, and "Good morning": Steve Appleford, "New GNR Gets Right Back in the Jungle," *Los Angeles Times,* January 2, 2001.

Scheduled summer 2001 tour canceled: Frank Meyer, "Guns N' Roses Cancel Euro Tour," knac.com, November 9, 2001.

Hair transplant rumor: Knac.com Pure Rock Newswire, May 10, 2001.

Slash being refused entry to see Guns in Vegas, and Axl being booed for insulting them: Frank Meyer, "Slash Turned Away at Guns N' Roses Vegas Show," knac.com, January 1, 2002; "Sun Tzu, Guns N' Roses Live in Las Vegas," knac.com, December 31, 2001.

Appetite sells 200,000 a year: Wilkinson, "The Lost Years"; and it was also confirmed that the album sells 5,000 copies a week with no promotion: Lyndsey Parker, "Chinese Fire Drill," *Guitar One,* June 2002.

"I heard so many": AI, Slash.

p. 364: "I'm washed up": Schwartz, "Smear Tactics."

"The eternal dudes rock on": Steve Hochman, "The Eternal Dudes Rock On and On," *Los Angeles Times,* April 6, 1995.

p. 365: "He was afraid": H. P. Newquist, "Push Comes to Shove," *Guitar,* January 1997.

Sammy stayed with his wife and the showdown with Eddie over the phone: Huff, "Ain't Talkin' Bout Love."

"I practically begged": Sutherland.

"Everything that Eddie": Huff.

"I've always been a solo artist": Rob Putnam, "Sammy Hagar," *Music Connection,* October 23–November 5, 2000.

p. 366: "The idea was not": Vic Garbarini, "Three of a Perfect Pair," *Guitar World,* March 1998.

Roth was forced to record his vocals in a separate room, and following: Jon Sutherland, "Van Halen," *Shockwaves,* Spring 1997.

"Half the album": Roth, *Crazy from the Heat.*

Van Halen falling apart at the MTV Awards, and David and Eddie fighting backstage: Reconstructed from accounts in Roth, *Crazy from the Heat;* Steven Rosen, "Eruptions," *Guitar World,* December 1996; Chris Willman and Dan Snierson, "Van Wailin'," *Entertainment Weekly,* March 20, 1998.

"I don't need that kind of": Rosen, "Eruptions."

pp. 366–367: "You don't know how much": Newquist, "Push Comes to Shove."

Roth's statement to the press was reprinted in its entirety in *Guitar* magazine, January 1997.

"a communist," and "We made Van Halen": Willman and Snierson.

"Eddie Sucks!": Paul Gargano, "Howard's Not-So-Private Side," *Metal Edge,* July 1997.

"I know they had already": Huff.

pp. 367–368: Eddie denied Cherrone was hired, and following: Willman and Snierson.

"If Gary's in": Ibid.

"I probably wouldn't have been": Greg Heller, "The Sounds of Sammy," *BAM,* March 26, 1999.

According to a report in *Rolling Stone,* and according to a source close to the band on Cherrone's departure: Richard Skause, "In the News," *Rolling Stone,* December 6–23, 1999; confidential source.

Late night meetings at Crazy Girls, and Van Halen with DLR: Frank Meyer, "Van Halen: Diamond Encrusted?," knac.com, January 31, 2000.

p. 369: "made the cancer seem": Frank Meyer, "Eddie Van Halen Comments on DLR Reunion," knac.com, July 10, 2001.

Van Halen lost their deal with Warner Bros: Kevin Raub, "Van Halen, Warner Bros. Records Part Ways After Twenty-five Years," allstarnews.com, January 25, 2001.

"wait for all this Seattle shit": Snowden, "Hair Today, Gone Tomorrow."

According to Rob Affuso: AI, Affuso.

pp. 369–370: Tom Keifer's vocal trouble and the record company told them to change their name and cut their hair: Geri Miller, "Still Climbing," *Metal Edge,* April 1995.

Affuso didn't totally blame, and following: AI, Affuso.

"We could have released": "Twenty Questions with Sabo."

Sabo and Bach had a bad falling out, and following: Ibid.

Affuso was furious with them, and following: AI, Affuso.

The band owed Doc money, which Hill denied: "Twenty Questions with Scotti Hill," *Metal Sludge,* 6/27/00.

p. 371: "You're wasting your time": Rob Brunner, "The Unlikely Return of Jon Rocker," *Entertainment Weekly,* July 21, 2000.

"This is not fun": DiPerna, "Of Life and Def."

p. 372: "I'll tell you right now," and following: AI, Elliott.

Details of Metallica trying to renegotiate their deal, and the lawsuit against Elektra: Stephen Fried, "Bad Vibes in Toon Town," *Vanity Fair,* February 1995;

Chuck Phillips, "Metallica Sues Label Challenging '7 Year' Contract Statute," *Los Angeles Times,* September 28, 1994.

"There were a lot," and following: AI, Paterno.

p. 373: Details of Metallica's new deal with Elektra: Ted Drozdowski, "Heavy Mettle," *Musician,* March 1997.

"The band that set," and "After reading": "The Sounding Board: Letters to *Guitar World*," *Guitar World,* September 1996.

"Admit it": Nick Bowcott, "Headbanger's Ball," *Guitar World,* December 1996.

"If you can step back": AI, Steffan Chirazi.

p. 374: "I believe that you don't": Jason Zasky, "Taking Care of Business," *Musician,* February 1999.

"Most of those hair bands": AI, Quintana.

"I've never seen a band": Tannebaum, "Playboy Interview."

"I have always suspected," and "Reading the Metallica interview": "Dear Playboy," *Playboy,* July 2001.

p. 375: "Whatever I had to do with Metallica": Newsted interview by John Harrell, quoted with permission.

pp. 375–376: "The last record that we made," and "Fuckin' A, we blew it": AI, Croucier.

Warren felt it was a blessing in disguise: Paul, "The Down Boys."

p. 377: "I think these bands can have": Scapelliti.

Pearcy left the group six days before the tour, promoters wanted their money back: Diana DeVille, "Bobby Blotzer from Ratt Spills the Beans," knac.com, February 10, 2000.

Pearcy claimed he didn't quit and wasn't fired: Frank Meyer, "Ratt Attack!!!", knac.com, April 12, 2000.

"I'm not gonna start from scratch": Geri Miller, "Ratt: Out of the Portrait Picture," knac.com, April 18, 2000.

Three members of Great White quit within a year: Frank Meyer, "Swimming With Sharks: Great White Lose Guitarist," knac.com, January 26, 2000; "Twenty Questions with Audie DuBrow," *Metal Sludge,* 9/26/00.

W.A.S.P./Motörhead fight: Uncredited, "For Immediate Release," *Rock City News,* July 24, 1997.

p. 378: "All those bands from the '80s": AI, Kalodner.

"Never forget your past": A full-page ad for Portrait Records with this tagline appeared in *L.A. Weekly,* July 2–8, 1999.

Dio refused to open for Ozzy: Stark.

Halford had to crouch on one knee and squint his eyes to see the lyrics: AI, Vinnie Appice.

p. 379: One critic made fun of the fact: Darryl Morden, Ozzfest '99 review, *Hollywood Reporter,* July 26, 1999. The reunited Sabbath performed at the Ozzfest that summer.

"Tony is still one of the": Jones.

"We rehearsed in some," and "And it was nice to": AI, Vinnie Appice.

"The scene changed," and following: AI, Brooks.

pp. 379–380: Details of the end of KNAC: Michael Wolffe, "KNAC's Final Fade to Black," *Los Angeles Times,* March 6, 1995.

KNAC signed off without a moment of silence: AI, KNAC DJ Anabella Marie Canto.

"the call letters of my youth": Wolffe.

What bands can make on the L.A. club circuit: AI, Jimmy D.

"There's been talk": AI, Jimmy D.

pp. 380–381: The changes in the Japanese market: AIs, Roy Z and John Harrell.

Bach blamed MTV for illiteracy: Snowden, "Hair Today, Gone Tomorrow."

"I think MTV": Dr. Fiorella Terenzi, "Steve Vai: Pretty Vai for a White Guy," knac.com, January 25, 2000.

"spoon-fed": This complaint was raised by Trixter's former manager, Chip Ruggieri, in Di Perna, "Who Killed the Hair Bands?"

"I think the pros": AI, Callner.

GIT's peak enrollment, and declining enrollment in 1997: Mark Small, "GIT: A Day in the Life," *Guitar Player,* August 1989; Joe Gore, "Declining Enrollment: Why Are Young Musicians Skipping School?", *Guitar Player,* September 1997.

"Rock stars were heroes": Tom Beaujour, "Metal Memories with Reb Beach," *Guitar World,* September 1999.

p. 382: "I can go": AI, McBurnie.

"Lemme buy ya a drink": AI, Sutherland, who was at the bar.

"I gotta tell ya": AI, Maglieri.

pp. 382–383: "A lot of the guys": confidential source.

"On Friday": AI, Alan Reiff.

"Let's put it this way": AI, Vicky Hamilton.

Bands like Iron Maiden had secret pouches, and following: AI, Anna Cartwright, a costume designer who worked with numerous metal bands, including Maiden and others.

"You have to use one sock": AI, Harrell.

"It was all the bands": Brunner, "The Unlikely Return of Jon, Rocker."

p. 384: "It wasn't real sincere": *It Came from the Eighties: Metal Goes Pop!*

"I wasn't really happy": Ibid.

"I was known as the metal guy": Snowden, "Hair Today, Gone Tomorrow."

Soundgarden made it clear during their acceptance speech: Ibid.

"not even slightly": Alec Foege, "The End of the Innocence: Chris Cornell," *Rolling Stone,* December 29, 1994–January 12, 1995.

"Eddie Vedder dressed up": Neely, *Five Against One.*

"Revenge of the Nerds": Snowden, "Hair Today, Gone Tomorrow."

p. 385: "A lot of bands from the '80s": AI, Sutherland.

"I kind of thought": AI, Werman.

"You probably sold": AI, Paul Shortino.

p. 386: "It's unfortunate that": Friend, John Kalodner A&R Guru.

"It's so much harder," and following: AI, Ian.

ACKNOWLEDGMENTS

THE WORLD OF HEAVY METAL was a hard one to penetrate and commit to paper, in fact this book went through a very tough, and often painful birth. A number of doors slammed in my face, research materials were hard to locate, and I had to overcome a number of obstacles to get to the finish this project.

Yet it seemed that for every door that was slammed in my face, there was another person who was willing to help me generously. First of all, without the incredibly kind and selfless efforts of Jon Sutherland, this book never would have been written. Jon was always available to speak to me, helped tremendously with locating research material I couldn't have found elsewhere, helped me reach and locate numerous people, and steered me into many great directions I never would have gone in without him. Thanks a million Jon, I hope you like the end result. I also have to give tremendous thanks to John Harrell, who has been very generous with sharing information (John allowed me to quote from several excellent interviews he did for *Burrn!* magazine, which include talks with Slash, Duff McKagan, and Jason Newsted) and has always there to make me laugh when I needed it. This book also wouldn't have come to be if it weren't for the help of Dan Starr, who through the many hours we spent talking about the music we loved, and telling me his memories of the 1970s and 1980s, inspired me to write this book in the first place. I am also honored to have the incredible photographs of Neil Zlozower, who in my view is the best metal / hard rock photographer there is, and John Harrell, in this book. I cannot thank all of you enough for everything you contributed to this project. And without the help of Paul

Duran, who is without question the best collaborator I've ever worked with, this book never would have been finished in a timely manner, or finished at all for that matter. Also thanks to Vera Anderson for her kindness and for letting me quote from her interview with Cameron Crowe. I also have to thank several publicists and friends who helped open a number of doors for me, and helped get me to crucial people I interviewed. I owe a tremendous debt to Doreen and Hernando Courtwright, Kelly Hammett, Ann Leighton, Rhonda Saenz, Karen Sundell, and Sue Tropio at Q-Prime, thanks to you all.

I spoke to many people during the course of this project, and this book could never have been written without their memories, insights and candor. I would especially like to thank Rob Affuso, Tom Allom, Vinnie Appice, Bill Aucoin, Marshall Berle, John Bush, Marty Callner, John Christ, John and Val Corabi, Al Coury, Kevin DuBrow, Joe Elliott, Bob Ezrin, Cherie Foglio, Scott Gorham, Byron Hantas, Beau Hill, Scott Ian, John Kalodner, Bruce Kulick, Mark Leialoha, Jim Lewis, Dave Lombardo, Mario Maglieri, Tom Maher, Larry Morand, Harald Ormen, Jeff Pilson, Tony Platt, Fritz Postelwaite, Neal Preston, Ron Quintana, Rudy Sarzo, Claude Schnell, Billy Sheehan, Slash (thank you for going the extra mile), Dee Snider, Vinni Stiletto, Steve Vai, Joey Vera, and Bill Ward.

I also wish to thank the following people for sharing their time and memories as well: Debbie Abono, Michael Alago, Uncle Joe Benson, Joe Burman, Mike Clink, Jimmy D, C. C. DeVille, Mike Fahley, Rik Fox, Lonn Friend, Rick Gould, Vicky Hamilton, Ross Hogarth, Chris Holmes, Steve Hunter, Grover Jackson, Del James, Danny Johnson, Patty Johnson, Mike Kelley, John Kornarens, Eddie Kramer, Borivoj Krigin, Greg Leon, Jim Lewis, George Lynch, Harvey Mandel, Cletus Nelson, Julia Nine, Eric Petersen, the late Bernie Rico, Steve Rosen, Karl Sandoval, Alex Solca, Jeff Stein, John Sykes, Diana Thompson, Michelle Young and everyone else I spoke to for this project. A special thanks to the memory of Frank Starr. It was great to know you, even though it was brief, rest in peace bro. Also thanks to Skylaire Alfegren, Lenn Fico,

Matthew Freeman at Lippman Entertainment, John Greenberg and Tim Heine at Tap Co., Geri Miller, Bob Ringe, Obi Steinman, Dieter Szcypinski at World Management.

This wasn't an easy project to find research materials on, but a number of people I came in contact with thankfully held on to a number of helpful magazines, books, and videos that greatly enhanced my research. I especially have to thank Stella Voche and Kristina Estlund for helping me locate long lost issues of *RIP Magazine,* probably the finest metal magazine of the 1980s. You ladies really saved the day for me, mucho kudos. Also thanks to Steve Darrow, Jim DeRogatis who got me great articles from *Creem* magazine I wouldn't have located otherwise, Darren O' Donnel at the MIT library, Allison Grochowski at *Rolling Stone,* The Margret Herrick Library, Dan Starr, and Adrianne Stone, Jon Sutherland. Thank you to Amel El-Zarou and Jill Matheson for transcription help. Special thanks to Dave Szulkin for great friendship and tremendous help with transcribing and research. I also have to give props to the most hilarious metal website there is, Metal-Sludge (www.metal-sludge.com), who I turned to a number of times for research help (their Twenty Questions interviews are amazing as well). Keep up the good work guys. Also thanks to Erik Bauer at Creative Screenwriting and the whole Creative Screenwriting crew (Christian Devine, Steve Ryfel, and Den Shewman), Lonn Friend, formerly of Knac.com, and Frank Meyer of Knac.com, Michael Gingold at *Fangoria,* Eric Lilleor at *Screentalk,* Greg Loescher at *Goldmine,* Steve Puchalski at *Shock Cinema,* Michael Stein and Jim Wilson at *Film Fax,* Brad Tolinski at *Guitar World,* and Rob Walton at Playboy.com.

For their friendship and kindness, I thank Gary Abramson, Ryan Angel, Deborah Attoinese, Greg Basic, Jeff Black, Max Fantozzi and the entire Fantozzi family, Bill Hill, Bill Huesser, Rodger Jacobs, Andrew Kersey, everyone at Mo's, Carly Osbourne, Siouxzan Perry, Chris Poggioli, R.A., and Lily Reyes.

I owe a tremendous debt of gratitude and thanks to my agent Rob Robertson, who in spite of our differences (or maybe because of them), this book came to be. Also if it were not for Rob, I would not have made such great strides as a writer. I also owe a great deal of gratitude and thanks to Carrie Thornton, who picked this project up and did a great job editing the manuscript. Her instincts and insights were invaluable. Special thanks to Maryann Palumbo, who has always been a tremendous mentor and friend. Thanks to Amelia Zalcman for wise counsel.

Last, but certainly not least, I have to thank my family who helped keep this project afloat long after most people's common sense would have allowed. Thank you to my father Steven, my mother Sandra, my brother Drew, and the new addition to the Konow family, Edward. Extra special thanks to my Grandmother Ginny, who I know I can count on no matter what.

INDEX